JOHN RUSKIN

RUSKIN
AT THE AGE OF FORTY-EIGHT, IN 1867

[Photo by Elliott and Fry]

JOHN RUSKIN

AN INTRODUCTION TO
FURTHER STUDY OF
HIS LIFE AND WORK

BY

R. H. WILENSKI, 1887-

NEW YORK / RUSSELL & RUSSELL

FIRST PUBLISHED IN 1933 BY FABER & FABER LTD., LONDON
REISSUED, 1967, BY RUSSELL & RUSSELL
A DIVISION OF ATHENEUM HOUSE, INC.
L. C. CATALOG CARD NO: 66-27182
PRINTED IN THE UNITED STATES OF AMERICA

This book is dedicated
to
HUGH MACDONALD
who has helped me
and to
S.S.
who has made it possible

CONTENTS

PREFACE   *page* 9

PART I: SYNOPTIC TABLES

SYNOPTIC TABLES   15

PART II: BIOGRAPHICAL

INTRODUCTORY COMMENTS   27

THE PROLOGUE   42

THE PLAY   103

THE EPILOGUE   177

POSTSCRIPT   180

PART III: CRITICAL

INTRODUCTORY COMMENTS   185

RUSKIN AS ART CRITIC   192
    His Theory of Art
    His Practice as Art Critic
    His Relations with Artists

RUSKIN AS SOCIAL AND POLITICAL ECONOMIST   279
    Introductory Comments
    Ruskin's Theory of Economy

RUSKIN ON WAR   303

RUSKIN'S RELIGION   329

RUSKIN AS A WRITER   357

APPENDIX

RUSKIN'S POSITION IN THE 'FIFTIES   369

INDEX   385

7

CONTENTS

ILLUSTRATIONS

RUSKIN AT THE AGE OF FORTY-EIGHT, IN 1867 *frontispiece*

RUSKIN, AGED SEVENTY-FOUR, IN 1893, ACCOMPANIED
BY HIS VALET AND DOG *to face page* 178

PREFACE

I must explain how this book has been given its present shape.

Some years ago I bought the thirty-nine volumes of the Library Edition of Ruskin's works and acquired the habit of referring to them on this topic and on that. As I read I became more and more puzzled. Ruskin always said something unexpected. It seemed impossible to capture his central attitude or to discover the real character of his work. Sometimes his dicta appeared part of a system, sometimes they seemed merely capricious; sometimes they appeared the result of thought and sometimes of feeling; sometimes the result of knowledge, and sometimes of prejudice. There were passages which revealed the wide range of real imaginative vision and others which were obviously pettish and parochial. There were moments when he seemed a man of first-rate mental powers and moments when he seemed quite unbelievably silly. His writing moreover was sometimes clear and sometimes muddled and obscure. And the most amazing thing of all was that these variations in character and quality were juxtaposed not only in the same book, or in the same chapter or lecture, but even on the same page and in the same paragraph.

After a time I thought that I had disentangled one or two threads which seemed to appear and reappear in all his writings and to bind them together. These threads—grouped ideas in the fields of art, social economics and war—seemed to me so vital and so serviceable at the present time that I decided to read Ruskin's books methodically and make an attempt to extract and submit them to my generation who show no disposition to read the thirty-nine volumes of his writings from cover to cover.

At that time I had read no biographies of Ruskin and I knew little of his life. I started to examine the biographical literature

9

in order to preface my comments on his ideas by a short biographical outline or table of outstanding dates. Immediately I began to examine the biographical data I realised that I had found the key to the strange varieties of character and quality and the astonishing inconsequence in the writings. For I discovered that there is hardly a page of his writings which can be properly apprehended until it is collated with the condition of his mind and the circumstances of his life not only at the general period within which the book falls, but on the actual day on which that particular page was written.

This meant that I had to start work on the main bulk of the biographical data and especially on some thousands of his published letters; and I soon found that my biographical introduction was an absorbing inquiry in itself—not only on account of its intrinsic interest, but also because I have been at work for a number of years on the collection of material for a book on the psychology of artistic production, and the examination of Ruskin's mental processes soon became intimately connected with my studies for the other book. For I had here a literary artist about whom far more is ascertainable than is usually the case with artists; a man from whose hand we have revealing letters and diary entries written almost daily all through his working life. Thus it came that the short biographical outline was developed to a study which now occupies a large proportion of this book.

There can be no doubt, I think, that Ruskin was not only a great man and a genius, but also a mental invalid all his life. As I explain in the Introductory Comments to the Biographical Part II, he appears to me to have suffered continuously from the malady now known to psychiatry as Manic-depression. I am not a psychologist, I have no clinical experience, and I have small acquaintance with the literature on this subject. I speak therefore under correction from the specialists.

I must add that I have not written this book in the spirit of W. P. Frith, R.A., who described St. Francis of Assisi as 'a weak-minded hysterical monk'. Nor have I written it as a disciple of Lombroso, Nordau, or Hyslop. I did not know what I should find when I embarked on the detailed examina-

PREFACE

tion of Ruskin's mental processes, and I collected the evidence as an introduction to Part III of my inquiry which contains, as I have said, an attempt to disentangle Ruskin's main contributions to the theories of art, sociology and war, from the discursions and digressions and incidentals which obscure them and can only be explained by the state of his mind and the circumstances of his life at the particular time.

The object of this inquiry is not to demonstrate that Ruskin was always a manic-depressive invalid—(though, as I have said, I believe that this is so)—but to indicate a way of studying his writings that makes every word in them comprehensible when we have found the necessary key—no such way, I submit, having previously been indicated by the official biographers or the well-known commentators.

I have compiled as Part I a set of Synoptic Tables—which I had by me as I wrote—in the hope that they may prove of the same convenience to the reader that they have proved to me.

At the end of the book I have added an Appendix dealing with Ruskin's position in the eighteen-fifties which his biographers, as I read the evidence, have misrepresented.

Many of Ruskin's biographers have not given references when they quote from his works and letters. This has caused me months of unnecessary labour. I have therefore given copious references, for which I trust succeeding students will bless me, and which everyone else can easily ignore. The references to paragraphs in the writings are, in all cases, to the numbering in the Library Edition. The text of all diary entries and letters is as given in that edition, except in the case of one or two letters to Macdonald Macdonald which were published in 1920 by Mr. J. H. Whitehouse in *Ruskin, The Prophet*, and several published last year by Dr. Greville MacDonald in *Reminiscences of a Specialist*. The student can verify my quotations from all letters and diary entries contained in the Library Edition by noting the date given in my footnote and referring to the Indices of Letters and Diary in Vol. XXXVIII (Bibliography) of that edition.

LONDON, *March*, 1933.

11

PART I
SYNOPTIC TABLES

SYNOPTIC TABLES

SECTION I
TO THE AGE OF THIRTY-FIVE (1819-1854)

EVENTS	PRODUCTIONS	REPUTE	HEALTH
Foreign travel, 1833–1835.	Miscellaneous verse, and prose essays, 1827-1842.	Repute and influence much smaller than is commonly supposed.	Four years before Ruskin was born his paternal grandfather became insane.
Oxford, 1837–1840, where he makes friends with Henry Acland afterwards Regius Professor of Medicine, and Henry Liddell afterwards Dean of Christ Church.	*Modern Painters*, I, published 1843. *Modern Painters*, II, published 1846. *The Seven Lamps of Architecture*, published 1849.	Known mainly among literary people. Name almost unknown to the general public. Small sale of his books which were very expensive.	His parents were first cousins. His father was thirty-four when he was born; his mother thirty-eight. Pleurisy at age of sixteen.
Foreign travel, 1840–1841.	*The Stones of Venice*, I, published 1851.	Writings not appreciated by artists and architects.	At twenty-one (1840) depression and physical breakdown following frustration in love affair; morbid condition of mind; consumption feared.
Begins a collection of works, chiefly watercolours, by Turner.	*The Stones of Venice*, II and III, published 1853.	Meets literary people and makes friends in society as a young man of letters. Helped in this by his wife's social activity in London and Venice.	Recovery eighteen months later after protracted foreign tour with his parents.
Marries a distant cousin, 1848.	Letters to *The Times* on the Pre-Raphaelites and pamphlet called *Pre-Raphaelitism*, 1851.		
Lives on a large allowance from his father. Has expensive establishments in London and Venice.	*Notes on the Construction of Sheepfolds.* A pamphlet on the Reunion of Protestant Sects, 1851.		Manic tone in his books 1843–1853. Confident that he has exceptional knowledge of the nature and intentions of God.
Architectural studies in France and Venice, 1848–1852.	Letters for *The Times* on *Taxation, Election and Education*, 1852.		Depression. Sees eels in sky. No pleasure in nature or society, 1847, till marriage, 1848.
Continues collection of Turner water-colours, which in 1860 numbered about 100; also collects mediæval manuscripts, engravings, drawings, minerals, etc.	Four lectures at Edinburgh, 1853. (Published as *Lectures on Architecture and Painting*, 1854).		Mental health during married life relatively good. Happy, enjoys social functions. Hyper-confident tendencies.
Defends Pre-Raphaelites, 1851.	*Giotto and his works in Padua.* Notes for Arundel Society's Reproductions (1853–1860).		Presumed to be virgin before and during his marriage, and for the rest of his life.
Aspires to be Art-Dictator.	Drawings—some used to illustrate his architectural books.		Abuse of Roman Catholicism in books due to fear of being seduced by R.C. ritual, 1846–1853.
His marriage annulled, 1854.			

SYNOPTIC TABLES

SECTION II
FROM THIRTY-FIVE TO FORTY-THREE (1854–1862)

EVENTS	PRODUCTIONS	REPUTE	HEALTH
Headquarters nominally at his parents' house in Denmark Hill, but frequently abroad.	*Academy Notes*, 1855–1859.	Still known only to a small public. Small sale of books.	Inability to concentrate for long on any type of work appears in 1855.
Seeks friendship with artists, notably Rossetti, whom he finances, 1854.	*The Harbours of England*. Notes on engravings of marine subjects after Turner, 1856.	Little influence in any field.	Recognition of his failure to capture Art-Dictatorship rationalised into defiance of artists and architects who are no longer considered worth teaching. Loss of interest in art 1857–1859.
Teaches at Working Men's College.	*Modern Painters*, III and IV, published 1856.	Looked on with disfavour as a pretentious dilettante by the official art world. Many enemies among architects and artists who regard him as a pretentious and malevolent amateur.	
Arranges water-colours in Turner Bequest at National Gallery, 1857–1858.	Notes and Catalogues of Turner Bequest, 1857–1858.		Species of climacteric with amorous impulses, 1858-1863.
Failure to achieve Art-Dictatorship.	Miscellaneous lectures, 1856–1859, afterwards published as *The Two Paths*, 1859, and *A Joy for Ever*, 1880.	Many acquaintances, but few friends.	Proclaims his personal religion, 1858.
Studies social and political economy. Work in this field discouraged by his father, 1855–1862.	*The Elements of Drawing*, 1857.	Henry Acland and Liddell his staunch champions in Oxford, where they procured a Gothic design for the Oxford Museum, to which Ruskin subscribed money.	Falls in love with child of eleven years old (Rose La Touche), 1859.
Wins friendship of Carlyle.	*The Elements of Perspective*, 1859.		Frequents girls' school at Winnington from 1859 to 1864.
	Modern Painters, V, published 1860.	Articles in *Cornhill* and *Fraser's Magazines* not taken seriously.	
	Four articles on Social and Political Economy in *Cornhill Magazine*, 1860 (republished 1862 as *Unto This Last*).		
	Four articles on Social and Political Economy in *Fraser's Magazine*, 1862—63 (republished as *Munera Pulveris*, 1872).		
	Drawings.		
	Letters to the Press.		

16

SYNOPTIC TABLES

SECTION III
FROM FORTY-THREE TO FORTY-FIVE (1862–1864)

EVENTS	PRODUCTIONS	REPUTE	HEALTH
Headquarters nominally at Denmark Hill; but almost continuously away. Mostly in High Savoy. Buys a property at Mornex and makes plans to settle there.		Repute and influence still small. A book of *Selections*, being purple passages from *Modern Painters* etc., was published in 1861. This increased his reputation as a 'word painter', much to his annoyance. Sale of other books very small.	Depression, languor, listlessness, indigestion, sense of failure. Flashes of persecution mania and inferiority complex. Hatred of the world at large. Insensibility to feelings of others. Blames parents for his self-indulgence. Writes many letters all about his condition. When in England continues to frequent the girls' school—staying weeks at a time. Rambling word-jingling and obscurantism in *Munera Pulveris*, 1862—1863. (N.B. — Depression sets in at end of 1862 and lasts to death of his father, March, 1864) Dabbles in spiritualism at Broadlands end of 1864.

SECTION IV
FROM FORTY-FIVE TO FIFTY (1864–1869)

EVENTS	PRODUCTIONS	REPUTE	HEALTH
Inherits a large fortune on the death of his father on March 3, 1864. Headquarters Denmark Hill, but much away after 1865.	Articles in the *Art Journal*, 1865 and 1866. Republished as *The Cestus of Aglaia* in *On the Old Road*, 1885.	*Sesame and Lilies* his first popular success. Thought suitable reading for young girls by their mothers and school - teachers all over the country.	The responsibilities of his new position and the work involved in the settlement of his father's estate pull him from depression for a time.

17

SYNOPTIC TABLES

EVENTS	PRODUCTIONS	REPUTE	HEALTH
France and Switzerland, April to July, 1866.	Miscellaneous lectures published as *Sesame and Lilies*, 1865, and *The Crown of Wild Olive*, 1866.	*The Crown of Wild Olive* a moderate success.	Feb., March, April, 1865, rambling word-jingling, and obscurantism in Art Journal articles.
English lakes, July and August, 1867.	Imaginary dialogues with the schoolgirls at Winningtonpublished as *Ethics of the Dust*, Dec., 1865.	*Ethics of the Dust* a complete failure.	February, 1866, proposes marriage to Rose La Touche, then eighteen, and is told to wait till her twenty-first birthday for her reply.
Dublin and Winnington, May, 1868.			
Northern France, September and October, 1868.			
France and Italy, April to September, 1869.	Letters on Ideal State in newspapers (1867), republished as *Time and Tide* in the same year.		Autumn, 1866, giddiness and physical distresses. Word-jingling letter to Winnington girl.
Appointed Slade Professor of Fine Art in Oxford — to begin work in 1870. (Appointment due to activities of Acland and Liddell on his behalf.)	Other letters to the Press on social, economic and political questions, (1864-1870)		1867. Alternates between hyper-confidence — when he makes plans for organisation to regenerate England (first scheme of St. George's Guild)—and depression with 'weird dreams', floating sparks in eyes, sleeplessness, nervous prostration. Begins to fear insanity.
	Articles in *Geological Magazine*, 1865, 1867-1870.		
	Rede Lecture in Cambridge: *Relation of National Ethics to National Art*, May, 1867.		
	Pamphlet on *Employment for the Destitute and Criminal Classes*, 1868, incorporated in *The Queen of the Air*, nominally a group of lectures on Greek myths, 1869.		Rose obsession. 1868. Return of confidence.
	Lecture on *Flamboyant Architecture of the Valley of the Somme*, Royal Institution, Jan., 1869.		1869. Ingenious rationalisations of sense of guilt at absenting himself from his mother, April to September.
	Drawings.		Beginning of Storm-Cloud obsession, May, 1869.
	Letters to the Press.		Irritability. Hatred of Italians. Insensibility. Summer, 1869.

SYNOPTIC TABLES

EVENTS	PRODUCTIONS	REPUTE	HEALTH
			Manic scheme to curb Alpine torrents, summer, 1869.
			Extreme mobility of interest(autumn,1869)
			Veiled attacks on Rose's pietistic theology in Ruskin's lectures and books, 1865-1869.
			'Discovers' Carpaccio's *St. Ursula*, summer, 1869.

SECTION V
FROM FIFTY-ONE TO FIFTY-FIVE (1870–1874)

EVENTS	PRODUCTIONS	REPUTE	HEALTH
Buys Brantwood,1871	Lecture on *Verona and its Rivers*, Royal Institution, Feb.,1870.	Increasing reputation as 'The Professor' (authority on art), as 'The Master' (director and financier of St. George's Guild), as social critic and friend of the poor (*Fors Clavigera*), as eccentric, and as 'fine writer'.	Serious attack of internal inflammation at Matlock. Dreams remembered ever afterwards, 1871.
Death of his mother, aged 90, Dec. 5, 1871.			
Inherits more money and property.	Oxford lectures, spring, 1870; published as *Lectures on Art*, 1870.		Increasing mobility of interest, manic projection and beginning of large schemes, moods of depression.
Disposes of Denmark Hill, spring, 1872.	Oxford lectures on Greek Sculpture, autumn, 1870; published as *Aratra Pentelici*, 1872.		
Three homes: Brantwood; rooms in Corpus Christi, Oxford; and in the Severn's house at Herne Hill.		New editions of his old books were published and began to be read by the general public.	Euphoria in 1872 and 1873.
	Fors Clavigera: Letters to the Workmen and Labourers of Britain. A monthly publication.		Storm - Cloud obsession.
Begins social action with *Fors Clavigera* and foundation of St. George's Guild in 1871.		Pirated editions read in America.	'Poor-Orphan' obsession.
Founds OxfordDrawing School; endows and equips it.	*Letters:* 1–12 (1871); 13–24 (1872); 25–36 (1873); 37–48 (1874).	Continued popularity of *Sesame and Lilies* and *Selections*.	Firefly and Fireworks obsessions.
Founds Sheffield Museum (Walkley); endows and equips it.	Oxford *Lectures on Landscape*, spring, 1871 (published,1898).		Rose obsession. (N.B.—Rose postpones decision again in 1870. Refuses to have anything to do with him in 1871. Meets him and definitely refuses to marry him in 1872.)
Street sweeping in Seven Dials, 1872.	Oxford lecture,*Michelangelo and Tintoretto*, June, 1871. Published 1872.		

SYNOPTIC TABLES

EVENTS	PRODUCTIONS	REPUTE	HEALTH
Paddington Tea Shop, 1874. Makes undergraduates build road, 1874. Abroad: 1870, April to July; 1872, April to August; 1874, March to October.	Oxford lectures, *The Relation of Natural Science to Art*, spring, 1872. Published as *The Eagle's Nest*, 1872. Oxford lectures on *Wood and Metal Engraving*, autumn, 1872. Published as pamphlets and then as *Ariadne Florentina*, 1876. Oxford lectures on *English and Greek Birds*, 1873. Published with other writings on birds as *Love's Meinie*, 1873 and 1881. Oxford lectures on *Tuscan Art*, autumn, 1873. Published as *Val d'Arno*, 1874. Oxford lectures on *The Alps and Jura*, Nov., 1874. Published in *Deucalion*, 1875. Oxford lectures on *The Æsthetic and Mathematical Schools of Art in Florence*, autumn, 1874. Published in the Library Edition, 1906. Drawings. Letters to the Press.		Veiled attacks on Rose's pietistic theology in Ruskin's lectures and books. Writes description of Carpaccio's *St. Ursula* in *Fors Clavigera*, 1872. Depression at beginning of 1874. Cannot face lecturing. Alternating moods. Marked perseverance in old activities in Italy, 1874. Begins to think of himself as 'a Brother of the third Order of St. Francis', 1874. Returns to early confidence in his exceptional knowledge of God.

SYNOPTIC TABLES

SECTION VI
FROM FIFTY-SIX TO FIFTY-NINE (1875–1878)

EVENTS	PRODUCTIONS	REPUTE	HEALTH
Driving tour in Yorkshire and Derbyshire and thence to London, Jan., 1875.	*Fors Clavigera: Letters* 49–60 (1875); 61–72 (1876); 73–84 (1877); 85–87 (1878).	Wide notoriety.	Rose dies. May, 1875.
Second driving tour, July, 1875, after death of Rose La Touche.	Oxford lectures on *The Discourses of Reynolds*, Nov., 1875.	Increased sale of his books. Selections from *Modern Painters* compiled by Susan Beever with title *Frondes Agrestes*,	Veiled allusions to her in obscurantist passages in *Fors Clavigera*. Dabbles in spiritualism at Broadlands.
Lectures in Oxford, Nov., 1875.	Pamphlet: *Academy Notes*, 1875.	published in 1875, a 'best seller', reprinted each year. *Mornings*	Half believes that Rose's ghost was seen beside him, winter, 1875–1876.
Driving tour, April, 1876.	Guide for English Travellers in Florence published in parts as *Mornings in Florence*,	*in Florence* much used by English travellers. More reprints of old books demanded.	Marked and rapid increase of mobility of interest and of all ob-
Abroad: August, 1876 to June, 1877.	1875–1877.		sessions, 1875–1877.
Oxford lectures, Nov., 1877.	*Letter to Young Girls* (*Fors* 65 and 66),1876.	Newspapers published bulletins during his 1878 madness.	Identifies Rose with Dante's Beatrice, with St. Ursula in Carpaccio's picture, and with
	Oxford, *Readings from Modern Painters*, Nov., 1877.		other figures in pictures. Has *St. Ursula's Dream* taken down and closets himself with it
	Guide to the Academy at Venice, 1877.		for weeks and copies every detail, 1876–1877.
	Begins a History of Venice, published in parts as *St. Mark's Rest*, 1877–1884.		Believes that Rose sends him messages through St. Ursula, 1877.
	Begins a new treatise on drawing. Published in parts as *The Laws of Fésole*, 1877–1879.		Firefly — Firework obsession expressed in panic attack on Fireworks picture by Whistler, 1877.
	Begins publication of Botanical papers as pamphlets called *Proserpina* (1875–1886).		Excited tone and attacks in *Fors Clavigera*, 1877.
	Begins publication of papers on geology as pamphlets called *Deucalion*, 1875–1883.		Excited tone, discursiveness, and eccentricities in delivery, Oxford Lectures, 1877.
	Begins scheme of educational publications for 'St. George's		Panic fears, extreme

21

EVENTS	PRODUCTIONS	REPUTE	HEALTH
	Schools' (to be called *Bibliotheca Pastorum*) with the publication of a new translation of Xenophon's *Economist* and *Rock Honeycomb: Broken pieces of Sir Philip Sidney's Psalter*, 1876 and 1877		mobility of ideas, the beginning of many new projects; alternating moods, obsessions, delusions, 1877–1878.
			First attack of madness, February to April, 1878.
	Drawings.		
	Letters to the Press.		

SECTION VII
FROM FIFTY-NINE TO SIXTY-SIX (1878–1885)

EVENTS	PRODUCTIONS	REPUTE	HEALTH
Whistler libel action, Nov., 1878.	*The Three Colours of Pre-Raphaelitism*. Articles in *Nineteenth Century*, November and December, 1878. Republished in *On the Old Road*, 1885.	The legend of the Prophet of Brantwood started during his 1878 madness and grew rapidly.	Second attack of madness, February and March, 1881.
Ruskin resigns Oxford Professorship, 1879. Nominal reason that the verdict in Whistler trial had gone against him.	*Letters on the Lord's Prayer and the Church*, Contemporary Review, winter, 1879–1880. Republished in *On the Old Road*, 1885.	First 'Ruskin Societies' for the study of his works established in 1879.	Third attack, March, 1882. Fourth attack, July, 1885.
Lives at Brantwood with visits to Herne Hill and travel, 1878–1885.	*Usury*, in the *Contemporary Review*, Feb., 1880. Republished in *On the Old Road*, 1885.	Greatly increased sale of his books of all periods which were read out of their order and without reference to or knowledge of circumstances of composition.	Marked increase of all characteristics: extreme mobility of interest, alternating euphoria and depression, increase of irritability; combative tendencies in hyper-confident happy moods, hostility to friends in depressed moods. Obsessions, delusions, eccentric conduct, 1879–1885.
Abroad: Northern France, August to October, 1880; Italy, August to December, 1882.	Lecture, *A Caution to Snakes*, at London Institution, March, 1880. Published in *Deucalion*, 1883.	*Sesame and Lilies* and books of *Selections* have the widest popularity. Four more editions of *Frondes Agrestes*. Large sales of *Mornings in Florence*, and *Letter to Young Girls*.	
Resumes Oxford Professorship, 1883.	*Fiction, Fair and Foul*. Five essays in the *Nineteenth Century*, 1880–1881. Republished in *On the Old Road*, 1885.		Starts controversies and begins work in several fields, 1879–1880.
Resigns Oxford Professorship, March, 1885.	*Elements of English Prosody*, 1880 (essay).		Euphoria on French journey, 1880.
Has spent most of his fortune, but now begins to have large and ever-increasing income from his books.			Nightmares precede second attack in which

SYNOPTIC TABLES

EVENTS	PRODUCTIONS	REPUTE	HEALTH
	Begins second grandiose scheme of educational publications: *Our Fathers have told us: Sketches of the History of Christendom for Boys and Girls.* Publishes chapters of *The Bible of Amiens* as first instalments, 1880–1885.		the delirium is 'terrific', 1881.
			Hostility to friends, perpetual plans for new activities, and 'hesitations, shifts, despairings' after 1881 attack.
	Fors Clavigera: Letters 88–89 (1880); 90–93 (1883); 94–96 (1884).		Alternating euphoria and depression on French-Italian tour, 1882.
	Oxford lectures on *The Art of England*, spring, 1883. Published in parts, 1883–1884; as book, 1884.		Excitement, extravagant extemporisations and attacks on scientists in Oxford lectures, 1884.
	Oxford lectures on *The Pleasures of Learning, Faith, Deed, Fancy*, autumn, 1884. Published in parts, 1884; republished as *The Pleasures of England*, 1898.		Extravagant purchases of minerals 'for Sheffield' and his own collection; extravagant commissions to artist-assistants to perseverate his former sketching in France and Italy, 1881–1884.
	Lectures at London Institution, *The Storm Cloud of the Nineteenth Century*, 1884.		Storm - Cloud obsession culminates in *Storm - Cloud* lectures at London Institution, 1884.
	A Knight's Faith. Comments on *A Year on the Punjab Frontier*, by Sir Herbert Edwardes. Expanded from a lecture at Coniston (1883) and published as the continuation of *Bibliotheca Pastorum*, 1885.		Imagines scientists are in league against him, 1884. Rose obsession persistent, especially in form of Rosie the child. Seeks company of girl children and young girls. Falls in love with Kate Greenaway's 'girlies' and a Rose-Ursula drawing by Francesca Alexander, etc., etc., 1879–1885.
	Further chapters of *Deucalion* and *Proserpina* published in parts 1880–1885. Drawings. Letters to the Press.		

23

SYNOPTIC TABLES

SECTION VIII
FROM SIXTY-SIX TO EIGHTY-ONE (1885–1900)

EVENTS	PRODUCTIONS	REPUTE	HEALTH
Drives from Brantwood to South Coast and stays at Folkestone and Sandgate, summer 1887 to spring 1888.	*Præterita:* an incomplete autobiography. Begun January to July, 1885. Published in parts, 1885–89. Last chapter written, summer, 1889.	Climax of fame, influence, and popularity of his books and selections from them. Eleven more editions of *Frondes Agrestes*, which reached 36th thousand in 1902.	Projects thirty-six chapters of *Dilecta* in extension of *Præterita*, 1886.
Visits to London, 1888.	*Dilecta:* notes and correspondence to illustrate *Præterita*, 1886. Three chapters only compiled.	*Sesame and Lilies* reached 64th thousand in 1903.	Fifth attack of madness, July, 1886.
Abroad: France, Italy and Switzerland, July to December, 1888.			Hostile depression, spring, 1887.
Continued large income from his books.	Last chapters of *Proserpina*, 1886.	*Letter to Young Girls* reached its 75th thousand in 1902. *Unto This Last*, of which barely 800 copies had been sold between 1862 and 1873, was in its 48th thousand in 1901.	Excitement and depression alternating, religious brooding, delusions, eccentric conduct, 1887–1888.
Summer, 1889, at Seascale.	Epilogue to *Modern Painters*, 1888.		Euphoria alternating with despondency on 1888 tour. Collapse into depression and delusions in Paris on the way home.
Retirement at Brantwood, 1889–1900.	Last letter, October, 1893.		
			Attack of madness, autumn, 1889.
			Thought concentration almost impossible in later years. Last chapter of *Præterita* written with great difficulty. Last private letter, one page took three hours.
			In last period alternating hostile and docile gloom; generally almost silent, occasionally excited and loquacious. Violent outbreaks. Sane periods.
			Dies in a sane period from influenza, January 21, 1900.

PART II
BIOGRAPHICAL

INTRODUCTORY COMMENTS

'And what am I, myself then, infirm and old, who take, or claim, leadership even of these lords? God forbid that I should claim it; it is thrust and compelled on me—utterly against my will, utterly to my distress, utterly, in many things, to my shame. But I have found no other man in England, none in Europe, ready to receive it,—or even desiring to make himself capable of receiving it. Such as I am, to my own amazement, I stand—so far as I can discern—alone in conviction, in hope, and in resolution, in the wilderness of this modern world. Bred in luxury, which I perceive to have been unjust to others, and destructive to myself; vacillating, foolish, and miserably failing in all my own conduct of life—and blown about hopelessly by storms of passion—I, a man clothed in soft raiment,—I, a reed shaken by the wind, have yet this Message to all men again entrusted to me: "Behold, the axe is laid to the root of the trees. Whatsoever tree therefore bringeth not forth good fruit, shall be hewn down and cast into the fire." '

Fors Clavigera,　Letter 58, 1875.

John Ruskin had a strange career. When he was forty-one, in 1860, he had written the five volumes of *Modern Painters*, *The Seven Lamps of Architecture*, the three volumes of *The Stones of Venice*, and *Unto This Last*. But he was still comparatively unknown to the general public, and the literary and artistic people with whom he had come in contact still looked upon him as a pretentious dilettante who drove about in a brougham and financed Rossetti with money provided by his father, and wore eccentric blue stocks to match his eyes, and super-elegant clothes from Stulz the most fashionable tailor. When he was seventy, an invisible and legendary figure with a flowing white beard at Brantwood, an exhausted organism shattered by long years of mental malady and six attacks of admitted madness, his name was revered by hundreds of thousands of people. On his eightieth birthday in 1899 he received addresses and messages of congratulation from all parts of the world. When he died the year after, the Dean and Chapter offered burial in Westminster Abbey; and there had been men who said that the nineteenth century would be chiefly memorable because he had lived and worked in it.[1]

What is the explanation of this strange career? What manner of man was Ruskin? What was his character? What was the constitution of his mind?

To begin with we must recognise that he was a great man and a genius. I call him a great man in the sense that he was a good man whose goodness was on a scale to be of use to a great many people. And I call him a genius because, at his best, he displayed a great imaginative grasp of first principles and refused to assume that a pretty blossom means a wholesome fruit.

He had a social conscience—the finest of a number of fine factors in his character. He was always rich; he always had enough money not only to procure his necessities and comforts and his chosen pleasures, but also to satisfy his extravagances and caprices. But he was never content to spend his money in these ways. From first to last there was a drive within him to serve his fellow-men. When he was twenty-six and travelling in his private carriage, with his courier and valet, he arrived at Champagnole and had supper of 'a couple of trout fried, just out of the river, of the richest flavour', followed by a roasted woodcock 'on delicate toast', and a small perfectly compounded *omelette soufflée;* with this he had half a bottle of *Sillery mousseux* 'very pure and in fine condition'; before he had finished he went out to look at the sunset, and in the evening he wrote home:

'As I came back to my soufflée and Sillery, I felt sad at thinking how few were capable of having such enjoyment, and very doubtful whether it were at all proper for me to have it all to myself.'[2]

'Prig', you may say. Not so. That was the real Ruskin with 'the ray of Heaven' that Carlyle saw in him.[3] At Cham-

---

[1] 'A hundred years hence,' Mr. Faunthorpe told them, 'the nineteenth century will be remembered only or chiefly because Ruskin lived and wrote in it.' *Pall Mall Gazette*, May 2, 1885.

[2] Letter to his parents, April 10, 1845.

[3] Letter from Carlyle to J. H. Froude, autumn, 1869.

INTRODUCTORY COMMENTS

pagnole on that evening the young man, who had just published the manic first volume of *Modern Painters*, looked at the sunset and found his soul. Forty years later writing his last book at Brantwood he remembered that moment. He speaks there of some political troubles which occurred in 1845 'while I sat over my trout at Champagnole'—words that mean nothing unless we are acquainted with that early letter and have read its significance.[1]

We must distinguish Ruskin's social conscience, the finest factor in his character, from his manic impulse to preach which derived from the abnormal constitution of his mind. He himself was often unable to draw that distinction. He often persuaded himself that his preaching—which he called 'my teaching'—was of necessity a form of service to his fellow-men. In his manic moments he always assumed that he stood alone in a world of wickedness and 'unendurable circumfluent fallacy'.[2] We get this in the passage which I have placed at the head of these notes. We get it in the use of the words 'were capable' instead of the words 'have the occasion' in the Champagnole letter, and we get it again and again, as we shall see, all through his career. But there were moments, even when he was indulging this impulse, when he recognised its character as an indulgence. Looking back on his life at the age of sixty-two he wrote as follows:

'Of all the chief characteristics legible of me, is an instinct for Teaching which resolves itself, as far as I can make out the thing under my own microscope, partly into an extreme dislike of folly absolute, and for the rest, into an almost inexplicable but strongly instinctive pleasure in the filling of empty heads and hearts, as if they were so many bottles, like to be broken for having nothing inside, or cells of honeycomb too hollowly fragile. And under the growling of this indignation at public folly the minor buzzing and murmuring of the hymenopterous instinct for pouring good conserve of eternal fact, sweet in the taste and nourishing in the substance, into every cell of human soul that will let it in, I have gone on throughout my life, print-

[1] *Præterita*, II, Chap. VI, para. 107.
[2] Letter *Concerning Glaciers* in *The Reader*, Nov. 26, 1864.

29

ing everything I could discover of such fact as fast as I could and snarling at foolish things and people as hard as I could; but often with no more sense of duty than the tide has in filling sandpits or a stone in rolling down hill.'[1]

There were people in his lifetime who resented his frequent satisfaction of this 'hymenopterous instinct'; and many readers to-day are, as the phrase goes, 'put off' his writings for this reason. It is therefore important to realise at the outset that his impulse to preach—as distinguished from his impulse to serve —was an aspect of the lifelong illness of his mind.

It is easy to call Ruskin arrogant. I have done it myself before I studied the workings of his mind. Now I know that he was not arrogant. What we mistake for the expression of his arrogance was sometimes manic exaltation, sometimes an effort to restart an engine which depression had almost paralysed, and sometimes a defiance of some personal or passing fear. Whenever it occurs, if we collate the passage with the circumstances in which it was written, we pardon at once because we understand.

For example. On February 17, 1875, he began a lecture at the London Institution as follows:

'It is at least ten years since I ceased to speak of anything but what I had ascertained; and thus becoming, as far as I know, the most practical and positive of men, left discourse of things doubtful to those whose pleasure is in quarrel:—content for my pupils and myself, to range all matters under the broad heads of things certain, with which we are vitally concerned, and things uncertain, which don't in the least matter.'[2]

Arrogance? No. We understand it when we know, that he was speaking after four years' experience as 'The Master' of his Guild of St. George which meant four years' experience of being called Utopian and unpractical; that he was speaking after four years' experience as the editor of his pugnacious, quarrelsome magazine called *Fors Clavigera;* that he wrote this lecture, a few months after the death of a girl whose personality

---

[1] Manuscript for a Preface to *Proserpina* II, written in 1881.
[2] *Deucalion* I, Chap. VII, *The Iris of the Earth*, para. 2 (cf. below, pp. 114 and 151).

had long been for him an obsession, in the house of a woman friend who was a spiritualist and was then assuring him that the girl's ghost had been seen beside him at dinner—which he half believed; and that it was just ten years since, after the death of his father, he had been half converted to spiritualism before.[1] Read in the light of this collateral knowledge the passage is seen to be an attempt to get back to terra firma, a pulling himself together, a sick man's effort to parade a façade of health.

Then again there are many people who cannot read without impatience the passages in his writings and in hundreds of his letters where he whines and moans and declares himself the most useless, the most thwarted, of mortals. Such people cannot tolerate his recurring complaints of listlessness and languor, his recurring laments that he can neither sleep, nor digest, nor walk, and his curious inability, at moments, to sympathise with the feelings of others.[2] But all this was really the other main aspect of his mental illness. He really had excellent health all his life; he had exceptionally good eyesight, he scarcely had any trouble with his teeth, and he never had headaches. His appetite was healthy—he was *gourmet* and almost greedy. But at times his mental illness brought on physical distresses.

From morbid elation he went to morbid depression and then back again, in a vicious circle, to elation. We see the circle in the passage which I have set at the beginning of these notes. And this went on continually, without ceasing, all his life. He had no attack of complete madness till he was just on sixty, and there were long periods when, on the surface, he was apparently quite sane. But in fact he rarely achieved a balance for any length of time between the two unhealthy positions. Sometimes his mind remained for months on end in one position or the other; sometimes the movement to and fro was perpetual and rapid.

It is habitually suggested by his biographers that he always worked exceptionally hard. But this is a mistake. Except in his spells of moral collapse and acute depression he always appeared, it is true, to be very industrious. He would sometimes

---

[1] Cf. below, pp. 133 and 134.
[2] Cf. below, pp. 70 and 88.

be up at sunrise and apparently occupied all day. But after the age of about thirty-six he could never work long at any one particular thing, the mobility of his interest became more and more conspicuous, and he turned continually from one activity to another. At all periods of his life he was always planning a large and complicated undertaking, and beginning work upon it, and then planning another large undertaking in a different field and beginning work on that, till in middle life he had a dozen impossibly large undertakings started, and he then passed his time pottering from one to another, with intervals when he really did nothing but indulge himself in various forms of play.

He was the victim of some curious and personal obsessions. In the days when he was writing the second volume of *Modern Painters* and the *Seven Lamps of Architecture* and *The Stones of Venice* (1845–1852) he was haunted by the fear of being seduced to Roman Catholicism by the æsthetic appeal of the Roman Catholic ritual which he encountered in the cathedrals of Italy and France—a fear which lay beneath his diatribes against Roman Catholicism in those books.[1] He was always afraid of speed in transport—a fear that accounts for the unbalanced nature of some of his references to railways. He had a morbid fear of light spots against blackness, of fireflies and fireworks— fear which probably underlay his uneasiness with Rembrandt's pictures and his panic outburst at the *Fireworks* picture by Whistler.[2] Sexual obsessions of a personal kind were persistently with him in adolescence and from just before forty to the end. He seems only to have been free from them during the five years of his married life. When about the age of forty he lost his delight in nature, he at first moaned over the loss as he moaned over his languor, his sense of failure and his indigestion. But by the age of fifty he had transferred the fault to nature herself, and thereafter he was haunted by the delusion that nature was deteriorating and that the world was cursed by a new kind of Storm-Cloud and Plague Wind.[3]

[1] Cf. below, pp. 226–227 and 330 *et seq.*
[2] Cf. below, pp. 138–143.
[3] Cf. below, pp. 97, 124–126, 168 and 169.

INTRODUCTORY COMMENTS

The procedures of rationalisation and transference, which were the mechanism, as it were, by which the Storm-Cloud delusion was evolved, were characteristic of his mental processes at all periods of his life. With the real chronic invalid's desperate desire for health—as distinguished from the malingering hysteric's desire for illness—he continuously rationalised his failures to capture mental health, and in the process he was often driven to transference of various kinds. He displayed a crazy ingenuity and audacity in his rationalisations. He evolved general theories and made transferences to make his actions and the conditions of his own life seem admirable and to invest his weaknesses with the appearance of strengths.

He had all his life a passion for collecting, picking up, hoarding and fiddling with small objects—small drawings, engravings, specimens of minerals, common pebbles, chips of marble, shells, botanical fragments, coins, and so forth. He would buy rare minerals for large sums of money and he would also pick up pebbles from the path, and shells on the seashore. When he observed, he liked to observe details; but he always found it difficult, and in later life he found it impossible, to relate and co-ordinate his observations. He always appeared to be working empirically—to be building up generalisations from accummulation of examples. But he was always really looking at each example as an isolated detail and his generalisations were not based on this experience at all. He surrounded himself with casually collected data with which he fiddled. He then turned his back on the data and made a generalisation on the basis of either his really fine imaginative grasp of first principles, or his desire to rationalise his own conduct, situation, or mental condition at the time. The generalisation made, he returned to the data and selected those which could be used to illustrate or reinforce it—ignoring, if necessary, the conflicting evidence of the others.

In his youth he reacted with effervescent passion to the broader aspects of natural phenomena and took a mobile interest in natural science. But by the age of forty, though the mobile interest remained, the passion was all spent. In his youth he also reacted with effervescent passion to certain manifestations

33

of the creative spirit in art. But this was frequently subordinated to his passion for and interest in nature; and after forty that passion also was all spent, and he could no longer make the effort required to react, even in a superficial way, to *contemporary* creativity in art. After forty he continued to look at skies, to look at *old* pictures, to travel to his favourite haunts in France, Italy and High Savoy, and make sketches—drawing being all his life his favourite play—but his reactions to nature and art were now automatic—forms of perseveration; and when, after his second attack of madness at the age of sixty-two, he no longer expected to see more sunsets at Chamonix, or to draw more corners of architecture at Abbeville and Verona, or to copy more fragments of Carpaccio's pictures of St. Ursula, he employed a whole troop of assistants, whom he sent over the old routes, with detailed instructions, to continue the perseveration.

He was always something of an exhibitionist. He always wore unusual and conspicuous blue ties, which oddly enough annoyed Matthew Arnold, who was a dandy himself.[1] He liked to have an audience. In his youth he read *Modern Painters*, as he wrote it, every morning to his parents at breakfast. Except in moods of extreme depression, or when he was doing his best work, he never liked to be alone. He liked to travel with a surrounding company of servants and assistants and pupils and guests. He was only happy in company which consisted of people whom he had himself selected and grouped about him. He was always unsatisfied in a company selected and grouped by other people where he was only one figure among the rest. He was a fluent and persistent talker when he found himself in a company of his own selection—a company selected because it would listen. He always liked public lecturing—a much larger proportion of his writings are lectures than is commonly realised—and he liked to 'hold the floor' in private life. He had a passion at all periods for writing letters and diaries about himself.

[1] 'Ruskin was there . . . He gains much by evening dress, plain black and white, and by his fancy being forbidden to range through the world of coloured cravats.' Letter of Matthew Arnold, Dec., 1877.

His mental malady—which as I have said above, I presume to have been Manic-depression—was at all times perfectly genuine. He was not a malingering hysteric. He always instinctively concealed his ill health and tried to keep it secret. In ordinary social intercouse it betrayed itself on the one hand by excessive expression of pleasure—he would clap his hands excitedly when anything pleased him—and, on the other, especially in later life, by insensibility and fits of silence, though in company he rarely exhibited depression. The apparent arrogance, so frequent in his writings—always explicable, I have submitted, as an expression of manic confidence or an attempt to defy depression—rarely appeared in ordinary social intercourse until after his first madness, when its intermittent appearance was partly an attempt to demonstrate that he had quite recovered and was capable of decided judgement, and partly the normal exploitation of a white beard, which, when we understand and therefore pardon it, we call 'the privilege of old age'.

There were always people who thought he was a madman. But such people belonged exclusively to two classes: the highly sensitive people who *sensed* his illness in the undue stresses which appeared against his will both in his writings and in his conduct and conversation—people that is to say, who knew him for a mental invalid in the same way that Cézanne knew that Van Gogh was a mental invalid the moment he saw one of his pictures; and the blunt-minded people who supposed him mad because he put down opinions which they had never met before and which it was against their interests to accept as important. From the ordinary intelligent man Ruskin successfully concealed his illness until that illness betrayed him by its own pressure in the period that led up to his first madness. And as he recovered from one attack after another he always made the same effort to be and to appear sane. He never exploited his attacks of madness to secure sympathy or other benefits. He never malingered at any stage. He never rationalised his madness.

We must distinguish the absolutely genuine character of his illness from the tortuous processes (resulting from the illness) by which he sought to rationalise the weak spot in his own character. I have called Ruskin a great man in the sense that he was a good man whose goodness was on a scale to be of use to a great number of other people, and I have called his social conscience the finest thing about him. Here I must add that he was a man who, it seems to me, had only one fault in his character—self-indulgence. In the thousands of his letters and diary entries that I have read, in the numerous accounts of his conduct at all times, in his voluminous writings, I can find no trace of meanness in him, no cruelty, no greed; I can find no record of a word spoken or a thing done in spite, or for revenge, or with deliberate attempt to wound. His behaviour when his wife deserted him, and always afterwards in regard to her, was perfect; and he never allowed the episode to influence in the slightest degree his published comments on the works of Millais which he praised on occasions; and a year or two after the desertion he had the courage to write that Millais had degenerated as an artist and to face the interpretation of the dictum which would inevitably be put upon it by the mean. He had physical courage also. In his boyhood he had not been allowed to ride because his mother indulged herself in a selfish fear that he would fall off the pony; and at that time also he was bitten on the lip by a dog—a disfigurement which led people to speak of him as a man with a hare-lip; but he was never afraid of animals, and was always kind to them—he picked up a wounded buzzard, and felt for its wound and dressed it, when his secretaries were frightened of its beak. He was naturally kind, and, except in gestures explicable by his malady, he was courteous and sensitive in dealing with all kinds of people— the letters which he wrote to accompany his many gifts being models of delicate consideration. That he was a lovable character, especially after his wife's desertion when he was thirty-five, is proved by the simple fact that thereafter he was loved by more and more people every year. He quarrelled with original artists, because as I show later, he could not understand them[1]; and he was always disliked by dons and other people with the academic mind because he looked on scholar-

[1] Cf. below, pp. 264–278.

ship as pottering and because such people were ill at ease with his originality. But—these mutually opposed types excepted —he could get on with everybody—men, women and children. He made friends whenever he wanted to and kept them all his life. Half the draughtsman-assistants whom he sent abroad in the 'eighties had worked for him for many years, and received countless kindnesses from him; some had been his pupils at the Working Men's College in the 'fifties. Allen who went out to him to Mornex in 1862, and published all his works from early in the 'seventies, had also been his pupil in the 'fifties, and he remained his devoted servant to the end. His secretary-assistants, Hilliard, Collingwood, Wedderburn and Cook were deeply attached to him. He only had three valets all his life. Scores of young women were sentimentally in love with him. When he established himself at Coniston he was soon loved by all classes for miles round. Dr. Greville MacDonald, who was a boy when Ruskin frequented the house of his father, George MacDonald, says that merely to look at his face and feel the grasp of his hand was 'to believe in him utterly'.[1] Carlyle loved him. Men like Norton, Acland, Liddell and Cowper-Temple, were his lifelong friends.

But his self-indulgence was a definite weakness in his character, quite independent, it seems to me, of his mental illness. He did countless kind actions when the spirit moved him, he frittered away thousands of pounds for the pleasure of giving and to satisfy his instinct of kindness and the 'rustling and grumbling' of his social conscience. But he always had more money than he required for his own pleasures; he never denied himself a pleasure; and he never did anything except the thing that he felt like doing at the time. Of work against the grain he had no experience; he was never compelled to do it, and he never put the compulsion on himself. He wrote the last three volumes of *Modern Painters* without really wanting to do so— that was as near as he ever came to disagreeable work. He never had to work for his living or encountered financial inconvenience when he ceased work for a week or six months or a couple of years. He never had to choose between doing

[1] *Reminiscences of a Specialist*, by Greville MacDonald, M.D. (1932).

the work he wanted to do and doing other work because it brought in necessary money. He had unusual freedom and unusual opportunities for indulging in his chosen pleasures. And all his life he took these opportunities and spent his money on his pleasures in the way that he confessed in a famous letter to Rossetti which I quote later. He always knew that he was living a life of self-indulgence and he was always ashamed of it; and, as will be seen, he was perpetually inventing elaborate excuses and making fantastic transferences to persuade himself that when he was indulging himself in this way, or in that way, he was really fulfilling some duty or working painfully against the grain. His reply in *Fors Clavigera* to a woman correspondent who charged him with this fault, is characteristic of these perpetual procedures.[1]

He was driven to these rationalisations of his self-indulgence because the sense of them was much more painful to him than to the ordinary plain man. I must reserve discussion of his valuable ideas in the fields of art and sociology for Part III. Here I must nevertheless indicate one idea which was with him from first to last, because it lay behind his sense of self-indulgence and influenced his conduct as well as his writing all his life.

He was brought up, as everyone knows, in a Puritanical creed by his mother, who was a religious bigot, and he early conceived the notion that the taking of any kind of pleasure was a sin. This notion was always with him; it coloured his attitude to æsthetics and to social economics; and though there were times when he worked through it to a broader vision, he always returned to it. We shall see this attitude when, as an adolescent, he was debating the choice of a career, and we meet it again at a later period when he wrote in *Fors Clavigera*:

'As you may neither eat, nor read, for the pleasure of eating or reading, so you may do *nothing else* for the pleasure of it, but for the use. The moral difference between a man and a beast is, that the one acts primarily for use, the other for pleasure. . . .'[2]

[1] *Fors Clavigera*, Letter 49, cf. below, pp. 117, 123 and 124.
[2] *Fors Clavigera*, Letter 61, Jan., 1876. The student should refer to the whole text of this passage which concludes with a reference to Revelation viii, 4 and 5.

38

INTRODUCTORY COMMENTS

It is essential to realise that Ruskin was not and never wanted to be and never pretended to be an artist content to set down enlargements of his experience without reference to the effect on other people; nor a scientist content to discover for the sake of discovery; nor a scholar content to escape from a living present which he cannot understand to a dead past which he can fashion as he will. To Ruskin his drawing and his intermittent studies of the past and of natural science were forms of play, and he could never pursue these activities without a sense of guilt—unless he could persuade himself that by his drawing or reading or measuring monuments he was in some way engaged in service to mankind. He indulged himself in these pastimes, as he indulged himself in everything, but we cannot understand his writings or his letters until we realise that he always really knew—when he was sketching at Abbeville, or drawing the monuments at Verona, or copying a corner of a picture by Giotto or Botticelli, or pottering among the archives in Venice, or chipping fragments from the Salève, or collecting minerals—that he *was* pottering and indulging himself in the forms of play which he happened to enjoy. Hence, as we shall see later, he had to persuade himself, in the 'sixties, that he was making necessary records that no one else could make, and to persuade himself and try to persuade others, in the 'seventies and 'eighties, that these activities were pursued 'for Oxford' or 'for Sheffield'.[1]

It was the same with the activities which are generally pursued as pleasures. He liked going to the theatre, and so he went frequently both in London and abroad. But he always had to find some excuse to himself for indulging in the pleasure. At the age of fifty he went to see Bancroft in Robertson's *Ours* and enjoyed it—but he had to write to the actor to explain that 'as regards myself, it is a duty no less than an indulgence ... for I get more help in my work from a good play than from any other kind of thoughtful rest'.[2] At sixty-five he went to see Wilson Barrett in *Claudian* 'three times from pure enjoy-

---

[1] Cf. below, pp. 106, 116, 122–123, 148–152 and 173–174.
[2] Letter to Squire Bancroft, March 16, 1871.

ment of it' as he confessed in conversation,[1] but he was only able to make the confession because he had already written to the actor to urge him 'to play all the noble parts of Roman and Gothic history in a series of such plays', and thus 'do more for art teaching than all the galleries and professors in Christendom'.[2]

Ruskin's pleasures at their best really were useful; and at their worst they were generally harmless. But we cannot understand his life or his writings unless we realise that since he knew them to be pleasures he could never pursue them in peace, and that he was always too self-indulgent to resist them. Carlyle who called him 'a bottle of beautiful soda-water' when he first met him early in the 'fifties, and who spoke in the 'sixties of the 'ray of real Heaven' that was in him, referred to him as a weak man.[3] And there can be no question that the charge was just. Ruskin was a great man in the sense of a good man; he had a social conscience, a sense of justice, inexhaustible funds of generous indignation, and he was a genius. He was also always a mentally sick man. And also, in character, a weak man. He was brave, but he was not of the stuff that martyrs are made of. He was never placed in the position of having to find where justice lay in any situation in which his personal safety was involved. He might have gone to the stake in a moment of manic exaltation had he lived in earlier times. It would not, however, have been his character that took him there, but a passing aspect of his mental ill.

The temptation to speculate on what he would have done, had the 1914–1918 war been perpetrated in the 'seventies, is, of course, irresistible to my generation who assess all values by their experience of good and evil, pleasure and suffering, strength and weakness, in those years. Would Ruskin have continued to hurl invective at the armament makers, at war waged 'by machinery and money'[4] and fought 'with a multi-

[1] With M. H. Spielmann, recorded in his *John Ruskin: a Sketch of his Life, his Work, and his Opinions*.
[2] Letter to Wilson Barrett, February 16, 1884.
[3] Letters from Carlyle to his brother, Dr. Carlyle, Nov. 27, 1855, and to Froude, autumn, 1869; Cook, *Life of Ruskin*, II, p. 562.
[4] *The Queen of the Air*, III, paras. 115 and 116 (cf. below, p. 322).

tude of human pawns'?[1] Would he have declared that the manhood of France and England should be sent to the frontiers armed with nothing but umbrellas as a demonstration that they were really Christians ready to meet 'powder and petroleum' as men and 'not as poisonous beasts may'?[2] Would he have told the munition makers that they '*must simply rather die* than make any destroying mechanism or compound'?[3] Would he have told the subscribers to the War Loan that it is only 'for an unjust war that men's bodies and souls have both to be bought and the best tools of war for them besides'?[4] Would he have thus defied the Defence of the Realm Act and taken the consequences? I think not. He would, I think, have found justice on his own side and told the world, as he did during the Crimean War, that the war was 'productive of good more than of evil', that it was not caused by any 'dim, half-avoidable involution of mean interests and errors' and that the Emperor of the Germans had been 'appointed' (as the Czar, he then said, had been 'appointed'), to launch the attack 'for conformation of all our greatness, trial of our strength, purging and punishment of our futilities' and so on and so forth.[5] Looking back upon it he might have said that in so doing he had indulged himself in a 'strongly instinctive pleasure'. But he would not, I think, have resisted the pleasure at the time.

In the biographical study, which follows, I try to show the operation of the several factors that I have just indicated: the drive of his social conscience, the perpetual rationalisations of his self-indulgence, and the influence on his thought and conduct of the mental malady that steadily destroyed him as the years went on.

Consideration of his valuable contributions to the theories of art, social economics and war is reserved for the Critical Comments in Part III.

[1] *The Crown of Wild Olive*, III, paras. 97 and 102 (cf. below, p. 317).
[2] *Fors Clavigera*, Letter 7 (cf. below, p. 367).
[3] *Fors Clavigera*, Letter 7.
[4] *Unto This Last*, IV, para. 76.
[5] *Modern Painters*, III, Part IV, Chap. XVIII, paras. 33–37 (cf. below, pp. 308 and 367-368).

THE PROLOGUE

John Ruskin was born in Hunter Street, Brunswick Square, London, on February 8, 1819.

His father was a wine-merchant who specialised in sherry; his mother's mother kept a Croydon public-house. The sherry busine s prospered; and when John was four his father moved from Hunter Street to a larger house and garden at He ne Hill.

Ruskin has told the story of his childhood in *Præterita;* and his biographers have given us accounts of his early years with portraits of his parents—of his father who had a taste for Byron's poetry and for pictures, and of his mother, an Evangelical Protestant, a stupid bigot and bully, who made him read aloud a chapter of the Bible every day and learn long passages by heart.

The mental troubles from which he suffered later were perhaps in part the result of bad heredity. His paternal grandfather was unstable, a man who 'seldom knew his own mind for two hours together' and who became insane in 1815.[1] His parents were first cousins. His mother, always intemperately narrow-minded and dogmatic, was thirty-eight when he was born, and his father was thirty-four. He himself was undoubtedly a prodigy with a brain that was exceptionally mobile and easily excited. Into this brain his mother forced, brutally, the text of the Bible day by day; and then his father made him listen to long extracts from the poets. While he was in the hands of a tutor at a small local school, he was encouraged, at home, to draw and to write in prose and verse; he was given specimens of minerals and encouraged to compile a mineralogical dictionary. When he was fifteen his birthday present

[1] Letters from his paternal grandmother about her husband, 1805–1817, quoted in Library Edition.

PROLOGUE

was a geological treatise—de Saussure's *Voyage dans les Alpes*.[1] He had little or no intercourse with other boys; when he was over forty and a widower he took to romping with schoolgirls[2]; but as a boy he never romped or rode or played outdoor games.

An unusual amount of travelling in England and abroad was another feature of his early education. His father was accustomed to leave London for two or three months in the middle of each year; he toured the country seeking orders for his sherry, and sightseeing at the same time; he travelled in a private carriage and took his wife and son with him:

'If there . . . were any gentleman's house to be seen—or better still a lord's—or, best of all a duke's—my father baited the horses, and took my mother and me reverently through the state rooms; always speaking a little under our breath to the housekeeper, major-domo, or other authority in charge; and gleaning worshipfully what fragmentary illustrations of the history and domestic ways of the family might fall from their lips.'[3]

In 1832, when Ruskin was thirteen, he was given a copy of Rogers' *Italy* with vignettes by Turner; and on a tour abroad with his parents in 1833 he began to look at mountain scenery with eyes influenced by these vignettes. On this tour, and on subsequent tours abroad, the family travelled in a carriage with four horses, and postillions, and a courier who rode ahead to make arrangements about rooms and relays of horses.[4] They looked at the outsides of buildings, and at the splendid scenery through which they drove. They rarely looked at pictures, and Ruskin learned next to nothing about the old masters on these Continental tours which preceded the writing of his first book.[5]

Turner was the only artist in whom he took any particular

[1] Cf. *Fors Clavigera*, Letter 4, para. 3, and *Præterita*, I, Chap. VII, para. 139.
[2] Cf. below, pp. 71–73.
[3] *Præterita*, I, Chap. I, para. 34.
[4] *Præterita*, I, Chap. VI, paras. 125 and 126.
[5] Cf. below, pp. 194–198.

43

interest at this time. When he was sixteen he saw some Turner water-colours depicting the kind of scenery which he knew, and he became so enthusiastic about them that, to please him, his father began to buy Turner water-colours for the drawing-room at Herne Hill. Thus it happened that at seventeen Ruskin became indignant when he read a hostile criticism of Turner's pictures in the Royal Academy of 1836 and that he wrote an essay in protest. His father sent the manuscript to Turner, who discouraged publication; and the essay was not published.[1]

At eighteen he went as a Gentleman Commoner to Christ Church, Oxford. He had with him a valet, as was customary at the time; he also had with him—which was no more customary then than now—his mother, who had insisted on taking rooms in Oxford, and his father who came up for weekends.

That Ruskin permitted his mother to come to Oxford was, of course, a blunder. He should have told his parents categorically that he would either not go to Oxford or else go in the same way as everyone else. But he did not make this troublesome stand. He allowed his mother to bully him and he went round to tea with her at seven every day.

In Oxford he won the Newdigate Prize at the third attempt with a poem called *Salsette and Elephanta*.[2] He dressed in an eccentric fashion with large neckcloth and a brown velvet collar to his coat.[3] A contemporary informs us that he was regarded as 'a kind of butt'.[4] He would have nothing to do with hunting or with games of ball. When the hunting and ball-playing gentlemen came round to 'rag' him, he bought them off with libations of the paternal sherry.[5]

The most important results of his stay in Oxford were the

[1] Cf. *Præterita*, I, Chap. XII, para. 243. The attack on Turner was in *Blackwood's Magazine;* the pictures attacked were *Juliet and her Nurse, Rome from Mount Adventure* and *Mercury and Argus*.

[2] Salsette and Elephanta are islands off Bombay with remains of temples.

[3] Letter written by Dean Liddell, 1837.

[4] Letter quoted by Dean Kitchin.

[5] Obituary notice on Ruskin in *The Times*, Jan. 22, 1900.

friendships which he began with Henry Acland, afterwards Regius Professor of Medicine, and Henry Liddell, afterwards Dean of Christ Church, who both became his champions in University circles, and eventually procured for him the Slade Professorship.[1]

When he came of age in February, 1840, he received from his father a water-colour by Turner and an allowance which brought him, as pocket money, the equivalent of about£600 a year in present values.[2] It seems moreover to have been understood that he could draw further for extra purposes, especially for specimens of minerals, which he collected, and for pictures. Both he and his father now became important customers for Turner's water-colours which they bought from Turner's agent, a dealer named Griffith, who in this same year introduced him to the artist himself.

In the late summer of this year, 1840, he had his first breakdown. This followed frustration in a love affair. He has told the story of his youthful passion very prettily in *Prœterita*.[3] The girl, whose name was Adèle, was one of the daughters of his father's French partner whom he had first seen in Paris when she was fourteen or fifteen. He himself was sixteen when he fell in love with her. He remained in love with her for four years. She was a Roman Catholic and his mother therefore would not allow the notion of a marriage to be discussed or considered. In 1840 she married someone else.

This passion had deep and lasting effects. Here is a poem written at the beginning :

ON ADÈLE BY MOONLIGHT

With what a glory and a grace
The moonbeam lights her laughing face,
And dances in her dazzling eye;
As liquid in its brilliancy
As the deep blue of midnight ocean,
When underneath, with trembling motion,
The phosphor light floats by.

[1] Cf. below, pp. 88–90, 99 and 100.
[2] The actual income then was something over £200 a year.
[3] *Prœterita*, I, Chap. X, paras. 205–210; Chap. XII, paras. 254–255.

And blushes bright pass o'er her cheek,
But pure and pale as is the glow
Of sunset on a mountain peak,
Robed in eternal snow;
Her ruby lips half-oped the while,
With careless air around her throwing
Or, with a vivid glance, bestowing
A burning word, or silver smile.[1]

I quote this, not to show that Ruskin at sixteen or seventeen was a good or a bad poet, but to draw attention to the images. Adèle, as I have said, was fourteen or fifteen at this time; all his life Ruskin was to take pleasure in contemplating girl children; and in middle life he fell in love with a girl of eleven. If we compare the images of eye and lip in this poem with those in the passages describing the children at Winnington and other passages which I quote later we see the furrows cut by this experience.[2]

It is always melancholy to contemplate the neurotic adolescent forced to painful expenditure of nervous energy if he (or she) is to escape parental tyranny at the right time. But it is still more melancholy to contemplate a neurotic adolescent like Ruskin who was too weak to effect the escape. Here for the second time he had allowed himself to be bullied by his mother and failed to establish himself on his two feet. Looking back on this period from his old age he wrote of 'the general mistake, mismanagement and misfortune of all my education, mind and heart' which characterised it.[3] But at the time he obeyed his mother with 'sullenness',[4] and fretted in secret, till he sank into depression and also became physically ill. The day came when he spat blood. The doctors diagnosed a threat of consumption; and advised a foreign tour.

In September, 1840, the family went accordingly to the South of France and Italy and remained there till June of the following year. Ruskin was in a melancholic condition, and

[1] 1836.
[2] Cf. below, pp. 71 and 73. The reference to 'phosphor light' is also significant; cf. below, pp. 139 and 142.
[3] MS. intended for *Præterita*.
[4] *Præterita*, I, Chap. XII, para. 256.

believed that he was dying.[1] But gradually his physical and mental condition improved. By the time he was twenty-three the fear of consumption had been proved to be unfounded, and he was back in Oxford to take his degree, while his parents moved to a new house at Denmark Hill—a large mansion with seven acres of garden, orchard and shrubbery.

He had now recovered his morale and he began to contemplate the various careers which seemed open to him. There was first the possibility of a career as a writer. He had already contributed some essays to the *Architectural Magazine* and the *Magazine of Natural History*. Referring to the first, *The Times* had written: 'This author has the mind of a poet as well as the eye and hand of an artist, and has produced a series of highly poetical essays';[2] referring to the second, the editor of the *Magazine of Natural History* had written to his father: 'Your son is certainly the greatest natural genius that ever it has been my fortune to become acquainted with...'[3] Secondly there was the possibility that he might become an artist. He had done a certain amount of amateur sketching and he might now concentrate his energy in that field. Thirdly there was the possibility that he might live the life of a gentleman with scientific tastes like White of Selborne.[4] Fourthly there was the possibility of the Church for which he had always been, as the phrase goes, 'destined' by his parents.

From the time of his majority till he was twenty-three he brooded on the possibility of the Church as his career. 'As long as we are doubtful of the state of *one* human soul of those among whom we dwell,' he wrote, 'any direction of our energies to any one end or object whatsoever except the saving of souls, is a merciless and execrable crime.'[5] But then he reflected that the energies of Galileo, Newton, Michelangelo, Handel, Wordsworth and Bacon had been 'employed more effectively to the glory of God' than if they had been

[1] *Præterita*, II, Chap. III, para 50 (first draft) and para. 51.
[2] *The Times* Feb. 2, 1839.
[3] Letter from J. C. Loudon to J. Ruskin, Nov. 30, 1838.
[4] *Præterita*, II, Chap. I, para. 204 and MS. addition to *Præterita*.
[5] Letter to the Rev. Thomas Dale, Sept. 22, 1841.

directed to 'priestly exertion'.[1] He himself was 'attached to the pursuits of art and science'. Was he justified in following them up when there were souls which he should save?[2]

The more he pondered the problem the clearer it became that he could not devote himself entirely to the Church or entirely to art, science and scholarship. He looked back wistfully to the days before such problems had perplexed him: 'What a nice thing it was at six years old to be told everything you were to do, and whipped if you did not do it! One never felt that one had got such a nasty thing as a conscience rustling and grumbling inside.'[3] In the end he broke away, for the first time, from his mother and decided definitely against the Church.

From the practical standpoint he was doubtless right. His father used to say with tears in his eyes, 'He would have been a Bishop.'[4] But Ruskin would never have been made a bishop. The matter would have been settled by his second sermon, if it had not been settled by his first. His religion was always, fundamentally, personal. He could never have had a career within an organisation of any kind, and least of all within the Church. There was never a time, once he began to think for himself, when in the recesses of his mind he looked to the Church or any section of it as an appointed intermediary between himself and God. It was thus sound wisdom that led him to defy his mother by deciding against Holy Orders.[5]

But even when he had decided against a career within the Church he could not decide to devote himself entirely to the Sirens called Art, Science and Scholarship. He had a talent for delicate descriptive drawing—(though, as he admitted, he was 'without power of design' and he could never compose a picture)[6]; he enjoyed drawing, but at the back of his mind he

[1] MS. for additions to *Præterita* and Letter to the Rev. Thomas Dale, Sept. 22, 1841.
[2] Letter to the Rev. Thomas Dale, Sept. 22, 1841.
[3] Letter to a College Friend, May 16, 1841.
[4] *Præterita*, I, Chap. I, para. 20.
[5] Cf. below, pp. 229 *et seq.*
[6] *Præterita*, I, Chap. VII, para. 139, and II, Chap. IV, para. 65.

PROLOGUE

always looked upon it as a relaxation and a form of play: 'I
find nothing equal to drawing', he wrote, 'for occupying the
whole mind without fatiguing of one's powers'[1]; and again
later: 'I am obliged often to give up thinking and take to
walking and drawing as mechanical opiates.'[2] He was happy
in geological and botanical studies, but he looked upon them
really in the same way. He had facility for writing sonorous
and decorative English; after every experience he 'had pleasure
in making some sort of melodious noise about it'[3]; he knew
that from boyhood he had always been capable of 'mere
rhythmic mewing and execration'[4]; but as he enjoyed perform-
ing in this manner he looked upon it as pleasure and so as self-
indulgence in yet another form. He believed from the outset
that art, science and scholarship, pursued for themselves, were
really drugs or forms of play; and when he lost himself in
drawing, or writing, or study, he was always haunted by a
sense of guilt.

Thus at twenty-two, he could not give himself completely
to the Church or to the Sirens; but life seemed to him impossible if either were thought away; it was *nec tecum nec sine
te vivere possum* in each case.

He was in this position when fate, in the shape of another
newspaper attack on Turner, made him decide to write another
answer—and to write it this time in the form of a book. That
book, the first volume of *Modern Painters*, was written when
he was twenty-three. It was published in May, 1843, when he
was twenty-four.

It is sometimes assumed that the book 'discovered' and
'made' Turner.[5] But Turner was nearly seventy at the time;
he had been an Academician for more than forty years; he had
long been recognised as an outstanding figure among the landscape painters; he had made a fortune by his paintings, and he

[1] Letter to a College Friend, May 16, 1841.
[2] Letter to C. E. Norton, July 31, 1859.
[3] *Præterita*, I, Chap. VII, para. 139.
[4] MS. for additions to *Præterita*.
[5] Thus Mr. David Larg in his *John Ruskin* (Davies, 1932) says: 'The
young graduate had lightly cast fame on the ageing shoulders of Turner.'

49

had twice refused £100,000 for the unsold works which he hoarded in his various houses. The critics of the day took the line that the celebrated J. M. W. Turner, R.A., had gone to pieces in his later years; Ruskin set out to prove that he had become a greater artist than he had ever been before. The book attracted a certain amount of attention—though less than is commonly supposed.[1] But it had no effect on Turner's position in his lifetime.[2]

I discuss later the strange manic character of this first volume of *Modern Painters*.[3] Here I need only consider its immediate effects on Ruskin's life. To begin with, it brought him the possession of Turner's oil painting *The Slave Ship* which his father gave him to celebrate the publication;[4] and it eventually brought about a species of intimacy with Turner himself. Ruskin had not made a very favourable impression on Turner at the first interview, referred to above, but the old artist had allowed him to keep in touch with him while he was writing the book, and after the publication he became a frequent visitor at Denmark Hill, being present regularly from 1844 to 1850 at Ruskin's birthday parties.[5] It was fifteen months, however, before he referred to the book, as we learn from Ruskin's diary:

'At Windus's on Thursday, to dine with Turner and Griffith alone, and Turner thanking me for my book for the first time. We drove home together, reached his house about one in the morning . . . vowed he'd be damned if we shouldn't come in and have some sherry. We were compelled to obey, and so drank healths again, exactly as the clock struck one, by the light of a single tallow candle in the under room—the wine by the way first-rate.'[6]

Ruskin now felt strong enough to put up some sort of fight

[1] Cf. below, pp. 369 and 370.
[2] Cf. below, p. 63.
[3] Cf. below, pp. 198–205.
[4] This picture is now in the Museum of Fine Arts, Boston, U.S.A. Ruskin sold it in 1869 for £2,042. (Cf. p. 383.)
[5] *Modern Painters*, II, Epilogue (1883), and *On the Old Road* (*My First Editor*), para. 8.
[6] Ruskin's Diary, Oct., 1844 (cf. below, p. 264).

against his mother. He announced that before he could write
the second volume of *Modern Painters* he must go to Italy—
and go without his parents. There was no open opposition.
But Turner (probably 'put up to it' by Mrs. Ruskin) tried to
dissuade him with 'There'll be such a fidge about you, when
you're gone.'[1]

Thus it came that in 1845, at the age of twenty-six, Ruskin
tasted freedom for the first time. He went through France and
Switzerland to Italy in his own carriage, with a Swiss guide,
and a valet. He made drawings; he stared at the scenery and at
sunsets; he worked at geology and architecture; and he began
for the first time really to study Italian painting.[2] He had
trained his valet, named George, to act as secretary and general
assistant in his work. If the sun was hot when he went out
sketching, the guide, or George, held an umbrella above his
head; if he wanted a manuscript fair-copied, or an inscription
or a relief traced, George was at hand to do it; when he went
for a ramble in the mountains the guide was in front, and
George was behind, with a hammer and a bag, ready to chip
off and carry home geological specimens. After six months of
this free and pleasant life he went home and wrote the second
volume of *Modern Painters* which appeared the following
year.

At Denmark Hill after the second volume was written he
was ill at ease. He was irritated by renewal of contact with
his mother who ruled the roost with stupidity and arrogance;
and he was also irritated by his father who, though sensible
and sympathetic, was unable to follow the workings of his
son's mind. On the surface there was harmony; the conflict
was not open but suppressed; and it was all the more harassing
because it was suppressed. At this time also he was disturbed
by unsatisfied sex desires. Another attack of depression now
made its appearance, and he again became physically ill, complaining of trouble with his eyes. A tour abroad with his
parents failed to relieve the situation; irritation appeared, and he
was rude, for the first time, to his father who had disturbed

[1] *Præterita*, II, Chap. VI, paras. 105–107.
[2] For these studies, cf. below, pp. 206, 213, 244 and 358.

him from a reverie with a question about the coachman's tip.[1] On the return to England he went away from home as much as possible—staying with friends in Oxford, at Ambleside, and in Scotland. He fell mildly in love with a Miss Lockhart (the daughter of Scott's biographer), who did not respond. On these visits he wrote depressed letters in sharp contrast with the manic self-confidence of his first two books:

'There is nothing for it but throwing one's self into the stream, and going down with one's arms under water, ready to be carried anywhere, or do anything. . . . I have not one moment of profitably spent time to look back to while I was here, and much useless labour and disappointed hope; and I can neither bear the excitement of being in the society where the play of mind is constant and rolls *over* me like heavy wheels; nor the pain of being alone. I get away in the evenings . . . and rest; but then my failing sight plagues me. I cannot look at anything as I used to do and the evening sky is covered with swimming strings and eels.'[2]

We must note here, with reference to this and other complaints about his eyes, that Ruskin all his life had excellent sight.

'I know not what is the matter with me, but the people seem to have put a chill on me and taken my life out of me. I feel alike uncertain and incapable of purpose. . . .'[3]

'I feel so utterly down-hearted to-night that I must get away to-morrow without going out again, for I am afraid of something seizing me in the state of depression.'[4]

'The sea by whose side I am writing was once to me a friend, companion, master, teacher; now it is *salt water* and salt water only.'[5]

'God knows that while I am eaten up with vanity and selfishness to the very heart's core there is not the lightest or lowest subject on which I could now utter a presumptuous word, so

[1] *Præterita*, II, Chap. X, para. 189.
[2] Letters to his father from Oxford, June 27, 1847.
[3] Letter to Miss Mary Mitford from Denmark Hill, June 19, 1847.
[4] Letter to his father from Dunkeld, Aug. 25, 1847.
[5] Letter to the Rev. W. L. Brown from Folkestone, Nov. 27, 1847

humbled have I lately been and so violently cast down from all high thoughts.'[1]

'I had not been long at home when I found nervous excitement returning on me violently, and as my father and mother wanted a little change of air they brought me down here, where, finding me better, they left me.'[2]

Meanwhile his mother had decided that he must be married at once and she selected a girl of eighteen, a distant cousin, Euphemia Gray, whom he had known from childhood. Here is a reference to this young lady written by Ruskin during the courtship:

'I love Miss Gray very much and therefore cannot tell what to think of her, only this I know, that in many respects she is unfit to be my wife unless she also loved me exceedingly. She is surrounded by people who pay her attentions, and though I believe most of them inferior in some points to myself, far more calculated to catch a girl's fancy. Still Miss Gray and I are old friends. I have every reason to think that if I were to try I could soon make her more than a friend, and if, after I leave her this time, she holds out for six months more, I believe I shall ask her to come to Switzerland with me next year, and if she will not, or if she takes anyone else in the meantime, I am sadly afraid I shall enjoy my tour much less than usual, though no disappointment of this kind would affect me as the first did.'[3]

He was clearly not very enthusiastic; he was obeying his mother, courting the lady, and doing his best to persuade himself that he was in love with her. Four months later he writes as follows:

'An old lady was telling me, but the day before yesterday, that if I was too particular about my wife I should assuredly get a bad one.'[4]

[1] Letter to William Macdonald Macdonald from Bowerswell, Perth, Oct. 5, 1847.
[2] Letter to William Macdonald Macdonald from Folkestone, Dec. 2, 1847.
[3] Letter to William Macdonald Macdonald from Bowerswell, Perth, Oct. 5, 1847.
[4] Letter to William Macdonald Macdonald, Feb. 20, 1848.

PROLOGUE

The old lady may or may not have been his mother. In any case six weeks after writing the letter, at the age of twenty-nine, he was married.[1]

He had planned a work on architecture as his next book; and he now went off with his wife for a tour of the English cathedrals. But he caught a feverish chill and decided that the English cathedrals were too cold to work in.[2] The couple went accordingly to Normandy, and there he began the study of French Gothic instead.

The marriage, it seems clear, was never consummated; and it has been frequently assumed that he was impotent; but a record of a perfectly authenticated conversation has recently been published in which Ruskin categorically denied this and stated that he did not claim the usual relations because, not being in love with his wife, he believed that he had no right to do so.[3]

The unusual relations with his wife did not make him unhappy. He was certainly happier in his married life than at many other periods. His wife, who was the daughter of a lawyer, was his social equal; she had beauty and social talents; but she had no special equipment in education, she was ten years his junior, and she had no money of her own. Ruskin in her company could indulge his manic impulse to preach and indulge in the pleasure of parading his erudition. Also he could indulge himself in the pleasure of being generous with money. He now had an annual allowance from his father equivalent to about £4,500 in present values with the faculty

[1] In conversation with George MacDonald years later Ruskin said that he had never been in love with his wife, but had hoped he might and thought he ought 'if only for her beauty'. (Cf. *Reminiscences of a Specialist*, by Greville MacDonald, M.D. Allen & Unwin, London, 1932.)

[2] *The Seven Lamps of Architecture*, Preface to the First Edition.

[3] *Reminiscences of a Specialist*, by Greville MacDonald, M.D. London, Allen & Unwin, 1932. The conversation was with the author's father, George MacDonald, with whom Ruskin was later intimate. (Cf. pp. 129 and 130). I am not competent to express an opinion as to whether his mental illness may or may not have played a part in this reluctance.

of procuring more from the same source whenever he required it.[1] His wife liked frocks and jewels, and he gave them to her. He provided her with a house in Park Street, Mayfair, and with an elegant apartment on the Grand Canal in Venice where, in addition to the ordinary servants and a private gondolier, she had an English maid—and he had George (who had now learned to make daguerreotypes of Venetian palaces). This generosity with money was a genuine satisfaction for Ruskin, as we know from a famous letter to Rosetti:

'My pleasures are in seeing, thinking, reading and making people happy (if I can consistently with my own comfort). And I *take* these pleasures. And I suppose if my pleasures were in smoking, betting, dicing and giving pain, I should take *those* pleasures. It seems to me that one man is made one way and one another—the measure of effort and self-denial can never be known, except by each conscience to itself. Mine is small enough.'[2]

In his married life he had all these pleasures and the ordinary pleasures of fashionable life as well. In London he and his wife were invited to dinners and parties and they were presented at Court, where he tells us they acquitted themselves well:

'I got through excellently well and I believe did what was right—and I *thought* that Prince Albert put something like markedness into his bow.... The Queen looked much younger and prettier than I expected ... but I only saw the profile—I could not see the front face as I knelt to her, at least without an upturning of the eyes, which I thought would be unseemly ... Effie ... heard people saying, "What a beautiful dress!" just as she got up to the Queen.'[3]

In Venice and the neighbourhood they mixed in the best and most expensive society, and they were informally presented to Austrian royalties. Here are some of his accounts of functions:

[1] The regular allowance paid to his account at the beginning of each year was £1,500; but Ruskin senior seems to have produced a good deal more for the purchase of pictures, expenses of publications and so forth.

[2] Letter to Dante Gabriel Rossetti, 1855.

[3] Letters to his mother, 1850, and Letters to his father from Park Street, May, 1850.

PROLOGUE

'Effie was well dressed and allowed by everyone to be the *reine du bal*. The old Marshal took her up the room himself to present her to the Maréchale, and then to the Archduke Charles Ferdinand. . . . The dancing was much more spirited than ours. . . .'[1]

'We are excessively petted here. Marshal Radetsky sent Effie his picture yesterday, with his own signature. . . . His chief of the staff . . . left his carriage for us . . . and the Marshal's two aides-de-camp and another young officer came to escort us in our drive in the evening.'[2]

'The Emperor announced himself for ten o'clock at night. Everybody on the Grand Canal was requested . . . to illuminate their houses *inside*. . . . We went out . . . and rowed down to the part of the Grand Canal nearest the railroad station . . . which was literally as full of boats as it could hold. . . . Presently the Emperor did come. We got pushed . . . and came crash up against the bow of the Emperor's boat. Effie and I were standing—I, of course, with my hat off . . . for half a minute, when we managed to slip clear of the Emperor who passed ahead, giving us a touch of his cap. We fell astern . . . but were pushed forward on the other side. . . . This time it was not a gondola on our other side, but a barge full of very ill-looking fellows, who, I thought, might just as well have me between them and the Emperor . . . so I let Beppo keep his place . . . for a quarter of an hour.'[3]

'The Austrian officers gave their last carnival ball last night. I took [Effie] there at nine, and left her, staying till ten myself. . . . Effie enjoyed herself very much and came home at half past one, which I thought very moderate.'[4]

Ruskin was clearly enjoying all this after his mother's regime at Denmark Hill. In Venice he felt important, and rich, and free. He could have these mundane pleasures when he

[1] Letter to his parents from Verona, Jan. 27, 1852.
[2] Letter to his parents from Verona, June 4, 1852.
[3] Letter to his father from Venice, Oct. 3, 1851. A characteristic rationalisation of his desire to have all the fun of the fair by keeping close to the Emperor's boat.
[4] Letter to his father from Venice, Feb. 19, 1852.

wanted them, and he could also draw and read, stare at Venetian architecture, measure the capitals of the Ducal Palace, work in the archives, and ponder on the Bible.[1] His work was not handicapped by shortage of money. He spent the equivalent of £3,500 on the production of *The Stones of Venice*[2]; and he bought expensive objects of art for his collections—specimens of minerals, mediæval manuscripts, and more Turner water-colours of which he had thirty in 1852 and nearly a hundred by 1860.

His marriage evidently cured him for the time being of the depression of 1847. While he was writing *The Seven Lamps of Architecture* and *The Stones of Venice* he was once more convinced that he had 'perfect judgement' of works of art,[3] and that he was an appointed reformer of his 'blind and wandering' fellow-men:[4] 'I could not write as I do unless I felt myself a reformer—a man who knew what others did not know and felt what they did not feel.'[5] At this time he published a pamphlet, *Notes on the Construction of Sheepfolds*, in which he set out to adjust the differences of all Protestant sects; and he wrote three letters for *The Times* on *Taxation, Election and Education*—which began by stating that the first principles of these problems are 'so clear and simple that he who runs may read them'.[6]

The letters intended for *The Times* were a result of Ruskin's manic impulse to preach. But in his luxurious married life his social conscience also had a word to say. While his wife was dancing with Austrian nobles and he was putting 'more verbiage' into '*Stones*',[7] he could not read an English newspaper without discomfort. In one he saw three parallel columns:

'The first gave an account of a girl aged twenty-one, being found, after lying exposed all night, and having given birth to

[1] Cf. below, pp. 336 and 337.
[2] The actual sum recorded is £1,200. The authority is C. A. Howell, who acted as his secretary from 1864 to 1866.
[3] Letter to his father from Venice, Jan. 9, 1852.
[4] *Ibid.*
[5] Letter to his father from Venice, Feb. 28, 1852.
[6] Cf. below, pp. 279 and 280.
[7] Letter to his father, April 4, 1852 (cf. below, p. 359).

a dead child, on the banks of a canal near Maidstone. The second was the fashions for November with an elaborate account of satin skirts; and the third the burning to death of a child—or rather a dying after burning—because the surgeon, without orders from the parents, would neither go to see it nor send it any medicine.'[1]

Ruskin was quite certain that God had not intended everyone to have suppers of soufflée and Sillery,[2] and to have gondoliers and valets, and jewels and satin dresses, and houses in Venice and Mayfair. He had no patience with the idea of 'Equality'; —'the laws of nature and the reason of man', he had written, 'are alike against it.'[3] Everyone should be taught in childhood 'the impossibility of equality among men, the good which arises from their inequality, and the compensating circumstances in different states and fortunes'.[4] But he was also quite certain that God had not intended young women to sleep out of doors in November or babies to be burned; and his social conscience told him that he should try to remedy these ills.

By the end of 1853 he was feeling quite embarrassed by the situation:

'My next birthday is the keystone of my arch of life—my 35th—and up to this time I cannot say that I have in any way "taken up my cross" or "denied myself"; neither have I visited the poor nor fed them, but have spent my money and time on my own pleasure or instruction. I find I cannot be easy in doing this any more. . . . I feel no call to part with anything I have, but I am going to preach some most *severe* doctrines in my next book, and I *must* act up to them in not going on spending in works of art. I won't make a vow that if, by any chance, I should hear of some exquisite thirteenth-century work being in the market, I may not consider whether I should be justified in buying it to take care of it.'[5]

We may note in passing that Ruskin's method of 'taking

---

[1] Letter to his father from Venice, Nov. 12, 1851.
[2] Cf. above, p. 28.
[3] *The Seven Lamps of Architecture*, Chap. IV, para. 28.
[4] *The Stones of Venice*, III, Appendix 7.
[5] Letter to his father, Nov. 16, 1853. The italics are Ruskin's.

care' of his considerable collection of mediæval manuscripts
was to annotate them in ink, and cut out pages,[1] and also that
shortly after writing this letter he bought the manuscript
known as the 'St. Louis Psalter'—the outstanding feature of his
collection.[2]

It was during his married life that he discovered the Pre-
Raphaelites and wrote letters in *The Times* and a pamphlet
defending them.[3] In the summer of 1853 he invited Millais,
who was then twenty-four, to stay with him and Mrs. Ruskin
at Glenfinlas in the Trossachs. He posed there to him for the
well-known full-length portrait (now in the possession of a
descendant of Sir Henry Acland) and he held an umbrella above
his protégé's head while he painted the mountain stream in the
background at six in the morning.[4] Mrs. Ruskin, who was
the same age as Millais, left Ruskin in April of next year, and
brought a suit for annulment of the marriage. Twelve months
later she married Millais.

Ruskin appeared to have taken this ending to his marriage
very well. The episode set the gossips' tongues wagging. But
he behaved with dignity and withdrew quietly from acquaintances who had been more his wife's friends than his own. At
this point nevertheless he made a fatal blunder. Though he
was now a man of thirty-five he went back to live in his
parents' house at Denmark Hill.

We may assume that he was lonely and that he indulged the
instinct which led him back to the old study where he had
worked before his marriage, and to the old audience to whom
he had formerly performed when he read aloud the purple

[1] Ruskin's Diaries: Dec. 30, 1853; Jan. 1, 1854; Jan. 3, 1854.
[2] *The Psalter and Hours of Isabelle of France*, a thirteenth-century
work, always referred to by Ruskin as the 'St. Louis Psalter'. He always
regarded it as his greatest treasure. Later he gave some leaves to Norton,
and lent some to his 'Standard' Collection in Oxford (cf. below, p. 105).
After his death the Psalter was reassembled and passed to the Yates
Thompson Collection. He bought the Psalter on Feb. 16, 1854, as
noted in his Diary.
[3] Cf. below, pp. 245–249.
[4] Ruskin's diary, 1853.

PROLOGUE

passages in the first volume of *Modern Painters* to his parents. But, once there, he wanted to get away again. In the next five years he wandered hither and thither in continual journeys that he might escape from the place where he was always ill at ease—his home. He was in Tunbridge Wells and Deal, ostensibly to cure a cough, in the summer of 1855; in France and Switzerland from May to October in 1854, 1856 and 1858; and away almost continuously in 1859. On his foreign tours he pursued his old occupations—he drew, he made notes, he looked at scenery and natural phenomena, pottered with geology, botany, history, architectural monuments and pictures. But now the mobility of his interest becomes conspicuous and a pronounced restlessness appears in his manner of work. He turns his attention continually from one thing to another. When he wakes in the morning he finds more crowding thoughts in his head than the day serves to recapture and put down.[1] And this character appears in the discursive and disjointed third, fourth, and fifth volumes of *Modern Painters* which were written in these five years.[2]

At this period he sought friendship with the Carlyles, the Brownings, Tennyson and other literary people; he kept in touch with some 'artistic' ladies—Lady Ashburton, Lady Waterford, Lady Trevelyan and Lady Canning—and gave them advice about their drawings. Above all he sought the company and friendship of the Pre-Raphaelite artists. With Millais, naturally, he could now have no personal relations. But he saw a good deal of Rossetti to whom he made an annual allowance.[3] He met Rossetti's master, Ford Madox Brown, and Rossetti's disciples, William Morris and Burne-Jones;[4] and he started the publication of an annual pamphlet on the Royal Academy exhibitions in order to help the Pre-Raphaelite movement and to demonstrate his 'perfect judgement' by separating the good pictures from the bad.[5]

[1] Letter to Mrs. Acland, July 10, 1855.
[2] Cf. below, pp. 227–230.
[3] Cf. below, pp. 270–272.
[4] Cf. below, pp. 272–275.
[5] Cf. below, pp. 250 and 377–379.

PROLOGUE

In *The Seven Lamps of Architecture* and *The Stones of Venice* he had put forward a theory that the happiness of the workman is a factor essentially connected with fine craftsmanship and art.[1] He now began more and more to take an interest in Social Economics and in the conditions of English artisans. He would order his brougham in the evenings and, escaping from his parents, he would drive to the newly founded Working Men's College in Red Lion Square where he entertained the workmen by talking to them and showing them the delicacy of a sprig of ivy and teaching them to draw it.

And thus he reached the age of forty in 1859.

It is important here to realise what seems to me a serious mistake made by all Ruskin's biographers. They all suggest that he was a kind of Art-Dictator of England in these years, the eighteen-fifties, which we have just been considering. They suggest that neo-Gothic buildings were going up all over England as a result of *The Seven Lamps of Architecture* and *The Stones of Venice;* that the officials in the art world were at his feet; that the general public devoured his writings; that his word was law in regard to modern painters and the old masters; that rich merchants rushed to buy the pictures which he praised; and that no painter could flourish without his helping hand. 'The world', says a recent biographer, 'watched *the* Ruskin piling books and articles and pamphlets one on top of the other.' 'He wrote . . . and taught', says another, '. . . and all England listened.'

All this, as I read the evidence, is greatly exaggerated if not indeed entirely wrong. The image created by his biographers must be the result of a confusion between his position and reputation at this time when he was under forty, and his position and reputation in the 'seventies, 'eighties and 'nineties; and it has its origin in Collingwood's biography, which was first published in 1892. In the Appendix I describe what I believe to be Ruskin's real position in the 'fifties.[2] Here I need only state in general terms that neither 'the world' nor even

[1] Cf. below, pp. 214, 216–218.
[2] Cf. below, pp. 369 *et seq.*

61

'all England' knew his name at this period. He was only known in literary and artistic circles. His books—*Modern Painters, I*, only to some extent excepted—had exceedingly small sales, and there were intervals of years between the editions, which were small. There were one or two people among his acquaintance who bought one or two pictures by the Pre-Raphaelites on his recommendation; but Millais always had his own patrons, and in the 'fifties Ruskin himself bought much more of Rossetti's work than he induced anyone else to buy. He was unable to make the general public buy the pictures which he praised, and still more unable to prevent them spending huge sums on works by Academicians and others to which he had referred in disparaging terms. He was detested by the Academy and by 90 per cent of all the other artists who had heard his name. The architects as a body regarded him as 'obnoxious to the profession'. He was disliked and had no influence at the National Gallery. At the end of the 'fifties he was so unpopular and without influence that he could write with almost perfect truth:

'I have so many enemies that it is enough to ruin any man that I should take the slightest interest in him. I assure you this is true—but I'll convince you of it when I see you.'[1]

He was also, we must remember, completely without official status. He had no appointment and no honours. When asked to give his exact position for official records he could only describe himself as 'Master of the Elementary and Land-scape School of Drawing at the Working Men's Institute'.[2]

He had started to praise Turner in 1843. But his praise had scarcely begun to have effect in 1858. Turner had died in 1851 and the National Gallery, under the settlement of his will, had received some two hundred of his oil paintings and nineteen thousand water-colours and drawings. But the galleries in which examples were exhibited were always empty and the Trustees sanctioned a catalogue in which Claude was described

---

[1] Letter to Coventry Patmore (probably 1859).
[2] Evidence before the National Gallery Commission, 1857. For his connection with this Commission, cf. Appendix, p. 375.

as superior to Turner—as though *Modern Painters* had never been written.[1]

The plain fact, as I read the evidence, was that Ruskin at the end of the 'fifties was still what he had been from the beginning —an isolated amateur in the art world.[2] By means of his father's money he had been able to act the part of an eighteenth-century dilettante with artistic tastes. He had travelled luxuriously abroad, moved in Continental society, made drawings, written about the arts as the spirit moved him. He was away from London for five or six months nearly every year, and the art world was unaffected by his absence. At home he had acted as an amateur patron of the arts whose pleasure it was to help a few protégés in various ways. He had, it is true, *aspired* to be Art-Dictator. In his periods of hyper-confidence he had been certain that he had 'perfect judgement' and that the position should be his by right. But he had not achieved the position at the age of forty in 1859. At that time he was still a dilettante who had made a bid for the position and had failed.

Ruskin was himself quite conscious of this failure, and the disappointment gradually grew upon him. For a time he met the situation with defiance. Art-Dictatorship, he decided, was not worth his while; the material with which he had to work was not worthy of his effort; he had told the architects and artists of England what they ought to do and they had not done it; their blood must be upon their own stupid, obstinate and empty heads.[3] Even the Pre-Raphaelites—who at one moment had shown signs of intelligent appreciation of his teaching—had now let him down; Millais, to say nothing of his conduct at Glenfinlas, had degenerated as an artist;[4] Rossetti himself was now doing the most absurd things 'in the

[1] Cf. *Modern Painters*, V, part IX, para. 11. *The Cestus of Aglaia*, para. 4. *Sesame and Lilies*, para. 101, and Letter to *The Times*, July 5, 1876.

[2] Cf. *Modern Painters*, III, Preface, para. 2, 1856.

[3] This tone is very apparent in the lecture called *Imagination in Architecture* which he delivered to the Architectural Association in 1857 (*The Two Paths*, IV).

[4] *Academy Notes*, 1857, and cf. above, p. 36, and below, p. 250.

midst of his beautiful ones'—Who ever heard of 'a Madonna with black hair in ringlets, like a George the 2nd wig, and black complexion like a Mulatto'?—and all the minor Pre-Raphaelites had gone quite crazy on mediævalism and the *Morte d'Arthur*.[1] It was clear that English art could not be regenerated by art criticism—even art criticism which had 'declared the perfectness and eternal beauty of the work of God' and 'tested all work of man by concurrence with and subjection to that'.[2] The trouble obviously was deep-rooted; to regenerate English art it was necessary first to regenerate English life; in the present state of English life the existence of art was simply an absurdity if not indeed a crime.[3] For his own part he would write art criticism no longer; the last volume of *Modern Painters* was his swan song in that field.[4] Henceforward he must strike at the real roots of the trouble. And indeed had he not in fact been so striking all the while? In his books about art and architecture the really important passages had always been the digressions on social and political questions and the passages directing attention to the necessary happiness of the men who carved and painted.[5] Those passages had always meant ten times as much to him as the passages in which he had revealed only 'selfish cultivation of critical acumen'.[6] He had learned to 'recognise the great fact that great Art is of no real use to anybody but the next great Artist: that it is wholly invisible to people in general . . . that one must begin at the other end with moral education of the people, and physical'.[7]

There were real grounds, of course, for the judgement that the Pre-Raphaelites had deteriorated and taken the wrong turn-

---

[1] Letters to C. E. Norton, Aug. 15, 1859, and Nov. 4, 1860, and to Mr. and Mrs. Browning, Dec. 11, 1859.

[2] *Modern Painters*, V, Preface, para. 8, 1860 (cf. below, p. 212).

[3] Letter to C. E. Norton, Aug. 15, 1859.

[4] *Modern Painters*, V, Part IX, Chap. I, para. 7, and Chap. XI, para. 15.

[5] *Modern Painters*, V, Part IX, Chap. I, para. 7.

[6] Cf. below, p. 204.

[7] Letter to Mrs. Browning, Nov. 5, 1860.

PROLOGUE

ing[1]; but the judgement nevertheless was mainly psychological in Ruskin's case—deriving from his mood and outlook at the time.

It was in this mood, as I show later, that he began to study economics, and that he wrote the lectures first entitled *The Political Economy of Art*.[2] The attitude held till he had written some articles for the Cornhill Magazine (*Unto This Last*, 1859–1860) and was half-way through some more for Fraser's Magazine (*Munera Pulveris*, 1859–1863); and there is marked hyperconfidence in letters which he wrote to *The Scotsman* on the Italian War in 1859.

This defiant attitude was supported by sexual impulses—a species of climacteric—for several years. In 1858 he suddenly became tired of the Alps, where he had gone to escape from Denmark Hill, and found himself attracted for the first time by the pleasures of urban life. The city was Turin. There he found himself rejoicing in the voluptuous paintings by the Venetians, and abandoning 'the old monkish pictures for their sakes'.[3] There he decided that 'to be a first-rate painter—you *mustn't* be pious, but rather a little wicked and entirely a man of the world'[4]; there he spent £100 'in grapes, partridges and the opera', and gave a £5 tip to a ballerina[5]; there he nearly ogled the Italian ladies round the bandstand on a Sunday morning[6]; and there possibly (and elsewhere possibly in the next few years) he indulged himself in other pleasures of which we have no records and which possibly he never confessed. 'I have more instincts of youth about me than when I was young', he wrote, towards the end of this climacteric, 'and am miserable because I cannot climb, run, or wrestle, sing or flirt—as I was when a youngster because I couldn't sit writing metaphysics all day long. Wrong at both ends of life . . .'[7]; and there were moments when he was 'seriously and despairingly thinking of

[1] Cf. below, p. 250.
[2] *A Joy for Ever*.
[3] Letter to Mr. and Mrs. Browning, Jan. 15, 1859.
[4] Letter to C. E. Norton, Oct. 24, 1858. Italics are Ruskin's.
[5] *Præterita*, II, Chap. II, para. 24.
[6] Letter to his father, Aug. 29, 1858.
[7] Letter to Dr. John Brown, Jan. 16, 1862.

going to Paris or Venice and breaking away from all modern society and opinion, and doing I don't know what'.[1]

It was at Turin also at this time that he went to a Waldensian chapel on a Sunday morning and walked out declaring to himself that henceforward his Evangelical beliefs would be 'put away, to be debated of no more'.[2] I discuss the significance of this gesture later, where I suggest that he had never really been a sectarian in religion. Here I need only note that in one of his descriptions of the episode he declares 'the courses of thought' which accomplished this to have been at work in his mind for a long time;[3] that at this moment he threatened to announce to the world that *all* churches were 'forms of idolatry'[4]; and was only restrained from this by a lady friend who made him promise to postpone the announcement for ten years[5]; and that all through the 'sixties, which we are now considering, he professed a personal 'Religion of Humanity'.[6]

This defiant attitude, thus evidenced in several ways, gradually gave place to depression. Disappointment at his failure to achieve art-dictatorship, ever-increasing conflict in his home, and the climacteric referred to above, were factors which contributed. In the period between the completion of *Unto This Last*, in 1860, and the death of his father in the spring of 1864, there were long months in which he evidently suffered from moral collapse and paralysis of will.

His letters of the period show him now quite out of touch with his parents and always ill at ease when he passed any length of time at Denmark Hill. He complains of 'unendurable solitude'[7] when he is there. 'I am at home,' he writes, 'or at least in the place which ought to be home'.[8] In another letter: 'Living with two old people, however good, is not good

---

[1] Letter to C. E. Norton, Feb. 25, 1861.
[2] *Præterita*, III, Chap. I, para. 23.
[3] *Præterita*, III, Chap. I, para. 23.
[4] Letter to Mr. and Mrs. Browning, March 29, 1858.
[5] Letter to his father, Feb. 21, 1863. The lady was Mrs. La Touche.
[6] Cf. below, pp. 340 *et seq*.
[7] Letter to C. E. Norton, Feb. 25, 1862.
[8] Letter to C. E. Norton, Jan. 19, 1862.

for a man'[1]; and in yet another: 'I must find a home—or at least the Shadow of a Roof of my own, somewhere; certainly not here.' He spent the greater part of his time abroad—in his favourite haunts at Chamonix and at Mornex on the Salève where he bought a property and made plans for settling altogether. On his visits to England he escaped as soon and as often as possible to stay with friends in various places and to a girls' school at Winnington to which I shall refer again in a minute.[2] Between 1862 and 1864 he hardly wrote anything at all.

In point of fact he had the advantages of fortune that had been his from the beginning. He had no money worries—he still had the large allowance from his father, and when he wanted an extra £1,000 to buy a property at Mornex, or any other money to satisfy a caprice, he could always get it. He lived in comfort at home and abroad, surrounded always by attendants and assistants.[3] He could afford to invite friends to stay with him on the Continent and pay their expenses; he took Burne-Jones and his wife for a trip to Italy in 1862, and he had a young American as his guest at Mornex for some months in 1860. He had no responsibilities; he was free to go anywhere and do anything he liked.

But from the summer of 1861 he began to feel more and more the most unfortunate, the most ailing, and the most thwarted of men. Till in the end he looked upon himself as one of the great victims in the history of the world.

In the letters of the period he complains continually about ailments. He has an earache, or indigestion, or a cough, and he whines for sympathy.[4] His 'poor 42-year-old feet' will scarcely carry him up the Salève.[5] If the wind gets up when he is out for a stroll his temper is out of control till the next day.[6]

[1] Letter to Rawdon Brown, May 10, 1862.
[2] Cf. below, pp. 71–75.
[3] At Mornex in addition to his servants he had George Allen who worked with him in various ways for fifty years.
[4] Letters to C. E. Norton, 1860–1863, *passim*.
[5] Letter to C. E. Norton, Aug. 26, 1861.
[6] Letter to his father, April 23, 1863.

PROLOGUE

He is 'pressed' by the bitter verse 'I am a worm and no man'.[1] He is so languid that he thinks he is dying—though Carlyle writes him that moulting would be the more appropriate word.[2] He has 'inferiority complex' and speaks of himself 'as a layman in the lower classes' when addressing Lord Elcho.[3] He has moments of persecution mania in which he regards himself as a man who had formerly 'taken all the abuse with poor Turner'[4]; who is now being martyred with Bishop Colenso for his religious thought—(there could be no other explanation of the Bishop of Oxford's rudeness to him at dinner);[5] and who in the path of sorrow where he now walks is suffering like the 'one man upon earth of whom we believe or profess to believe that he knew all things and did no sin . . . of whom it is recorded that he sorrowed constantly, fasted often, wept and agonised'.[6] Looking back on his past work it now seems to him to have been a waste of effort and ill-done. 'I have written a few second-rate books', he says, 'which nobody minds.'[7] He feels 'intense scorn of all he had hitherto done or thought'.[8]

This last dissatisfaction was not, of course, entirely morbid. With the collapse of his manic confidence he saw the real character of his past work and his present position with greater accuracy than he had ever done before. He now saw that his system of art-criticism was unworkable, and he knew that *Modern Painters* had stopped at the end of the fifth volume but had never been finished, because it never could be finished in the grandiose form in which it had been planned.[9] He now saw also the fictional character of the laws of history as set forth in *The Stones of Venice*.[10] 'There is no law of history,' he writes, 'any more than of a kaleidoscope. With certain bits of glass—

[1] Letter to Mrs. Browning, May 13, 1861.
[2] Letter to Dr. F. J. Furnivall, Sept. 26, 1863.
[3] Evidence before Royal Academy Commission, June, 1863.
[4] Letter to his father, May 4, 1863.
[5] Letter to Henry Acland, June, 1863 (cf. below p. 341).
[6] Letter to his father, May 16, 1863.
[7] Letter to C. E. Norton, Feb. 25, 1861.
[8] *Ibid.*
[9] Cf. below, pp. 227–230.
[10] Cf. below, pp. 221 and 222.

68

shaken so, and so—you will get pretty figures but what figures, Heaven only knows . . . the wards of a Chubb's lock are infinite in their chances. Is the Key of Destiny made on a less complex principle?'[1] In the same way he now saw that his scientific studies had been amateurish; that while he and George had been chipping bits off the mountains in High Savoy, specialists had been really adding to geological knowledge; that since his time 'crystallography alone' had 'become a science for nine lives' and that there were 'seven new elements or so' in chemistry.[2] Moreover he had real cause for disappointment in the failure of his last writings to win appreciation. The *Cornhill* and *Fraser's Magazine* articles were serious and valuable contributions to social and political economy; but they had not been taken seriously at all.[3]

Insensibility to the feelings of others and a general hostility to mankind are other characteristics of his attitude at this time. He not only felt 'intense scorn' when he looked at himself and his doings, but 'still intenser scorn of other people's doings and thinkings'.[4]   His American friend, Charles Eliot Norton,

[1] Letter to J. A. Froude (beginning of 1864?).
[2] Letters to C. E. Norton, June 2, 1861, and Oct. 6, 1863.
[3] Ruskin's biographers habitually refer to the reception of these articles (afterwards published in book form as *Unto This Last* and *Munera Pulveris*) in terms which suggest that all England was roused to rage by their publication. 'The scandal, outrage and tumult which was caused', says one biographer for example, 'was extreme'. But England as a whole never heard of these articles, and there was no tumult. The articles, printed in magazines, were reviewed at intervals of time by various newspapers in offensive terms, and subscribers to the magazines seem to have written to the editors protesting against them. In both cases the editors told Ruskin that the articles must be discontinued. To Ruskin, in his state of mind at this time, it doubtless appeared as though England had risen up against him. But he and the editors were the only people who saw the hostile press-cuttings collected together. Other people only saw one or two. The articles had not been taken seriously;— that was all that had really happened. And when *Unto This Last* was republished in book form in 1862 (*Munera Pulveris* was not republished till 1872) the only thing that happened was that hardly anybody read it. It took eleven years to sell 880 copies at 3s. 6d. (say 10s. 6d.); cf. below, p. 177.
[4] Letter to C. E. Norton, Feb. 25, 1861.

writes to announce the birth of his son, and Ruskin is incapable of even an ordinary polite reply, and rationalises his insensibility into rhetoric:

'I would have rejoiced with you if I could have rejoiced in anything . . . I am still very unwell and tormented between the longing for rest and for lovely life and the sense of the terrific call of human crime for resistance and of human misery for help.'[1]

The same insensibility is seen in his letters to his parents, now aged respectively seventy-eight and eighty-two. He sends them alarmist accounts of his health, and informs them that people comment on the 'jaded, bilious look' in his face and think he has heart disease.[2] Now, when it is too late, he proclaims his right to independence: 'the one thing I can have is liberty.'[3] He flings reproaches at his parents for the way in which they had brought him up. His self-indulgence, he says, is all their fault, they gave way when they should have thwarted and thwarted when they should have given way; and he spares them nothing in his frequent references to his present refusal to accept their religion.[4]

Mental disorder was, of course, the main explanation of these letters. But we must remember that the malady had possibly been aggravated by the long-existing conflict with his parents from whom he had not emancipated himself twenty-five years earlier at the appropriate time. The frustration from this quarter was not all imaginary. There is ample evidence

[1] Letter to C. E. Norton, July 29, 1863.
[2] Letter to his father from Winnington, March, 1861, and Letters to the same, 1861–1863, *passim*.
[3] Letter to his father from Milan, July 22, 1862.
[4] Letter to his father from Winnington, Dec. 16, 1863. It has been suggested that, in extenuation of the insensibility in Ruskin's letters to his parents at this time, we ought to set the fact that he always wrote them a letter every day when he was away from home. But writing about himself was a pleasure, a form of exhibitionism, for Ruskin, and his letters to his parents are for the most part all about himself. After his father's death he went on with the pleasure by writing letters to his mother. After her death he continued writing about himself in thousands of letters to other people; and he indulged himself more and more in this as his malady got worse year by year.

from records left by people who visited Denmark Hill that his mother still bullied him as though he were a schoolboy; that she habitually contradicted him on matters of which she knew nothing; that she insisted upon expressing her views to everyone who came to the house; and that she repeatedly told him that his ridiculous ideas were the result of listening to people like Carlyle, Froude and Bishop Colenso.[1]

It is also clear that his father disapproved of his writings outside the field of art and not only expressed his disapproval, but actively impeded his work in the social-economic and political fields. In the 'fifties he had suppressed some letters on political problems which Ruskin had destined for *The Times*;[2] and now he vetoed another letter (on Gold)[3] and exacted a definite promise that Ruskin would not publish anything in the Press without previously submitting the text to him.[4] Ruskin senior was unable to follow his son's real studies or understand his attitudes; but he was a shrewd and sensible man; he probably realised at this time that his mind was not in a healthy condition; and he wanted to restrain him from publishing anything which in his judgement would make him look ridiculous. His action, that is to say, was perhaps defensible; but it was real obstruction all the same.

And now we must look at the most important result of the species of climacteric—some of the symptoms of which have already been noted in Ruskin's conduct at Turin. From the beginning of this disturbance Ruskin had been seeking subconsciously for a point of fixation to allay a recrudescence of

[1] Letter to his father from Winnington, Dec. 15, 1863. 'His mother', say the Editors of the Library Edition, 'was affectionate, but also exacting and somewhat censorious; she was firmly persuaded that only the pernicious influence of ill-chosen friends had seduced her son from the evangelical principles which she had inculcated in his youth. She liked, too, to be mistress . . . in her own house; and in that capacity she was a great martinet.' Other accounts are given by Lady Burne-Jones and an artist named Smetham.
[2] Cf. above, p. 57, and below, pp. 279 and 295.
[3] Cf. below, p. 295.
[4] Letter to his father Nov. 23, 1863.

amorous desires. He had been looking subconsciously for the wet eyes and half-opened lips of the child Adèle.[1] He found them in another child, Rose La Touche, who was between nine and ten when he first saw her in 1858 and who gradually became more and more an obsession in his life.

Rose La Touche lived in Ireland. Her father was a rich banker and landowner who was converted by Spurgeon. Her mother seems to have been an average worldly woman whose interests were mainly social—she gave a *déjeuner* to eighty people to meet the Prince of Wales in 1861.[2] Ruskin at this time saw the child but rarely. He went once or twice to Ireland and she came with her parents now and then to London. We have thus, on the one hand, a child in Ireland and, on the other, a man thirty years her senior, whose mind was in a morbid condition, who was suffering from a climacteric, who was obsessed by her image, and who added frustration in this desire to his sense of frustration in other fields. We must realise this to understand what is otherwise the most extraordinary feature of these distressing years—his repeated visits in this period to a girls' school at Winnington.

The school, called Winnington Hall, was in Cheshire. There were some fifty girls aged from nine upwards. And in these girls Ruskin saw substitute images of his absent Rosie as she developed year by year.

He met the principal of the school, a Miss Bell, in 1859; he went to Winnington for the first time some months later; and he was there frequently for weeks at a time in the next few years. Miss Bell kept a room for him and allowed him continual contact with the girls, who were evidently encouraged to treat him partly as a juvenile uncle—he was still little more than forty, still beardless, still a dandy with a blue stock-tie to match his eyes—and partly as a learned man who condescended to give them informal drawing lessons and informal instruction in the various subjects in which he had specialised.

His letters from, and referring to, Winnington make astonishing reading. The man who had already written not only

1 Cf. above, pp. 45 and 46.
2 Letter from Ruskin to his father from Harristown, Aug. 29, 1861.

Modern Painters, *The Seven Lamps of Architecture* and *The Stones of Venice*, but also *Unto This Last* dances with the girls and plays baseball with them.[1] The girls 'run or dance or ball-play me out-of-breath all day long'[2]; the new girls are shy and the romps suffer in consequence[3]; 'the girls don't play with half the fire and romp when I am not among them'[3]; the best fun of all is 'breaking-up' time when half the girls have gone home for the holidays and only fourteen are left: 'We had such a game of hide-and-seek yesterday in the attics and empty rooms, I was as hot at last as if I had been up and down the Montanvert.'[4] In calmer moments he sits on the lawn or by the fire and the girls cluster round him 'in a close circle' as he talks to them;[5] or he acts Lowell's poems with them—('I had studied curtseying all the afternoon in order to get myself nicely up as Venus')[6]; or he strolls in the garden and listens to their silvery voices as they sing for him indoors in choir.[7]

And all the time he was looking at them. In the park and gardens he watched them running about 'like hares' and dancing 'like will-o'-the-wisps'[8]; when they cluster round him some look 'as lovely as one could well see on a summer's day'[9]; and when their sensibility is aroused by music it is 'beautiful to see the . . . faces . . . the eyes all wet with feeling, and the little coral mouths fixed into little half-open gapes with utter intensity of astonishment',[10] or, as he put it elsewhere, 'the eyes wet, round open, and the little scarlet upper lips, lifted, and drawn slightly together, in passionate glow of utter wonder'[11]—the old images of the poem on Adèle.[12]

---

[1] Letter to his father, March 22, 1861.
[2] Letter to Sir John Murray Naesmyth, April 5, 1861.
[3] Letter to his father, March, 1861.
[4] *Ibid.*, Dec. 16, 1863.
[5] *Ibid.*, Aug. 31, 1863.
[6] Letter to J. R. Lowell, Dec. 5, 1859.
[7] Letter to Sir John Murray Naesmyth, April 5, 1861.
[8] Letter to Miss Julia Richmond, March 23, 1860 (cf. p. 142).
[9] Letter to his father, Aug. 31, 1863.
[10] Letter to his mother from Winnington, undated.
[11] *Cestus of Aglaia*, Chap. II, para. 27.
[12] Cf. above, pp. 45 and 46.

But he was not only looking at them, but also through them to his Rosie. 'You need not think', he writes to his father from Winnington, 'I'm in love with any of the girls here . . . Rosie's my only pet.'[1] This was both true and untrue. He was in love with none of them; but he was also in love with them all—for they were all aspects of Rosie as she changed each year. 'I shall not see her', he writes to Mrs. Burne-Jones, 'till November. Nay, I shall never see *her* again. It's another Rosie every six months now.'[2] At the same time he writes of the changes in the girls at Winnington: 'How one feels the *current* of human life in such a place—the child of last year is the woman of this; and the faces seem to change almost from day to day—it is like a dream.'[3] Depression comes upon him when he remembers that he is thirty years older than the children who are the same age as his 'Rosie-Posie'.[4] And when he wrote to an old friend to explain that—though he was, of course, of service to the children—the children were also of great service to him, he was merely stating a plain fact.[5]

But what, I here ask myself, was Miss Bell about to permit and encourage these proceedings? The editors of the Library Edition imply that she thought Ruskin's presence a good advertisement for her establishment, especially as he brought distinguished people there—including Burne-Jones and his wife; and that the school was not financially successful and she was glad to receive from Ruskin both loans and gifts of money. Perhaps that was the whole story. Perhaps not. Perhaps Ruskin felt exquisitely wicked in organising some of the romps and clusterings behind her back—just as years later when he was Slade Professor in Oxford he organised a secret tea-party with the daughters of his old friend the Dean of Christ Church when the Dean and his wife had gone out to dinner.[6] Perhaps Miss Bell was herself in love with him and believed that he came to

---

[1] Letter to his father, March, 1861.
[2] Letter to Mrs. Burne-Jones, July 20, 1861.
[3] Letter to Sir John Murray Naesmyth, April 5, 1861.
[4] Letter to his father, Nov. 23, 1863.
[5] Letter to Miss Ellen Heaton, Nov. 13, 1863.
[6] *Præterita*, III, Chap. II, para. 30.

Winnington because he was in love with her, in the same way
that (as I shall mention again later) Mrs. La Touche, Rose's
mother, was apparently in love with him and may have believed
for years that he was in love with her—not Rose.[1] But one
thing at any rate is certain, Miss Bell did not know and could
not know, as we know, that Ruskin at this period was suffering
a species of climacteric and was also mentally in a really dangerous state. She did not and could not know that in 1860 he was
'seriously and despairingly thinking of going to Paris or Venice
and breaking away from all modern society and opinion, and
doing I don't know what'—and that a few days after writing
the letter, where he confessed it, he went to Winnington instead.[2]

It may well be that the visits to this girls' school saved him
from an attack of madness in this period. Winnington was
much better for him than Denmark Hill, where he was always
irritated by his parents, and much better than Mornex or
Chamonix, where he was lonely. It provided a refuge and at
the same time substitute gratification of his obsessional desire to
talk to Rosie, and touch her, and look upon her lips and eyes.
And *The Ethics of the Dust*, in which all this is most charmingly
sublimated, is thus a kind of thank-offering for the service
which Winnington had rendered.[3]

The death of Ruskin's father, in March, 1864, pulled him
from the depression of 1863. In the first place it gave him a
real cause for distress to replace the imaginary causes, and in

---

[1] Cf. below, p. 82.

[2] As stated above (p. 66) the letter is dated February 25, 1861. It
was written at Denmark Hill. I find letters written at Winnington dated
March.

[3] The children with whom the dialogues take place in this book (written in 1865) are aged from nine to eighteen, and evidently symbolise different ages and aspects of Rose—all except 'Mary', aged 20, who is a kind of
monitress. 'Isabel', aged eleven, who is clearly the 'lecturer's' favourite, is
called 'Mousie', one of Ruskin's pet-names for Rosie (cf. p. 82). In one
passage he speaks of the children clustered round him as 'a lovely group
of rosy sugar-candy' (II, para. 14). For passages in the book directly intended for the eye of Rose cf. below, pp. 345–351.

the second it gave him new responsibilities and placed him in a position which improved his morale. The death was sudden and a shock. In spite of their differences there had been real friendship between the two men, and a species of alliance between them against the stupid tyranny of Ruskin's mother.[1]

Ruskin senior had always been most generous to him with money; and in his will he left him three-quarters of his fortune with what amounted to a reversion of the rest. At forty-five Ruskin thus found himself transformed, from a man living on a large allowance from his father, to a man with a large independent fortune of his own. There was much business to be attended to. His inheritance was equivalent to about £360,000 in present money, with various leaseholds and freeholds and other property valued at the equivalent of something over £30,000. The equivalent of £111,000 and the house at Denmark Hill had been left to his mother for life.[2]

He had planned to take Burne-Jones and his wife away with him on a Continental tour. As he was unable to go he arranged at once (the day after his father's death) that they should go without him—he providing the funds and a courier who would see that they had every comfort.[3] The next thing was to find

[1] Ruskin made no parades of grief at the death of his father and discouraged people from coming to the funeral. The day after, he wrote: 'I'm used to live in pain and *this* kind of pain does not kill by withering as other sorts of pain do; I have no feeling of weakness, nor of fever and slept without dreaming last night.' (Letter to Burne-Jones, March 4, 1864.) A few days later he writes of his father 'who would have sacrificed his life for his son and yet forced his son to sacrifice his life to him and sacrifice it in vain' (Letter to Acland, March 9, 1864). He displayed no grief when other friends died. After the death of Rose La Touche he was merry on the coaching tour to which I refer later (cf. below, p. 116).

[2] The actual figures of the will were: £120,000 and the properties to Ruskin and £37,000 and the house at Denmark Hill for life to his mother. Mrs. Williams Ellis writes (in *The Tragedy of John Ruskin*) of a further £200,000 (equivalent say to £600,000 now) realised later by the sale of his father's interest in the sherry business, but states that her authority for this further sum is only gossip recorded by William Rossetti; and I have not found any other authority for this additional amount. The other figures were published by Ruskin himself (*Fors Clavigera*, Letter 76).

[3] Letter to Burne-Jones, March 4, 1864.

76

someone to look after his mother so that he would not be continuously chained to Denmark Hill. This turned out to be easy.
A cousin called Joan Agnew (afterwards Mrs. Severn) came on
probation. The old lady liked her and told her to stay; so she
stayed. The next step was to do something for the various
poor relations to whom Ruskin senior, the only rich man of
the family, had left nothing:

"As I was very fond of some of them,' he tells us, 'I indulged
myself and relieved my conscience at the same time by giving
seventeen thousand pounds [say £51,000 in present money] to
those I liked best. Money which turned out to be quite rightly
invested and at a high interest; and has been fruitful to me of
many good things and much happiness.'[1]

In the eyes of those who knew of him Ruskin was now a
very rich artistic dilettante who was reputed to have a socialistic
and philanthropic turn of mind. He was accordingly besieged
by people begging for money and by people asking him to
lecture in aid of this good cause or that. For a year or two he
indulged himself in the bestowal of capricious and indiscrimin-
ate charities, and he kept a special secretary to act as almoner.
Also he lectured here and there—at Manchester in aid of funds
for a library and some new schools (lectures afterwards published as *Sesame and Lilies*) and at Camberwell in aid of funds
for a new Working Men's Institute (a lecture included in *The
Crown of Wild Olive*). But eventually he found that even his
large resources could not stand up against these demands for
charities and that he 'must retire from the position necessarily
now occupied by a publicly recognised benevolent—or simple
—person'[2]; and he tried characteristically to reconcile this retirement with his conscience:

'I am certain there is no man, whatever his fortune, who is
now engaged in any earnest offices of kindness to . . . sufferers,
especially of the middle classes, among his acquaintance, who
will not bear me witness that for one we can relieve, we must
leave three to perish. I have left three, myself, in the first three
months of this year . . . The knowledge of all this distress, even

[1] *Fors Clavigera*, Letter 76.
[2] Letter to his secretary, C. A. Howell, Nov. 9, 1866.

when I can assist it—much more when I cannot—and the various thoughts of what I can and cannot, or ought and ought not, to do, are a far greater burden to me than the mere loss of money . . . the sight of pain is not good for me . . . I like a quiet life . . . and I don't like seeing people cry or die.'[1]

At Denmark Hill he filled his time by directing elaborate alterations in the gardens; by drawing; and by miscellaneous geological and botanical pottering. He escaped from time to time for Continental travel where he pursued his habitual occupations over the old ground.

He was still quite decided that his career as an art critic was finished; he no longer took pleasure in his own collection of miscellaneous works of art.[2] He tells a correspondent that he had nothing more to say about art,[3] and in a lecture of this time he said:

'I am weary of all writing and speaking about art and most of my own . . . I have seceded from the study not only of architecture but nearly of all art.'[4]

For this loss of interest in art he still blamed the artists and the general state of England. Already in 1860 his behaviour in artists' studios had been so captious that the artists turned him out of their rooms 'in haste'[5]; and he now forced quarrels with his few remaining artist friends. He called Brett a fool and ended that friendship in 1864.[6] Burne-Jones was now almost the only artist with whom he remained intimate. He took little or no interest in other modern painters. In 1865 Swinburne (whose poems he much admired) sent him his poem called *Before the Mirror* written about a painting by Whistler; in the covering letter Swinburne said that the poem was 'not so complete in beauty, in tenderness and significance, in exquisite execution and delicate strength as Whistler's picture', and asked him to come to Whistler's studio to see it. But Rus-

---

[1] *Time and Tide*, XIX, paras. 116 and 117, April, 1867.
[2] Letter to C. E. Norton, Aug. 8, 1867.
[3] Letter to Captain Brackenbury, Jan. 19, 1864.
[4] *The Study of Architecture*, 1865.
[5] Letter to C. E. Norton, Nov. 4, 1860.
[6] Letter to Rossetti, July, 1865 (cf. below, p. 276).

kin did not even have the curiosity to want to see the work thus praised, though Burne-Jones was to be of the party.[1] In the same year there is an acrimonious correspondence with Rossetti ending in a letter where Ruskin said:

'There are many things in which I always have acknowledged and shall acknowledge your superiority to me. I know it, as well as I know that St. Paul's is higher than I am. There are other things in which I just as simply know that *I* am superior to you. I don't mean in writing. You write, as you paint, better than I . . . You know nothing of me, nor of my knowledge, nor of my thoughts, nor of the sort of grasp of things I have in directions in which you are utterly powerless . . . I do not choose any more to talk to you until you can recognise my superiorities as *I* can yours.'[2]

In a man of Ruskin's peculiar mentality a letter of this kind was really an encouraging signal. It meant that he was recovering his morale and that his mind was swinging away from the depressed position, when he was morally paralysed, to the hyper-confidence which impelled him to action. And indeed from the autumn of 1865 to the autumn of 1866 his mind seems to have been, relatively speaking, balanced. He had not given up his interest in social, economic and political questions which had begun in the 'fifties. In the darkest days of his depression he had always been haunted by the call to action in these spheres. Even in those days he heard 'the terrific call of human crime for resistance and of human misery for help'. 'The folly and horror of humanity', he had written from Mornex, 'enlarge to my eyes daily'; his peace there was only as if he had buried himself, 'in a battle-field wet with blood'.[3] At that time these calls had moved him only to rhetoric in his letters; his will was then too paralysed for action; the thought of the work he ought to be doing had then only increased his depression:
'As soon as I see or hear what human creatures are suffering

[1] Letter from Swinburne to Ruskin, Aug. 11, 1865.
[2] Letter to Rossetti, July, 1865. For Ruskin's relations with Rossetti and other artists, cf. below, pp. 264–278.
[3] Letters to Norton, Nov. 4, 1860, Aug. 26, 1861, March 10, 1863, and others.

PROLOGUE

of pain, and saying of absurdity, I get about as cheerful as I
should be in a sheep-fold strewed hurdle-deep with bloody
carcases, with a herd of wolves and monkeys howling and gib-
bering on the top of them.'[1]

With the return of confidence he began once more to feel
himself an appointed reformer. He wrote letters to the Press
on social, economic and political questions in 1864 and 1865[2];
and he was feeling confident when he wrote *The Ethics of the
Dust* at the end of 1865 and the later essays for the *Art Journal*
in 1866.[3] He now writes:

'I shall speak more and more strongly as I can get a hearing
—every word of truth spoken to the English public at present
is answered by a stone flung at you—and I can't take a cartload
all at once.'[4]

It was in this mood that on February 2, 1866, he formally
proposed marriage to Rose La Touche. The reply was that he
must await her decision for three years when she would be
twenty-one. The nominal reason given was that Rose regarded
his personal 'Religion of Humanity' as a form not of Christianity, but of scepticism.[5]

To understand this we must look behind the scenes.

Rose as a child had been mentally precocious, and had written him enormously long letters (one of which he published
nearly twenty-five years later in *Præterita*)[6]. She was by nature
rather wild[7]; but at thirteen she was already subject to melan-

[1] Letter to Dr. John Brown, August, 1862.
[2] On *The Position of Denmark* (*Morning Post*, July 7, 1864); *The Law
of Supply and Demand* (*Daily Telegraph*, Oct. 28, Oct. 31 and Nov. 3,
1864); *Work and Wages* (*Pall Mall Gazette*, April 21, April 25, May 2,
May 9, May 22, 1865); *Domestic Servants* (*Daily Telegraph*, Sept., 5,
Sept. 7, Sept. 18, 1865); *Our Railway System* (*Daily Telegraph*, Dec. 8,
1865); and the *Jamaica Insurrection* (*Daily Telegraph*, Dec. 20, 1865).
[3] These essays, afterwards republished as *The Cestus of Aglaia*, were
written partly in the early part of 1865 and partly in 1866. I comment
later (pp. 360 *et seq*.) on the rambling style of the early ones; the later
ones are more reasonably written.
[4] Letter to Joseph Toynbee, Feb. 8, 1866.
[5] For Ruskin's religion at this time, cf. below, pp. 340–348.
[6] *Præterita*, III, Chap. III, para. 57.
[7] Letter from Ruskin to his father from Harristown, Aug. 29, 1861.

PROLOGUE

cholic moods. Ruskin describes her at that time as 'like patience on a monument', and as walking 'like a little white statue through the twilight woods, talking solemnly'.[1] At sixteen she was usually animated and active and her mother wrote of her: 'The Wild Rose is very well, but wilder than ever. I sometimes wonder if she will ever be a civilised being . . . All day long she is in and out let the weather be what it may and not one single thing that girls do does she do—except a little music when she pleases. She has the run of all the cottages and cabins about, gets fed from the labourers' dinners and is an exception to every rule and custom of society.'[2]

Into the head of this child her parents had pumped orthodox religion (just as Ruskin's mother had pumped it into his), and at the same time Ruskin himself had pumped into it his personal 'Religion of Humanity', in long letters written in the years which followed the episode in the Waldensian Chapel.[3] As a result she had now become a neurotic, continually brooding on religion, a prey to headaches, sometimes on the verge of 'brain fever'. Now at eighteen, in 1866, when Ruskin proposed to her, she was in a state of morbid religious mania. At a party in that year she knelt down and prayed for the recovery from illness of one of her girl friends and 'prayed so that' the whole company 'could not but join with her'.[4] She had thus imagined herself unable to accept Ruskin's proposal of marriage because she was horrified at the thought of marrying a man whom she looked on as a sceptic.

In suggesting the postponement she had been supported by her parents. Her father, as already noted, had been converted by Spurgeon; and Spurgeon had recently preached as follows against Ruskin:

[1] Letter from Ruskin to his father from Harristown, Sept. 2, 1861.
[2] Letter from Mrs. La Touche to Mr. and Mrs. George MacDonald (1865), published in Dr. Greville MacDonald's *Reminiscences of a Specialist*. Rose's philanthropy was due to the influence of Ruskin (cf. below, p. 130, where her diary entries are quoted).
[3] Cf. above, p. 66, and below, pp. 338–340. It was Mrs. La Touche, it will be remembered, to whom he had promised to postpone for ten years his announcement that all churches were idolatrous (cf. above, p. 66).
[4] Letter from Ruskin to Kate Greenaway, Jan. 23, 1884.

81

PROLOGUE

"I had some time ago a conversation with a very eminent man . . . who was once a professed believer but is now full of scepticism. He said to me in the course of our argument: "Why, how foolish you are, and all the company of preachers. You tell people to think about the next world, when the best thing they could do would be to behave themselves as well as they can in this." '[1]

Rose's father, following Spurgeon, doubtless supported Rose in regarding Ruskin as a lost soul—and he may have also disliked him personally, and have been jealous of his correspondence with and friendship with his wife.

To Mrs. La Touche the proposal had come as a shock. She may have imagined that all the time he had really been in love with her. She herself had apparently been in love with him, as we see from a letter written during his depressed period:

'Nothing will ever get me right save getting him right—for somehow if he were holding on to a straw and I to a plank, I must leave my plank to catch at his straw . . . I don't care what becomes of me so long as anyhow he can be brought to some sort of happiness and life. He knows that very well and is welcome to know it.'[2]

But Ruskin had not known this. His mind had been on Rosie:

'I can't love anybody except my Mouse-pet in Ireland who nibbles me to the very sick-death with weariness to see her.'[3]

And here we must note that in this reference to Rose as his 'mouse-pet' he was really thinking of her as the child with

<hr/>

[1] Sermon by Spurgeon, March 27, 1864 (*Metropolitan Tabernacle Pulpit*, No. 562). A copy of this sermon was marked by Ruskin 'Spurgeon on me'. In the conversation referred to Ruskin had said that St. Paul was a liar and no gentleman, and that Spurgeon was a fool (*C. H. Spurgeon: an Autobiography by his Wife*, 1898). In the 'fifties, before the episode of the Waldensian Chapel, Ruskin had attended Spurgeon's sermons and appreciated them and sent him a cheque for £100.
[2] Letter from Mrs. La Touche to Mr. and Mrs. George MacDonald, 1863. Published by Greville MacDonald, *op. cit.*
[3] Letter from Ruskin to George MacDonald, Feb. 8, 1864. Published by Greville MacDonald, *op. cit.* (For Ruskin's use of the pet-name 'Mousie' in *The Ethics of the Dust*, cf. above, p. 75, and below, p. 173.)

whom he had fallen in love. 'Mousie' in *Ethics of the Dust* is only eleven.[1] When Ruskin proposed marriage to Rose aged eighteen in 1866 he was not really in love with her at all; he was still in love with the child-image of Rosie. He had never forgiven her for growing up. Already in 1861 when she was thirteen he had written 'I shall never see *her* again. It's another Rosie every six months now.'[2] Now that she was a young woman who adopted a superior theological attitude towards him he really hated her. But he believed he was still in love with Rose because he was still in love with Rosie, and was destined to remain so to the end.[3]

This explains not only the attacks upon her pietistic attitude which abound in Ruskin's writings between 1865 and 1872,[4] but also a celebrated passage known to all those who read their Ruskin in *Selections:*

'I am going to tell you what I was thinking . . . in Covent Garden Theatre as I was looking, and not laughing, at the pantomime of "Ali Baba and the Forty Thieves" . . . The forty thieves were girls. The forty thieves had forty companions who were girls. The forty thieves and their forty companions were in some way mixed up with about four hundred and forty fairies, who were girls. There was an Oxford and Cambridge boat-race, in which the Oxford and Cambridge men were girls. There was a transformation scene, with a forest, in which the flowers were girls, and a chandelier, in which the lamps were

[1] Cf. above, p. 75.

[2] Cf. above, p. 74.

[3] It is possible that Rose knew this and that it played a part in her reluctance to marry him (cf. below, p. 131). In *Præterita*, Ruskin says nothing of Rose. But he writes about Rosie and prints her *first* letter (cf. below, pp. 134 and 137). The letters exchanged between Ruskin and Rose were, unfortunately, destroyed by Professor Norton and Mrs. Severn acting as literary executors with authority under the Will to destroy letters. We have only one or two of Ruskin's to her, of which he sent copies to his parents, at the beginning of the acquaintance; the one from her printed in *Præterita;* another intended for *Præterita* published by Cook; and one or two quotations. These fragments of the correspondence make it clear that as she grew up she filled her letters with texts from the Bible and theological pretensions (cf. below, p. 346).

[4] Cf. below, pp. 345–351.

girls, and a great rainbow which was all of girls . . . The forty thieves . . . there being no thieving to be presently done, and time hanging heavy on their hands, arms, and legs . . . proceeded to light forty cigars . . . Whereupon the British public gave them a round of applause . . . There was a little actress of whom I have chiefly to speak, who played exquisitely the little part she had to play . . . The little lady . . . eight or nine years old dances a *pas-de-deux* with the donkey—she did it beautifully and simply as a child ought to dance . . . She did nothing more than any child, well taught, but painlessly, might easily do. She caricatured no older person—attempted no curious or fantastic skill . . . she danced with . . . sweetness and self-forgetfulness. And through all the vast theatre, full of fathers, mothers, and children, there was not one hand lifted to give her sign or praise but mine.'[1]

This passage read without knowledge of the circumstances when it was written is naturally regarded in one of two ways. Either the reader images the white-bearded Prophet of Brantwood taking relaxation from his service to mankind by visiting the pantomime and conspicuously applauding from his box the child dancer in a grandfatherly way to the delight of the stalls who knew who he was—or else the reader regards it less sentimentally as a piece of entertaining journalism and leaves it at that. But both interpretations are equally wrong. Ruskin when he went to that pantomime was not the white-bearded Prophet of Brantwood. What the audience saw in the box was an unknown, tall, slim, fashionably dressed man, who had certainly drunk champagne on his forty-eighth birthday a few days before, who always enjoyed the ballet and had given presents to a ballerina[2] and who was watching this pantomime exactly a year after Rose's refusal to decide to marry him. In this passage he contrasts, on the surface, the child dancer with the girl dancers, but what he was really contrasting, unknown to himself, was Rosie who had danced so *sweetly* and in *self-forgetfulness* with an old donkey when she was a child and a Mouse-pet, and who now like these cigar-smoking wenches

[1] *Time and Tide*, V.
[2] Cf. above, p. 65.

was self-conscious and self-centred and *caricaturing older people* with her confounded theological pretensions.[1]

This interpretation may be thought to be too far-fetched. But consider this. More than twenty years later when he was painfully attempting to concentrate and writing the last three pages of his last book describing Joan Severn's dancing, the word 'Rosina' appeared upon the page and automatically with it the image of *little Rosie dancing* and with that automatically the image of the child dancer in Ali-baba to which he refers in a footnote.[2]

After Rose's decision at the beginning of 1866 he left his mother in April and went to Switzerland for four months with various friends. He returned at the end of July. He seems to have been mentally and physically well in the autumn. But then physical distresses appear. I find reference to morbid humours and indications of mental flittering in a letter to one of the children at Winnington on November 19:

'Yes, it is nice that Venice is free from the Austrians, but Venice and all Italy are still enslaved to an emperor they know not of—and there is no hope for them till they have broken his yoke asunder and cast *his* cords from them. For as *our* true monarch is not Victoria but Victor Mammon, so theirs is Victor—ah—not Emmanuel but Belial—

> "To vice industrious—but to nobler deeds
> Timorous and slothful ."

And the only idea of the Venetians in regaining what they imagine to be liberty, is not to recall the Toil of Venice—by which she Rose—but the Pleasures by which she Perished.'[3]

Here we have automatic use of remembered words and phrases—(the Psalmist's 'Let us break their bands asunder, and cast away their cords from us,' and *Paradise Lost*)—and word-jingling, and automatic use of the capital letter for the *verb*

---

[1] We get exactly the same type of automatic subconscious contrast when years later he contrasted Kate Greenaway's 'girlies' with Raphael's *St. Cecilia* (cf. below, p. 174).

[2] *Præterita*, III, Chap. IV, para. 84.

[3] Letter of Nov. 19, 1866, to Lily Armstrong, aged 13, the 'Lily' of *Ethics of the Dust*.

'rose'—rationalised immediately afterwards by a pendant capital for 'perished'.[1]

He seems to have realised that he was in a bad state at this moment and to have consulted doctors. For on December 28th he writes in a letter that the doctors say that there is nothing the matter 'but what it isn't their business to deal with'.[2]

At the beginning of 1867 entries in his diaries show 'various morbid conditions', record 'many weird dreams', and refer to 'floating sparks in his eyes', despondency, sleeplessness and nervous prostration.[3]

This is the moment of the visit to the pantomime just described. In the summer he numbers his days till the date when Rose's answer is due,[4] and describing the ceremonies when he received his degree in Cambridge (to which I refer again in a minute) he writes to his mother:

'The Orator . . . delivers a Latin laudatory speech . . . some ten or fifteen minutes long; . . . I wished that the young ladies present could better understand that learned language . . . (N.B.—One a very sweet, though short-coming, likeness of Rose, with her *very* smile, so that it made me start) . . . The Oration finished, he takes your hand . . . and gives it to the Vice-Chancellor (but it made me think of Somebody else— whom it much more belongs to).'[5]

He now begins to have serious doubts of his own sanity:

'In 1867 the first warning mischief to my own health began to show itself, giddiness and mistiness of head and eyes, which stopped alike my drawing and thinking to any good purpose. I went down into Cumberland and walked and rowed till I was well again.'[6]

---

[1] We get similar automatic use of the word 'Rose' in the Preface to *Sesame and Lilies* (1865): 'I could watch the Rose of Italy flush in the first morning light'.

[2] Letter to C. E. Norton, Dec. 28, 1866.

[3] Editors of the Library Edition.

[4] Letter to Miss Joan Agnew, Aug. 18, 1867.

[5] Letter to his mother from Cambridge, May 23, 1867.

[6] Obituary notice of Arthur Burgess in *The Century Guild Hobby Horse*, 1887.

PROLOGUE

This visit to the Lakes (where his attendants included the Denmark Hill gardener named Downs) was in July and August. He had some peace there. Rose sent him a rose, and wrote him that she had refused another lover.[1] But he was far from cured of his mental ills. In September he had to come back to London and take a rest cure in a doctor's house.

When the pendulum swung the other way he conceived vague plans for using his resources in direct social action. He did not, I fancy, contemplate any definite step as long as his mother was still alive; but she was now eighty-six and it was not unnatural that he should look ahead. We get these plans indicated in a letter as follows:

'I think . . . that any one of us who have hearts sound enough must verily and indeed draw together and initiate a true and wholesome way of life, in defiance of the world—I do not in the least propose any onslaught on public opinion or custom in any violent way—and with laws which we will obey and endeavour to make others, by our example, accept. I think it must come to this, but accidents in my own life have prevented me until lately from being able to give to such a plan any practical hope; but now I might with some help be led on to its organisation. Would you join it and vow to keep justice and judgement and the peace of God on this earth?'[2]

At such moments he was determined not to write or speak another word about art, and to set out, when the moment of release came, to regenerate the world:

'I utterly disdain to speak a word about art in the hearing of any English creature—at present. Let us make our Religion true and our Trade honest. *Then* and not till then will there be even so much as *ground* for casting seed of the Arts.'[3]

'I am entirely convinced that the spirit (*body* I would more sadly say) of the age is such as to render it wholly impossible for it to nourish or receive any great art whatsoever . . . I have no hope for any of us but in a change in the discipline and framework of all society . . . and therefore it is that I do not

[1] Letter to his mother from Keswick, July 24, 1867.
[2] Letters to an unnamed correspondent, May 15 and 21, 1867.
[3] Letter to Acland, Sept. 20, 1867.

87

care to write more or to complete what I have done, feeling it all useless. . . . Not in despair nor in sick sloth but in deep though stern hope, and in reserve of what strength is in me, I refuse to talk about art . . . The weapons with which such evil may be stayed before the end thereof are not camel's-hair pencils. Camel's-hair raiment might do something.'[1]

And once more we find him defiantly rationalising his in-sensitiveness to the feelings of others, in a letter where the Rose obsession also appears:

'You must remember that I am engaged in the investigation of enormous religious and moral questions in the history of nations; and your feelings or my own or anybody else's, at any particular moment are of very little interest to me—not from want of sympathy, but from the small proportion the individu-ality bears to the whole subject of my inquiry. I have no affec-tions, having had them three times over torn out by the roots—most fatally the last time, within the last year. My word "affectionately" means only—that I *should* have loved people, if I were not dead. I have no *pleasure* myself, now, in any human relation.'[2]

It was thus that he began to plan the social gesture which was later to be called St. George's Guild; and he sketched some of its principles in the letters to Thomas Dixon published in the *Scotsman*, the *Leeds Mercury*, the *Manchester Daily Examiner and Times* and afterwards in book form as *Time and Tide*.

But meanwhile fate was working in another direction.

From about 1860 he had apparently toyed with the idea of seeking a University appointment—preferably in Oxford, or failing that in Cambridge, or at one of the other Universities. In 1861 he had given about twenty-five Turner drawings to Oxford and as many to Cambridge—partly perhaps to buy his way into the good graces of the Universities; partly perhaps to silence the malicious who had doubtless suggested that the praise of Turner in *Modern Painters* (of which there was much

[1] Letters to Ernest Chesneau, Feb. 13, 1867, and to Acland, Sept. 22, 1867.
[2] Letter to William Ward, Oct. 31, 1867 (cf. below, pp. 277 and 278).

in the last volume which appeared in 1860) was designed to increase the value of his own collection of a hundred examples of that artist's work[1]; partly perhaps to ease his conscience which made him doubt if it were at all proper for him to have a hundred Turners all to himself[2]; and partly perhaps because, as he wrote to Norton, he was not taking any pleasure in these years in his art collections. He had always kept in touch with Acland and Liddell and other Oxford friends of his undergraduate days. Acland was now Regius Professor of Medicine in Oxford, and Liddell was Dean of Christ Church; both were disturbed at their friend's despondencies and the singular vacillations of his mind; and they judged, doubtless, that the best thing for him would be an appointment in Oxford where he would have a little light regular work to do, and intelligent men for his companions, and where he would presumably forget his schemes for regenerating the world and settle down to be a professor and drink port. With other friends they now began to make great efforts to bring this about. As a first step, I fancy, they must have pointed out to Ruskin that he must be prepared, if he got an appointment, to talk about the Greeks—that being the recognised occupation of a professor in the school of Humanities—and atone for the exaltation of Christian art and religion above pagan art and religion which had hitherto distinguished his writings. As a result presumably of this, Ruskin from about 1864 onwards began to work at Greek mythology and at Greek vases and coins in the British Museum —wasting no time, it must be said to his credit, on the Museum's array of concoctions known as Græco-Roman sculpture.[3] These studies form the basis of the fantastic passages on Greek mythology which alternate with his views on social and economic problems in the extraordinary book called *The*

---

[1] Cf. Appendix, p. 383.

[2] Cf. above, p. 28.

[3] For these concoctions cf. *The Meaning of Modern Sculpture*, by R. H. Wilenski (Faber & Faber), Part II, Sec. 9. Ruskin at this time seems, however, to have liked the so-called *Townley Venus* (cf. *The Cestus of Aglaia*, IX, para. 108), which is one of the things 'restored' by Nollekens (cf. below, p. 104).

Queen of the Air, which contains a lecture delivered as a *ballon d'essai* at University College, London.

In 1866 Acland and other Oxford friends, including the Rev. St. John Tyrwhitt, procured for him the refusal of the Professorship of Poetry about to be vacated by Matthew Arnold. Ruskin after some hesitation declined the offer.[1]

Meanwhile other people were working on his behalf in Cambridge. His friends there included Dr. Whewell, the Master of Trinity, whom he had known for fifteen years and who shared his views on John Stuart Mill; Robert Willis, Jacksonian Professor of Applied Mechanics and inventor of an instrument for tracing the outline of mouldings, whom he had known as long; and the Rev. William Kingsley of Sidney Sussex College, an intimate with whom he had stayed in 1858 and 1863 and who remained one of his close friends throughout his life.[2] In 1867 he was offered an LL.D. degree by Cambridge; this he accepted, and he delivered the Rede Lecture of the year in the Senate House in May.[3]

In September, as noted, he was having a rest cure in London; and Acland determined on a bold stroke to get him immediately to Oxford—he offered, that is to say, to resign his own place as one of the Curators of the University Galleries if Ruskin would agree to stand for the vacancy. But Ruskin only flirted with this proposal as he had done with the Professorship of Poetry, and nothing came of it.

And so 1867 came to an end with Ruskin once more at Denmark Hill spending his evenings by the side of his mother.

The next year, 1868, was better. An invitation came from a Lecture Club in Dublin asking him to lecture on some subject connected with the arts. Ruskin replied that he would come and speak on *The Mystery of Life and its Arts.* He took great pains with the preparation of this lecture and enjoyed

---

[1] Letter to his mother from Interlaken, June 11, 1866, and Letter to Carlyle, Feb. 17, 1867.

[2] Cf. *Fors Clavigera,* Letter 80, and Letters from Ruskin to Kingsley, April 21, 1885.

[3] *The Relation of National Ethics to National Art.*

the work—for was it not in Dublin that he was to recite it, and might not Rose herself come from Newbridge for the occasion?[1] In the event Rose did not come; but she sent him a letter —enough, he said, to keep him happy for the remainder of the year.[2]

This lecture was delivered on May 13th. The text was incorporated in some later editions of *Sesame and Lilies* and it figures there in the Library Edition. Read without knowledge of the circumstances it seems a rather flatulent sermon padded with references to Milton, Dante and Shakespeare and rendered emotive by forty-nine quotations from the Bible. But if we have enough collateral knowledge of the circumstances we realise that it should have been entitled *Generalisations about Life and Religion, addressed to a Young Lady preoccupied with orthodox Protestant Religion who was hesitating to marry the author because his Religion was too personal.*[3]

Ruskin's suit it will be remembered had been opposed by her parents, who would not take her to this Dublin lecture. The letter which she sent him was smuggled to him with the aid of a woman friend[4]; and he not unreasonably looked upon it as a good omen.

The visit to Dublin was encouraging also in another way. When he arrived he found that—the hall where he was to lecture having proved too small to accommodate the audience, —he was to speak in the Concert Hall of the Exhibition Palace; and when he stepped on the platform he saw two thousand people before him.[5] He had never lectured to an audience approaching this size before—two or three hundred having been probably the average attendance on previous occasions. This greatly increased interest in his personality was due to two causes: Firstly a book of *Selections*, consisting of purple descriptive passages from *Modern Painters* and his other books, com-

---

[1] Her parents' house was at Harristown, Brannackstown near Newbridge, Kildare, and so not far from Dublin.
[2] Letter to his mother, Dublin, May 14, 1868.
[3] Cf. below, pp. 348–349 and 365.
[4] Letter from Ruskin to his mother, May 14, 1868.
[5] *Daily Express*, May 14, 1868.

piled by W. H. Harrison (who saw all the early books through the press for him), had been published in 1861, and gone into a second edition the year after. This had introduced his writing to a new public and extended his reputation as a 'word painter' much to his annoyance.[1] Secondly the book called *Sesame and Lilies* (containing the texts of two earlier lectures already referred to[2]) which had been published in 1865 had proved a real popular success. Mothers all over the country were regarding it as suitable reading for their daughters; and schoolmistresses thought it suitable for prizes. The book, already then in its fourth edition, was what we call to-day a 'best seller'. Ruskin's name had suddenly reached the average middle-class home.

The effect of these experiences in Ireland was characteristic. The pendulum swung once more to the right, and hyper-confidence appeared. Ruskin felt impelled to action, but he was perplexed at the thought of what his action should rightly be. His social conscience and his manic impulse to preach urged him to deal with 'unendurable circumfluent fallacy' in the social and economic fields; but then there were all these people who had come to this concert hall because they had been told that the celebrated art critic and 'word painter', the author of *Modern Painters* and *Sesame and Lilies* was going to lecture about art.

Thus he writes from Dublin:

'There is so much misery and error in the world which I see I could have immense power to set various human influences against, by giving up my science and art, and wholly trying to teach peace and justice; and yet my own gifts seem so specially directed towards quiet investigation of beautiful things that I cannot make up my mind . . .'[3]

On the way back he stopped at Winnington, and there the mental conflict was continued:

'If I chose to give up my own studying and writing and to use my social influence now to the utmost, I see I could do no

[1] Cf. below, pp. 203–4, and 357 *et seq.*
[2] Cf. above, p. 77.
[3] Letter to his mother from Dublin, May 25, 1868.

end of good. It is curious that in these days in which I do no work of my own, but all for other people, though I have no *pleasure* in the day, I have no serious despondency. But when I am at work, I *enjoy* my work as long as I can go on, exceedingly—but am wholly depressed and melancholy afterwards.'[1]

In the end he decided that social service had the major claim; and on his return to Denmark Hill he set to work. He had been for some time a member of a body called 'The National Association for the Promotion of Social Science'; and he now attended two meetings of the Association in the large room at the Society of Arts in the Adelphi and made speeches (beneath the paintings by Barry) on *Trade Unions and Strikes*[2]; and he followed this by letters in the *Daily Telegraph* about the *Ownership and Management of Railways.*[3]

He was quite confident that he could solve all these problems and impatient at the stupidity of people for not hastening to apply his solutions:

'In all that is necessary at present to be taught of political economy all men who can think and who will think honestly must soon agree . . . I have separated distinctly the productive occupations, which maintain life, from those which refine it, and shown how the common political economy fails in enunciation even of the first. I have been not a little provoked with . . . you for not helping me long ago to beat at least *this* into people's heads—that very different consequences are likely to result from making a cannon ball—or a pudding.'[4]

But two months at Denmark Hill with his mother were as much as he could stand. At the end of August he packed up and went to France where he amused himself by making notes and drawings at Abbeville and spent some time with his American friend, Professor Norton, who was now in Europe.

At Abbeville in addition to his valet he had with him the gardener, Downs, and an assistant named William Ward to

[1] Letter to his mother, Winnington, May 29, 1868.
[2] July 4 and 15, 1868.
[3] July 31, August 6 and August 10, 1868. (For the point of view expressed in these letters, cf. below, p. 298.)
[4] Letter to Frederic Harrison, July 8, 1868 (cf. below, p. 293).

make drawings. The result of these occupations appeared in a lecture called *The Flamboyant Architecture of the Valley of the Somme*, delivered at the Royal Institution in the following year. At Abbeville he also went on with his social work and wrote a paper on *The General Principles of Employment for the Destitute and Criminal Classes* which he had printed as a pamphlet and communicated to the *Daily Telegraph*.[1]

When he returned to London in the autumn he joined a 'Committee for studying problems connected with Unemployment', of which Cardinal (then Archbishop) Manning was a member. But of course he could not work with a committee:

'Getting things through Committee . . . is like threading many needles not in a line (and some restive) with a thread fluffy at the end . . . I've never found two heads better than one, unless neither could be much worse for being alone, or unless the weakest was uppermost.'[2]

And so he retired to his study and looked through his plans for a reforming body with the best head, i.e. his own, in sole command of it, which he had been meditating for eighteen months.[3] And then he went downstairs and spent another Christmas with his mother.

In the first three months of 1869 he remained at Denmark Hill. His mother was now eighty-eight and almost blind. 'My simple duty . . .', he wrote later referring to this period, 'was to have stayed with my widowed mother at Denmark Hill doing whatever my hand found to do there.'[4] He felt this also at the time. But by March his self-indulgence again got the better of his conscience, and he went off to Venice and Verona, where he remained for five months.

The mental characters that appear in these months in Italy are: conceit, extreme mobility of interest, hostile irritability and insensibility, sense of guilt at remaining away from his mother,

---

[1] Dec. 26, 1868. The substance of the pamphlet was subsequently reprinted in *The Queen of the Air*.
[2] Letters to Mrs. C. E. Norton, October and November, 1868.
[3] Cf. letter quoted above, p. 87.
[4] Obituary notice of Arthur Burgess (1887).

the starting of a grandiose enterprise, and the beginning of a new obsessional delusion. Depression rarely appears.[1]

He meets Longfellow and his daughter at Verona and remarks in two letters that some people in England and America would have liked a photograph of such a meeting on the old square[2]; he meets Holman Hunt in front of Tintoretto's *Annunciation* and makes the same remark.[3] He is irritated to rage by two American girls in a railway carriage who were oppressed with the Italian heat in August and who moaned 'and fidgeted and frowned and puffed and stretched and fanned, and ate lemons, and smelt bottles, and covered their faces, and tore the cover off again, and had no one thought or feeling during five hours of travelling in the most noble part of the world, except what . . . poor beasts would have had, in their den in a menagerie, being dragged about on a hot day'.[4] He was equally incapable of sympathy with the Italians themselves:

'The Italians have not even sense or patience enough to taste a ripe peach . . . They are so sunk beneath all sympathy and have become detestable—down to the very children.'[5]

And again:

'The horror of living among these foul Italian wretches and seeing them behave exactly like dogs and flies among the tombs and churches of their fathers, is more than I can bear, with any power of rational speech left about anything . . . There are the vilest wretches of ape-faced children riding on my griffins all day long or throwing stones at the carving—that ever were

---

[1] At this time Ruskin, I fancy, was indulging the hope that Rose's letter smuggled to him in Dublin was an omen of a favourable answer at the end of the year. Also he may have heard from Acland that he would probably get the appointment in Oxford.

[2] Letters to his mother, June 4, 1869, and to C. E. Norton, June 13, 1869.

[3] Letter to his mother, July 1, 1869.

[4] Letter to C. E. Norton, Aug. 9, 1869. The episode is referred to again in *Fors Clavigera*, Letter 20, in 1872, with a specimen of the girls' conversation: 'Don't those snow-caps make you cool?' 'No—I wish they did.'

[5] Letters to Miss Jean Ingelow, July 19, 1869, and Miss Constance Hilliard, May 9, 1869.

left to find the broad way to Hades without so much as blinker, let alone a bridle.'[1]

It may be objected that these outbursts of hatred are semi-serious. But, I submit, the objection will not hold when the letters are compared with those written later when he was in a still more abnormal state,[2] or with letters by other people in a similar condition. The passages quoted are records of insensitiveness, irritability, and hostility to his fellow-men—feelings of which he became a little ashamed *in the process of writing*, and which he therefore tries to palliate by semi-serious flourishes at the end. The tail piece about Hades is a typical flourish of this kind—a sort of apology for 'the vilest wretches of ape-faced children' which records a flash of real hostility.

He was accompanied on this trip by his valet and two assistants. He pottered round the monuments making notes and sketches and finding this and that for his assistants to do. One of these assistants, Arthur Burgess, took photographs and made drawings. The other, J. W. Bunney, did 'the most lovely work—large coloured drawings of the buildings' while Ruskin did the details.[3] For the rest he looked up old friends and the sacristans in his favourite churches who all loved him for his generous tips, and he drove up into the hills and stopped the carriage to admire the views.

But all the time his conscience plagued him for the desertion of his mother and he rationalises this desertion in several characteristic ways in his letters:

'All these things do not make me happy—nothing will ever do that; and I should be ashamed if anything could, while the earth is so full of misery.'[4]

'You seem to think I do not like coming home while you are alone; but you never were more mistaken. If life and time

---

[1] Letters to C. E. Norton from Verona, June 13, and June 24, 1869. Ruskin was amusing himself by trying to draw the griffins sustaining the pillar on the Cathedral porch. He had drawn one of them before in 1852, and had it engraved as an illustration to *Modern Painters*, Vol. III.

[2] Cf. pp. 123–4.

[3] Letter to his mother from Verona, June 10, 1869.

[4] Letter to his mother from Verona, June 17, 1869.

were unlimited I would come home instantly, and never leave you, but for little changes of air. But I am fifty, and my sight *may* fail soon in its present power—and I am quite certain that my duty is just as much here, and not at Denmark Hill, as if I were a rector ordered to a foreign church, or a colonel sent abroad on active service.'[1]

Here we must note the transference to himself of his mother's failing sight—though his own was in fact excellent. On other days he excuses his desertion by persuading himself that he was recording monuments that were fast crumbling to dust or being ruined by restorers and that he was justified in pottering month after month over the old ground because he alone in the world could appreciate the pictures, monuments, and scenery of Italy:

'I am so anxious at least now to spend my last ten years well —and so puzzled what to choose out of the much I can do that no one else can . . . Tintoret or Turner—neither of them visible to anyone but me—nor the colours of architecture— nor of skies . . . All the knowledge I have gained in these seventeen years only makes me more full of awe and wonder at Tintoret. But it *is* so sad—so sad—no one to care for him but me . . .'[2]

Here again we see the transference of his mother's condition to himself. She at eighty-eight was faced with the thought of her last years—he was only fifty.

Moreover the old delight in landscape had now really gone from him. Just as formerly he had persuaded himself that it was the artists' fault that he had lost interest in modern art, so now he persuaded himself that, if he no longer delighted in the scenery, it was the fault of the scenery itself. He now began to imagine that the natural phenomena which he had loved had deteriorated:

'The light which once flushed those pale summits with its rose at dawn, and purple at sunset, is now umbered and faint . . . The light, the air, the waters all defiled.'[3]

This notion which seems to make its appearance here for

[1] Letter to his mother from Venice, July 16, 1869.
[2] Letters to his mother from Venice, July 2 and Aug. 3, 1869.
[3] Preface to *Queen of the Air*, written at Vevay, May, 1869.

the first time was to become a regular obsession; and I shall trace its development as the years go by.[1]

It is at this time also that a manic scheme for curbing the mountain torrents in the Alps first makes its appearance. He had often pondered on the waste of water-power in mountainous regions and he had rejoiced in the annexation of Savoy to France in 1860 because he observed that French engineers set to work at once on embanking the Arve, thus dowering Savoy with 'millions of acres of fruitfullest land and healthy air instead of miasma'.[2] And now he embarked on grandiose plans to induce the inhabitants of the Alpine regions to construct reservoirs against inundations. He started off with megalomaniac confidence:

'The whole upper valley of the Rhone, sixty miles long and two wide with three or four miles of hill on each side—say some 700 square miles of land—is a mere hotbed of pestilence (marsh fever) and barren of all food, owing to the ravages of the river. Now I see perfectly how this could be prevented, and it only needs a little good engineering, and employment of idle hands . . . Here is a motive and an employment which will last to the end of my days . . . It is to arrest the Rainfall, that I mean to work. I will take a single hillside; and so trench it that I can catch the rainfall for three average years at once . . . it shall all go into reservoirs . . . Of course to deal with the *rain*fall is easy . . . the great devastations are caused by snow melting, and for that I must have a great work of Fortification at the narrowest point of every lateral valley . . . I know I can do it, but I must succeed in the less thing first . . . When I have done this for one hillside, if other people don't do it for other hillsides, and make the lost valleys of the Alps one Paradise of safe plenty, it is their fault—not mine.'[3]

He consulted engineers and made plans for negotiating a loan of 4,000,000 francs for an aqueduct to Venice;[4] and he tried

---

[1] Cf. below, pp. 124–126, 168 and 169.

[2] Letter to Dr. John Brown, Aug. 6, 1860.

[3] Letters to Miss Joan Agnew, May 12, 1869; Mrs. John Simon, May 28, 1869; C. E. Norton, June 14, 1869.

[4] Letter to C. E. Norton, Aug. 9, 1869.

PROLOGUE

to interest the Alpine Club and the banker, Carlo Blumenthal of Venice.[1]

From this he derived, of course, a double satisfaction: he indulged a manic desire to start a vast project, and found an excuse for remaining away from his mother at one and the same time.

But what of his social and economic and political work in England? He thought of that now as in 1859 he had thought of his work in the world of art. He had told he economists the truth and they had simply ignored it. Their blood must be on their own stupid, obstinate and empty heads:

'*Don't tell me* any more about good and wise people "giving their lives" to the subject, and "differing from me". *They don't differ* . . . from me . . . They are absolutely contrary to and in *Collision* with me; they don't know the *alphabet* even of the science they profess; they don't know the meaning of one word they use . . . the miserable wretches haven't brains enough to be prologue to an egg and butter, and you talk of their giving their lives! They haven't lives to give; they are not alive—they are a strange spawn begotten of misused money, senseless conductors of the curse of it, flesh-flies with false tongues in the proboscis of them. Differ from *me* indeed. Heaven help me! I am bad enough and low enough in a thousand ways, but you must know the "difference" between them and me, a little better, one day . . .'[2]

Such was Ruskin's position, such his activities and such the condition of his mind, when news reached him in Lugano that he had been elected to the newly created post of Slade Professor

[1] Letter to Charles Eliot Norton. It was optimistic of Ruskin to imagine that he could interest the Alpine Club in his scheme seeing that he had offended the members by writing in *Sesame and Lilies:* 'The Alps . . . you look upon as soaped poles in a bear-garden, which you set yourselves to climb and slide down again, with shrieks of delight.' He had returned to the attack in the Preface to the Second Edition (1865) and was very definitely *persona ingrata* with the club

[2] Letter to C. E. Norton, Aug. 18, 1869. This letter was a little bit too much even for Norton who used the word 'arrogance' in his reply (cf. Ruskin's letter to Norton from Dijon, Aug. 30, 1869).

of Fine Art in Oxford—if he cared to accept the appointment.

The Election Committee had included his old friends, Acland and Liddell and two other friends—the Rev. G. Rawlinson (a Curator of the University Galleries) and the Rev. H. O. Coxe (Bodley's Librarian). The other members were Grote the historian (in his capacity as President of University College, London); Sir Francis Grant (President of the Royal Academy); and a representative of Felix Slade who had endowed the Professorship. Rival candidates were put forward—(doubtless by the President of the Academy and Grote (of whom Ruskin had spoken as 'a vulgar materialist'). But Acland and Liddell had their way.

It was mainly vanity that made Ruskin accept the appointment—satisfaction that he had at last achieved an official status, that mere Mr. Ruskin had now become 'The Professor'. But the appointment also appealed to him because it provided an excuse (better than the necessity of 'change of air' or the alleged duty to draw griffins at Verona or curb mountain torrents) for escaping from Denmark Hill and his mother. He persuaded himself, by a characteristic rationalisation that he was accepting it to please his mother, that he was able to teach 'more sound necessary things than anyone else'[1]; and that his real work—social service—could only be accomplished by means of the upper classes. Looking back nearly twenty years later he wrote: 'Mixed vanity, hope of wider usefulness, and her [his mother's] pleasure in my being at Oxford again, took me away from her, and from myself.'[2]

He promised Acland and Liddell that he would not put forward his social, economic and religious views to the undergraduates:

'I believe you will both be greatly surprised ... at the caution with which I shall avoid saying anything with the University authority which may be either questionable by, or offensive to, even persons who know little of my subject ... I shall scrupulously avoid the expression of any of my own peculiar opinions when I speak by permission of the University . . .'[3]

[1] Letter to the Rt. Hon. W. Cowper-Temple, Sept. 4, 1869.
[2] Obituary notice of Arthur Burgess (1887).
[3] Letters to Acland, Aug. 19, 1869, and to Liddell, Sept. 2, 1869.

The first lectures were to be delivered at the beginning of the following year. He thus had the autumn in which to arrange his plan of work.

How did he set about it? We find an answer in an account of a visit to Denmark Hill by a young lady, a Miss Roberts, who procured an introduction to him in connection with her botanical studies in the middle of November. When she arrived he was teaching something to 'a poor little school girl' in one room and superintending the sketching of something by a Miss Lizzie White, a sister of one of the Winnington girls, in another. He talked to young Miss Roberts for an hour. He told her 'of a kind of society he wished to form of right-minded, right-hearted people ... who would determine to try and do some good in the world'; he described his scheme for curbing the Alpine torrents; he told her that many people made a real *idol* of the Bible 'calling it the Word of God—a great mistake'; and that he never went to church. And then he kept her to luncheon.[1]

A letter gives us another glimpse of him on the next day. He is engaged, he writes, in botany, in translating 'Chaucer's Dream' and de Queux de Saint-Hilaire's *Cent Ballades* into 'intelligible and simple' English, in writing two papers on agates, in giving an unnamed young lady lessons in Italian and 'directing her as a vowed sister of our society with one or two more', in reading Marmontel's *Memoirs* to his mother, in taking music lessons twice a week and practising scales for half an hour a day, as well as in making drawings and notes for his new duties at Oxford.[2]

[1] This account is inserted by the editors of the Library Edition in the Introduction to the volume containing *Sesame and Lilies* and *Ethics of the Dust*—and Ruskin's preoccupations are thus made to appear less inappropriate to the work on hand. But it is important to remember that the interview did not take place in 1864–5 when he was writing those volumes, but at the end of 1869 when he ought to have been preparing his Oxford *Lectures on Art* to be delivered at the beginning of 1870.

[2] Letter to Norton, Nov. 17, 1869. The geological writings referred to are the papers called *Banded and Brecciated Concretions*, published in the *Geological Magazine*, Dec., 1869, and Jan. 1870. At this time he was also preparing a lecture, *Verona and its Rivers* (illustrated with drawings and a catalogue), which he delivered at the Royal Institution a day or two

It is also clear that he had not given up his scheme for curbing Alpine torrents:

'I'm not going to make Oxford the main business of my declining life . . . I'll bridle that Rhone or I'll know why.'[1]

And a fortnight before he was due to lecture he wrote a letter to the *Daily Telegraph* about field-sports in which he said:

'Foxhunting . . . is entirely futile . . . The real evils . . . are that it wastes the time, misapplies the energy, exhausts the wealth, narrows the capacity, debases the taste, and abates the honour of the upper classes of this country . . . The athletic training given by foxhunting is excellent . . . but such training . . . ought always to be . . . in personal agricultural labour at the head of tenantry.'[2]

Thus Ruskin at fifty became 'The Professor'. Thus the author of *Unto this Last*, this genius who was at the same time a mental invalid, this man who had long been unable to work consecutively at any one thing, who had produced very little in the past seven years but had made plans for forming a body that would regenerate England and plans to curb the Alpine torrents, this man who had repeatedly protested that nothing would induce him to utter another word about art—suddenly became 'The Professor' in Oxford, charged with the duty of talking about the 'self-contemplating, self-contented Greeks'[3] and the art of the past to young men, who, 'like children of seven or eight years old' were mainly concerned with 'bats and balls and oars'[4] and to young women who recalled that their last school prize had been a book called *Sesame and Lilies* in which they had been told that they must braid their minds as well as their hair each morning before their mirrors.[5]

before he started his first lectures in Oxford in February of the following year. For his musical activities, cf. below, p. 161.

[1] Letter to the Rt. Hon. W. Cowper-Temple, Sept. 4, 1869.

[2] Letter to *Daily Telegraph*, Jan. 15, 1870. Ruskin had made earlier pronouncements on the subject in *Modern Painters*, II (cf. below, p. 213) and other works. The curious will find the references collected in a note to *Modern Painters*, V, Part IX, Chap. VI, para. 22, in the Library Edition.

[3] *The Seven Lamps of Architecture*, III, para. 18.

[4] *Aratra Pentelici*, II, para. 52.

[5] *Sesame and Lilies*, 1871, Preface.

THE PLAY

'One day . . . at Oxford, as I was going in at the private door of the University Galleries, to give a lecture on the Fine Arts in Florence, I was hindered for a moment by a nice little girl, whipping a top on the pavement. She was a *very* nice little girl; and rejoiced wholly in her whip and top; but could not inflict the reviving chastisement with all the activity that was in her, because she had on a large and dilapidated pair of woman's shoes which projected the full length of her own little foot behind it and before . . . There were some worthy people at my lecture, and I think the lecture was one of my best . . . But all the time I was speaking I knew that nothing spoken about art, either by myself or other people, could be the least use to anybody there. For their primary business, and mine, was with art in Oxford, now; not with art in Florence, then; and art in Oxford now was absolutely dependent on our power of solving the question— which I knew that my audience would not even allow to be proposed for solution—"Why have our little girls large shoes?" '

Fors Clavigera, Letter 37.

The curtain now rises on the strange performance which living men associate with the name of Ruskin. It began in February, 1870, in Oxford. 'The Professor', still blue-stocked and beardless, and dressed with an affectation of the old-fashioned in style, gave the first of his inaugural lectures to a large audience of undergraduates and of ladies and gentlemen from 'North Oxford'; and Acland, in the front row, was weeping with pleasure.[1]

At the beginning Ruskin made an effort to do what was expected of him. There were even moments when he showed signs of being influenced by his environment. For example, in using Vasari, he had hitherto worked from the Italian text, and his comments on Greek vases had hitherto been based on the study of specimens in the British Museum; but now he became 'terribly nervous' lest he should be caught out in some point of

[1] Ruskin's letter to his mother, Feb. 16, 1870.

scholarship, and he bought an English translation of Vasari and the standard book on Greek vases.[1] Moreover he planned to explain the art of Apelles[2] as though he were one of the tribe of professional propagandists for the Greek prejudice who see nothing ludicrous in talking of the style of an artist whose works have all perished. He also projected a course of lectures on Greek sculpture for the autumn, though he really thought Greek 'idealism' dull,[3] and he had hitherto never written any silly eulogies of the non-existent works by Myron, Polyclitus, Scopas, Praxiteles, and Lysippus.[4]

But even in his first course of lectures he wandered from his official brief. References to social conditions, tilts at orthodox religious teaching, and startling extemporisations soon made their appearance;[5] and his friends and the University authori-

---

[1] Letters to F. S. Ellis, Feb. 17 and 25, 1870. Later he began to collect Greek vases himself. Norton brought thirty for him in Italy in May, 1871 (Letter to C. E. Norton, May 18, 1871).

[2] Letter to C. E. Norton, March 26, 1870 .

[3] *Modern Painters*, II, Part III, Sec. I, Chap. XIII, para. 3.

[4] He had been saved from this error by early reading of Barry's Lectures (cf. *Modern Painters*, I, Part I, Sec. I, Chap. I, para. 2). There is a reference to 'ideal lines carried out with the science of a Praxiteles' in *Modern Painters*, I (Part I, Sec. I, Chap. VII, para. 3), but that is the only slip—(the *Hermes* it will be recalled was not excavated till 1877). He mentions the subject of an *Apollo Sauroctonos* statue (*Modern Art*, 1867), but does not ascribe it to Praxiteles. In the Oxford lectures of autumn, 1870, he quoted Lucian on Myron and Polyclitus (*Aratra Pentelici*, II, para. 36), but made no other reference to those sculptors. Already in 1845—when the professional admirers of Greek sculpture still looked on the *Apollo Belvedere* as the touchstone of 'ideal beauty' in sculpture—he had denied that character and called the statue vulgar (*Modern Painters*, II, Part III, Sec. II, Chap. V, para. 19). Once his juvenile days were over he had always looked on the Venus dei Medici as an 'uninteresting little person' (*Præterita*, II, Chap. II, para. 29, and *Modern Painters*, II, Part III, Sec. I, Chap. XIII, para. 3). At one time nevertheless he liked the *Townley Venus*, concocted by Nollekens (cf. above, p. 89), and he was always bluffed by the contemporary propaganda which shamelessly described Phidias as the architect of the Parthenon and sculptor of the Elgin Marbles (cf. my *The Meaning of Modern Sculpture*, pp. 36 and 37 and 71–73), and he always wrote about Phidias on this assumption.

[5] Letters of J. R. Green to W. Boyd Dawkins and E. A. Freeman, 1870.

ties came 'with grave faces to remonstrate against irrelevant and Utopian topics being introduced into lectures on art'.[1]

Most of his audience were bewildered by the indiscretions. But everyone was impressed by his plans to make the Slade Professorship an important feature of University life. For he had started at once on the formation of a reference collection of works of art for the students. He began by presenting miscellaneous drawings, photographs, engravings, and so forth, as a Reference Series of Examples. Then the idea expanded into three collections—'Standard', 'Educational' and 'Rudimentary'. Then he founded a Drawing School, equipped it, and endowed it, complete with a Drawing Master responsible to the Professor.[2]

When his first course of lectures had been delivered he was faced with the return to his mother at Denmark Hill. He postponed the unwelcome moment by pottering for some weeks with his 'Standard', 'Educational' and 'Rudimentary' Examples. But all the time his tiresome conscience was 'rustling and grumbling inside'. What right had he to be making drawings of this and that and writing catalogues of engravings and explaining chiaroscuro for the ball-playing foxhunting young gentlemen of England, when England was sunk in crime and suffering? Was it not 'the vainest of affectations to try to put beauty into shadows while all real things that cast them are left in deformity and pain'?[3]

Then he remembered that his friend Mrs. Hilliard, 'a most refined gentlewoman, good and sweet, and infinitely sensitive in all right ways' had never seen Italy.[4] Clearly to show her Italy, and especially Venice and Carpaccio's *St. Ursula*,[5] would be, if not a relief of 'deformity and pain' at any rate a kind

[1] *Fors Clavigera*, Letter 42.

[2] His endowment gift was £5,000 (say £15,000 in present money). He calculated that the drawings, engravings, and so forth, which he had presented to the school by 1875 were worth more than £2,000 (*Fors Clavigera*, Letter 49); but that was probably an exaggerated estimate even without translating the figure into the modern equivalent of £6,000.

[3] *Notes on the Educational Series*, April, 1870.

[4] Letter to C. E. Norton, June 20, 1870.

[5] Cf. below, p. 135.

action—and one which would be more agreeable to execute than a kind action at Denmark Hill. He would take Mrs. Hilliard to Venice, and with her should come her daughter Connie, and with Connie should come Joan Agnew (his mother could doubtless spare her); and he would take his valet, and a courier, and a maid for the ladies; and as, on the way, they would pass by Alpine torrents he would be able to return to his old project and 'redeem some of their barren slopes'; this would be a task with 'just enough difficulty to make it a sublime piece of manual work',[1] and when he had made some reservoirs, he would plant flowers round their banks—and for that purpose he had better add Downs, the gardener, to the party.

The party, thus constituted, started on April 26th. They went to Pisa and Florence, Verona and Venice, and Ruskin made sketches and copied fragments of this and that, as he had always done before—with this difference, that now this amusement could be described as serviceable work, because the sketches might come in useful for the Reference, or the Rudimentary, or the Educational Series of Examples in Oxford. Then kindness demanded that he should take the whole party to stay with his friend Norton who had a villa in Siena, and the needs of Oxford demanded that he should draw the lioness and her cubs at the base of the pulpit in the cathedral. Thus May and June passed, and July began with a visit to the mountains to show Downs Alpine roses, and it looked as though the return to Denmark Hill could be postponed till it was time to go back to Oxford. But then the Franco-Prussian War broke out, and the party had to hurry home—though Joan and Connie wanted to go down the Rhine and be taken prisoners for fun.[2]

Ruskin had now to prepare his Oxford lectures on Greek sculpture for the autumn; and in order to get into the atmosphere he went to the British Museum and fiddled with Greek coins. From September to the end of the year he was in Oxford concerned with 'mere art work'.[3] He took comfort in the thought that *he only* could 'put true life into those dead Greek

[1] Letter to his mother, May 13, 1870.
[2] Letter to W. H. Harrison, July 17, 1870 (cf. below, p. 323).
[3] Letter to a journalist, Aug. 20, 1870.

forms'[1] and he let off steam by writing to the *Daily Telegraph* about the war.[2]

This second bout of talking about the Greeks and consorting with the dons and parsons and ladies of Oxford convinced him that he could never hope to capture peace of mind by such procedures. Was he not with Carlyle in 'a minority of two' in a world to which they had to reveal 'the vital laws and mortal violations of them which regulate and ruin states'?[3] The lessons given the country by 'this marvellous and ghastly war' might render it possible to do what otherwise it would have been vain to think of'[4]—it was no good waiting for the end at Denmark Hill. The time had come for action. He would wait no longer. On the last day of the year he wrote as follows:

'I begin this next year in the fixed purpose of executing—at least of beginning the fulfilment of—many designs long in my mind, up to such point as I may.'[5]

And this time he was as good as, and better than, his word. The first number of *Fors Clavigera: Letters to the Workmen and Labourers of Great Britain* was published the next day.

Between January, 1871, and February, 1878, he produced eighty-seven of these 'letters' as a monthly magazine. They were published at his own expense in editions of a thousand and fifty. They were sold at first at sevenpence (one and ninepence in present values) and subsequently at tenpence (half a crown). They excited a good deal of comment, and they much increased the circle of interest in his doings. When, later, the tide of his popularity set in they were swept into it and reprinted as separate numbers and eventually as bound volumes.

Ruskin has clearly stated his mental attitude when he started *Fors Clavigera:*

'I began the writing of Fors, as a bye work to quiet *my* conscience, that I might be happy in what I supposed to be my

---

[1] Letter to C. E. Norton, Sept. 30, 1870.
[2] October 6 and 7 (cf. pp. 323 *et seq.*).
[3] Letter to a journalist, Aug. 20, 1870 (cf. below, p. 186).
[4] *Ibid.*
[5] Letter to John Simon, M.D., Dec. 31, 1870.

THE PLAY

own proper life of Art-teaching at Oxford and elsewhere; and through my own happiness, rightly help others.'[1]

But the magazine was also intended to be 'Morning, Noon and Evening Advertiser of what things appear verily noteworthy',[2] and to serve the scheme of direct social action, the foundation of a miniature Utopia, which he had been meditating, as we have seen, since 1867.[3] The cat popped out of the bag in the fifth number:

'Are there any landlords—any masters—who would like better to be served by men than by iron devils?

'Any tenants, any workmen, who can be true to their leaders and each other? . . .

'Will any such give the tenth of what they have, and of what they earn—not to emigrate with, but to stay in England with; and do what is in their hands and hearts to make her a happy England? . . .

'The tenth of whatever is left to me, estimated as accurately as I can (you shall see the accounts) I will make over to you in perpetuity, with the best security that English law can give, on Christmas Day of this year, with engagement to add the tithe of whatever I earn afterwards. Who else will help with little or much?'[4]

But he could not wait till Christmas. He started 'St. George's Fund' three months later with a contribution from his own resources of the equivalent of £3000,[5] and invited contributions, saying that 'the money is not to be spent on feeding Woolwich infants with gunpowder; it is to be spent in dressing the earth and keeping it—in feeding human lips—in clothing human bodies—in kindling human souls'[6]; and at Christmas he converted his contribution to the equivalent of £21,000.[7]

[1] *Fors Clavigera*, Letter 61.
[2] *Fors Clavigera*, Letter 61.
[3] Cf. above, pp. 87 and 94.
[4] *Fors Clavigera*, Letter 5 (May, 1871).
[5] £1,000. *Fors Clavigera*, Letter 8 (August, 1871).
[6] *Fors Clavigera*, Letter 8. The 'Woolwich infant' was a new large gun made at Woolwich in 1870 (cf. *Fors Clavigera*, Letters 2, 42, 45 and 73).
[7] £7,000. *Fors Clavigera*, Letter 12.

Thus was founded the celebrated 'Guild of St. George' which exists to this day. The scheme started as a kind of Order—the 'Companions of St. George' with an inner Order, as the heart of it, called—significantly—The Society of Mont Rose.[1] The Companions were to acquire land and work it on principles laid down in a creed composed by Ruskin, who soon began to call himself 'The Master'. They were to undertake service, to be honest, and kind, and helpful to one another. They were to be graded in ranks. They were not to prattle of 'liberty' or 'equality', but to work and obey The Master. They were to be, as it were, adult Boy Scouts and Girl Guides building, and living in, their own Garden Cities. They were to use hand power, air power, water power, and electric power, but no coal power—with its filthy smoke—unless other power was not available; and no machine power was to be used when hand power could do the work.[2]

The scheme was partly practical and partly fantastic. The Master soon began to embroider it with decorative details—special nomenclatures, special costumes, special coinage and so forth. As the arts were to be cultivated in the model settlements he started a Reference Collection for the use of the Companions; and before long he had opened a St. George's Museum in a cottage at Walkley on the top of a hill outside Sheffield, and endowed it, and equipped it with a Curator, and provided partly from the Guild's funds and partly from his own resources a miscellaneous collection of drawings, engravings, photographs, minerals and so forth.[3]

He expected the Company of St. George 'to extend its opera-

[1] *Fors Clavigera*, Letter 17.

[2] *Fors Clavigera*, Letters 49 and 58, and *General Statement of St. George's Guild* (1882). Ruskin had foreshadowed this in *Munera Pulveris*, I, para. 17 (1861), and in *Notes for the Employment of the Destitute and Criminal Classes*, written at Abbeville in 1868 (cf. above, p. 94).

[3] The Museum was subsequently installed in Meersbrook Park, Sheffield, where it exists to-day. Negotiations with the City of Sheffield for the purpose of establishing the Walkley Museum in larger premises took place over a number of years. When the transfer eventually took place Ruskin had fallen into his final illness and he never saw it. The Guild of St. George is still the owner of the contents of the Museum. For these contents cf. below, pp. 148 *et seq*.

tions over the Continent of Europe and number its members ultimately by myriads'.[1] This, in his case, was a manic scheme. Yet such things have been done. Only five years earlier William Booth had taken his Bible and his umbrella, approximately all he possessed, and, standing on Mile End Waste, had begun an organisation which was, in fact, destined to spread across the world.[2] In our own day, my old school friend, the Rev. P. B. Clayton has founded a companionship which now has 'lodges' all over the British Empire. The thing might have been done. But Ruskin was not the man who could do it— though he had his Bible and a large fortune against Booth's Bible and umbrella. He could not concentrate upon the work. And he knew this before he embarked on it: 'Though I can almost infallibly reason out the final law of anything if within reach of my industry,' he had confessed in 1867, 'I neither care for, nor can trace, the minor exigencies of its daily appliance.'[3]

Nevertheless, as a propaganda-gesture, as a means of bringing his ideas of social reform before the public, the scheme was a very considerable success. Like *Fors Clavigera*, the Company of St. George was widely talked about. Some people stared and scoffed and giggled, others (and those were for the most part the keener minds and more generous spirits) stared and marvelled at this crazy but inspiring creature who said that when a thing was right it was always possible, and who brushed aside objections with: 'I have nothing to do with its possibility but only with its indispensability.'[4]

He now embarked on other gestures which also had what

[1] *Master's Report of the Guild of St. George* (1881).

[2] Cf. *The Great Victorians*. Essay on General Booth, by St. John Ervine.

[3] *Time and Tide*, XIX, para. 117.

[4] *Lectures on Art*, IV, para. 123 (1870). He had said the same thing twenty years earlier in *The Seven Lamps of Architecture* (VII, para. 6). It is noteworthy that though Ruskin's social action was partly the result of his admiration for Carlyle (with whom he had now been intimate for many years), Carlyle himself disapproved of the Guild of St. George. He thought it, at first, 'a joke' and 'utterly absurd', and then a dangerously exciting adventure for Ruskin (cf. Carlyle's letters to W. Allingham, March 11, 1878, and to Dr. John Carlyle, Nov. 6, 1875).

we should describe to-day as 'publicity value' in disseminating
his ideas. In 1872 he hired some unemployed men and got
leave from the parish of St. Giles to make them sweep a piece
of pavement in Seven Dials—as a demonstration of what a
properly cleaned street should look like.[1] The operations were
directed by the gardener, Downs, and Ruskin himself would
drive up from time to time in his carriage and take a broom to
show his subordinates 'how to finish into depths of gutter'.[2]
And then he would explain to the men exactly how much more
they were paying for their boots when they bought them by
instalments than they would pay if they were thrifty and saved
enough money to buy their boots outright.[3]

Then there was the Tea Shop which he opened in Marylebone in 1874. He put fine china tea pots in the window, a
pretty sign outside, and two old Denmark Hill servants inside
as managers; he announced that he would sell unadulterated
tea to the poor in the neighbourhood 'in packets as small as
they chose to buy, without making a profit on the subdivision'.[4]
The tea shop did not pay. As Ruskin put it: 'The result of this
experiment has been my ascertaining that the poor only like to
buy their tea where it is brilliantly lighted and eloquently tick-
eted; and as I resolutely refuse to compete with my neigh-
bouring tradesmen either in gas or rhetoric, the patient subdivision of my parcels by the two old servants of my mother
. . . passes little recognised as an advantage by my uncalcula-
ting public.'[5] But the shop, like the Guild and the street sweep-
ing, served a purpose, as a propaganda gesture.

It was the same with the celebrated episode of the Hincksey
road-making of 1874. Ruskin despised the public-school system, and games and foxhunting, because, as he explained, they
resulted in the idealisation of play, 'so that the word "manly"
has come to mean practically, among us, a schoolboy's charac-

[1] Letter to W. H. Harrison, Nov., 1871, and *Fors Clavigera*, Letter 48.
[2] *Præterita*, II, Chap. X, para. 197.
[3] Appendix to *Fors Clavigera*, Letter 26.
[4] *Fors Clavigera*, Letter 48.
[5] *Fors Clavigera*, Letter 48. For the two old servants, and the servants
at Denmark Hill generally, cf. below, note, p. 281.

ter and not a man's'.[1] He talked of 'our damned athletics . . .
which have made schoolboys of all our public men—and end
in horse-racing—and the devil's work, of all sorts'.[2] Years before he had told the cadets at Woolwich[3] that if they put their
backs into their work they would capture 'a glorious and en-
larging happiness, not such as can be won by the speed of a
horse or marred by the obliquity of a ball'. Now he told the
undergraduates of Oxford that 'like children of seven or eight
years old' they were interested only 'in bats, balls and oars';[4]
that they must leave their games and hunting and convert a
muddy lane into a decent road. And he actually induced them
to go and do it—under the supervision of the gardener Downs,
who had *carte blanche* to meet all expenses—except the purchase of spades and pickaxes, which the undergraduates were
to provide for themselves and take care of as of 'pet rifles' and
have adorned 'in time to come . . . with a little coquetry of
iron work and devices for various grip'.[5]

The road, when made, was not a particularly good one. But
the making of it was a splendid advertisement for Ruskin and
so for his ideas, which in the end became so well known that
nobody in Oxford was surprised when in 1877 he told the undergraduates to make scholars of themselves in term by reading,
and men of themselves in the vacations by doing rough sailor's
work and sea fishing, and ploughing and helping woodmen and
shepherds at their labours.[6]

There was obviously a foundation of sound sense in all these
gestures. But Ruskin's mind nevertheless was really becoming
more and more unbalanced all through the 'seventies. His biographers usually suggest, and it was suggested at the time, that
his first collapse into recognised madness in February, 1878,
was the result of overwork—of attempting to combine his pro-

[1] *The Study of Architecture*, para. 13 (1865).
[2] Letter to Dr. W. C. Bennett, Feb. 16, 1873.
[3] *The Crown of Wild Olive*, III, para. 127 (cf. below, pp. 303 and 327 *et seq*).
[4] *Aratra Pentelici*, II, para. 62.
[5] Letter to J. R. Anderson, April 5, 1874.
[6] *Readings in Modern Painters*, Dec. 1, 1877.

fessorship in Oxford with *Fors Clavigera*, and with the organisation of St. George's Guild, and with the preparation of the books that he published in these years. But, as I have pointed out earlier, he had long been unable to work hard or continuously; between 1855 and 1870 he had only really concentrated for a few months on working out the Economic doctrines for *Unto This Last* and *Munera Pulveris*—pottering for the rest of the time from one form of self-indulgence to another; and between 1871 and 1878 he worked even less than he had habitually done before. His Oxford lectures soon ceased to give him much trouble. After 1873 he lectured less and less and at longer and longer intervals; in 1874, 1875 and 1877 he lectured only in November; in 1876 he did not lecture at all; and in the later years, in place of the carefully prepared texts of the early courses, he delivered impromptu harangues from short notes and gave readings from his earlier books. He wrote his magazine articles in *Fors Clavigera* when he felt in the mood and wherever he might happen to be at the time; and he could write one (as anybody else could, who could write one at all, if any such person could be found) in a couple of mornings with the greatest ease. The other books which he published in this period were mainly the texts of his Oxford lectures, new editions of old books, notes on botany (*Proserpina*) and geology (*Deucalion*) published in parts over a number of years, and discursive guide books to the pictures in Venice and Florence, also published in parts as the spirit moved him.[1]

The organisation of the Guild of St. George was not a great labour because he evaded work at it, and when he was wanted he was rarely to be found. He spent a lot of his time making drawings 'for Oxford' and 'for Sheffield'; but drawing of all his occupations was the one that tired him least,[2] and, as we shall see when we look more closely, his drawing in Italy at this period was partly perseveration in old habits and partly the

---

[1] The little guide book called *Mornings in Florence*, for example, which he could have written comfortably in three weeks was already planned out and begun in September, 1874 (Letter to C. E. Norton, Sept. 7, 1874), it was on the stocks till July, 1877, and then 'revised' in 1882 (cf. p. 260).

[2] Cf. above, p. 49.

relief of his obsessional brooding about Rose. Moreover, when we look behind the scenes, we find that he was now always surrounded with assistants, that he took long and frequent holidays, and that he spent a good deal of time in making himself comfortable in various new homes.

When he first went to Oxford he lived in Acland's house and he had rooms also in 'The Crown and Thistle' at Abingdon, where he retired for a few days whenever he felt like a little country air. At the beginning of 1871 he hinted to a friend in Corpus Christi that he would like to have rooms in that College, and later in the year he was made a Fellow, and given rooms which thereafter became his Oxford home—a home which he at once began to fill with some of the results of his incessant purchases of miscellaneous objects and works of art, so that a year later the contents were insured for the equivalent of £90,000.[1] And in these rooms there were times when he was happy and comfortable:

'I am to-night in a very comfortable room—all my own; have four wax candles and a nice fire; a college dinner about to be brought up in state, admirably cooked. A Titian portrait in the corner, Turner's *Bolton Abbey* over the chimney-piece, fifteen sketches by Mantegna under my table, any book in London that I like to send for, and a balance of about a thousand pounds ready money at my bankers. And I think in claiming, or even expecting, any extraordinary share of pity or condolence from my fellow-mortals I am perhaps a little exacting.'[2]

While he was arranging this home in Oxford he had also bought a house called Brantwood with sixteen acres at Coniston. This happened by accident—or, as he always said in his later years, 'As Fors would have it'.

In May, 1871, he had abandoned his mother and gone to stay with the Cowper-Temples at Broadlands, whence he wrote characteristically:

'Domestic matters very bad with me. My mother steadily declining. I obliged to leave her in patient solitude sinking

[1] £30,000.
[2] Letter to Joan Agnew (Mrs. Severn), Dec. 6, 1873.

towards less and less possibility of pleasure or exertion.'[1]

From there he had gone to Matlock, where he had a severe attack of internal inflammation accompanied by delirious fever which nearly killed him. During this illness he had dreams to which I refer later[2] and among them one about Coniston Water. Brantwood was offered him the next day by the owner (an engraver with ideas on social reform) and Ruskin interpreting the dream as an omen bought the place, without seeing it, for the equivalent of £4,500.[3]

When he recovered, the inspection of this property made a good excuse for leaving his mother throughout August and September. He found the house 'a mere shed of rotten timber and loose stone' and he set about repairing and furnishing it. 'For old acquaintance sake,' he wrote later, 'I went to my father's upholsterer in London (instead of the country Coniston one, as I ought) and had five pounds [fifteen] charged me for a footstool'; and he states that before he had his first cup of tea there (with his servants installed in a newly built lodge) he had spent the equivalent of £18,000.[4]

He was due back in Oxford to lecture in the autumn, but his mother was now visibly dying, and Joan Agnew had become Mrs. Severn and left Denmark Hill. So he returned there till, on December 5, his mother died in her ninety-first year.

The old tyrant's will consisted of one sentence: 'I leave all I have to my son'; and thus the equivalent of £110,000, with the value of the lease of the Denmark Hill property, came to replenish his exchequer.[5]

Some years before, he had bought the old house at Herne Hill where he had passed his childhood. This he now presented to the Severns, who allocated some rooms in it for him that he might stay there when he pleased. As he had Brantwood, and his rooms at Corpus, and these rooms at the Severns, he disposed of the Denmark Hill house—which he had hated for years—and finally left it in the spring of 1872.

[1] Letter to C. E. Norton from Broadlands, May 28, 1871.
[2] Cf. pp. 157 and 352.
[3] £1,500.
[4] £6,000 (Fors Clavigera, Letter 76).
[5] £ 7,000 was the actual amount (Fors Clavigera, Letter 76).

Thereafter he resumed his long annual visits to his favourite haunts abroad. In 1872, after lecturing in Oxford, he went for four months to Italy, taking with him Mrs. Hilliard and Connie, Joan and Arthur Severn, an artist assistant named Albert Goodwin, and the usual attendants. In 1873, though he lectured in Oxford and was sometimes at Herne Hill, he spent most of his time at Brantwood, where he received a number of visitors and showed them his new estate. In 1874 as soon as he had started the Oxford road-making, he went off again to Italy with courier, valet, and (for part of the time) an artist assistant, and remained there for six months—looking at this and that and sketching this and copying that in Pisa, Assisi, Rome, Naples and Sicily. At the beginning of 1875, with his continual desire to perseverate in old occupations, he felt impelled to drive about England in the old way. He hired a carriage and drove 'leisurely' from Brantwood to Yorkshire and Derbyshire and thence to London.[1] In the summer he continued the driving on a larger scale, saying to the Severns at Herne Hill: 'I will take you in a carriage and with horses and we will ride the whole way from London to the North of England'; and he built a posting carriage like the one in which he had toured abroad with his parents, and found, with some difficulty, a postillion, and drove to Brantwood—stopping at Sheffield to talk to the local authorities about St. George's Museum.[2] In the spring of 1876 he again drove the Severns from London to Brantwood spending the equivalent of £360 on the diversion.[3] From August, 1876, to June, 1877, he was abroad ten months, mainly in Verona and Venice, surrounded by a whole troop of artist assistants whom he set to copy this and that—'for Oxford' or 'for Sheffield'.

When we consider these numerous holidays and retirements to pleasant places in these years we cannot but sympathise

[1] *Fors Clavigera*, Letters 50 and 52.

[2] This happened immediately after the death of Rose La Touche (cf. pp. 76 and 131). According to an account written by Mrs. Severn, Ruskin at times was merry on this tour; he had a portable chess board and they played in the carriage when the scenery was dull. For Ruskin's chess playing cf. below, p. 309.

[3] £120. *Fors Clavigera*, Letter 66.

with the sensible female, a subscriber to *Fors Clavigera*, who wrote to him:

'I will join St. George's Company when you join it yourself. . . . Above all things you urge our duties to the land, the common earth of our country. It seems to me that the first duty anyone owes to his country is *to live in it* . . . Almost every month you date from some new place, a dream of delight to me; and all the time I am stopping at home, labouring to improve the place I live at, to keep the lives entrusted to me, and to bring forth other lives in the agony and peril of my own. And when I read your reproaches and see where they date from I feel as a soldier freezing in the trenches before Sebastopol might feel at receiving orders from a General who was dining at his club in London . . .'[1]

It was thus not overwork that brought on the collapse of 1878, and, indeed, Ruskin himself never pretended that it was. 'The doctors said I went mad . . . from overwork. I had not been then working more than usual, and what was usual with me had become easy. But I went mad because nothing came of my work . . .[2] It is not work but the sorrowful interruptions of it, that overthrow me.'[3] That was part of the truth. We get another part in a letter to Acland immediately after his first recovery: 'I am getting round, I believe really . . . Nor am I much farther out of my wits than I always was, as far as I can judge myself.'[4]

Writing later of his illness he said, 'The enduring calamity under which I toil is humiliation—resisted necessarily by a dangerous and lonely pride.'[5] That was very near it, when we add that the sense of humiliation and the dangerous pride were chronic attitudes of mind to which circumstances could only

[1] *Fors Clavigera*, Letter 49. Ruskin's reply, printed in the same number is very characteristic of the way his mind was working at this period. I refer to parts of it below, pp. 123 and 124.
[2] *Fors Clavigera*, Letter 88.
[3] *Notes on his own Drawings*, 1878.
[4] Letter to Henry Acland, May 1, 1878.
[5] *Fors Clavigera*, Letter 88.

contribute. But circumstances, undoubtedly, did contribute. Disappointment at the contrast between his grandiose plans and the actual results of his activities in the 'seventies was a factor in the 1878 collapse just as disappointment at his failure to capture art-dictatorship, the lack of interest shown in his social-economic writings, and the friction with his parents, had been factors in the breakdown at the beginning of the 'sixties. As before, the frustration was not all imaginary, but partly real.

He had really been a failure in Oxford. It was true that he was much talked about and had made himself a conspicuous figure; that a few undergraduates had succumbed to his magnetic personality, that many young ladies had succumbed to his blue stock and his blue eyes and the melodious cadence of his voice when he lectured; and that a great many old ladies liked his lectures because, though he said some bewildering things about religion, he always finished his sentence with a quotation from the Bible.[2] But after the inaugural series when he was a novelty most of the undergraduates gave up going to his lectures, and the seniors in the University, Collingwood tells us, 'were always conspicuous by their absence'. In his diaries he laments thin attendances at the lectures,[2] and he could never get more than a dozen or fifteen undergraduates to work in his Drawing School or copy his Standard, Educational and Rudimentary Examples even when he was there himself, and when his back was turned the number dropped to two or three.[3] Moreover many of the dons were definitely hostile. 'In Oxford', Ruskin said, 'I was looked upon as a lively musical box instead of a man who knew his science and his business.'[4] This was perfectly true.

His social action had also provided real ground for disappointment. He had written at the top of his voice in *Fors*

---

[1] Cf. below, pp. 342 *et seq.* and 362–365.

[2] For example, Oct. 23, 1873, 'Displeased at having thin audience'; Nov. 9, 1873, 'Thinnest audience I ever had at a lecture'.

[3] Collingwood, *Life and Work of Ruskin*. Cf. also *Ariadne Florentina*, I, paras. 1 and 2, and E. T. Cook's *Studies in Ruskin* (Allen, 1890), pp. 65 and 66, where we learn that the Drawing School was better attended at the times when it was open to the young ladies of North Oxford.

[4] Letter to the *Oxford University Herald*, June 7, 1880 (cf. below, p. 162).

Clavigera, month after month, and drawn attention to the Company of St. George, but the Roll of Companions remained ridiculously small. There were only twenty-five Companions at the beginning of 1876.[1] A year later he laments the 'entire cessation of all serviceable offers of Companionship'.[2] In March, 1877, the accession of three schoolmistresses was an event.[3] The gifts and subscriptions were equally disappointing. Ruskin had some rich friends and many rich acquaintances. He expected them to come forward with subscriptions. But they did not do so. In 1876 the Company had only received two small properties as gifts.[4] These were at Barmouth in Merioneth, and Bewdley in Worcestershire. The rest of the Guild's landed property, bought by Ruskin out of the Guild's funds, consisted mainly of thirteen acres with farmhouse and buildings at Totley (near Abbeydale in the parish of Mickley) in Derbyshire, which cost the equivalent of £6,600; a cottage near Scarborough;[5] and the Sheffield Museum in the cottage at Walkley. Some Companions were found to work the Abbeydale property—under the supervision of our old friend the gardener, Downs.[6] But in 1876 The Master had to admit that his 'collected subscriptions for the reform of the world' had amounted in five years to approximately only £700 (£2,100).[7] His friends, Acland and Cowper-Temple, had acted as Trustees of St. George's Fund from the beginning. But in the summer of 1877 they felt bound to resign. The Company had now become The Guild in The Master's mind, but it was still not a legally constituted body. The Master was generally inaccessible—driving about the country with a postillion, or away in Venice. Moreover the accounts were always in confusion. Ruskin would buy this or that, or commission a drawing or a series of drawings, before deciding whether he intended to give the things to the Oxford or the Sheffield collection or keep

[1] *Fors Clavigera*, Letter 61.
[2] *Ibid.*, Letter 73.
[3] *Ibid.*, Letter 75.
[4] *Master's Report*, 1885.
[5] £2,200. *Fors Clavigera*, Letter 80 and the *Master's Report*, 1879.
[6] The *Master's Report*, 1879 and 1881.
[7] *Fors Clavigera*, Letter 62.

them himself. There may have been Companions who could not make out how much St. George's Company and how much Ruskin himself were paying for the services of Downs, which figured so frequently in the Accounts published as appendices[1] in *Fors Clavigera;* and these accounts showed singular mistakes in arithmetic which were detected by a Companion in the Isle of Man.[2] Even the Editors of the Library Edition are baffled by the Guild's finances and suggest that only a Royal Commission 'with firms of Chartered Accountants as Assessors' could conceivably reduce them 'to complete transparency'. In 1877 Acland and Cowper-Temple probably realised that his mind was in a precarious state. They had their reputations to consider, especially as many of the Companions were poor people. When The Master absented himself month after month in Italy in 1877 they thought it necessary to remind him that St. George's Company after all was his affair, not theirs.[3] But Ruskin took their defection very much to heart. Then a faithful follower, Miss Octavia Hill, who had managed house property for him extremely well, on philanthropic lines, felt bound to warn one of her own friends that he was quite incapable of managing and carrying out the details of practical schemes, and she thus diverted a possible Companion and a possible subscription. Some foolish or spiteful person told Ruskin of the matter and he took this also very much to heart. This second blow came at the end of 1877. Ruskin published the correspondence (in spite of Miss Hill's request that he should not do so) and behaved with a caddish brutality which made it clear that he was rapidly approaching a collapse.[4]

When we examine his letters and diaries of the 'seventies we find the mental characters, observed before, now very definitely increased, and with them some new features that are obviously morbid. We find extreme mobility of interest, manic projec-

[1] The *Master's Report*, 1879, and *Fors Clavigera*, Letters 62, 63, 66–70, 72–74.
[2] *Fors Clavigera*, Letters 65 and 65.
[3] *Fors Clavigera*, Letter 78.
[4] *Fors Clavigera*, Letter 86 (February, 1878).

tion of grandiose schemes, and moods of depression; and with these characters the growth of old obsessions and delusions, and the appearance of new ones.

He spent little time in Oxford, as we have seen, and while there he pottered from one thing to another, fussing about his Standard, Reference, and Elementary Examples, and with his Drawing School. The subjects of his lectures—apart from the extempore digressions into sociology and religion—ranged from Greek coins and myths to mediæval art and history and Italian painting; and from landscape and natural phenomena to Greek and English birds. At this period he also started the publication of papers on geology and botany eventually collected as *Deucalion* and *Proserpina*.

The manic tone in *Fors Clavigera* and the manic character of the scheme for St. George's Guild are obvious. And to the main scheme of the Guild he added others including a scheme for a chain of St. George's Schools with libraries of books prepared by himself; and he started the libraries by commissioning two of his Oxford followers, Wedderburn and Collingwood, to translate Xenophon's *Economist*. He published this translation as the first volume of a *Bibliotheca Pastorum;* and then added a second volume, *Rock Honeycomb*, which was 'Broken Pieces of Sir Philip Sidney's Psalter.'

At times he exhibited extreme satisfaction with everything. At the end of 1872 and in 1873 he was delighted with Brantwood; he enjoyed showing it and the surrounding country to his guests, and his diaries refer to 'divinest walks', 'the rosy light on the Old Man reflected in *utter* calm by the lake' than which he has never seen anything more lovely, etc., etc. He enjoyed making changes and improvements on his property; he would spend an hour superintending the construction of a harbour for the mooring of his boat, and then he would go indoors to 'Birds, *Fors*, Flowers and Botticelli all in a mess',[1] and translate some lines from *Le Roman de la Rose*. It was at the end of 1873 that he wrote the contented letter from his rooms in Oxford quoted above.[2]

[1] Diary, March 3, 1873.
[2] Cf. p. 114.

THE PLAY

In the spring of 1874 he was so listless and depressed that he could not summon energy to lecture in Oxford. On his Italian wanderings which lasted from March to October of that year, he was accompanied only by his courier and valet, and he amused himself in the old ways, copying bits of familiar frescoes in Florence and Rome. He had a commission from the Arundel Society to superintend the copyists of Giotto's frescoes in Assisi and he climbed up scaffolding and copied fragments himself. The following letter shows the mobility of his interest and the trivial character of his activities in these places:

'I must tell you exactly how this last day but one in Florence has passed. It has been a nice active one.

'Up at six. Red dawn. Bothered in shaving by aphorisms coming into my head. Dressed by ten minutes to seven. Read Esdras II, xiv, to verse 15.

'Coffee. Put down bothering aphorisms. Put on boots. Walk to Santa Croce quietly. Set to work thinking over Giotto's fresco of St. Francis before the Soldan. Sketch Soldan's crown. Do eyes. Feeble attempt at beard.

'Sketch draperies of Soldan's discomfited Magi. A. Magus giving in. B. Magus shut up. C. Exit Magus . . . Proceeded to examine St. John in Patmos. Sketched Woman, Baby, Dragon, and Moon, and thought it time to go to breakfast. Found letters from Joanie . . . *Fors* for October, proof. Ate breakfast, read letters and *Fors* proof, out at eleven for Spanish Chapel. Drew Pope Clement and his mitre. Ditto, Geometry's back hair coming loose in an infinite curve. Deciphered inscription in St. Thomas Aquinas' book.

'Got ladder in green cloister. Examined picture of St. Anne and baby. Came back and had a final try at Logic's white jacket. Had to give in—no use. I never yet have been able to draw a girl's shoulder . . . Then . . . had to finish Zoroaster's beard, and Tubal-cain's anvil . . . and then went home to dinner and wrote to Di Ma.

'Then drove up to Bellosguardo and saw sunset, and walked home, and wrote out notes till ten o'clock . . . Must go to bed.'[1]

These potterings he rationalised into:

[1] Letter to Mrs. Severn from Florence, Sept. 18, 1874.

'My time is passed in a fierce steady struggle to save all I can every day, as a fireman from a smouldering ruin, of history or aspect.'[1]

Irritability and hostility of the same character as chronicled of 1869 appear on this tour. For example:

'A beggar boy—half idiot, whole devil, greatly irritates me. The quantity of wretches of this sort whom wholesale earthquake would swallow like Korah and make manure of! Korah was the mere representation of millions equally insolent and far more nasty who remain unburied.'[2]

And this hostility revived in him when he looked back in memory the year after:

'By day or night . . . in the streets of every city . . . entirely monstrous and inhuman noises in perpetual recurrence. The violent rattle of carriages, driven habitually in brutal and senseless haste, or creaking and thundering under loads too great for their cattle, urged on by perpetual roars and shouts; wild bellowing and howling of obscene wretches far into the night; clashing of church bells . . . as if rung by devils . . . filthy, stridulous shrieks and squeaks, reaching for miles into the quiet air, from the railroad stations at every gate; the vociferation, endless, and frantic, of a passing populace whose every word was in mean passion or in unclean jest.'[3]

'Florence is . . . a place of torment day and night for all loving, decent and industrious people; for every face one meets is full of hatred and cruelty; and the corner of every house is foul . . . what is said here of Florence is now equally true of every great city of France or Italy.'[4]

The last quotation comes from his reply to the Companion's letter commenting on his frequent long sojourns abroad in agreeable places, referred to above (p. 117). Ruskin defended himself by saying that his visits to Venice, Florence, etc., were torture to him and only undertaken in fulfilment of stern duty

[1] Letter to Miss Susan Beever from Florence, Aug. 25, 1874.

[2] Letter to Mrs. Severn from Assisi, June 4, 1874.

[3] *Deucalion*, I, Chap. V, para. 7. Written in 1875 of his 1874 stay in Italy. Cf. also *Mornings in Florence*, V, para. 89 quoted below, p. 260.

[4] *Fors Clavigera*, Letter 49, January, 1875.

to Oxford and Sheffield. And he concludes with a threat to punish the world for its ingratitude 'by staying at home among my plants and minerals and forsaking the study of Italian art for ever'.

There are also rapid alternations from extreme satisfaction to depression:

'An extraordinary fit of wellness has succeeded the extra-ordinary fit of illness. At Genoa I felt as if I could do nothing; and here I have suddenly great appetite, enjoyment of my work, and capability of thinking and directing without fatigue.'[1]

We get 'glorious afternoon', 'the Carrara hills . . . one glow of calm glory', 'the most wonderful walk to-night that I've yet found in Italy', 'Rosy sunset intense; beyond all glows I ever remember', 'the best day for work I ever had in my life', etc., and then depression. One entry on his way home in October reads, 'Walked to Bonneville . . . there at first all was sweet: then a cloud seemed to come over my mind and the sky to-gether.'[2]

We must now examine the obsessions and delusions that grew upon him in the 'seventies.

The first was a notion that a new kind of Storm Cloud and Plague Wind had come to destroy the beauty and pleasantness of the physical world; the second was a notion that he was a lonely and pathetic orphan; the third was a series of images connected with Rose La Touche; and the fourth an obsessional fear connected with fireflies and fireworks.

(i) The Storm-Cloud notion had begun in 1869 as noted. He had already then conceived the idea that nature had deterio-rated, that the sun no longer shone with the same brilliance, and that the skies had lost their radiance. While he was perform-ing with conspicuous manic confidence as The Professor in Oxford and as The Master of St. George's Company, this idea was becoming an obsessional delusion. He ascribed the dark-ness of the imaginary new Storm Cloud in part to the foul smoke of coal fuel, but the whole thing, Storm Cloud and

[1] Letter to Mrs. Severn from Assisi, April 12, 1874.
[2] Diary, Oct. 18, 1874.

Plague Wind together, he thought of fundamentally as a change of climate sent by the Devil to thwart God and persecute man. He refers to this several times in *Fors Clavigera*. In one place he says that the new cloud looks 'as if it were made of dead men's souls'[1]; in another he refers to 'the black-plague wind which has now darkened the spring for five years, veiling all the hills with sullen colour'.[2] He makes frequent entries of the same kind in his diaries. On July 4, 1875, he notes that the range of power of this plague-wind is from the North of England to Sicily. He divides thunderstorms into normal storms and others 'dirty, weak foul' with the new kind of 'thin, scraggy, filthy, mangy, miserable' plague-cloud and a new 'poisonous', 'fretful', 'fluttering' plague-wind.[3]

In 1871 he writes:

'Everything is infinitely sad to me—this black east wind for three months most of all. Of all the things that oppress me, this sense of the evil working of nature herself—my disgust at her barbarity—clumsiness—darkness—bitter mockery of herself—is the most desolating.'[4]

While he was driving about the country behind the postillion in 1875 he wrote in his diary:

'An exquisite morning sky, all fretted with sweet white cloud seen only here and there through miserable rack of the foul storm smoke. Why does, how *can*, God do it and spoil His own work so wretchedly? At the moment, whistling wind, calm luminous sky and the black Devil cloud all contending for mastery.'[5]

I find the same obsession in his correspondence in these years—whether he is in England or Italy.

Here are some references:

'Nature herself traitress to me—whatever Wordsworth may say.'[6]

[1] Letter 8 (August, 1871).

[2] Letter 53 (May, 1875). Cf. also Letter 12 (Dec., 1871) and Letter 29 (April, 1873).

[3] He gives quotations from these diaries in *The Storm Cloud of the Nineteenth Century* (cf. p. 169).

[4] To C. E. Norton from Denmark Hill, April 3, 1871.

[5] Aug. 16, 1875.

[6] Letter to C. E. Norton from Brantwood, Jan. 15, 1873.

'The weather . . . appals me; it is a plague of darkness such as I never believed nature could inflict or suffer.'[1]

' I have learned . . . not to despise even the worst darkness of England, or storm of Coniston, as evils of baser climate. That accursed wind takes them all over earth, and the orange groves are all blighted here by the same storms that made me ill in passing the Cenis.'[2]

'I . . . am literally frightened at this unnatural darkness and cold . . . the bitter, blighting black-clouded *wind* . . .'[3]

'I really begin to think there is some terrible change of climate coming upon the world for its sin, like another deluge.'[4]

'The deadliest of all things to me is my loss of faith in nature. No spring and no summer. Fog always and the snow faded from the Alps.'[5]

'Everything that has happened to me . . . is *little* in comparison to the crushing and depressing effect on me, of what I learn day by day as I work on, of the cruelty and ghastliness of the *Nature* I used to think so divine.'[6]

'Nothing could beat me except the plague of darkness and blighting wind—perpetual, awful—crushing me with the sense of Nature and Heaven failing as well as man.'[7]

'The difference to me between nature as she is now and as she was ten years ago is as great as between Lapland and Italy, and the total loss of comfort in morning and evening sky the most difficult to resist of all spiritual hostility.'[8]

(ii) The notion that he was a pathetic orphan, was, I take it, a kind of transference to himself of the deserted state in which he had left his mother, equivalent to his former transference to himself of her failing sight and her nearness to the grave[9]; it was a rationalisation of a sense of remorse not only for

[1] To an Artist from London, June 15, 1873.
[2] To Mrs. Severn from Sicily, April 22, 1874.
[3] To Dean Liddell from Rome, May 23, 1874.
[4] To Miss Susan Beever from Rome, May 23, 1874.
[5] To C. E. Norton from Herne Hill, Feb. 13, 1875.
[6] To Susan Beever from Kirkby Lonsdale, Jan. 21, 1875.
[7] To C. E. Norton from Brantwood, March 25, 1875.
[8] To Miss Susan Beever from Broadlands, Dec. 11, 1875.
[9] Cf. above, p. 97.

126

THE PLAY

the real desertion of his mother, but also for imaginary past shortcomings in his duty to his father.

The refrain, 'Father gone, Mother gone', occurs repeatedly and it is clear that he imagined himself the victim of some special punishment because, though he was already approaching sixty, he had been abnormally robbed of parents who had died, the one at seventy-nine and the other at ninety. To this he assimilated the loss of an old nurse who had remained at Denmark Hill till she died when he was fifty-two.[1] So we meet the refrain, 'Father gone, Mother gone, Nurse gone' frequently in his letters.[2]

We also get it in *Fors Clavigera*:

'I have no home . . . because my father, and mother and nurse are dead . . .'[3]

'Now father and mother and nurse all dead, and the roses of spring, prime or late—what are they to me?'[4]

In regard to the first of these quotations we must observe that Ruskin at this time had three homes—Brantwood, Corpus Christi, and his rooms at Herne Hill; and in regard to the second we must note the association of the word 'roses'.

(iii) Rose, it will be recalled, had postponed her answer to his proposal of 1866 till her majority in 1870. She continued her religious broodings; her parents continued to oppose the marriage; and she relieved her feelings by writing a volume of devotional poems called (as though it were a chapter in *Modern Painters*) *Clouds and Light*. There we read:

'Oh, dearer than my failing words express,
Is nature's beauty to this heart of mine;
Yet for the soul's utter weariness
She has no balm nor any anodyne;
Her "changeful glories" may not heal or bless
The human heart which cries for the divine.'

At the beginning of 1870 she again postponed her decision.

[1] Cf. below, pp. 187 and 281.
[2] For example: Letters to Carlyle, October, 1873; to Dr. John Brown, Dec. 29, 1873; to C. E. Norton, Oct. 30, 1875.
[3] *Fors Clavigera*, Letter 49, Jan., 1875.
[4] *Fors Clavigera*, Letter 41, April 1, 1874. (Cf. *Fors Clavigera*, Letter 28, April, 1873).

127

Ruskin who was at work on his inaugural Oxford lectures was so angry that he rewrote some parts of the text at the last minute in order to scold her.[1]

I find the Rose obsession frequently in 1870. In August he spent the equivalent of £600[2] on a 'providential'[3] find of a four-teenth-century *Roman de la Rose*—'. . . very typical of the course of all *my* Roman, and therefore exquisitely sweet in feeling—not particularly wise in execution'.[4] In the autumn in Oxford he hoped for a decision, but none came.[5] In 1871 a woman mischief-maker told Rose's mother something seriously detrimental to his character; Mrs. La Touche (whose personal feelings towards Ruskin I have already noted)[6] repeated this to Rose who believed it and decided to have nothing more to do with him. Ruskin heard of the accusation and wrote categorically denying it. But the letter was withheld from Rose. These facts, recently revealed by Dr. MacDonald,[7] explain the singular Preface added in 1871 to *Sesame and Lilies*, where Ruskin reproaches Rose and defends his own character:

'No man ever lived a right life who had not been chastened by a woman's love, strengthened by her courage, and guided by her discretion. What I might myself have been so helped, I rarely indulge in the idleness of thinking; but what I am, since I take on me the function of a teacher, it is well that the reader should know . . . Not an unjust person; not an unkind one; not a false one; a lover of order, labour, and peace. That, it seems

[1] Letter to C. E. Norton, March 26, 1870. For passages in these inaugural Oxford lectures directed at Rose, cf. below, pp. 349 *et seq.* As an example of the persistence of the Orphan obsession we may note here that in a Preface added to the 1887 edition of these inaugural *Lectures on Art*, Ruskin said that they were written 'while my mother yet lived and had vividest sympathy in all I was attempting'—though as we have seen she was in her ninetieth year at the time, almost blind, and then, as always, not competent to advise on the composition of Oxford lectures; and he had been mainly occupied in finding excuses to get away from her.

[2] £200.

[3] Letter to C. E. Norton, Aug. 26, 1870.

[4] Letter to C. E. Norton, Aug. 14, 1870.

[5] Letter to his mother, Oct. 1, 1870.

[6] Cf. above, p. 82.

[7] Cf. *Reminiscences of a Specialist*, by Greville MacDonald, M.D.

to me, is enough to give me right to say all I care to say on ethical subjects.'[1]

This Preface was of no avail. Carlyle records that Ruskin in the beginning of 1872 had 'fallen into thick, quiet despair again on the personal question; and meant all the more to go ahead with fire and sword upon the universal one'.[2] Meanwhile Rose herself was very unhappy as we see from her letters to George and Mrs. MacDonald (who were friends both of her and of Ruskin):

'I have nothing in the world to do from day to day but what I like. All my parents want from me is that I should be well and happy. This seems a slight requirement, but I cannot fulfil it ... My daily life is simply hour after hour of pondering, wishing, praying, enduring ... I go about among the poor people here and come back in despair sometimes. They lead a life so much more like Christ's than mine, and I go jingling off from their doors in the carriage with my ponies and bells, but with a sadder heartache than many of them could know ... My mother hates the place and does not interest herself at all in it— and cannot bear me to talk to her on the subjects I feel most strongly upon ... She is not happy with me ... Can you give me a word of counsel? For I believe you will understand although I have expressed myself so dimly.'[3]

'... Friends I have met in strange ways, very poor and suffering people, curious characters that have temptations I can't understand, form half of a strange clasp that draws my heart to them. I love what I cannot have and desire what I can't do ... Last night I sat down at my mother's feet and laid my head on her knee aching to rest my heart there too. But she said I was a baby instead of a young woman of twenty-four ... If it could have been so that I could have kept the friend who has brought such pain and suffering and torture and division among so many hearts—if there had never been anything but friendship between us—how much might have been spared ...'

[1] Cf. below, p. 351.
[2] Letter from Carlyle to John Forster, Dec. 20, 1872.
[3] Letter of April 20, 1872, to Mr. and Mrs. George MacDonald. (From Greville MacDonald, *op. cit.*) How strangely the style echoes Ruskin! That 'dimly' could have no other source.

'I want to say some things to you, please. I know what the misery of believing the "evil reports" I have heard of him have been to me. I cannot trust him as you do. Remember the words and belief of my parents and the advisers and counsellors who have brought me up *must* weigh with me, and come to me as they could not to you; for they are in some measure the divinely appointed guardians to whom I must give heed.'[1]

As a result of such letters, the MacDonalds who were satisfied of Ruskin's innocence of the specific charge and of his physical normality,[2] decided to arrange a meeting in spite of the attitude of Rose's parents. Ruskin at the time was in Italy with the Hilliards and Severns.[3] His feeling on the matter at the moment was that of the Preface of *Sesame and Lilies*. 'Let her read that,' he wrote to the MacDonalds. Then on June 30 he telegraphed from Venice: 'I will not move unless in certainty of seeing her. If you and Mrs. MacDonald can bring her to Italy I will meet you at Geneva'; and he followed this with letters:

'I will have no talking ... I trusted her with my whole heart; she threw it to the dogs to eat and must be satisfied. But we might at least contrive that we could each think of the other without horror.'

[1] Letters to Mr. and Mrs. George MacDonald, 1872. (From Greville MacDonald, *op. cit.*) Here again we get the Ruskinian ring: 'I love what I cannot have and desire what I can't do' is an echo from words addressed indirectly to her in Ruskin's inaugural lectures in Oxford (published 1870), cf. below, p. 350. Compare also Ruskin's letter to his father on his honeymoon (Aug. 9, 1848): 'I seem born to conceive what I cannot execute, recommend what I cannot obtain, and mourn over what I cannot save'. And with 'I want to say some things to you, please,' compare Ruskin's favourite beginnings of letters such as 'Please, I want to know this' (to Dr. John Brown, June 25, 1874); 'I want really to tell you now, something ... (to Mrs. Severn, June 25, 1877); 'I am not doing as you bid me' (to C. E. Norton, June 25, 1873), etc. It is clear that though Rose resisted Ruskin's personality she had been dominated by it from childhood. It was his influence that made her visit the poor. Cook has published entries in her diary: 'I think it was Mr. Ruskin's teaching when I was about twelve that made me first take to looking after the poor.' 'The letters Mr. Ruskin wrote me only helped me, and did me no harm, whatever others may say' (cf. above, p. 81).

[2] Cf. above, p. 54.

[3] Cf. above, p. 116.

And:

'I wrote with absolute openness to her aunt. They burn my letters and then ask me to write more. I am not a saint. Rose is —but a cruel one.'[1]

Eventually a meeting took place at the MacDonald's house in Hammersmith. Ruskin had 'three days of heaven' and the position was made finally clear. He could not induce her to marry him, and he realised that she was a sick woman 'her entire soul being paralysed by the poisoned air'.[2] Rose on her side wrote: 'His last words to me were a blessing. I felt too dumb with pain to answer him . . . I cannot be to him what he wishes, or return the vehement love which he gave me which petrified me and frightened me.'

Perhaps she knew that Ruskin was not really in love with her but with the remembered image of Rosie, and perhaps also she sensed the madness behind his vehemence and depression.

They met again at Cowper-Temple's at Broadlands, again in the house of other mutual friends at Toft (where Rose complained of a tone of levity in parts of *Fors Clavigera*);[3] and again in London in 1874. Rose's mental and physical state grew steadily worse. Dr. MacDonald describes her condition as an acute case of psychasthenia.[4] In December, 1874, Ruskin wrote in *Fors Clavigera*: 'One of my best friends has just gone mad.'[5] In January, 1875, he wrote: 'The woman I hoped would have been my wife is dying.'[6] On May 29 she died.

Meanwhile in *Fors Clavigera* he had been railing against pietistic religion. When Rose was dying, he wrote a number entitled 'Platted Thorns' (*'When they had platted a crown of thorns, they put it upon his head'*), and he told the world that Lady Jane Grey had thanked God that she had 'sharp and severe' parents, and 'a gentle schoolmaster' with whom, though

---

[1] From Greville MacDonald, *op. cit.*

[2] Letter to George MacDonald, Aug. 11, 1872 (from Greville MacDonald, *op. cit.*).

[3] *Fors Clavigera*, Letter 21, and Ruskin's Diary for Aug. 17, 1872.

[4] Greville MacDonald, *op. cit.*

[5] *Fors Clavigera*, Letter 48.

[6] *Fors Clavigera*, Letter 49.

THE PLAY

she delighted in his lessons, she was not in love. And he concluded with this passage:

'That her father and mother, with whatever leaven of human selfishness, or impetuous disgrace in the manner and violence of their dealing with her, did, nevertheless, compel their child to do all things that she did—rightly, and no otherwise, was, verily, though, at that age she knew it but in part—the literally crowning and guiding Mercy in her life—the platted thorn upon the brow, and rooted thorn around the feet, which are the tribute of Earth to the Princesses of Heaven.'[1]

The significance of all this is obvious. So also, I take it, is the confused punctuation.

In July, after Rose's death, he writes in *Fors Clavigera* that if the true discipline of the Church were carried out 'though still the various passions and powers of the several orders would remain where the providence of Heaven placed them—and the useful reed and useless rose would still bind the wintry waters with their border, and brighten the May sunshine with their bloom—for each, their happy being would be fulfilled in peace in the garden of the world; and the glow, if not of immortal, at least of sacredly bequeathed life, and endlessly cherished, memory, abide even within its chambers of the tomb'.

And below this he placed a drawing of a tomb with roses growing from the centre.[2]

[1] *Fors Clavigera*, Letter 54.

[2] In October, 1875, Ruskin calls himself 'a reed shaken by the wind' in the passage in *Fors Clavigera* which stands at the head of my Introductory Comments. There had been the same juxtaposition of *Broken Reeds* and *Rose Gardens* in *Time and Tide*, Letters XIX and XX, at the time when Rose had first postponed her answer. There we read that 'whosoever is wise, patient, unselfish and pure' is kept maid or bachelor; and there too we read the celebrated suggestion that youths and maidens should have to qualify for marriage by a period of probation and then be crowned 'Bachelors' and 'Rosières'—a suggestion which is, of course, incomprehensible until we realise that it is all subconsciously ironical—a *reductio ad absurdum* of the probation imposed by Rose the Rosière on her Bachelor, the Bachelor of Arts once known as 'The Graduate of Oxford'. In *Mornings in Florence* and in all his later writings he always used the word 'rosy', for 'pink' when describing the colours in pictures: Giotto 'dreamed of angels that were rosy', the flesh tints in the Spanish chapel are 'rosy' and so forth.

132

THE PLAY

In 1870 Ruskin had written:

'I have been endeavouring this morning to define the limits of insanity. My experience is not yet wide enough. I have been entirely insane, as far as I know, only about Turner and Rose.'[1]

His experience now was to be tragically widened. From an early stage in his courtship he had identified Rose with Beatrice and himself with Dante. Before he had met Rose he had decided that Dante's Beatrice was a real person and one who did not marry (and therefore not the same person as Beatrice Portinari who eventually married Simon de Bardi).[2] He had also long been attracted by Dante's image in the *Paradiso* of the White Rose in the midst of heaven:

> 'Rosa sempiterna
> Che si dilata, rigrada, e ridole
> Odor di lode al sol.'

He quoted the lines, which he soon came to associate with Rose, in *The Queen of the Air* (1869)[3] and he refers to the image in his Oxford Lectures (1870).[4]

After Rose's death he went to stay with the Cowper-Temples at Broadlands. Mrs. Cowper-Temple was a spiritualist, who had persuaded him after his father's death in 1864 to attend the séances of the fashionable medium, Daniel Douglas Home. In 1875 and 1876 at Broadlands she again induced him to dabble in these perilous waters. Traces of the results appear in his letters:

'I have heard wonderful things this very afternoon. I have seen a person who has herself had the Stigmata . . . she had the wounds more than once, but on one occasion conveyed instantly by a relic of St. Catherine of Siena. And I'm as giddy as if I had been thrown off Strasbourg steeple and stopped in the air; but thing after thing of this kind is being brought to me . . .'[5]

---

[1] Letter to C. E. Norton, July 29, 1870.
[2] Letter to Rossetti (1855).
[3] *Queen of the Air*, II, para. 78.
[4] *Aratra Pentelici*, III, para. 72 (cf. also *Proserpina*, I, Chap. XI, para. 18.
[5] Letter to C. E. Norton from Broadlands, Dec. 14, 1875.

'At Broadlands either the most horrible lies were told me, without conceivable motive—or the ghost of Rose was seen often beside Mrs. —— or me—which is pleasantest of these things I know, but cannot intellectually say which is likeliest . . .'[1]

'To me personally, it is no common sign that just after the shade of Rose was asserted to have been seen beside Mrs. T. and beside me, here, I should recover the most precious of the letters she ever wrote me, which, returned when we parted, she had nevertheless kept . . .'[2]

Thereafter he always carried this letter between thin plates of gold in his breast pocket.

From 1869 onwards he had identified Rose not only with Dante's Beatrice, but also with St. Ursula in Carpaccio's pictures in Venice.

He had not paid any particular attention to Carpaccio when he began to study Italian painting in 1845, nor had he when working on *The Stones of Venice* at the beginning of the 'fifties. He slipped the name into the revised version of *Modern Painters, I*, which I discuss later,[3] and he mentions it twice in the *Venetian Index* appended to *The Stones of Venice;* but in these references he describes the pictures as topographical records of old Venetian architecture. In 1869, when Burne-Jones had drawn his attention to other aspects of Carpaccio's work, he 'discovered' him—and St. Ursula lying in her bed in the picture called *St. Ursula's Dream*.[4]

We see what happened in the very first reference to Carpaccio thereafter. 'Carpaccio's work is faultless. When done it is a mouth; and a perfect one'[5]; and later he tried 'twelve times over' to copy it.[6] In 1870 when he had persuaded himself that he must leave his mother to show Mrs. Hilliard Italy and curb

---

[1] Letter to C. E. Norton, Jan. 13, 1876.
[2] Letter to C. E. Norton from Broadlands, Feb. 1, 1876.
[3] Cf. pp. 206–208.
[4] Letter to Burne-Jones from Venice, May 13, 1869, and *Fors Clavigera*, Letter 20 (August, 1872).
[5] *Verona and its Rivers*. Lecture delivered at the Royal Institution, Feb. 4, 1870.
[6] Cf. below, p. 173.

THE PLAY

the mountain streams with the help of Downs, it was really
Carpaccio's picture of St. Ursula sleeping that he was impatient to revisit.[1] He could not get to Italy in 1871, but he was
in Venice again in 1872 staring at the Rose-Ursula images. He
was thus engaged when he telegraphed and wrote the suggestion that Rose should come out to him with the MacDonalds.[2]
While he was waiting for the answer he wrote a detailed description of *St. Ursula's Dream* for *Fors Clavigera*[3]; and he
somehow contrived to identify Carpaccio with Dante and thus
St. Ursula with Beatrice, and both groups with himself and
Rose.[4]

On his 1874 tour in Italy the St. Ursula obsession seems for
a time to have lost its power. On that occasion he fell in love
with the figure of Zipporah by Botticelli (in the Sistine Chapel)
—doubtless because he saw in her a likeness to Rose—and he
made a detailed copy of the figure. When he was tired of the
copying he went 'among the roses' in the Pincio gardens or
made a sketch of some roses against a Byzantine pillar in the
cloisters of San Paolo.[5] In Florence at the same time we get
this in a letter:

'To-day I've been up to my dear Spring drawing the roses
by measure for my book vignette. They are so altogether in-
imitable, I try again and again till I fall asleep with trying.'[6]

This copying of the roses in Botticelli's *Spring* was for the
rose vignette on the title pages of his book. But in 1874 the
copying was sheer perseveration because the work had already
been done and the vignette was in use, as we know from *Fors
Clavigera* in 1872:

'The little vignette stamp of roses on title page . . . is copied
from the clearest bit of the pattern on the petticoat of *Spring*,
where it is drawn tight over her thigh . . . I drew it on the wood

[1] His notes for the continuation of *Præterita* make his study of Carpaccio the feature of this tour (cf. above, p. 105).
[2] See above, p. 130. He records study of Carpaccio as the feature of
this tour also in his notes for the continuation of *Præterita*.
[3] *Fors Clavigera*, Letter 20 (Venice, July 5, 1872).
[4] *Fors Clavigera*, Letter 18 (Pisa, April, 1872).
[5] Letter to Mrs. Severn from Rome, June 4, 1874.
[6] Letter to Mrs. Severn from Florence, Sept. 3, 1874.

135

myself and Mr. Burgess cut it; and it is on all my title pages, because whatever I now write is meant to help in founding the society called "Monte Rosa".[1]

He was not abroad in 1875. But after Rose's death and the spiritualist experiences at Broadlands came the ten months' Italian holiday of 1876–1877. On this occasion he surrendered himself most dangerously to the St. Ursula obsession. He arranged for *St. Ursula's Dream* to be placed in a private room where he spent four months copying the picture and making separate studies of the head, the hand, and the slippers on the floor.[2] He also copied the *Martyrdom and Funeral of St. Ursula* where the girl lies not asleep but dead on her bier; and he employed his assistants to make separate copies of every detail in *St. Ursula's Dream* and to copy other pictures in the St. Ursula series.

'I've been having a quite glorious day with St. Ursula . . . Fancy having St. Ursula right down on the floor in a good light and leave to lock myself in with her . . . There she lies, so real, that when the room's quiet I get afraid of waking her . . . Then there's the one of St. Ursula asleep—that other way.'[3]

He knew that this was perilous and he read *The Memoirs of Casanova* in the evenings 'to prevent St. Ursula having it all her own way'.[4] But he continued all the same. He published the whole story of St. Ursula in *Fors Clavigera*—Ursula, the 'Bud of Flowers', who at fifteen was a light of wisdom, and a glass of all beauty, and a fountain of scripture and of sweet ways; the maiden whose speech was 'so full of all delight that it seemed as though an angel of Paradise had taken human flesh', the maiden who would not wed her suitor till he had changed his religion to make it as her own, the maiden who asked her suitor to postpone the marriage for three years, the maiden who served God and went to God wearing a martyr's crown.[5]

[1] *Fors Clavigera*, Letter 22, October, 1872. For Burgess cf. above, p. 96. For the Society of Monte Rosa as the heart of St. George's Guild, cf. p. 109.
[2] Letter to C. E. Norton, Jan. 16, 1877.
[3] Letter to Mrs. Arthur Severn, Sept. 19, 1876.
[4] Letter to C. E. Norton, Oct. 5, 1876.
[5] *Fors Clavigera*, Letter 71 (Nov., 1876).

THE PLAY

This was written while he was closeted with the picture and on the day before he wrote to Norton that he was reading Casanova as an antidote. On Christmas Day, 1876, he wrote in *Fors Clavigera:*

'Last night, St. Ursula sent me her dianthus "out of her bedroom window with her love" . . . She sent me the living dianthus (with a little personal message besides, of great importance to *me* . . .), by the hands of an Irish friend now staying here: but she had sent me also a dried sprig of the other flowers in her window, the sacred vervain.'[1]

The passage continues with the explanation that the one flower is Wild and the other Domestic—and reading between the lines we see that he was thinking of 'hedges of virgin's bower and wild rose'.[2]

The following year when he had returned to London he fell to brooding on the picture of *St. Ursula blessed by the Pope.* He had already had copies made of the central group; and as he pondered on them he saw a strange significance:

'It signifies the essential truth of joy in the Holy Ghost filling the whole body of the Christian Church with visible inspiration, sometimes in old men, sometimes in children; yet never breaking the laws of established authority and subordination— the greater saint blessed by the lesser, when the lesser is in the higher place of authority.'[3]

This interpretation doubtless came to him because he recalled another scene—a scene between a maiden and a man thirty years her senior who had raised his hand in blessing, in George MacDonald's morning room at Hammersmith, as described by Rose: 'His last words to me were a blessing . . .'[4]

[1] *Fors Clavigera,* Letter 74.

[2] *Fors Clavigera,* Letter 72. Cf. also *Præterita,* III, Chap. III, para. 59, 'My cousins the moorland roses nodded at me as I passed and . . . couldn't understand why Irish hedge roses bloomed in July instead of March'—a passage from Rosie's letter to him of March 16, 1861, which when he wrote *Præterita* he had carried in his pocket between gold plates for years and doubtless knew by heart (cf. above, p. 134).

[3] *St. Mark Rest,* X, para. 205. Written immediately after Ruskin's return to England in 1877.

[4] Cf. above. p. 131.

(iv) We must now note the obsessional images connected with Fireflies and Fireworks—images inducing a kind of panic which explains, incidentally, Ruskin's attack on Whistler in July of 1877.

People who associate Ruskin's name with the Pre-Raphael-ites often suppose that he only admired pictures painted in 'niggling' Pre-Raphaelite technique. But this is a mistake. We must remember his admiration of Tintoretto among the old masters and of Turner in the modern schools. He enjoyed especially the broad effects of Turner's late-middle manner seen in *The Slave Ship* (Boston) which he owned for many years, and in *The Snow Storm* (London, National Gallery). Moreover Turner's words had weight with him, and he knew that Turner had said: 'Indistinctness is my forte'[1] and 'An artist ought to paint his impressions.'[2] In a notable passage he him-self had said:

'A painter . . . is . . . incapable of conceiving anything at all, except as a phenomenon or a sensation . . . That which is not an appearance, or a feeling, or a mode of one or the other, is to him nothing.'[3]

It is true that he did not like Whistler's pictures, that he thought them careless in execution, and that he looked on Whistler's use of musical terms in his titles as an affectation. And he had already attacked Whistler in an Oxford lecture in 1873.[4] But the celebrated outburst which caused Whistler to bring an action for libel must be looked on as a gesture of an-other kind. It was not, I feel certain, the deliberate expression of an artistic judgement, but the involuntary expression of automatic panic.

To understand the panic we must realise that Ruskin was always both fascinated and frightened by spots of light sur-rounded with darkness. Such phenomena affected him in mor-bid moments with a kind of horror. He liked pictures with

---

[1] C. R. Leslie's *Autobiographical Recollections*, 1860.

[2] *Modern Painters*, IV, Part V, Chap. XV, para. 33.

[3] *The Range of Intellectual Conception proportioned to the Rank in Animated Life*. Paper by Ruskin read to the Metaphysical Society, April 25, 1871 (cf. below, pp. 189 and 190).

[4] *Val d'Arno*, III, para. 79.

light backgrounds and light distances; and he was disagreeably
affected, to the degree of horror, by pictures consisting of light
spots on a black background.[1] He detested and was horrified
by Rembrandt's spotlight and candlelight convention. Though
he recognised Rembrandt's greatness and his power as a tech-
nician,[2] he shrank from his 'abysses of obscurity' illumined
only by 'guttering, sputtering' spots of 'rushlight material and
spiritual'[3]; he was distressed and uneasy with 'Rembrandtesque
gradations of gloom', and 'glitterings of sword-hilt and arm-
our'[4]; and with the 'rather *alarming* than dignified *explosions*
round the stable lantern which sometimes take place in a Rembrandt Nativity'.[5] And by a transposition of his own uneasiness he ascribed Rembrandt's fondness for these effects to a
fear of light.[6] Thus it came that he placed Rembrandt's etching, *The Angel appearing to the Shepherds* (with its cascade of
Cupids in a light rent against a black sky) in his Educational
Series of Examples in Oxford as an example of 'every kind of
badness', and of 'an ignoble attempt to get a candlelight effect',
and that he described it elsewhere as an 'unsightly *firework*',
adding that 'the less we walk . . . by such *fatuous fire* . . . such
phosphoric glow . . . the better it may be for us'.[7]

It was with the same kind of fascinated horror that he regarded fireflies and fireworks. The last words of his last book
are as follows:

'We . . . walked together . . . on the hills. . . where the fireflies among the scented thickets shone fitfully in the still un-
darkened air. *How* they shone! moving like fine-broken star-
light through the purple leaves. How they shone! through the
sunset that faded into thunderous night as I entered Siena . . .

[1] *Modern Painters*, II, Part III, Sec. I, Chap. V, para. 6.
[2] *The Cestus of Aglaia*, V, para. 62 (June, 1865).
[3] *The Cestus of Aglaia*, V, paras. 60 and 61.
[4] *Mornings in Florence*, III, para. 52 (1875).
[5] *Præterita*, II, Part IX, para. 171 (1886). (Italics are mine.)
[6] *The Cestus of Aglaia*, V, para, 63.
[7] *Notes on the Educational Series*, No. 236 (1872), and *The Cestus of
Aglaia*, V, paras. 61 and 63. The etching is No. 120 in A. M. Hind's
catalogue. The italics in the quotations are mine.

fireflies everywhere in sky and cloud rising and falling, mixed with the lightning, and more intense than the stars.'[1]

My notes give his earliest published reference to fireflies as occurring in a letter to his mother written in 1845:

'I have just come in from an evening walk among the stars and fireflies. One hardly knows where one has got to between them, for the flies flash . . . like stars on the sea, . . . and the impression to the eye is as if one was walking on water . . . They dazzled me like fireworks, and it was very heavenly to see them floating . . .'[2]

The same impression comes two years later:

'At evening . . . fireflies glance . . . silent and intermittent, like stars upon the rippling of mute soft sea.'[3]

Then comes a passage in a letter to the Press on the Italian War of 1859 when he drags in a reference to 'fireflies by the Mincio'.[3]

The note of fear is sounded in the book recording the unstable days with the schoolgirls at Winnington:

Lecturer: 'The fireflies fly round the edge of the forests all night long; you wade in fireflies, they make the fields look like a lake trembling with reflections of stars; but you must take care not to touch them, for they are not like Italian fireflies, but burn like real sparks . . . You ought to be little fireflies yourselves and find your way in twilight by your own wits . . .'

Isabel: 'But you said they burned, you know?'

Lecturer: 'Yes: and you may be fireflies that way too, some of you before long, though I did not mean that . . . I meant them for the light, unpursued vanities which yet blind us confused among the stars.'[4]

In 1870 he writes of the fireflies in Siena (to which he was to refer again in *Præterita*):

[1] Concluding passage of *Præterita* written in 1889. The italics are Ruskin's.
[2] Letter to his mother from Pistoja, May 28, 1845.
[3] Review of Lord Lindsay's *History of Christian Art* in the *Quarterly Review*, 1847.
[3] *The Italian Question*, in the *Scotsman*, July 20, 1859.
[4] *Ethics of the Dust*, I, para. 6, written 1865, and Note VI added in 1877.

'The stars burning like torches all over the sky, the fireflies flying all about, literally brighter than the stars. One came into the railroad carriage and shone clear in full lamplight, settling above my head . . .'[1]

'The fireflies are almost awful in the twilight in and out of the dark cypresses.'[2]

'A climate like the loveliest and purest English summer, with only the somewhat, to me, awful addition of fireflies innumerable which . . . light up the dark ilex groves with flitting torches, or at least, lights as large as candles, and in the sky larger than the stars . . . We got to Siena in a heavy thunderstorm . . . incessant flashes and showers of fireflies between made the whole scene look anything but *celestial*.'[3]

Then during the period of his spiritualistic experiments at Broadlands after Rose's death, when his mind was in a very bad state and Mrs. Cowper-Temple was throwing people into trances, and Frederic Myers was of the company, Ruskin notes in his diary:

'Heard the most extraordinary evidence of the other state of the world that has ever come to me; and am this morning like a flint stone suddenly changed into a firefly and ordered to flutter about in a bramble thicket.'[4]

The reader will observe in the quotations referring to Rembrandt's pictures the use of the words 'fireworks', 'fatuous fire', 'phosphoric glow'; and in the quotations referring to the fire-

[1] Letter to his mother from Siena, June 25, 1870.

[2] *Ibid.*, June 26, 1870.

[3] Letter to W. H. Harrison from Airola, July 8, 1870. Italics are Ruskin's.

[4] Diary, Dec. 14, 1875. It is noteworthy that when he was making this entry in his diary he was probably preparing the lecture for the London Institution (from which I quote above, p. 30), where he held in his hand a flint-stone which he had picked up in Hyde Park (*Deucalion*, I, Chap. VII, para. 4). There is also a reference to fireflies in *Mornings in Florence*, I, para. 16. The date may be anything from 1874 to 1882 (cf. above, p. 113).

These references to fireflies are, of course, only those which have caught my eye. There are doubtless many others in the published writings and letters, and probably still more in unpublished letters and diaries.

flies the use of the words 'fireworks', 'candles' and 'torches'. He will recall the use of the words 'phosphor light' in the early poem on Adèle;[1] the likening of the Winnington girls among the dark trees to 'will-o'-the-wisps'[2]; the description of Rosie walking like 'a little white statue through the twilight woods'[3]. He will also remember that when Ruskin was in a morbid condition he complained of 'floating sparks in his eyes' and said that the evening sky appeared 'covered with swimming strings and eels'.[4] We must now observe his habit of referring to the horror of instruments of destruction in modern war as 'fireworks':

'First you spend eighty millions of money in fireworks, doing no end of damage letting them off. Then you borrow money to pay the firework maker's bill from any gain-loving persons who have got it . . .'[5]

'Society discovering itself to derive satisfaction from pyrotechnics, turns its attention more and more to the manufacture of gunpowder . . . till at last the labourers . . . discover that no amount of currency will command anything Festive except Fire. The supply of rockets is unlimited, but that of food, limited . . .'[6]

'When the civilised mob wants to spend money for any profitless or mischievous purposes—fireworks, illuminations, battles . . . it sets its money-collecting machine to borrow the sum needful for these amusements from the civilised capitalist . . . the civilised mob spends the money forthwith in gunpowder, infernal machines, masquerade dresses . . .'[7]

The last quotation with its juxtapositions of the words 'fireworks', 'illuminations', 'battles', 'gunpowder', 'infernal machines' and 'masquerade dresses' was written just before his expedition to Venice when he closeted himself with the picture

[1] Cf. above, p. 46.
[2] Cf. above, p. 73.
[2] Cf. above p. 81.
[4] Cf. above p. 52.
[5] *Fors Clavigera*, Letter 8, August, 1871.
[6] *Munera Pulveris*, II, paras. 47 and 48, written 1862–1863; revised, 1872.
[7] *Fors Clavigera*, Letter 67, July, 1876.

of St. Ursula; it was written about eighteen months before the collapse into admitted madness; and, less than a year after it was written Ruskin went to the Grosvenor Gallery and saw Whistler's picture called *Nocturne in Black and Gold: The Falling Rocket*—which represented fireworks watched by 'masqueraders' in Cremorne Gardens; and he experienced, I submit, a rush of subconscious panic anger as he looked at this cascade of glittering light spots surrounded with the black gloom of the night sky.

I offer no explanation of the source of Ruskin's fear of light spots surrounded with darkness. He records that as a child he was frightened by the smooth blackness of the dark pools of Tay, and by tombstones seen at night (*Præterita*, I, Chap. III, paras. 74 and 75)—which may or may not have been abnormal. He may, of course, have been frightened in very early life by fireworks. It is also possible that the fear was really connected with his early fear of being attracted by Roman Catholic ritual associated with images of grouped candles flickering in dark cathedral chapels.[2] But clinical experience may provide some different answer altogether.

Ruskin was moved to 'height of black anger' by Whistler's picture as he had been moved thirty-five years earlier by the critic who said that Turner's pictures were painted as by a man who had thrown paint at the canvas, 'letting what would stick, stick'[3]; and unconsciously transposing the recollection he sat down and wrote:

'I . . . never expected to hear a coxcomb ask two hundred guineas for flinging a pot of paint in the public's face.'[4]

And thus what Ruskin had called 'this sickly, muddy, half *eau sucrée* and half poisoned wine—which is my River of Life'[5] flowed on. To the casual observer the flow was still not conspicuously uneven. At the end of 1877 Ruskin must have been

---

[1] *Præterita*, I, Chap. III, paras. 74 and 75.
[2] Cf. below, p. 335.
[3] *Literary Gazette*, May 14, 1842.
[4] *Fors Clavigera*, Letter 79, July, 1877 (cf. below, p. 198).
[5] Letter to C. E. Norton, Sept. 24, 1871.

envied by many men. He was 'The Professor' widely talked about as a result of the Hincksey road-making and his popularity with the ladies of Oxford. He was a celebrated political pamphleteer and journalist, the Editor of *Fors Clavigera*. He was a notorious apostle of social reform about to convert St. George's Company into a legally constituted St. George's Guild with himself legally appointed as 'The Master'. He was the author of books which were now being read by a really wide public. He had just collaborated with a Venetian nobleman, a Morosini, in what was destined to be a successful campaign to stop the destruction of the West Front of St. Mark's on the plea that it needed restoration—pointing out incidentally that there was real danger that the Campanile might collapse.[1] And he was expected to give a good account of himself when the action which Whistler had just started should come up for hearing.[2]

On New Year's Day, 1878, he was staying at Windsor Castle with his Oxford pupil, Prince Leopold (afterwards the Duke of Albany). On January 15 he was at Hawarden with Gladstone. Next month dreaming comes upon him. 'I *must* get to work or I shall get utterly into dream-land.'[3] He was writing at the time a catalogue of his own collection of Turner's work which evoked many old episodes and which, he tells us later, greatly excited him.[4] The jostling of flying thoughts within his brain, which had begun as early as 1855, now becomes overwhelming. Despairs and the old obsessional images and new panic fears crowd upon him. He is defenceless against the Devilish Storm Cloud and Plague Wind, and the Devilish fireworks of Whist-

[1] *Open Letter to Count Zorǳi* (1877), published as a foreword to the Count's pamphlet on the Restorations. See also Ruskin's private letters to Count Zorzi of the same year. The Campanile collapsed, it will be remembered, two years after Ruskin's death.

[2] The celebrated libel was in *Fors Clavigera*, July, 1877. Whistler started proceedings in November. Ruskin was looking forward to the fun. 'It's mere nuts and nectar to me . . . the whole thing will enable me to assert some principles of art economy which I've never got into the public's head.' (Letter to Burne-Jones, autumn, 1877.)

[3] Diary, Feb. 15.

[4] *Fors Clavigera*, Letter 88 (1880).

ler; he has been robbed of father, mother, nurse and Rose: Rose who had been a Wild Rose on earth, and was Dante's Eternal White Rose in Heaven, and who now sends him spirit messages through St. Ursula.[1] He is 'down in dreamy scatterment and bewilderment' and 'shame of my own selfishness and faithlessness'.[2] He dreams that the police are pursuing him, and that he is 'left by an express train without courage to get into the carriage—everyone going faster and faster past him'.[3] And at last action follows the wild racing thoughts. Naked in the middle of the night he fights the Devil in the shape of his black cat, which had sprung out from behind the mirror. . . .

The next morning he was found 'in a state of prostration and bereft of his senses'; and he remained completely mad in almost constant delirium for two and a half months.[4]

[1] Letter to Miss Anderson, Feb. 17, 1878.

[2] Diary, Feb. 12, 1878.

[3] Diary, Jan. 31, 1878. He always had a fear of speed and this was a cause contributing to his dislike of railways. But for the rest that dislike appears to me in no way abnormal—founded as it was (a) on the view that railways spoil the landscape (which is undeniable), and (b) on his own preference for travelling by road in a private carriage (a preference which in these days of motor cars we all share).

[4] Ruskin's own account of the onset and decline of this first attack was published after his death in the *British Medical Journal*, Jan. 27, 1900. He states that the voice of his fowls and his peacock's croaking at the approach of rain were terrible torments to him. He knew the sounds, but immediately, 'so quickly flew my thoughts', he imagined that he was in a farmyard and impelled by 'some tyrant Devil' to do some fearful wrong; that he passionately and vainly resisted and, every time he yielded 'the voice of the Demon'—that is, the peacock—gave forth a loud croak of triumph. He also states 'all ugly things assumed fearfully and horribly hideous forms and all beautiful objects appeared more lovely', and that his Turner drawings—appeared 'a thousand times more lovely, looking in their added brightness of colour more like pictures of Heaven than of earth'. This document is printed on pp. 172 and 173 in Volume XXXVIII (Bibliography) of the Library Edition.

His insistence here on the morbid intensity of his vision during his madness gives, it seems to me, pathological significance to his confessions of this type of experience in the criticism of Hunt's *The Awakening Conscience* in 1854 and elsewhere in 1857 (cf. pp. 188 and 251 *et seq.*).

I find no evidence of any peacock obsessions before or after this first illness. The only passage in my notes which suggests it is in a letter of

THE PLAY

But the play was not yet done. After three months he re-covered and resumed, from Brantwood, his actions as Master of St. George's Guild.

August, 1867: 'If an angel all over peacocks' feathers were to appear in the bit of blue sky now over Castle Crag, and to write on it in star letters, "God writes vulgar Greek," I should say, "*You* are the Devil, peacocks' feathers and all." '

Ruskin made many references to his attacks of madness, some of which I quote (cf. pp. 156 and 157, 163 and 164, 168). The following is in the first number of *Fors Clavigera*, when he restarted the magazine in 1880:

'For a physician's estimate of it, indeed, I can only refer them to my physicians. But there were some conditions of it which I knew better than they could: namely, first, the precise and sharp distinction between the state of morbid inflammation of brain which gave rise to false visions (whether in sleep, or trance, or waking, in broad daylight, with perfect knowledge of the real things in the room, while yet I saw others that were not there), and the not morbid, however dangerous, states of more or less excited temper, and too much quickened thought, which gradually led up to the illness, accelerating in action during the eight or ten days preceding the actual giving way of the brain (as may be enough seen in the fragmentary writing of the first edition of my notes on the Turner exhibition); and yet, up to the transitional moment of first hallucination, entirely healthy, and in the full sense of the word "sane"; just as the natural inflammation about a healing wound in flesh is sane, up to the transitional edge where it may pass at a crisis into morbific, or even mortified, substance. And this more or less inflamed, yet still perfectly healthy, condition of mental power, may be traced by any watchful reader, in *Fors*, nearly from its beginning—that manner of mental ignition or irritation being for the time a great additional force, enabling me to discern more clearly, and say more vividly, what for long years it had been in my heart to say' (cf. below, p. 366).

Ruskin's attack on the cat at the beginning of this first madness is thus described in the article in the *British Medical Journal* referred to above: 'As I put forth my hand towards the window a large black cat sprang forth from behind the mirror. Persuaded that the foul fiend was here at last in his own person . . . I darted at it . . . and grappled with it with both my hands and, gathering all the strength that was in me, I flung it with all my might and main against the floor . . .'

At the end of 1877 he seems to have begun to think of himself as a man with 'cattish' characteristics (Letter to Susan Beever, Dec. 27, 1877); in 1878 he writes to Susan Beever that her five cats were all at the door when he called 'and I should have made six, but they ran away'. In June, 1879, he signs himself 'Cat' in a letter to Susan Beever. Five or six weeks before his fifth attack of madness in 1886 he writes to Susan Beever, 'Isn't that a nice amusing categorical, catalogueical, catechismic, catcataceous plan'

His lawyers—who had been trying for some time past to get legal status for the unusual association—received, at the end of 1878, a licence to hold lands granted by 'The Lords of the Committee of Privy Council appointed for the consideration of matters relating to Trade and Foreign Plantations', in accordance with the 23rd section of the Companies Act of 1867; and the Guild was thus legally constituted.

For this purpose Ruskin had written an *Abstract of the Objects and Constitution* at the end of 1877, and the Civil Servants who filed the document must have been astonished at the first sentence:

'The St. George's Guild consists of a body of persons who think, primarily, that it is time for honest persons to separate themselves intelligibly from knaves, announcing their purpose, if God help them, to live in godliness and honour, not in atheism and rascality . . .'

At the end of 1878 he resigned the Oxford Professorship. In 1879 he remained at Brantwood and Herne Hill; and he was well enough in October to show Prince Leopold over St. George's Museum.

In order to conform to the requirements of the Guild's legal constitution he wrote and issued in this year a *Master's Report*, where we read that the radical cause of the 'general resistance to St. George's effort is the doctrine . . . that you serve your neighbour best by letting him alone, except in the one particular of endeavouring to cheat him of his money'; that St. George's Guild aims at securing 'excellent quality not merely in goods to be delivered, but in the persons by whom they are enjoyed; which the modern British public is indeed satisfied may be presently effected by the instruction of its operatives in atheism and molecular development and by its own industrious novel-reading, but which the British public will assuredly find to its

(Letter of May 31, 1886). He always had not only a favourite dog, but also a favourite cat at Brantwood. One cat has been thus described by a lady who visited Brantwood as a child in August, 1880: 'In the wood at dusk . . . suddenly his big cat—a fierce animal that I was always afraid of—sprang from a dark bush . . . and alighted upon his arm, where she stayed, during the remainder of the walk' (*A Sketch of John Ruskin* by Peggy Webling; privately printed). Cf. below, p. 172.

cost and sorrow can only be effected . . . by training their children in the way they should go, and being sure, primarily, that they are not out of that way themselves'. Other reports and statements of accounts followed from 1881 to 1886.

Ruskin's expenditure of the Guild's funds in these years is only explicable by the condition of his mind; and in relation to that I must examine his proceedings in some detail.

The Guild it will be remembered was a scheme of agricultural settlements for working men. At the end of 1880 the 'Companions' numbered about sixty. Its resources consisted of the small landed properties mentioned above, and the Sheffield Museum at Walkley[1]; of the interest on about £5,000 in Consols, and of subscriptions. The year 1881 started with a cash balance of £970. Between 1881 and 1886 Ruskin spent large sums of the Guild's money in the most singular purchases for the Sheffield Museum. For a year or two, between 1881 and 1886, he charged the Guild with £120 a year for water-colours done on his instructions in Abbeville, Amiens, and elsewhere by one of his artist protégés and assistants named W. Hackstoun, and with £160 a year for others made for him by another named Frank Randal in Amiens, Auxerre, Avallon, Bourges, Senlis, Verona, etc. In 1883–1884 he charged the Guild with £190 for water-colours made for him in France, Italy, and High Savoy by another named T. M. Rooke; with £105 for similar work in Rome, Pisa, Venice, Verona, etc., by Angelo Alessandri, and with £187 for 'mixed drawings'. Others to whom he gave commissions at the Guild's expense for drawings, photographs, and casts made in his old haunts and for copies of his favourite pictures included C. Fairfax Murray, Arthur Burgess, J. W. Bunney, and H. N. Newman. In this period he also charged the Guild with £550 for a twelfth-century Lectionarium of the monastery of Ottobeuren; with £500 for a Queen of Scots Missal, and with £600 for an illustrated book and manuscript called *Roadside Songs of Tuscany*, by a lady called Miss Francesca Alexander.[2] In 1884 he further charged the Guild with £340 for specimens of minerals and

[1] Cf. above, pp. 109 and 119.
[2] Cf. below, p. 174.

with £25 for specimens of shells. And we must remember that all these sums must be multiplied by two and a half or three to get modern equivalents.[1]

As his Sheffield Museum was already full, he had to store these purchases here and there, keeping some at Brantwood, and depositing others as permanent or temporary loans from the Guild at a girls' school in Chelsea (Whitelands), at Somerville College, at a training school for governesses (Felstead House), at his Drawing School in Oxford and elsewhere.

To understand this performance we must realise that these purchases were not, of course, really in the nature of building up the contents of a museum, as he persuaded himself, and hoped to persuade other people. They were the continuation of his personal habits, as it were by proxy, through the person of the Guild. He sent his assistants to sketch bits of architecture and so forth, and to copy bits of pictures in his favourite haunts in France and Italy, and thus continued his old occupations by proxy through them. In the *Master's Report* for 1885 (dated January, 1886) he stated that 'upwards of two thousand pounds' worth of drawings executed for the Guild' were avail-

---

[1] Thus in 1883 he spent the equivalent of £1,200 of the Guild's money on the water-colours by his protégés; he spent the equivalent of £4,000 on the mediæval manuscripts and Francesca Alexander's book; and the equivalent of £1,455 in one year on the purchases of minerals, shown in the *Master's Report*, 1884, as follows:

	£	s.	d.
Jan. 9. Wright, Topazes and Russian Emerald ..	158	0	0
Mar. 6. Wright, Emerald, Santate	50	0	0
July 31. Damon, Emeralds and Chalcedones ..	14	7	0
June 21–Dec. 19. Butler, Mixed Silicas	43	17	0
Nov. 28. Wright, Finest Australian Opal	46	0	0
	£312	4	0

Additional items were:			
Shells	25	0	0
Purple velvet to display Silicas	5	0	0
	£342	4	0

Wright, Damon and Butler were dealers.

able for the Museum.[1] But these drawings, made in fulfilment of precise instructions from himself, were not really executed 'for the Guild' or 'for the Museum'. When he wrote his protégés precise instructions as to where they were to go and what they were to do and how they were to do it, and read their letters in reply, and saw their drawings, he perseverated in the satisfaction formerly experienced when he had himself pottered in these same places and made sketches and copies in the same places. He had given two hundred of his own drawings to his Oxford Drawing School; but he still had over a thousand more and hundreds of photographs which would have served the nominal purpose of the Guild expenditure in the 'eighties equally well or better.[2]

He might also have earmarked for the Guild other things from his own accumulation of works of art, minerals, and miscellaneous objects at Brantwood. He had always been both a collector and a 'picker up'. The contents of his rooms at Corpus Christi, Oxford, had been insured for the equivalent of £90,000.[3] In the 'sixties he gave twenty-five Turner drawings to Cambridge and about as many to Oxford, and he gave a collection of minerals to Winnington and Harrow Schools. At the end of the 'seventies he had given some minerals to Sheffield. But at the beginning of the period, which

[1] For Ruskin's claim to the powers of assessing the money value (exchange value) of works of art cf. below, p. 241. For £2,000, say £4,500 in present values.

[2] Over two thousand drawings by Ruskin are recorded. At the last Brantwood sale many cases full of Daguerreotypes and photographs of French and Italian buildings were sold.

In *Mornings in Florence*, V, para. 89 (1874–1877) we read: 'The small detached line of tombs on the left I would fain have painted, stone by stone: but one can never draw in front of a church in these republican days: for all the blackguard children of the neighbourhood come to howl, and throw stones on the steps, and the ball or stone play against these sculptured tombs is incessant . . . ' To this he added as a note in 1882: 'I have since bought for St. George's Museum a drawing of these three arches, carried out with more patience than I possessed, by Mr. Henry R. Newman.'

[3] £30,000. Cf. above, p. 114.

we are now considering, he still had more than eighty Turners,[1] more than twenty mediæval manuscripts, (including the St. Louis Psalter),[2] some Scott manuscripts, pictures which he ascribed to Titian and Tintoretto, Gainsborough and Reynolds, drawings by Prout, Rossetti, Burne-Jones and other living artists, numerous engravings, fragments of sculpture, and a picture by Meissonier for which he paid £1,000, in 1869 or 1870.[3] He still had also three thousand specimens of minerals —for which he had paid thousands of pounds (one group alone having cost him the equivalent of £9,000)[4]—and quantities of shells and miscellaneous geological and botanical fragments, which he had picked up or chipped off and pocketed at various times.[5] He added to these miscellaneous collections all the time. In August, 1877, he had written in *Fors Clavigera* that he would buy no more Turners[6]; but by June of the same year he 'felt it his duty for various reasons', to buy three expensive Turner drawings at the sale of Munro of Novar.[7] In 1880 he bought a Della Robbia, *Madonna and Child*, which all visitors to Brantwood in the later years recall. In 1884 he bought a diamond for which he paid £1,000 (say £2,500) and a ruby for which he paid £100 (say £250).[8]

[1] *Fors Clavigera*, Letter 76.
[2] *Ibid.*, Cf. above, p. 59.
[3] *Fors Clavigera*, Letter 1. All these works are mentioned in accounts of Brantwood at this time by W. G. Collingwood and M. H. Spielmann. (For Ruskin's subsequent sale of the Meissonier cf. below, p. 383.)
[4] *Fors Clavigera*, Letter 76.
[5] In 1876 he lectured on a blunt pebble picked up and pocketed in Hyde Park (cf. p. 141). In the last sale at Brantwood boxes of common shells and pebbles were among the 'lots'.
[6] *Fors Clavigera*, Letter 76.
[7] *Fors Clavigera*, Letter 85.
[8] By 1879 he had such an accumulation of minerals, shells, and so forth, at Brantwood, that he did not know what to do with them, especially after he moved those which were in his Oxford rooms to Brantwood. He gave a number to Susan Beever (Letter to Susan Beever, February, 1879). He lent both the diamond and the ruby bought in 1884 to the British Museum and gave them to the Museum in 1887. The diamond is known as the *Colenso Diamond* and the ruby known as the *Edwardes Ruby*, in memory of his friends, Bishop Colenso and Sir Herbert Edwardes. (Cf. pp. 68, 71 and 303). The inscriptions on the jewels read:

He could obviously have allocated some of these things for the eventual benefit of St. George's Guild, had it really been St. George's Guild that he was thinking of when he spent these hundreds of pounds on sketches of his old haunts, and on Russian and South American emeralds and opals and shells for the Sheffield Museum which he had planned as a collection to illustrate iron work, the natural history round Sheffield and 'more especially the geology and flora of Derbyshire'.[1] He did not do so because the collecting activity which he persuaded himself was 'for Sheffield' was really but an excuse for and rationalisation of the continuation of his own collecting. Just as he was now sketching in Abbeville, Amiens, and Verona, and copying Carpaccio and so on by proxy through the troop of Guild draughtsmen whose labours he directed, so also when he was spending the Guild's money on more minerals and shells, of the kinds which he had always collected, he was really buying by proxy for himself.

Even before the specially absurd purchases of 1883—1884 there was already so great an accumulation of things 'for Sheffield' that he began to plan extensions of the building, with a cloistered hostelry for the students. Then he let his mind fly to the project of a new building at Bewdley, and had plans drawn and met the architect of the London School Board in Italy, where he selected marbles for the exterior.[2] At the same time he projected further schemes for writing and editing a library of general knowledge and universal history for St. George's Schools.

He had started this in 1876 and 1877 with the publication of Xenophon's *Economist* and *Rock Honeycomb* ('Broken pieces of Sir Philip Sidney's Psalter') which he called the first two

'The Colenso Diamond presented in 1887 by John Ruskin in Honour of his Friend, the loyal and patiently adamantine First Bishop of Natal.'
'The Edwardes Ruby, presented in 1887 by John Ruskin, in Honour of the Invincible Soldiership and Loving Equity of Sir Herbert Edwardes' Rule by the Shores of Indus.'
[1] *Fors Clavigera*, Letters 56 and 59.
[2] At Lucca in 1882 (cf. below, p. 168).

THE PLAY

volumes of a *Bibliotheca Pastorum*, as already noted. He now embarked on a series of works called *Our Fathers have told us: Sketches of the History of Christendom for Boys and Girls*. The scheme was nothing less than a vast history of mediæval Christianity and mediæval architecture with sections devoted to Amiens, to Rouen, and to Chartres, to the Foundations of the Papal power, to the monastic architecture of England and Wales, to the pastoral forms of Catholicism from early times to the present day, the pastoral Protestantism of Savoy, Geneva, and the Scottish border, and so forth. But *The Bible of Amiens* (1880) was almost the only part produced.[1]

Nor was it only as the Master of St. George's Guild that Ruskin continued to perform. In the summer of 1880 he seemed to be so much better that he went to Northern France. It was on his return that he wrote the lecture on *Cistercian Architecture* (*Mending the Sieve*) and the first chapter of *The Bible of Amiens*—a good deal helped, I suspect, as in all work after 1878, by his secretaries, Lawrence Hilliard and Collingwood, who were now attached to him.[2] In February and March 1881, he had a second attack of acute madness; and he had a third attack in March, 1882. By August, 1882, he was considered well enough to go with Collingwood for a six months' Continental tour over his favourite ground in France, Italy, and High Savoy. During this tour he so far recovered that he intimated his desire to resume his Professorship in Oxford, and Acland and his other friends were foolish enough to bring about his re-election.[3]

On March 9, 1883, he reappeared as Slade Professor in Oxford and gave a lecture on Rossetti and Holman Hunt, the first of the series afterwards published as *The Art of England*.[4] He

[1] The student will find the whole scheme in an 'Advice' appended to *The Bible of Amiens*, 1880. The lecture on Cistercian Architecture (*Mending the Sieve*) and the papers collected in the Library Edition under the titles *Ara Cœli* and *Valle Crucis* were also fragments in execution of this scheme.
[2] Cf. below, pp. 165 and 166.
[3] His place had been taken by W. B. Richmond who now resigned that he might be re-elected (cf. below, p. 158).
[4] Cf. below, p. 254-5.

153

THE PLAY

was now sixty-four and much aged as the result of three attacks
of madness. He had grown a beard during the first attack, and
it was a bent and grey-bearded figure that replaced the blue-
stocked Professor of former days.[1]

He had written out the text of his first lecture, which is poor
in quality, and he refrained from impromptu digressions in the
delivery. The audience was the same as for the more successful
lectures in the old days. There were a certain number of undergraduates who came out of curiosity hoping for a 'show', and
many young and old women from North Oxford. But heads
of houses, fellows, and tutors were 'chiefly conspicuous by
their absence'.[2] On this occasion, however, the Vice-Chancellor attended with the proctors, and spoke some words of
welcome.

Meanwhile in the five years that had passed since the last
Oxford lectures the Ruskin Legend had been set on foot. The
sale of his books, old and new, which had increased all through
the 'seventies, had increased still more rapidly since the 1878
breakdown had led the public to assume that his writing days
were done. Ruskin Societies for the study of his works began
to be formed from 1879 onwards. And the new generation of
young women who attended this second series of lectures had
been taught to think of the figure before them as a haloed prophet with a vague divine message to the world. Here is an
account written by one of the audience at this course:

'Youth and maiden, matron and scholar, artist and scientist,
all pressed shoulder to shoulder, listening with hushed intensity almost trance-like,—their common gaze focussed upon
the gracious stooping figure of the lecturer—who, golden-
voiced, with flowing gown flung back from eager, nervous
hands—hands ever moving in suppressed gesticulation, stood

[1] He dressed with rather baroque elegance till he was fifty. As 'the
Professor' in Oxford he had affected old-fashioned elegance and old
clothes, and indulged in eccentricities of manipulation of his cap and
gown, especially as he approached his first breakdown. In the last period
he clung to the old-fashioned styles, and in the end he let his beard grow
to abnormal length. In company he seems never to have neglected his
appearance.
[2] Collingwood, *Life of Ruskin*.

in the warming sunshine of that wintry afternoon, telling us brave things of art in this our England . . . The grave benedictory voice died away into an unbroken silence. Then a girl, sitting hand in hand with her lover, gave a little sob, and the great audience loosed its pent-up enthusiasm.'[1]

This course of lectures was spread over the three terms of 1883. He did not lecture again in Oxford till the autumn of 1884 when he announced a grandiose programme called the *Pleasures of England*, which was to describe the history of Christian England from the earliest times to the evil atheism and mechanism of the nineteenth century. In this course, which is within the memory of living men, he indulged in many extravagant extemporisations and digressions and attacks, and excitement appeared in the delivery. He held his audience by his dithyrambic eloquence, but it was hard if not impossible to find the main argument, and the more sensitive listeners were uneasy and distressed. His friends persuaded him to substitute readings from his earlier works for the last three lectures on the programme and, as Collingwood says, 'they breathed more freely when he left Oxford without another serious attack.'[2]

Three months later, March, 1885, he resigned his Professorship, giving as his reason the University vote endowing vivisection, of which as a lifelong lover of animals he passionately disapproved.

In this second period in Oxford he continued to add to the collections of Examples in this Drawing School—apart from the Guild purchases which were deposited there—and shortly before resigning he had applied for a grant for larger premises and for the purchase of two drawings by Turner. Later he removed from Oxford a number of his loans; but at the end the Drawing School had nevertheless a collection amounting to two thousand miscellaneous drawings, engravings, photographs, and so forth, some of interest and value, which can be seen there to-day.[3]

[1] 'Happy Memories of John Ruskin', by Mrs. Allen Harker, in *The Puritan*, May, 1900.
[2] For Ruskin's own account of this cf. below, p. 167.
[3] The Library Edition contains a catalogue of this collection. Some

THE PLAY

After the break with Oxford, Ruskin spent most of his time at Brantwood and Herne Hill. A fourth attack of madness came on him in July, 1885, a fifth in the same month in 1886. He suffered from hostile depression in 1887, alternating euphoria and despondency in 1888, and he had a sixth attack of madness in 1889.

Of his mental processes from the 1878 attack to the end of his working days there is considerable evidence—apart from his actions—in his letters and writings, and in contemporary accounts. I find still more marked mobility of interest and chronic inability to work continuously at any one thing—'a stitch here and a patch there'[1]—being the habitual procedure; and more and more reliance on help from his secretaries and assistants. Manic confidence and planning of large schemes alternates with depression, inertia and sense of guilt. There are also flashes of hostility to the world at large, and persecution delusions which in these later years become definitely more frequent. There is a continuance of obsessions—notably the Storm-Cloud delusion and the Rose obsession—with a new delusion that the *scientists* are in league against him.

Immediately after the recovery from the 1878 attack he describes it as 'one continued vision to me of my selfishnesses, prides, insolences, failures, written down day by day, it seemed to me, with reversed interpretation of all I had fondly thought done for others, as the mere foaming out of my own vanity'.[2] A few months later he writes:

"I am, as far as I can make out, quite myself again, and for the present *one* self only, and not one—beside myself. I never understood the meaning of that phrase before, but indeed I was a double, or even treble, creature through a great part of that dream.'[3]

illustrated notes upon it by Mr. Albert Rutherston, the present Master of the Ruskin Drawing School, appeared in *Art Work*, Spring Number, 1931.

[1] Diary, Dec. 18, 1881.

[2] Letter to the Rev. J. P. Faunthorpe, April 17, 1878. For his own full account of his illness cf. above, pp. 145 and 146.

[3] Letter to Mrs. John Simon, May 15, 1878.

A month later:

'It was more wonderful yet to find the madness made up into things so dreadful, out of things so trivial. One of the most provoking and disagreeable of the spectres was developed out of the firelight on my mahogany bed-post . . . But the sorrow-fullest part of the matter was, and is, that while my illness at Matlock encouraged me by all its dreams in after work, this one has done nothing but humiliate and terrify me . . . and leaves me nearly unable to speak any more except of the nature of stones and flowers . . . Nevertheless I am working out some points in the history and geography of Arabia.'[1]

In July he writes to Norton:

'The Doctors say it was overwork and worry, which is partly true and partly not. *Mere* overwork or worry might have soon ended me, but it would not have driven me crazy. I went crazy about St. Ursula and the other saints—chiefly young-lady saints . . . But the Doctors know nothing either of St. Ursula or St. Kate or St. Lachesis—and not much else of anything worth knowing . . . The chief real danger . . . was . . . during the first stages of recovery . . . The (quite usual, I believe, in such cases) refusal to eat anything; not that I didn't want to, but I wouldn't take it out of a cup with a rose on it, or the like . . .'[2]

In September there is an agitated letter with 'the excitement of conversation breaks me or bends me, banefully always.'[3] In October he writes: 'I was at Hawarden last week . . . but I *cannot* now go into society. People are continually trying to dis-

[1] Letter to Thomas Carlyle, June 23, 1878. For the disturbance caused by the flickering firelight, cf. my notes on Ruskin's Firefly-Firework obsession above, pp. 138 *et seq.* For his illness at Matlock in 1871, cf. above, p. 115. He describes three of his dreams there in the published version of his Oxford lecture (1872) on Florentine Engraving (*Ariadne Florentina,* VI), which he revised at Assisi in 1874, and states there also that they had helpful significance to him and led him to repeat to himself '*Tu ne cede malis, sed contra fortior ito,*' cf. below, p. 352.

[2] Letter to C. E. Norton, July 23, 1878. For the admission that over-work was not the cause of the breakdown, cf. above, p. 117. The reference to the rose on the teacup is of course significant.

[3] Letter to Miss Mary Gladstone, Sept. 30, 1878.

cuss things with me of which I know the bottom and all round, and have *told* them the bottom and all round twenty years ago; and the deadly feeling of the resilience and immortality of the undintable caoutchouoc of which most people's heads are made is too much for me.'[1] In November: 'I am entirely hopeless of any good whatever against these devilish modern powers and passions; my words choke me if I try to speak.'[2] Later in November there are letters about his botanical studies where he is planning names and classifications of his own invention ('All my pretty flowers have names of girls'), and playing with word-jingling as follows:

'The representative type (now *Sagina procumbens*) is to be in—

> *Latin:* Mica amica.
> *French:* Miette l'amie.
> *English:* Pet pearl wort.'[3]

The Whistler trial took place in this month and he speaks of it at first as 'comic'.[4] But he was very angry that the judgement went against him: 'I'll make them remember it or my name's not mine';[5] and he gave the result as his official reason for his first resignation from Oxford.[6]

In January, 1879, he is 'curiously oppressed by many things',[7] but his spirits revive when the danger months of February and March are passed. At Easter he is out on Coniston Lake in a new boat specially built for him, and by May he is in confident mood:

'It is a hard trial for a man to be forced to think himself wise in his generation above others, but God knows I don't want to be so, and would make every soul on earth wiser than I if I

[1] Letter to Dr. John Brown, Oct. 22, 1878.
[2] Letter to Hall Caine, Nov. 8, 1878.
[3] Letters to Susan Beever, Nov. 19 and 26, 1878. For similar word-jingling, cf. above, pp. 85 and 146.
[4] Letter to C. E. Norton, Nov. 26, 1878.
[5] Letter to George Allen, Nov. 28, 1878.
[6] Cf. below, p. 254. He recommended Herkomer as 'a gentleman . . . of supreme innocence, honour and healthy genius' to succeed him (Letter to Liddell, Jan. 4, 1879). But Richmond was elected (cf. above. p. 153).
[7] Letter to Miss Mary Gladstone, Jan., 1879.

could—but so it is, that in matters of *abstract* principle (I don't mean unpractical! but as distinct from the subjects of debate in one's own conduct) I know that I am at one with the wisest men of all ages, and that the other thinkers of the day are fearfully divided from them, and I know that it will be well for those who listen to me, in the degree they obey.'[1]

On June 8 he writes to Norton:

'It is only in utter shame and self-reproach that I ever allow myself (or cannot help myself) in despondency; and the very wildness of howling devilry and idiocy in the English mob around me strengthens me more than it disgusts—in the definiteness of its demoniac character.'[2]

A few days later:

'With the persons whom I most loved, joy in the *beauty* of nature is virtually dead in me, but I can still interest myself in her doings.'[3]

A week after that:

'I wrote in my diary this morning that really I never felt better in my life. Mouth, eyes, head, feet, and fingers all fairly in trim.'[4]

Then comes confidence and plans for more work: translations of all the Odes of Horace and Plato's Laws:

'I'm doing the *Laws* of Plato thoroughly. Jowett's translation is a disgrace to Oxford and how much to Plato . . . cannot be said, and I must get mine done all the more.'[5]

And then irritability:

'In my present state of illness, nearly every word everybody says, if I care for them, either grieves or astonishes me to a degree which puts me off my sleep, and off my work, and off my meat. I am obliged to work at botany and mineralogy and put cotton in my ears.'[6]

[1] Letter to F. W. Pullen, May 22, 1879. This strikes the same note as the passage in *Fors Clavigera*, Letter 58 (October, 1875), quoted above (p. 27).

[2] Letter to C. E. Norton, June 4, 1879.

[3] Letter to Dr. John Brown, June 22, 1879.

[4] Letter to Susan Beever, June 27, 1879.

[5] Letter to C. E. Norton, July 9, 1879.

[6] Letter to Miss Mary Gladstone, July 28, 1879.

His doctors forbade him all exciting work and he tried to limit himself to botanical and geological pottering for *Proserpina* and *Deucalion*, which, as noted, he had begun to issue in parts in the 'seventies, and which he was now continuing when the spirit moved him and with help from his secretaries and assistants. But he could not restrain himself or suffer himself to be restrained. In 1879 he had already started a series of *Letters to the Clergy on the Lord's Prayer and the Church*. The next year, 1880, opens with a Diary entry: 'Utterly jaded and feverish with nearly sleepless night and crowding thoughts—wonderful in sudden call upon me for action, and I so feeble but must answer a little.'[1] And he answered the call by entering into controversy with the Bishop of Manchester on Interest and Usury,[2] and by resuming *Fors Clavigera*.[3]

Nor was this all. In March, 1880, he gave a lecture at the London Institution on Serpents (*A Caution to Snakes*)—a most lively, interesting and entertaining paper.[4] In May he began a series of essays on Scott, Byron and Wordsworth, called *Fiction, Fair and Foul*, which he published in the *Nineteenth Century*.[5] In the same year he wrote an essay called *The Elements of English Prosody*, which Tennyson and Patmore found interest-

[1] Diary, Jan. 2, 1880.

[2] *Usury. A Reply and a Rejoinder* in *Contemporary Review*, February, 1880. The controversy had been started by Ruskin in *Fors Clavigera* before it was suspended. Ruskin returned to the attack in his *Letters to the Clergy on the Lord's Prayer and the Church* in 1879. The Bishop then replied and Ruskin wrote this article.

[3] Not however as a monthly magazine, but as a pamphlet to appear as and when he might be disposed to write one. The first number of the new series appeared in March, 1880, the second in September (after which none appeared till May, 1883). The first 1880 number contains some very interesting comments on the causes and premonitory symptoms of his 1878 breakdown from which I have already quoted (cf. p. 146). The second is addressed to the Trade Unions and urges them to call themselves Labour Unions because men 'don't and can't live by exchanging articles, but by producing them' (cf. below, p. 299).

[4] The lecture was delivered from notes; but he afterwards produced a text which he entitled *Living Waves*. This can be read in *Deucalion*, II (1883). I refer again to the substance and form of this piece (cf. below, pp. 188 and 363).

[5] Republished in *On the Old Road*.

ing; and he composed some music including a setting to Herrick's *Comfort to a Youth that had lost his Love*—a significant selection of poem, as the Rose obsession was all the time with him, as we shall see.[1]

This activity in 1880 was accompanied by irritability. To the Rev. F. A. Malleson, to whom the *Letters on the Lord's Prayer* were addressed, he writes: 'I've told you now twenty times, if once, that I *won't talk*. I see people whom I can teach, or who can teach me—you can be neither pupil nor master. You come simply to amuse *yourself*.'[2] Then he writes to William Morris: 'Please recollect—and hereafter know—by these presents—that I am old, ill, and liable any day to be struck crazy if I get into a passion. And therefore, while I can still lecture—if I choose—on rattlesnakes' tails, I can't on anything I care about.'[3] And the same tone appears in a letter to the *Oxford University Herald:*

[1] Cf. letter to Coventry Patmore, April 20, 1880, where he quotes the lines:

> 'In endless bliss
> She thinks not on
> What's said or done
> In earth.
> Nor doth she mind,
> Or think on't now
> That ever thou
> Wast kind.'

And he fears 'it is too true'.

The curious will find examples of Ruskin's musical compositions in Vol. XXXI of the Library Edition. His taste in music was personal. He was brought up on Italian opera and always liked it. He disliked Mendelssohn and thought that Beethoven sounded 'like the upsetting of bags of nails with here and there a dropped hammer' (Letter to Dr. John Brown, Feb. 6, 1881). At Winnington he enjoyed 'Home Sweet Home' played on the piano with variations by Hallé—'quite the most wonderful thing I have ever heard in music' (Letter to his mother, 1864). He disliked 'The Meistersingers' to which he was taken in 1882 and which he abused and called formless in a well-known letter to Georgiana Burne-Jones (June 30, 1882) in the cumulative word-piling style of his private correspondence in the later years. He was inclined to look on music as intensified speech.

[2] Letter to the Rev. F. A. Malleson, May, 1880.

[3] Letter to William Morris, May 27, 1880 .

'Had I announced myself as a discoverer or doctor of new things I should instantly have had a following, and been amicably received by my fellow-sectarians. It is precisely because I utter nothing of my own, and therefore virtually hint to them that they had better utter nothing of theirs that they unite in ignoring or abusing me. The theology I teach is not mine, but St. Bernard's and St. Francis's; the philosophy I teach is Plato's and Bacon's; the art, Phidias' and John Bellini's; the economy Xenophon's; the geology Saussure's . . . (In Oxford) I was looked upon as a lively musical-box instead of a man who knew his science and his business . . .'[1]

In August, 1880, as noted above, he went to Beauvais, Amiens, and Chartres, with his secretary and various friends including the amateur artist Brabazon. He was away till November, and most of the time in extremely good spirits, up at sunrise to the crown of Chartres spire, 'in perfectly good health',[2] drinking champagne,[3] delighting in everything, sketching (with his valet holding his paint box open for him in the old way), and making plans and notes for *Our Fathers have told us*.[4]

His letters show a state of extreme elation: 'One thing is lovelier than another':

'We really do see the sun here! And last night the sky was all a spangle and delicate glitter of stars, the glare of them and spikiness softened off by a young darling of a moon. And I'm having rather a time of it in boudoirs turned into smiling instead of pouting service.'[5]

'Nearly everything I have ever done or said is as much above the present level of public understanding as the Old Man is above the Waterhead.'[6]

'I suppose I'm the grand Monarque! I don't know of any other going just now, but I don't feel quite the right thing with-

[1] Letter in the *Oxford University Herald*, June 7, 1880 (cf. above, p. 118).
[2] Diary, Sept. 10, 1880.
[3] Letter to Susan Beever, Sept., 1880.
[4] Cf. above, p. 153.
[5] Letter to Susan Beever, Sept., 1880.
[6] Letter to Susan Beever from Paris, Sept. 4, 1880.

out a wig. Anyhow, I'm having everything my own way just now . . .'[1]

He enjoys Paris, finds the French peasants clean and amiable, and even appreciates the views from the train.

By Christmas the excitement has exhausted him.[2] In January, 1881, he writes to the Rev. J. P. Faunthorpe, the Principal at Whitelands, telling him to master *Munera Pulveris* and teach the girls that 'persons who have money in quantities, can employ armies in assassination, fools in machine making, whore-mongers in painting lewd pictures, and horse-breeders in destroying the morals of every boy in England'.[3] Then come insomnia and 'grotesque, terrific, inevitable' dreams.[4] In February he is urging his bookseller in London to buy him every Scott manuscript that appears in the market '*carte blanche* as to price'.[5] Then comes the second madness with 'terrific delirium'.[6]

Afterwards he writes:

'My illness was partly brought on by the sense of loneliness —and greater responsibility brought upon me by Carlyle's death, that and a course of saintly studies for Amiens which I fancy the Devil objected to—but I'm getting quietly into work again, for all that, and hope he'll get the worst of it, at last— nor even now has he done me much harm, in teaching me what kind of temper Blake worked in . . .'[7]

---

[1] *Ibid.* from Hotel du Grande Monarque, Chartres, Sept. 8, 1880.

[2] Letter to C. E. Norton, Jan. 20, 1881.

[3] Letter to Rev. J. P. Faunthorpe, Jan. 5, 1881.

[4] Diary, Jan. 9, 1881.

[5] Letter to F. S. Ellis, February, 1881.

[6] It is perhaps noteworthy that almost the last letter that he wrote before his first attack in 1878 contains instructions to friends to buy him Bewick drawings *carte blanche* as to price. (Letter to H. S. Marks, R.A., February, 1878.)

[7] Letter to George Richmond, May 20, 1881. Ruskin bought a portfolio of Blake drawings when he was twenty-four, in 1843, for £100, intending to ask his father to treat the purchase as an 'extra' on his allowance (cf. above, p. 45). But he was afraid his father would not agree, and he got the dealer to take the portfolio back. He particularly admired then the *Horse*, the *Owls*, the *Newton*, the *Nebuchadnezzar* . . . the *Satan and Eve*, the *Goblin Huntsman* and *Search for the Body of Harold* (Letter to

'I don't *anger* my soul nor vex my *own* heart, I relieve it, by all violent language.'[1]

'When I have growling to do or can't help, I write like that (scrawl on page), and get blacker and blacker all down the page.'[2]

'It is all nonsense what you hear of "overwork" as the cause of my two illnesses . . . These two times of delirium were both periods of extreme mental energy in perilous directions.'[3]

At the same time there is a reference to his attacks of 1878 and 1881 in a manuscript intended as a Preface to *Proserpina*, II:

'So far as I can trace the effects of the illness on my mental powers, it leaves them only weaker in the patience of application, but neither distorts nor blunts them, so long as they can be used. I cannot now write as long as I could nor deal with any questions involving laborious effort; but in ordinary faculties of judgement, modes of feeling, or play of what little fancy I ever had, I cannot trace more than such slackness or languor as age itself accounts for . . .'

In the same document he states that he experienced no physical suffering during the attacks, felt rested on his recovery, and gained physical strength more rapidly than after a bad attack of influenza or 'the slightest attack of low fever'; and he describes his condition during the attacks as 'prolonged dream—sometimes of actual trance, unconscious of surrounding objects, sometimes of waking fantasy, disguising or associating itself with the immediate realities both of substance and sound'.[4]

George Richmond, 1843). He actually kept some drawings. In 1880 he is said to have owned the drawing *Let Loose the Dogs of War*. He refers to *The Ghost of a Flea* and Blake's poems and madness in the Preface to the *Cestus of Aglaia* (1865). Later in the same articles he speaks of Blake's 'conscientious agony of beautiful purpose and warped power' and contrasts Blake's insanity with that of Haydon due to 'weakness of insolent egotism' (VI, para. 85). There are many other references to Blake and his works in Ruskin's writings. Richmond who in his youth, had known Blake, showed Ruskin his drawings about 1840.

[1] Letter to the Rev. J. P. Faunthorpe, July 20, 1881.
[2] Letter to Mrs. La Touche, Aug. 3, 1881.
[3] Letter to the Rev. J. P. Faunthorpe, Dec. 6, 1881.
[4] Cf. above, pp. 145 and 157.

THE PLAY

From this second attack to the end of 1881 he was increasingly unable (his secretary, Lawrence Hilliard, records) 'to keep any one settled train of thought or work'. He was perpetually planning new schemes of activity while noting in his Diary 'hesitations, shifts, and despairings'. At the same time marked hostility to his friends appears, irritability with his devoted secretaries, and refusal to be influenced by those around him.[1]

In January, 1882, he writes 'terribly languid' in his Diary. When he approached the danger month of February in 1882 he tried London distractions, staying at Herne Hill: 'I'm going to all manner of wicked plays and pantomimes and filling up my days with flirtations.'[2] But he could not steer clear. At this time he sent a letter to the *Morning Post* protesting against the selling of Old Jumbo, a Zoo elephant, to Barnum, the showman. The elephant having been bad-tempered the Zoo wanted to get rid of him; and the Council of the Zoo had excused themselves in a statement saying that they shared the regret felt by the Fellows in parting with the old animal. Ruskin, who was a Fellow, wrote as follows:

'I, for one of the said Fellows, am not in the habit of selling my old pets or parting with my old servants because I find them subject occasionally, perhaps even "periodically", to fits of ill temper; and I not only "regret" the proceedings of the Council, but disclaim them utterly as disgraceful to the City of London and dishonourable to humanity.'

So far so good. And not only good but excellent—driving words of generous indignation that call forth responding indignation in the reader. But then he goes on:

'If the Council want money let them beg it—if they want a stronger elephant's house let them build it; there is brick and iron enough in London to keep a single beast safe with, I suppose, and if there are not children in London brave enough to back him in his afternoon walk, let them look at him and go to their rocking horses.'[3]

[1] Letters from L. Hilliard and W. G. Collingwood to C. E. Norton, Oct. 15, 1881, and March 7, 1882.
[2] Letter to the Rev. J. P. Faunthorpe, Feb. 9, 1882.
[3] Letter to the *Morning Post*, Feb. 22, 1882. Jumbo was nevertheless

THE PLAY

Which is not so good—especially as Ruskin when a child was never allowed to back even a docile pony, let alone a bad-tempered elephant.

A few days later when he is near to the next attack I find this:

'I am better, but almost dead for want of sleep and fearful cough; and all my friends are throwing stones through my window, and dropping parcels down the chimney, and shrieking through the keyhole that they must and will see me instantly, and lying in wait for me if I want a breath of fresh air, to say their life depends on my instantly superintending the arrangement of their new Chapel, or Museum, or Model Lodging-House or Gospel steam-engine. And I'm in such a fury at them all that I can scarcely eat . . . In Heaven's name *be quiet* just now.'[1]

The importuning was, in fact, imaginary. For his secretaries under doctors' instructions kept from him at this time nearly all correspondence—(the letters from Hilliard and Collingwood to Norton, from which I have quoted, being written to explain why communications from him had not been handed on).

The recovery from the third madness in March, 1882, seemed especially good. In August, as already noted, he went abroad with Collingwood for the rest of the year, and he was then believed to be well enough to return to Oxford.

But, of course, he was not really in a state to undertake such exciting work in the presence of an audience. On the tour with Collingwood, whatever the outward appearances may have been, he was rapidly alternating, all the time, between morbid elation and morbid depression. One day he records that he has never been happier, never felt more disposed for work, etc.; shortly afterwards that he is 'depressed and useless', 'extremely languid and low but not ill', and suffering alternately from nightmare and from insomnia, when he lies awake delivering imaginary lectures.[2]

sold to Barnum; and he was killed three years later on the Grand Trunk Railway when he was struck by a train while his keeper was leading him and other elephants along the track.

[1] Letter to the Rev. J. P. Faunthorpe, March 3, 1882.
[2] Diaries, September and October, 1882.

I have already described the debacle in Oxford. Here I must add that in the later stages there he imagined that the scientists were plotting against him. The end there is thus summarised in a letter to Kate Greenaway:

'I gave a fourteenth, and last for this year, lecture this afternoon with vigour and effect; and am safe and well (D.V.), after such a spell of work as never I did before. I have been thrown a week out in all my plans by having to write two new lectures, instead of those the University was frightened at. The scientists slink out of my way now, as if I was a mad dog, for I let them have it hot and heavy whenever I've a chance at them.'[1]

[1] Letter to Kate Greenaway from Oxford, Dec. 1, 1884. This notion that the scientists were plotting against him had its origin I fancy in a long-standing jealousy of Faraday. We meet this as early as 1854: 'I don't say that I wouldn't care for reputation if I had it, but until people are ready to receive all I say about art as "unquestionable", just as they receive what Faraday tells them about chemistry, I don't consider myself to have any reputation at all worth caring about . . . I have no authority yet, such as I want to have, or such as I feel I deserve to have' (Letter to F. J. Furnivall, June 9, 1854). Then we get this in 1856: 'It is as ridiculous for a person to speak hesitatingly about the laws of painting who has conscientiously given his time to their ascertainment, as it would be for Mr. Faraday to announce in a dubious manner that iron has an affinity for oxygen, and to put the question to the vote of his audience whether it had or not' (*Modern Painters*, III, Preface). The next year when he appeared before the National Gallery Site Commission he found that Faraday was one of the members, and he must have been especially annoyed at having his ignorance of the German galleries revealed before the man whom he regarded as a rival (cf. below, p. 375). After Faraday's death he continues to be jealous and tilts at him as 'little Mr. Faraday' (he was, in fact, a very short man) in various lectures. In *Fors Clavigera* in 1874 we read, 'Your simple Queen of May, whom once you worshipped for a goddess—has not little Mr. Faraday analysed her, and proved her to consist of charcoal and water? . . .' (Letter 41). In the same year he writes in a private letter: 'I'm going to have a go at Faraday! this time at Oxford. Perfectest of men, wasn't he? Domestic, Orthodox, Episcopal, Enchanting, Accurate, Infallible, Modest, Merry-making! Well, I'm going to have a go at him for all that; but I want to know first, please, how orthodox he was? or was by *way* of being. Did he do his church regularly?—expect to go to heaven?—think chemistry a Divine operation? It is of great importance to me to know this as accurately as I can' (Letter to George Richmond, R.A., March 6, 1874). And then we get him associated in odium with Watt in *Mornings in Florence* (1874–1882): 'It is impossible to overrate the sagacity, patience

I must also chronicle a letter written in March, 1883, at a moment when he seemed to be particularly well and had just delivered the first lecture after his return to Oxford. The letter looks back on the attack of the year before:

'In this little room, where the quite prosy sunshine is resting quietly on my prosy table—last year, at this very time, I saw the stars rushing at each other—and thought the lamps of London were gliding through the night into a World Collision. I took my pretty Devonshire farm-girl Nurse for a Black Vision of Judgement; when I found I was still alive, a tinkly Italian organ became to me the music of the Spheres . . .'[1]

This if examined closely is a significant letter because it reveals the presence of two of his old obsessions. The London lights moving through the night are the old Firefly obsession, and in the actual wording of this letter he had wanted to write 'rosy' sunshine, then pulled himself up and written 'prosy' instead, and then rationalised it by 'prosy table' where the adjective is appropriate.[2]

Secretly all the old obsessions were at work. There are Storm Cloud entries in his Diary in 1879 and 1880. The sky is now 'a raging enemy',[3] and references to it abound during the long tour with Collingwood in 1882. While he seemed so well and was choosing marbles at Lucca for the exterior of a new Sheffield Museum (for which no site yet existed and no money was yet forthcoming),[4] he was writing in his Diary:

'Here I am, at last, again—in the eighth year from 1874—when I had precious letters, and went home by Chamouni—and

and precision of the masters in modern mechanical and scientific discovery But their sudden triumph . . . may not in anywise be attributed to their own power . . . the universal and overwhelming consequences of the facts . . . proclaimed indicate only the crisis of a rapture produced by the offering of new objects of curiosity to nations who had nothing to look at, and of the amusement of novel motion and action to nations who had nothing to do.' *Mornings in Florence*, II, paras. 33 and 34.

[1] Letter to C. E. Norton, March 15, 1883.
[2] Cf. above, p. 85; where he rationalised the irrational use of the capital for the verb Rose by a capital for the verb which followed.
[3] Letter to Susan Beever, 1879.
[4] Cf. above, p. 152.

Champagnole, St. Cergues, Geneva, Bonneville, Sallenches, Annécy, Turin, all seen once more. But how different it would have been but for this plague-cloud, which yesterday with its following wind darkened and tormented all Val di Serchio. To-day having slept well—curiously well—I can scarcely see to write; the sky is settled, stern, gapless doom.'[1]

A few days before he had written to Norton:

'The Mont Blanc *we* knew is no more. All the snows are wasted, the lower rocks bare, the luxuriance of light, the pleni-tude of power, the Eternity of Being, are all gone from it . . . But no one is sad for it but only I, and you, I suppose, would be.'[2]

There is more Storm Cloud in a letter to Norton in August, 1883, and then this long-standing delusion culminates in two lectures to the London Institution in February, 1884: *The Storm Cloud of the Nineteenth Century*. There he quoted from his diaries and informed his audience that the sunsets had become 'unnatural and terrific' but had no connection with the new and far more fearful 'Storm Cloud and Plague Wind'. A peroration at these lectures was as follows:

'Blanched sun,—blighted grass,—blinded man . . . What is best to be done, do you ask me? The answer is plain—Whether you can affect the signs of the sky or not, you *can* the signs of the times . . . The paths of rectitude and piety once regained, who shall say that the promise of old time would not be found to hold for us also? "Bring ye all the tithes into my storehouse, and prove me now herewith, saith the Lord God, if I will not open you the windows of heaven, and pour you out a blessing, that there shall not be room enough to receive it!" '[3]

[1] Diary, Sept. 30, 1882. The 'precious letters' of 1874 were of course from Rose.

[2] Letter to C. E. Norton from Sallenches, Sept. 11, 1882. Compare with this letter the lament of the old days, 'so sad—so sad' I only can care for Tintoretto (cf. above, p. 97).

[3] To the numerous references to the Storm Cloud and Plague Wind in the diaries and letters we must add, of course, references in conversa-tion which are not recorded. In an account of a visit he paid to Farnley in December, 1884, however, his host records: 'Mr. Ruskin talked at break-fast about the clouds and the study of the sky, and the fact that the last

The Rose obsession in these years was also very persistent; and it was multiple in form. We have first indirect references like the following: Asked to suggest a name for a Ruskin Society in Manchester he replied that they might 'with grace and truth take the name of the Society of the Rose—meaning the English wild rose';[1] he still used a rose device as heraldic emblem on his books; when he spent such large sums of the Guild's money on emeralds and so forth for Sheffield in 1883 he extracted one piece—a Rose quartz—which he could not part with—and credited the Guild with its price. In May, 1883, he told the world in *Fors Clavigera* that 'extremely good girls— usually die young', that 'no lover should have the insolence to think of being accepted at once,' that 'no girl should have the cruelty to refuse at once' and that if she was not certain she should send him away, for three to seven years on probation.[2]

Then we get direct references like the following:

'It's very pretty of you to give me those lovely lines ('On Aprile', *Paracelsus*): I like them because that child I told you of, who died, who wasn't usually by way of paying me compliments, *did* once say, "Those eyes" after looking at them a while.'[3]

'Got in my evening thoughts into a steady try if I couldn't get Rosie's ghost at least alive by me, if not the body of her . . .'[4]

In October, 1883, he was again in contact with Frederic

ten years had been marked by such great absence of sun and so much cloud and fog . . .' ('Mr. Ruskin at Farnley', by E. M. Fawkes, *Nineteenth Century*, April, 1900).

[1] Letter to the Secretary of the Manchester Ruskin Society, 1879.

[2] *Fors Clavigera*, Letter 90 (May, 1883).

[3] Letter to Miss Mary Gladstone, Feb. 1, 1879. In *Præterita*, Ruskin says that 'the main good of my face, as of my life, is in the eyes—and only in those, seen near' (*Præterita*, II, Chap. III, para. 43).

[4] Letter to C. E. Norton, April 26, 1881. The omissions after the last word quoted are Norton's. Such omissions, which occur in all Ruskin's letters to Norton, as published by Norton, are much to be regretted. It is also regrettable that Norton did not see fit to publish *all* Ruskin's letters to him, and that as literary executor he destroyed all Ruskin's letters to Rose and all hers to him—though he was technically within his rights as Ruskin in his Will left the destruction of papers to his discretion and that of Mrs. Severn (cf. note, p. 83).

Myers and doubtless once more dabbling in spiritualism.[1] The result appears a little later in a letter to Kate Greenaway where he relates the story of Rose making the company at a party all pray for a girl friend who was ill[2]; and adds that he has just received an envelope from the sick girl's daughter, who was dying and had written him on her deathbed 'in my own old Rosie's hand'.[3]

It will be observed that in the first letter quoted above, he refers to Rose as 'that child'—and it was the passion for the child Rosie for which he sought relief at the beginning of the 'eighties, just as he had sought relief from it before at the beginning of the 'sixties at Winnington and again at the pantomime in 1867.[4] Sublimating this desire into a general passion for girl children he now surrounds himself with little girls on every possible occasion and goes out of his way to be in their company. He pretends when writing to his aged neighbour Susan Beever that she is a 'dear good little girl', who is 'really thirteen',[5] and indulges periodically in this significant playfulness for years. He has the girls from Coniston Parish School once a week to tea with him at Brantwood and potters repeatedly in and out of the school. He plays the role of the old Uncle at Whitelands Training College for Girls in Chelsea, where he deposits Guild minerals and pictures as already noted.[6] He also gives sixty prints and pictures to Whitelands and institutes there a May Queen Festival, with songs and dances like the old songs and dances and May Queen Festival at Winnington. For the Cork High School for Girls he institutes a Rose Queen Festival with a gold rose-brooch designed by Burne-Jones to be annually given. He corresponds with the 'Queens' and

[1] Cf. above, pp. 133 and 134.
[2] Cf. above, p. 81.
[3] Letter to Kate Greenaway, Jan. 23, 1884. Here, as in the case of the Storm-cloud obsession, we must add to the frequent references in letters, the references in conversation which are not recorded. There is evidence that Ruskin talked about Rosie frequently to a number of people in the 'eighties.
[4] Cf. above, pp. 71–75 and 83.
[5] Letter to Susan Beever, Nov. 27, 1878.
[6] Cf. above, p. 149.

keeps in touch with them. In 1880 he attended the dramatic entertainment of some little girls called Webling. One of these children was called Rosalind. He invited her and her sister Peggy to Brantwood and kept them there for seven weeks. He gave Rosalind a gold rose-brooch and corresponded with her frequently afterwards. In his first letter of invitation to their father he said 'Tell Miss Rosalind that the only toilettes needed at Brantwood are a rose in the hair and a frock that won't tear —or won't matter if it does.'[1]

When he was about to deliver his *Storm Cloud* lectures at the London Institution in February, 1884, some girl students at the Academy Schools wrote and asked for tickets. He replied that this was impossible, but could he come to tea with them? He went to tea and invited them all back to tea and a talk at Herne Hill. In preparing for this lecture to the girls he was 'all of a flutter'. Though he was now sixty-five and knew, one would have thought, enough about the old masters for a talk to a dozen young students, he made a special visit to the National Gallery and 'went all over it noting things for lecture to the Academy girls on Saturday'. Then he went off to buy coffee and teacups for the girls, and then he spent half an hour choosing toys for a little girl model of Kate Greenaway's. Another day he goes to Sanger's Amphitheatre and sees 'a pretty girl ride *haute école*' and then goes home where 'pretty ——' boils eggs for his supper.[2] At this time he also made presents to Girton, and frequented Somerville College where he said that he was glad to be old enough to take tea with the 'girlies'. He deposited Guild minerals at Somerville, and gave the College other minerals, and his own copies of the head and the hand of Carpaccio's *St. Ursula*, which he made when he was closeted with the picture in 1876.[3] He made the presentation publicly during the last distressing course of Oxford lectures in the autumn of 1884. On that occasion he harangued, significantly, as follows:

[1] Letter published by Miss Peggy Webling in *A Sketch of John Ruskin* (cf. above, p. 147).
[2] Letters to W. G. Collingwood from London, February, 1884.
[3] Cf. above, p. 136.

THE PLAY

'Here is a Spectral Girl—an idol of a girl—never was such a girl. Ask the sweetest you can find to your college gardens, show your Phyllis the brightest flowers *qua crines religata fulget*, she will not look like this one . . . Never was twisted hair like hers—twisted, like that of all Venetian girls, in memory of the time when they first made their hair into ropes for the fugitive ships at Aquileia. You will never see such hair, nor such peace beneath it on the brow—*Pax Vobiscum*—the peace of heaven, of infancy, and of death. No one knows who she is or where she lived. She is Persephone at rest below the earth; she is Proserpine at play above the ground. She is Ursula, the gentlest yet the rudest of little bears; a type in that, perhaps, of the moss rose, or of the rose *spinosissima*, with its rough little buds. She is in England, in Cologne, in Venice, in Rome, in eternity, living everywhere, dying everywhere, the most intangible yet the most practical of all saints—queen, for one thing, of female education, when once her legend is understood. This sketch of her head is the best drawing I ever made. Carpaccio's picture is hung, like all good pictures, out of sight, seven feet above the ground; but the Venetian Academy had it taken down for me, and I traced every detail in it accurately to a hair's breadth. It took me a day's hard work to get that spray of silver hair loosening itself rightly from the coil, and twelve times over had I to try the mouth. And to-day, assuming Miss Shaw Lefevre's indulgence, I present it to the girls of Somerville Hall.'[1]

He had already astounded his Oxford audience by announcing that he was proposing to reprint 'for my younger pupils' a tale called *Little Downey, or the History of a Field-Mouse* from *Evenings at Home*, a publication of the 'twenties—they not knowing that 'Mousie' had been one of his pet names for Rosie.[2] And he had further astounded them by extravagant praise of Kate Greenaway's 'girlies', and by exhibiting in the same frames which he used to protect drawings by Turner a series of drawings by an American amateur, Francesca Alexander.[3]

[1] *The Pleasures of England*, V. The Pleasure of Truth; lecture delivered in November, 1884.
[2] Cf. above, pp. 75 and 82.
[3] *The Art of England*, Lecture I, III, and IV, 1883.

They did not know that he delighted in Kate Greenaway's 'girlies' of different ages, because, when he looked at them, he was really looking through them to memories of the real children at Winnington who had all been aspects of Rosie. They did not know that in one of the first letters he ever wrote to Kate Greenaway (when he was still addressing her as 'Miss Greenaway') he had told her that the little girl on her Christmas card was 'a greater thing than Raphael's *St. Cecilia*',[1] and that this was not an art judgement but the equivalent of saying, 'This little girl reminds me of Rosie—the child I fell in love with—a much sweeter Rosie than the pietistic Rose with eyes turned up to Heaven (like Raphael's *St. Cecilia*) who made me miserable in her later years.'

Nor did they know that he had fallen in love with Francesca Alexander's work because the first thing he saw of hers was a drawing of a frail girl leaning back on her pillow, with closed eyes, in bed, who died a month later—a Rose-Ursula image.[2]

[1] Letter to Kate Greenaway, Dec. 26, 1880.

[2] This drawing entitled *In the Last Ray of Sunset, and the Last Day of the Year*, 1872 is reproduced as Plate I in Vol. XXXII of the Library Edition. It was drawn for *The Story of Ida* which was both written and illustrated by Francesca Alexander. The wording as well as the drawing must have evoked Rose-images in Ruskin's mind. He became very excited when he saw the manuscript and the drawings and bought them immediately; he published the book and the first drawing with a Preface of his own in 1883. Then he bought Francesca's other illustrated book, *Roadside Songs of Tuscany*, for £600 (say £1,500), charging it to St. George's Guild (cf. above, p. 148). *Roadside Songs of Tuscany* contains sentimental drawings and legends of Italian peasants whom he had so often abused in his letters at various periods of his life. But now we read in his Diary 'well pleased with myself for having bought Miss Alexander's book, showing all I want to say about Italian peasantry' (Diary, Oct. 10, 1882); and, referring to the book in his Oxford lectures, he describes the Italian peasants as 'gracious and blessed creatures—God's own poor' (*Art of England*, I, para. 25, March, 1883)—thus at one and the same time rationalising his fantastic expenditure of Guild money and making atonement for 'the vilest wretches of ape-faced children', and similar abuse of Italian peasants in 1869 and 1874 (cf. above, pp. 95 and 123). Francesca Alexander was, not unnaturally, delighted with this open-handed patron, and later she drew for him a *Santa Rosa*—a little girl with a halo round her head.

THE PLAY

After the fourth attack of madness in 1885 he was only able to work 'between the storms'. He had started his Autobiography, *Præterita*, at the beginning of that year and he went on with it at intervals, and with ever-increasing difficulty in concentration, between the attacks that followed. The attack of 1886 seems to have been very damaging. But he still forms projects for new work. *Præterita* was to be in thirty-six chapters. By 1886 he has already projected and started on an accompanying work, *Dilecta*, containing notes and correspondence illustrative of *Præterita*. On January 9, 1887, he writes in his diary: 'Sixteen letters written on Friday; eleven yesterday. Mineral ticketing. Chess playing. Botanical lesson to Gussie, musical to Annie, painting to Robert Hedhead. Miss Murray found out; and promised support in bird drawing. *Cœli Enarrant* begun again with "Institutes of Mineralogy"; and *Præterita* in full speed; and article on art for *Chambers' Encyclopædia.*'

During 1887 he was hostile to his friends and showed alternating euphoria and despondency accompanied by delusions.[1] In the summer he drove down to the South Coast and lived at Folkestone till the end of the year. Then he went abroad with friends over the old ground in France, Italy and High Savoy, where the usual moods alternated; and he collapsed into acute depression with delusions on the way back at the end of 1888 in Paris.

We get a characteristic glimpse of him on his return to Brantwood:

'He looked an old man ... but his eyes were the youngest I have ever seen in an adult face, blue and clear like a child's, with the child's large direct gaze. By tea time, every table, chair, and most of the floor would be littered with ... sketches, photographs, missals, Greek coins, and uncut gems. "Now we begin to look comfortable," he would say ... He talked much and brilliantly, laughing heartily, an infectious, chuckling laugh when anything amused him.'[2]

---

[1] E. T. Cook, *Life of Ruskin* (London, Allen, 1911).

[2] *John Ruskin in the 'Eighties*, by Mrs. Allen Harker, in the *Outlook*, Feb., 1899. We know from various visitors to Brantwood in the 'eighties that Ruskin frequently had favourite songs played to him in the evenings

In the summer of 1889 he was for some time at Seascale in Cumberland. In the autumn he had another attack of madness, and after that he lived in retirement at Brantwood.

With *Præterita* he received help from his assistants who collected material—old letters, diaries, and so forth—and these assistants doubtless pruned the text a good deal, extracting from it all polemical and unbalanced discursions. As it stands it is a prettily written gossiping narrative, easy to read, and it is now the fashion among people who cannot be troubled to work through the tangled jungle of his life's writings to describe it as his 'best book'. It appeared in instalments from the early part of 1885 and it was still far from finished when he wrote the last instalment at Seascale in the summer of 1889. When that was published the curtain came down, as far as the public was concerned, on what Ruskin himself had called 'the not, I hope, unentertaining history of the Don Quixote of Denmark Hill'.[1]

and that when he was in cheerful mood he would sing and clap his hands and dance about. Miss Peggy Webling in *A Sketch of John Ruskin*, writes: 'The swinging lilt of the Scotch song, "*Wi*' *a hundred pipers and a*' *and a*' ", whenever I chance to hear it, transforms my surroundings into the drawing-room at Brantwood, where a lady sang it nearly every night . . . the Professor laughed and clapped his hands . . . joined in the chorus and even danced a few wild fantastic steps to express his pleasure.' Already in 1875 he had astounded his Oxford audience by dancing and singing in an attack on Mendelssohn's setting of *Oh! for the wings of a dove* which he introduced into a lecture on *The Discourses of Reynolds* (Cook, Vol. II, p. 269, where contemporary accounts are given).

[1] *Financial History of St. George's Guild* (1884). It will be observed that he writes of himself as the Don Quixote of *Denmark Hill*, though his Denmark Hill days had been over since 1872 (and he had not, of course, been born there). The explanation is doubtless that he had begun to think of himself as Don Quixote in the 'sixties and that the phrase 'The Don Quixote of Denmark Hill' was an oral image of long standing, so that its use in 1886 was automatic. On Aug. 9, 1870, he had written to Norton:

'*Don Quixote* always affected me throughout to tears, not laughter. It was always *throughout real* chivalry to me; and it is precisely because the most touching valour and tenderness are rendered vain by madness . . . and because *all* true chivalry is thus by implication accused of madness, and involved in shame, that I call the book so deadly.'

THE EPILOGUE

During the last years of his secluded life the legend of the Aged Prophet of Brantwood grew apace. In the 'nineties there were no artists in England and relatively few in America and on the Continent who had not read some parts of *Modern Painters* and *The Stones of Venice;* and there was no middle-class schoolgirl in England who was not plagued with *Sesame and Lilies* which reached its sixty-fourth thousand in 1903. Books of *Selections* were read everywhere—*Frondes Agrestes* (the purple passages selected from *Modern Painters* by Susan Beever in 1875) was in its thirty-sixth thousand in 1902; the *Letter to Young Girls* (a reprint from *Fors Clavigera*, Letters 65 and 66) was in its seventy-fifth thousand in the same year; and translated *Selections* were read in France, Italy, Spain, Germany and Sweden. All his books and lectures, his early poems, all the letters that he had sent to the Press, were now republished, and edition after edition was called for.[1] *Unto This Last,* of which barely nine hundred copies had been sold between 1862 and 1873, was in its forty-eight thousand in 1901. *Ethics of the Dust* (which was a complete failure when it appeared in 1866 and had not gone into a second edition till 1877) was in its twenty-fourth thousand in 1903.[2]

And all this was without Press advertisement and without reviews in the Press, from the beginning of the 'seventies onwards, when he established George Allen as his own publisher

[1] A collection of his letters to the Press from 1851–1880 was published as *Arrows of the Chase*, in 1880. The Library Edition extends the book to 1896.

[2] The first authorised American edition of Ruskin's works (the Brantwood Edition consisting of twenty-two volumes) was produced with introduction by Norton between 1891 and 1893. Till then his books had been much pirated in America, greatly to his annoyance; he complained in *Fors Clavigera* that not a penny had ever come to him in royalties from America.

and sent no review copies to the Press. Allen published all the reprints of his old books and all the new ones from 1871 onwards. His establishment was in Kent and run by his own family and local labour. Everyone, booksellers and private individuals, had to get the books from him and pay the same price, and, except in the case of well-known booksellers, to pay cash. In 1882 the arrangement was modified to give booksellers a fixed discount. When the expenses were paid, Ruskin received the remaining retail price as 'royalty' on each copy. On two thousand copies of a reprint of *The Seven Lamps of Architecture* he made £991 (say £2,375), on three thousand of *Sesame and Lilies* at five shillings he made £345 (£860). On the 1886 reprint of *The Stones of Venice* he had made £3,069 (£7,672) by 1890. Between 1880 and 1889 he made £3,200 (£8,000) on *The Seven Lamps of Architecture*. In 1886 over 10,000 copies of his books were sold, many of them at high prices. And thus in his later years the income from his books was equivalent to £10,000 a year in present money.[1]

This income from his books was bread that had been cast upon the waters. Because by the beginning of the 'eighties he had frittered away the whole of his own fortune by extravagancies, gifts, losses and bad investments. In *Fors Clavigera*, Letter 76 (April, 1877), he gave an account of the way in which his inheritance had by that time dwindled to less than a third of the original £157,000 (to keep to the figure of the time). He had by 1877 given £17,000 to relations, spent £12,000 on the Oxford Drawing School and the Guild of St. George, and lost £15,000 in financing the business of relations, and £20,000 in bad investments. He calculated that he had spent £15,000 on 'harness and stable expenses', and £70,000 in other living ex-

---

[1] £4,000 is the actual average figure of the 'eighties given by Cook in his *Studies in Ruskin* from which the above details are extracted. The figures in the 'nineties must have been higher. Before he started Allen as his publisher, Ruskin had published his books with Smith, Elder & Co., and both he and his father had contributed to the expenses in many cases —Ruskin having spent the equivalent of £3,500, as noted on the illustrations, etc., to *The Stones of Venice* (cf. above, p. 57). His final income from his books was of course only rendered possible by his expenditure in establishing Allen in the way detailed.

RUSKIN, AGED SEVENTY-FOUR, IN 1893

ACCOMPANIED BY HIS VALET AND DOG

[Photo by Courtesy of Messrs. B. F. Stevens and Brown]

penses—the upkeep of Brantwood, where he had nine servants, and secretaries, and so forth, and his perpetual travelling with servants, guests and assistants. He had therefore at that date only about £7,000 in Bank Stock and various properties, including Brantwood, and some freeholds and leaseholds, and his Turners and other collections which he estimated at £45,000. 'When one is living on one's capital,' he wrote, after giving the figures, 'the melting away is faster than one expects.' Between 1878 and 1885 most of this residue melted further in capricious extravagancies, the expenses of illness, and the upkeep of Brantwood (where the Severns and their children eventually came to look after him). And thus in his old age he was dependent on the income from his books which provided him with plenty of money to the end. His effects when his Will was proved were sworn at £10,662 2s. 8d.

His mental condition in these last years seems to have been the continuation in aggravated forms of the earlier conditions. There were long periods in which he was depressed and almost speechless, sometimes docile and sometimes gloomily hostile, not recognising most people at all. But I am told that there were times when he became excited and talked without ceasing; and times when he was so violent that he had to be strapped to his chair. In the last period there were also times when he temporarily recovered and was sane.

On January 18, 1900, he showed symptoms of influenza (with which several of his servants were suffering). He was sane at the time, scoffed at the danger, and ate a dinner of sole and pheasant accompanied by champagne. He died on January 21.

POSTSCRIPT

In the analysis of Ruskin's action and of the progress of his
mental malady which I have attempted in the foregoing
pages I have not suggested that the memory of his wife's
desertion might have been a suppressed irritant with important
effects. I have omitted reference to this possibility because I
have tried to avoid pure speculation altogether and to restrict
myself to the statement and interpretation of evidence; and on
this point there is no evidence at all. Ruskin does not mention
his wife's name in *Præterita*, and there are, as my knowledge
goes, no references to her after 1854 in his published letters;
moreover, as the reader will see, I find no indirect references to
her conduct or to his married life in the autobiographical mosaic of his writings which I discuss in Part III.

A recent biographer has suggested that the whole of Ruskin's later activities were the result of subconscious resentment at his wife's desertion; that his social-economic work was
'a passing on of the indictment of Effie, a suit for nullity proclaimed against England'; that when he proposed marriage to
Rose La Touche 'he did not want to marry so much as to prove
that he could be accepted as a suitor in marriage', and to give
'the only real reply to Effie, another woman'; and that when he
wrote 'I wanted my Rosie *here*. In Heaven I mean to go and
talk to Pythagoras and Socrates and Valerius Publicola. I
shan't care a bit for Rosie there, she needn't think it. What will
grey eyes and red cheeks be good for *there?*'[1]—'the reproach of
Effie was passed on to the dead Rose and taken out of the world
altogether'.[2]

The complex problem of Ruskin's psychosis cannot be
solved by this unduly simplified hypothesis. On the other hand,

[1] Letter to Susan Beever, June 25, 1874.
[2] David Larg. *John Ruskin* (London, Davies, 1932).

though Ruskin wrote nothing about Euphemia, and, by all accounts, never spoke of her from the age of thirty-five onwards, it does not follow that he never thought about her or that he was completely unaffected by the annulment of his marriage. It is clear that his wife never penetrated to the inner circle of his life. He had known her from childhood, but the child Euphemia had not supplanted the image of the child Adèle. We have his direct statement to George MacDonald that he was not in love with her at the time of the marriage or during his married life. He was not affectionate in early manhood, and there is no evidence that there was ever affection between them. We can safely assume that his wife's departure left no place empty in his heart. But even so he may have felt resentment at her departure. And I think it possible that this and the annulment of his marriage did have some psychic results.

The mobility of his thought and interest, and his difficulty in concentration first became marked in 1855. Suppressed friction with his parents was one of the several factors aggravating the growth of his mental illness at this point, as we have seen; the collapse of his marriage may well have been another. Reflection upon the non-consummation of his marriage may have been a factor in the recrudescence of sexual impulses, which I have called a species of climacteric, and in the formulation of the broader outlook which began about 1858. The proposal to the grown-up Rose, whom he hated, in 1866, may have been as much a defiance of Effie as an attempt to recapture the image of Rosie that he loved. But for all this we really have no evidence. And if there was an Effie obsession, it was, as we have seen, only one strand in the complex cord that pressed upon his sanity and finally destroyed it; and I doubt if, as an obsession, it had any existence after 1858.

PART III
CRITICAL

INTRODUCTORY COMMENTS

Ruskin's writings fill thirty-three volumes in the Library, Edition. Of these the major portion consist of lectures essays, pamphlets, notes and journalism. The 'books' properly so called are *Modern Painters, I, Modern Painters, II, The Seven Lamps of Architecture, The Stones of Venice, Unto This Last* (with *Munera Pulveris*), *Ethics of the Dust*, and the long autobiographical fragment, *Præterita*. Most of these books are to some extent constructed. The other writings are all irregular, if not chaotic, in form.

Laurence Binyon has said that Ruskin was 'driving all one way'.[1] This is true of his central contributions in all fields. But much reconstruction and pruning are necessary before we can discover what those central contributions are. Ruskin built up polygons of doctrine for the study of Art, Social and Political Economy, and the problem of War, which were valuable in his own day, and, as I see things, are still valuable to-day. But his polygons are not in constructed formation ; they exist only as isolated blocks scattered over the thirty-three volumes; and they are obscured and overlaid by incidentals. Before we can arrive at the real character of these valuable polygons we have first to distinguish the main theories from the incidentals—a task that can only perfectly be accomplished by complete knowledge of the circumstances of his life and the workings of his mind—and we have then to set aside the incidentals and collect the scattered parts of the main figures and assemble them in the forms that were always in Ruskin's mind, though he himself could never assemble them. Or, to put it differently—before we can understand what he wanted us most to understand in

---

[1] Essay in *Ruskin the Prophet*, edited by J. H. Whitehouse (London, Allen & Unwin. New York, Dutton. 1920).

his writings we have to rearrange them all and rewrite most of them.[1]

To separate the essential from the incidental in a book or a page by Ruskin is often very difficult. In his writings the confusing irrelevancies and discursions are as *real* and *organic* as the essentials. The incidentals are branches from the main trunk of his personal psychosis—they are not pseudo-branches tied on with string. Ruskin's writing was always genuinely personal. He never decked himself with other people's ideas. When we examine most people's writings—as when we examine most people's pictures or sculpture—we find that 80 or 90 or 100 per cent of the content is derived from other people. I find a large proportion of derivative content in Ruskin's drawings—and I regard most of them as negligible for that reason. But I do not find it in his writings at any period of his life.

After 1852 he learned a lot from Carlyle. But learning from a man is one thing, and stealing his ideas is another. Ruskin was susceptible to a powerful influence like Carlyle's; he called him 'my Master' and it was many years before he ceased to write to him as 'Dear Mr. Carlyle'. But Carlyle never referred to Ruskin as 'my imitator' or 'my follower' or 'my pupil'; he referred to his 'flightiness'[2] (meaning the flittering of his thoughts caused by his mental weakness), but he recognised his originality and accepted him as a brother, saying: 'We stand in a minority of two.'[3]

Ruskin was influenced by other people as well as by Carlyle

[1] For Ruskin as a writer cf. below, pp. 357–368.
[2] Letter from Carlyle to his brother, Dr. Carlyle, Nov. 17, 1874. ('He is aiming as if at the very stars; but his sensitive, flighty nature disqualifies him for earnest conversation and frank communication of his secret thoughts.')
[3] Carlyle in a letter to Ruskin quoted by Ruskin in a letter to 'A Journalist', Aug. 20, 1870 (cf. above. p. 107). At the beginning of his friendship with Carlyle, Ruskin wrote him: 'People are continually accusing me of borrowing other men's thoughts, and not confessing the obligation. I don't think there is anything of which I am more utterly incapable, than of this meanness . . . How much your general influence has told upon me, I know not, but I always confess it, or rather boast about it . . .' (Letter to Carlyle, Jan. 23, 1855.)

—by Plato, Xenophon, Dante, Turner. But he always set their ideas to the service of his own. At all periods he used data provided by scholars. In his later years he would send his assistants to collect such data saying, 'What else are the professors there for?'[1] In the 'forties and the early 'fifties he read some art history and did some research work himself; and he liked to make a parade of scholarly erudition. But he was never a scholar. He always looked on scholarship in itself as a playlike activity.[2] Driven by the mobility of his interest he indulged in the pastime when the spirit moved him; but he never used any data in his writings except such as could be made to serve his personal ideas. Every word that he wrote had become *his own word* before it appears as an extract from archives or as a paraphrase from some ancient dictionary of heraldry,[3] or as a quotation from Dante or Blake or Anatole France.[4]

The digressions, discursions, and irrelevancies that abound in his writings are never 'padding'. They have a life of their own which often conflicts with or obscures or partially destroys the central theme. Even his lightest and most bantering and journalistic passages have this quality. They are never trivial. And this applies not only to his public writings, but

---

[1] Collingwood, *Life and Work of Ruskin*, 1900, p. 329.

[2] Cf. above, pp. 39 and 49.

[3] For example, *Deucalion*, I, Chap. VII, *The Iris of the Earth*, *passim*.

[4] *Le Crime de Silvestre Bonnard*. Ruskin was very fond of this book and identified himself with the old Professor. In a manuscript intended as an addition to *Deucalion* he refers to Anatole France's creation as 'an old philosopher (who is amazingly like one I know of)'. He identified *la gouvernante* in the book with his old nurse (cf. above, p. 127, and below, p. 281), and quotes a passage about her in his notes on *Roadside Songs of Tuscany*, 'Life of Santa Zita' (Library Edition, Vol. XXXII, p. 71). He marked, characteristically, in his copy the following passage: '*Si cette enfant m'était confiée je ferais d'elle, non pas une savante, car je lui veux du bien, mais une enfant brillante d' intelligence et de vie, et en laquelle toutes les belles choses de la nature et d 'art se refléteraient avec un doux éclat. Je la ferais vivre en sympathie avec les beaux paysages, avec les scènes idéales de la poésie et de l'histoire, avec la musique noblement émue. Je lui rendrais aimable tout ce que je voudrais lui faire aimer.*' Rosie submitted, but Rose would not.

also to his letters. As a rule when we read a man's letters in order to get at his mind and heart we can 'skip' a great proportion which is conventional nothingness or light gossip. But, except in his early years and during his married life in Venice, Ruskin never wrote gossip in his letters, and even at that early period he never wrote a conventional line. If we skip three lines of any of the thousands of his published letters we miss three lines of the real man. He says somewhere that he could never indulge in the pleasure of saying 'nothing worth'. It is true. It was one of the pleasures to which he was not drawn and in which, therefore, he never indulged.

Even in the lighter incidental passages in Ruskin's books, sentence after sentence is a book in itself—with a life of its own independent of the sentence before and the sentence following. Again and again we meet pages where each sentence reveals that curious intensity of idea *at the moment* which seems to go with morbid mobility of interest and must be parallel to that morbid visual hyper-reaction to detail to which Ruskin confessed as early as 1854 in his comments on Hunt's *The Awakening Conscience*, and which he tells us was a characteristic of his vision during his attacks of madness.[1] Anyone can quote Ruskin in any sense on any topic he has touched upon. Ruskin calendars can be compiled by Tories, Fascists, and Communists, by photographic painters and Cubist artists, by Chauvinists and Pacifists, by parsons and agnostics. All can claim him as their man. And yet Binyon is right—he was really driving all one way. The incidentals always bear relation to the man's attitudes even though they may bear little or no relation to their immediate context. In the lecture on serpents, *A Caution to Snakes*, for example, which he wrote in 1880, we read:

'A serpent is a honeysuckle with a head put on. . . . Nothing is more mysterious in the compass of creation than the relation of flowers to the serpent tribe [especially] in carnivorous, insect-eating and monstrous insect-begotten structures. . . . In the most accurate sense, the honeysuckle is an "anguis"—a strangling thing.'[2]

[1] Cf. above, p. 145, and below, p. 253.
[2] *Deucalion*, II, Chap. I, 'Living Waves', para. 32. The lecture as

This is an incidental remark in his discussion of the movement of serpents (Living Waves), but it is closely related to the doctrine of Typical and Vital Beauty—the doctrine of the Universal Analogy—which he had put forward thirty-five years earlier, in his Theory of Art—as we shall see.

Then again in the same lecture we get this:

'I endeavoured to find out some particulars . . . in my scientific books; but though I found pages upon pages of description of the scales and wrinkles about snakes' eyes, I could come at no account whatever of the probable range or distinctness in the sight of them; and though extreme pains had been taken to exhibit, in sundry delicate engravings, their lachrymatory glands and ducts, I could neither discover the occasions on which rattle-snakes wept, nor under what consolations they dried their eyes.'[1]

This from another speaker would be merely wit. From Ruskin it symbolised a lifelong attitude to scholarship and science, allied to the attitude which led him in Social Economics to differentiate Wealth and Illth, and to set aside the postulate of the Economic Man as useless and absurd.[2]

Or consider this—from a paper which he read to the Metaphysical Society in 1871:

'A painter . . . may, I think, be looked upon as only representing a high order of sensational creatures, incapable of any but physical ideas and impressions; and . . . we should be much more docile than we are if we were never occupied in efforts to conceive things above our natures. To take an instance, in a creature somewhat lower than myself. I came by surprise the other day on a cuttle-fish in a pool at low tide. On being touched with the point of my umbrella, he first filled the pool with ink, and then finding himself still touched in the darkness, lost his temper, and attacked the umbrella with much psyche or anima, hugging it tightly with all his eight arms, and making

delivered was entitled *A Caution to Snakes*. The title was changed to *Living Waves* for the published version. (For other references to this lecture, cf. above, p. 160, and below, p. 363.)

[1] *Deucalion*, II, Chap. I, 'Living Waves', para. 9.
[2] Cf. below, pp. 290, 291–2, 300.

efforts, like an impetuous baby with a coral, to get it into his mouth. On my offering him a finger instead, he sucked that with two or three of his arms with an apparently malignant satisfaction and, on being shaken off, retired with an air of frantic misanthropy into the cloud of his ink. . . . It seems to me not a little instructive to reflect how entirely useless such a manifestation of a superior being was to his cuttle-fish mind, and how fortunate it was for his fellow-octopods that he had no command of pens as well as ink, nor any disposition to write on the nature of umbrellas or of men.'[1]

From an Oxford don this would be just academic banter. From Ruskin, in April, 1871, it was related to his concept of that 'incredulity . . . of help given by any Divine power to the thoughts of men' of which he had written:

'This form of infidelity merely indicates a natural incapacity for receiving certain emotions; though many honest and good men belong to this insentient class, they are not to be thought of except as more or less mechanical or animal forces, which must be dealt with by similar forces, not by reasoning.'[2]

Then again the compelling power of the incidentals often derives from the aspect of his mental illness which drove him to use his pen as a means of rationalising his self-indulgence or of relieving his obsessions. Such passages are real and organic because they are autobiography disguised. And it is such passages which give quality to a poor book like *Mornings in Florence*, and even sometimes to the fragments in books of *Selections*.

Nevertheless before we can arrive at Ruskin's main contributions to the study of Art, Social and Political Economy, and War, we have to disengage the digressions and the discursions from the main theories. And when we have done that we find autobiography also in the formulation of the main ideas.

Ruskin, as I have said, was a genius in the sense that he had a great imaginative grasp of first principles and refused to assume that a pretty blossom means a wholesome fruit. But even

[1] *The Range of Intellectual Conception proportioned to the Rank in Animated Life.*

[2] *Time and Tide*, VIII, para. 36, March, 1867 (cf. below, p. 344).

for his central contributions the jumping-off point was frequently a rationalisation of his self-indulgence, when its character was not determined either by his social conscience working in conjunction with or in conflict with his manic hyper-confidence or in conjunction with or in conflict with his sick mind's need to persuade itself of health. The factors that we have followed in his action—the drive of his social conscience, the manic impulse to preach, the rationalisations of his self-indulgence, the obsessions—all appear not only in the confusing digressions and excursions but also in his central work.

He was always learning—or rather he was always learning by fits and starts. He learned as the imaginative genius learns, by suddenly piercing to the heart of a thing and understanding it. In his manic moods he boasted of this power. Even in his depressed moods he very seldom doubted it. And he really had it.

But because of his manic hyper-confidence he always assumed that no further leap was necessary or possible until he was ready to leap again. In the field of Art he knew all that he ever was to know by the time he was forty. Thereafter he merely restated and reillustrated fragments of his earlier theories, corrected some minor errors, and used the contemplation of works of art as a means of satisfying his morbid impulse to perseverate and of relieving his obsessions. As far as art was concerned his receptivity closed down in 1859. But he had already begun to leap from point to point in another field. He began to know something of Social and Political Economy at the age of thirty, and he knew all he was to know by the age of forty-two. But again he had already started on another exploration—the exploration of the problem of War. In that field he had realised nothing at all till he was forty; but from 1859 onwards he leapt from comprehension to comprehension. And the points at which he arrived—at forty, forty-two and sixty— in these three fields, are points beyond which, as my knowledge goes, few men, if any, have far advanced to-day.

RUSKIN AS ART CRITIC

HIS THEORY OF ART

'A Spirit does actually exist which teaches the ant her path, the bird her building, and men, in an instinctive and marvellous way, whatever lovely arts and noble deeds are possible to them.'

Lectures on Art, IV, para. 125.

Ruskin's art criticism, as it stands, is an appalling muddle. Students have always found it impossible to work back to an underlying system of artistic doctrine from his varied pronouncements on particular works of art. Even when it is suggested that he changed his doctrines from time to time all attempts to examine the pronouncements and deduce the changes of doctrine from them have always broken down. Moreover as his pronouncements on particular works are so various in character, and often appear merely silly or capricious, it is sometimes assumed by those who cannot be troubled to read the corpus of his writing that he never evolved a system of artistic doctrine which can be usefully applied at the present time to the contemplation of works of art; and that his contribution to the study of the artistic activity was already complete in the short sermon which he delivered at the age of four, when, mounted on the drawing-room sofa, he said with solemnity: 'People be good.'[1]

His contribution in this field was really more than this; and more people would understand it were it not that so many start to look for it at the wrong end. It is impossible to extract his artistic doctrines from the books and lectures of the later periods or from his pronouncements on particular monuments and pictures. His entire contribution to the study of art was made between 1843 and 1859 when he fashioned a polygon of doc-

[1] *Præterita*, I, Chap. I, para. 22.

trine as an answer to the question: 'What is the nature of the creative activity called Art?'

That answer can be found in eleven volumes which he published in the 'forties and 'fifties: the five volumes of *Modern Painters; The Seven Lamps of Architecture;* the three volumes of *The Stones of Venice; Lectures on Architecture and Painting* and *The Two Paths.*

After 1859 he wrote practically nothing about art for ten years. Then come the *Queen of the Air,* the successive courses of Oxford Lectures, *Mornings in Florence,* and so forth. These later writings contribute little or nothing to the theoretical work of the 'fifties. We get an added felicity of phrase here, an extension or a reservation or a new illustration there, and some arresting aphorisms. But fundamentally these later performances are the work of a man who has long lost faith in art as a worth-while activity, and who is entirely convinced that anything he may say of importance will fall upon deaf ears.[1] They are the work of a man who has long been unable to react to contemporary artistic creativity, whose mind is more and more disposed to flitter, and whose so-called 'art studies' have long been nothing but pleasant holidays with morbid perseveration in old grooves. The performances were effective; but the performer was an old actor who had played the part too often, and who either spoke and moved automatically, or else sought to relieve the tedium by fantastic gestures and improvisations on the text.[2]

[1] Cf. quotation at the head of p. 103.

[2] The last-named character appears in the *Queen of the Air,* 1869. Ruskin here invented fantastic interpretations of Greek myths because he realised that very little Greek art was in existence, and he had always found most of the surviving fragments uninteresting. He had to learn to talk about the Greeks in preparation for a University appointment, and he relieved his boredom by the fantastic inventions (cf. above, p. 89.) These inventions seem to me different in character from the rambling obscurantism in *Munera Pulveris,* 1863, and the word-jingling word-associations of the essays in the *Cestus of Aglaia,* spring, 1865 (cf. below, p. 360 *et seq.*). I imagine that many of the improvisations in the Oxford Lectures in the 'seventies and 'eighties—of most of which we have no records—were also something like the old actor's boredom with his part and contempt for his audience. Herkomer described them as follows: 'It was

To the student of art who wants to discover Ruskin's theory of the artistic activity the later lectures and writings are thus quite useless, unless he is already acquainted with the early thesis as a whole, and can recognise the scattered references to it. Students will therefore do well to leave on one side not only all Ruskin's pronouncements on particular pictures but also all his later writings about art; and to begin the examination of his contribution to the subject by seeking the central theory in the early books.

That theory is ascertainable and is well worth seeking. To understand it we must follow him as he arrived at one doctrine after another in the 'forties and the 'fifties; and to do this we must begin at the beginning of the eleven volumes and work through them to the end.

We must begin then at the beginning with the boy Ruskin driving in his father's carriage through the English counties, and behind his father's postillion in France and Italy and High Savoy. It is usually suggested (even the Editors of the Library Edition are not guiltless) that as a result of this driving, Ruskin had acquired familiarity with most of the works of art in private collections in England and in the museums and churches in France and Italy by the time he wrote *Modern Painters, I*, at the age of twenty-three. But this is an error. It is impossible for a trained adult to acquire any real knowledge of pictures shown by a housekeeper for a few minutes beneath a half-lifted dust cloth in a half-shuttered room; and Ruskin was a child of five when he was first shown the English noblemen's pictures under these conditions, and on the later tours in England he was not concerned with pictures at all.[1] Nor in fact did he acquire much knowledge of the old masters on the early Continental tours, as we see if we examine these travels in detail.

The first considerable tour was in 1833 when he was four-

painful to his friends who . . . so plainly saw how he played to the gallery, how, in the perversity of spirit that sometimes overtook that brilliant mind, he seemed only to wish to arouse hilarity among the undergraduates . . .' (*The Herkomers*, Vol. II, p. 87).

[1] *Præterita*, I, Chap. XII, paras. 244 and 245.

teen. He had Rogers' *Italy* in the carriage and went from Calais to Brussels, thence to Aix-la-Chapelle and Cologne; then Heidelberg, Strasbourg, to Schaffhausen; then Constance, the Splügen, to Como, Milan, Maggiore, Turin, the great St. Bernard, Chamonix; and back through Paris, where he was sent to the Louvre with the courier and made a sketch from Rembrandt's *Supper at Emmaus*.[1]

He kept a diary of this tour which he worked up, on his return, into an illustrated prose and verse account in imitation of Rogers' *Italy*. In this account, called *A Tour on the Continent*, there are only two references to pictures: the first is to a work, said to be by Michelangelo, seen 'when it was pitch dark', in a place where no work by Michelangelo has ever existed—the Hôtel de Ville at Aix-la-Chapelle[2]; and the second is to a picture by Rubens which, he states, he did not go to see.[3]

The next tour was in 1835. The party went from Calais to Abbeville, Rouen and Paris; thence Dijon and Geneva, Chamonix, the Great St. Bernard, the Swiss Oberland, Innsbruck, the Stelvio, Como, Verona, Venice, Salzburg, possibly Munich, Strasbourg, and back home by Paris. Ruskin, now sixteen, kept an illustrated diary and wrote poems, some of which he sent to relations in letters; he sketched, made geological charts in an exercise book, and recorded the variations of blue in the sky with a cyanometer of his own construction.[4] On his return he wrote more poems, including one called *Venice* and another called *A Tour through France*. There seem to be no references at all to pictures in these productions. And this is comprehensible, firstly because he had been ill with pleurisy before he started on this tour and he was, of course, treated as an invalid by his parents and not allowed to tire himself in museums and churches;[5] and secondly because, as can be seen by the itinerary, the opportunities for studying the old masters on this tour

[1] *Præterita*, I, Chap. IV, para. 94.
[2] *A Tour on the Continent*, 'Aix-la-Chapelle'.
[3] *A Tour on the Continent*, 'Cologne'.
[4] *Præterita*, I, Chap. VIII, para, 176.
[5] *Præterita*, I, Chap. VIII, para. 176.

consisted of two days in Paris on the way out, four days in
Venice, and two or three in Paris again on the way back. There
was plenty for a boy of sixteen to see on a first four-day visit
to Venice without examining old pictures; there was also plenty
to see in Paris, as we know from his own words:

> 'When you've walked up the Rue de la Paix at Paris,
> Been to the Louvre, and the Tuileries,
> And to Versailles, although to go so far is
> A thing not quite consistent with your ease,
> And—but the mass of objects quite a bar is
> To my describing what the traveller sees.
> You who have ever been to Paris, know:
> And you who have not been to Paris—go!'[1]

Moreover in Paris there were the daughters of his father's
French partner, one of whom proved more attractive than the
pictures in the Louvre.

Ruskin's passion for Adèle, his new life in Oxford, and his
youthful 'craze' for Turner occupied him till the nervous breakdown in the summer of 1840. Then, as will be recalled, the
family started in September for the South and remained abroad
till June of the following year.

They went straight down, this time, without touching Paris,
to Nice; thence to Italy, where they remained for eight months
visiting most of the Italian towns, with a fortnight in Florence,
a week in Venice, six weeks in Naples and two months in Rome.
But Ruskin did not spend his time in detailed and daily study
of the old masters. It is true that he now had opportunities for
this study; but he did not take them. The journey had been
undertaken to cure him of an illness feared to be consumption;
he was treated as an invalid, not permitted to fatigue himself,
and not allowed to work or even 'saunter' in cold galleries.[2] He
was melancholic and believed himself to be dying. His main
interest was his own health and his own dejected morale; his
main occupation was not looking at pictures, but seeking relief
from thought in the way that he was to seek it all his life—the
sketching of 'picturesque bits'.[3] Moreover his bigoted mother

[1] *A Tour through France*, Canto I, Stanza 14.
[2] Letter to the Rev. Thomas Dale, Rome, Dec. 31, 1840.
[3] *Præterita*, II, Chap. III, para. 50 (first draft), and Chap. II, paras. 37
and 38.

was in charge of the proceedings; approaching Rome she had 'observed with triumph that every mile the road got worse';[1] she did not intend to permit her son to stand about and stare at pictures in Roman Catholic churches and catch yet another disease from Italian peasants;[2] and as for the pagan pictures of naked women—the less time he spent with them also the better. Nor at that time had Ruskin himself any impulse towards such studies. He was frightened by the pagan pictures, convinced that Papist art was naturally evil, and that the guilt of the Papacy was the cause of the malaria in the Campagna.[3] And he set aside all the religious painting in Italy, 'frescoes, tempera, what not' as 'mere zero' and not worth looking at.[4]

It is clear that he learned practically nothing of the old masters on this journey. When his health improved he walked through some of the galleries, but made no attempt at study; and he did not go to see the frescoes in the churches. His interest in old pictures of all kinds was languid. In Rome he still had Turner in his head: 'He is the epitome of all art, the concentration of all power; there is nothing that ever artist was celebrated for, that he cannot do better than the most celebrated.'[5] At Pisa he did not go to the Campo Santo to see the frescoes byOrcagna and Gozzoli but got giddy instead 'on its nasty, squinting tower'.[6] At Genoa he did not hunt out Van Dyck's portraits in the palaces,[7] but bought velvet[8] and made sketches of the port.[9] In Florence he waved aside the whole collection in the Uffizi as 'an unbecoming medley got together by people who knew nothing and cared less than nothing about the arts';[10] and his interest was not aroused by the Primitives, or

[1] Præterita, II, Chap. II, para. 30 .
[2] A Tour through France, Canto I, Stanza 7.
[3] Præterita, II, Chap. II, para. 33.
[4] Præterita, II, Chap. II, para. 29.
[5] Letter to a College Friend, from Rome, Dec. 3, 1840.
[6] Ibid. and Epilogue (1883) to Modern Painters, II.
[7] Præterita, II, Chap. II, para. 24.
[8] Letter to a College Friend, from Rome, Dec. 3, 1840.
[9] Præterita, II, Chap. II, para. 24.
[10] Præterita, II, Chap. II, para. 29.

Fra Angelico, Perugino or Botticelli.[1] In Venice he had no desire to look at the works of the Venetian masters and he did not 'see anything particular in the flesh colour of Titian'.[2] In Rome he merely looked long enough at Domenichino to pronounce him abominable,[3] long enough at Michelangelo to decide to rank him with the great names (i.e. with Rubens, Sir Joshua Reynolds, Gainsborough, Van Dyck, Velasquez and Turner),[4] and long enough at Raphael to decide that he might possibly admire him later.[5] That was the extent of his knowledge of the old masters when in 1841 at the age of twenty-two he returned to England and took his degree.

In the following year he went with his parents to Chamonix, and it was there that he determined to write a book in answer to the critics who had said of Turner's pictures in the 1842 Academy that they were produced 'as if by throwing handfuls of white and blue and red at the canvas, letting what chanced to stick, stick'.[6] And it is curious to note that he thus began his career as an art critic by protesting against this type of criticism, and that he encountered his chief rebuff as an art critic when, in the panic outburst against Whistler's *Nocturne in Black and Gold: The Falling Rocket*, he used almost the same words.[7]

A. C. Benson tells us that Ruskin sat down to write the first volume of *Modern Painters* 'in a light-hearted fashion . . . with his mind as clear as light'.[8] But, as we have seen in the Biographical Section, his mind was not clear; it had already been

[1] *Ibid.*, para. 34.
[2] *Ibid.*, para. 37.
[3] *Ibid.*, para. 34.
[4] MS. addition to *Præterita*.
[5] *Præterita*, II, Chap. II, para. 28.
[6] *The Literary Gazette*, May, 1842. Turner's pictures in the 1842 Academy included *Venice: View across the Grand Canal and Giudecca* (London, National Gallery, No. 372). *Snow Storm* (N.G., No. 530). *Peace: Burial of Wilkie* (N.G., No. 528). *War: the Exile of the Rock Limpet* (N.G., No. 529). For Turner's own attitude to hostile criticisms cf. below, pp. 265–6.
[7] 'I . . . never expected to hear a coxcomb ask two hundred guineas for flinging a pot of paint in the public's face' (cf. above, p. 143).
[8] A. C. Benson, *Ruskin, A Study in Personality*. London, Smith Elder, 1911.

much troubled; and he had already had one collapse into prolonged and serious melancholia with physical distresses. It was 'in height of black anger', impelled partly by his sense of justice, partly by his manic hyper-confidence, and partly by his manic impulse to preach, that he sat down to write the book: 'I heard falsehood taught', he said later, 'and was compelled to deny it.'[1]

He called the book, at first, *Turner and the Ancients*. But later he evolved, with the aid of his publishers, the more impressive title—*Modern Painters: Their Superiority in the Art of Landscape Painting to all the Ancient Masters proved by examples of The True, The Beautiful and the Intellectual, From the Works of Modern Artists, especially from those of J. M. W. Turner Esq., R.A.* And thus eventually the book appeared. The author's name, as everyone knows, was not given; he was described as 'A Graduate of Oxford'.

He began to write it at Chamonix in June, 1842. But he soon found himself in difficulties, because he found he knew scarcely anything about 'The Ancients' whose inferiority he had set out to prove. So he put the manuscript on one side, and chipped off bits of granite from the rocks for his geological collection, and stared at the snow landscapes and at the sunsets, instead.[2]

He resumed work in the winter in his new study at Denmark Hill; and in order to find examples of the inferiority of 'The Ancients' he paid visits to the Dulwich Gallery, which was near his home, and to the National Gallery, which, like the Dulwich Gallery, consisted, at that time, mainly of seventeenth and eighteenth-century pictures.[3]

[1] *Modern Painters*, V, Preface, para 8, and *Præterita*, I, Chap. XII, para. 243.

[2] Letters to W. H. Harrison, June 20, 1842, and to the Rev. Osborne Gordon, March 10, 1844.

[3] The National Gallery had been opened to the public five years before. In 1843 it consisted of less than two hundred pictures. The Dulwich Collection had been brought together at the end of the eighteenth century by a dealer for King Stanislas of Poland who lost his throne before paying for it. It had subsequently been enriched by various gifts and bequests including the celebrated Linley and Moody portraits by Gainsborough

RUSKIN AS ART CRITIC

Six months later the book was finished and Ruskin wrote as follows in the Preface:

'It is proper for the public to know that the writer is no mere theorist, but has been devoted from his youth to the laborious study of practical art. Whatever has been generally affirmed of the old schools of landscape painting is founded on familiar acquaintance with every important work of art from Antwerp to Naples. But it would be useless, where close and immediate comparison with works in our own Academy is desirable, to refer to the details of pictures in Rome and Munich; and it would be impossible to speak at once with just feeling, as regarded the possessor, and just freedom, as regarded the public, of pictures in private galleries. Whatever particular references have been made for illustration have been therefore confined, as far as was in my power, to works in the National and Dulwich Galleries.'[1]

Why, we may ask, did Ruskin not write the truth—instead of this series of pretentious and misleading statements? Why did he not write:

'The author, who is now twenty-three, has from childhood made picturesque sketches of landscape and buildings in imitation of Turner, Samuel Prout and David Roberts; and he has made a drawing of ivy round a tree.[2] But other interests and ill health have prevented continuous labour in practical art. The pictures by the ancient masters referred to in this book are mainly seventeenth- and eighteenth-century works in the National and Dulwich Galleries, because the author has little acquaintance with any others.'

The reader who has followed the account of Ruskin's mind given in my Biographical Section will know the answer. When Ruskin wrote this book his mind was in the manic position. When he wrote that nonsense in the Preface he was already so crazy that he believed it true,—already so crazy that he also

which arrived between 1820 and 1835. Records of visits to these galleries in 1843 are in Ruskin's Diary for Jan. 26, Feb. 9, etc.

[1] *Modern Painters*, I, Preface to first edition, reprinted in all others.
[2] *Modern Painters*, II, Epilogue (1883), paras. 1 and 4, and *Præterita*, II, Chap. IV, paras. 74 and 77.

believed it within his power to 'declare and demonstrate, wherever they exist, the essence and the authority of the Beautiful and the True'.[1]

In letters written immediately after its publication we see that, by mental processes which were to be repeated again and again later, the scope of this first book was expanded in the making to grandiose proportions:

'I undertook not a treatise on art or nature, but . . . a small pamphlet defending a noble artist against a strong current of erring public opinion. The thing swelled under my hands; before the volume was half-way dealt with it hydra-ized into three heads, and each head became a volume. Finding that nothing could be done except on such enormous scale I determined to take the hydra by the horns and produce a complete treatise on landscape art. Then came the question, what is the real end of landscape art? and then the conviction that it had been entirely degraded and mistaken, that it might become an instrument of gigantic moral power, and that the demonstration of this high function . . . was an end worthy of my utmost labour. . . .'[2]

What happened is apparent if the book be carefully read. Ruskin started out to defend Turner against the unjust critics. How was this to be done? By comparing Turner's work with that of other artists and showing the inferiority of the others. Where could he find the inferior artists? In the Dulwich and National Galleries which were full of Claude, Gaspard Poussin, Salvator Rosa, Cuyp, Berghem, Both, Ruysdael, Hobbema, Teniers, P. Potter, Canaletto 'and the various Van somethings and Back somethings'.[3] But then what was to be the standard of comparison? Superiority in conveying The True, The Beautiful and The Intellectual. And what is The True? What 'The Beautiful? What The Intellectual'? To those questions also he would provide the answers. . . .

Here he paused for breath and reserved the discussion of

[1] *Modern Painters*, I. Preface to the first edition, reprinted in all others.

[2] Passages run together from letters to the Rev. Osborne Gordon, March 10, 1844, and the Rev. H. G. Liddell, Oct. 12, 1844.

[3] *Modern Painters*, I, Part I, Sec. I, Chap. I, para. 4.

The Beautiful and The Intellectual for future volumes.[1] He must begin with The True because the critics had said that Turner's pictures were 'untrue'. He would show that 'The Ancients', whom the critics praised, were 'untrue' and that Turner was 'true'.

How could he prove that Turner's pictures were true? Obviously by proving that they were 'true to nature'. Was this possible? Assuredly—for John Ruskin. Had he not stared at sunsets from his childhood, noted the blue of the sky with his cyanometer,[2] studied geology, gazed into streams and glaciers? Had he not examined nature in every mood and on every scale? Had he not drawn landscapes and a sprig of ivy round a tree? And here he thought of Wordsworth's lines:

'Accuse me not
Of arrogance . . . .
If, having walked with Nature
And offered, far as frailty would allow,
My heart a daily sacrifice to Truth,
I now affirm of Nature and of Truth,
Whom I have served, that their Divinity
Revolts, offended at the ways of men,
Philosophers, who, though the human soul
Be of a thousand faculties composed,
And twice ten thousand interests, do yet prize
This soul, and the transcendent universe,
No more than as a mirror that reflects
To proud self-love her own intelligence.'[3]

Thus the stage was set—Claude and Gaspard Poussin, the proud philosophers on the one side, and himself and Nature on the other.

Himself and Nature. Ruskin had started to prove that Turner's work was true to nature. But before he knew what had happened he was proving that he, John Ruskin, had 'walked with Nature' and 'offered daily sacrifice to Truth'. Before he knew what he was doing he was claiming the right and the power to 'explain in what real truth, as far as it is ex-

[1] *Modern Painters*, I, Part I, Sec. II, Chap. III, para. 6.
[2] *Præterita*, I, Chap. VIII, para. 176.
[3] This quotation appeared on the title page of the *Modern Painters*, Vol. I, First Edition.

plicable, consists' and to illustrate the explanation 'by those pictures in which it most distinctly occurs or from which it is most visibly absent'.[1]

Thus he was led to those singular and celebrated performances in which he describes his own experiences of natural phenomena, and tests by that standard the degree of truth in the pictures by Claude, Gaspard Poussin, and the Dutchmen on the one hand, and in those by Turner on the other.

He takes the reader up the Alban Mount and describes his own impressions of the rocky slopes of La Riccia and the light on the landscape and in the sky; and then says: 'Tell me who is likest this, Poussin or Turner? Not in his most daring and dazzling efforts could Turner himself come near it.'[2]

Elsewhere he takes the reader up another mountain and gives him his own impressions of 'morning on the plains', 'noon with gathering storms', 'sunset in tempest', and 'serene midnight', exclaiming after each description: 'Has Claude given this?' And then he asks: 'When you are bowed down with fear and love of the Maker and Doer of this, tell me who has best delivered this His message unto men?'—a rhetorical question to which the answer is neither 'Claude' nor 'Turner'—but 'John Ruskin'.[3]

[1] *Modern Painters*, I, Part II, Sec. III, Chap. IV, para. 29.
[2] *Modern Painters*, I, Part II, Sec. II, paras. 2 and 3.
[3] *Modern Painters*, I, Part II, Sec. III, Chap. IV, paras. 30–34.

The central absurdity of the whole thing—Ruskin's identification of his personal experiences with 'the True', and his attempt to assess degrees of truth in works of art by comparison with that 'Truth'—is not apparent when the purple passages describing phenomena are removed from their contexts and printed in books of *Selections*. In these books the comparison between 'the True' (i.e. Ruskin's descriptions) and the pictures of Claude and his confrères on the one side and Turner on the other, are habitually *left out*. In Susan Beever's selections called *Frondes Agrestes*, for example, the refrain 'Has Claude given this?' is deleted throughout the passage referred to above. Thus isolated, the passages lose their original meaning and become fragments of literary art. But it was not so that Ruskin wished them to be judged—either when he wrote them or at any other time. When Susan Beever was compiling the book he implored her not to choose such passages. 'It is the chief provocation of my life', he wrote her, 'to be called a "word painter" . . . I hope you haven't filled your book with descrip-

RUSKIN AS ART CRITIC

In the early part of the book he had merged Turner with the prophets and the angels:

'Turner ... glorious in conception—unfathomable in knowledge—solitary in power—with the elements waiting upon his will, and the night and the morning obedient to his call, sent as a prophet of God to reveal to men the mysteries of His universe, standing like the great angel of the Apocalypse, clothed with a cloud, and with a rainbow on his head, and with the sun and stars given into his hand'.[1]

Then insensibly the image changed to John Ruskin as the Divinely inspired revealer. And the book ends with this new angel-prophet pouring 'good conserve of eternal fact, sweet in the taste and nourishing in the substance' into the ears of Turner himself, who is exhorted to 'utter nothing lightly', and 'do nothing regardlessly', to spend no more time on sketches, and to take more trouble to use only colours that will not crack or fade.[2]

Ruskin's mind was at the top of its vicious circle when he finished this first volume. In letters immediately after its publication we see him convinced that his own experience is 'Truth', that the degree of truth in works of art can be tested by comparison with that 'Truth'; that the parade of his own experience is the proclamation of 'the perfectness and eternal beauty of the work of God',[3] and that God had sent him into the world to exhibit and explain that perfectness and beauty to all mankind, including the artists:

'I am not engaged in selfish cultivation of critical acumen ... Consider whether the years from four to seven-and-twenty could be, on the whole, much better employed—or *are* on the whole much better employed by most men—than in ... exhibiting the perfection, desirableness and instructiveness of all features, small or great, of external nature, and directing the

tions. I thought it was the thoughts you were looking for' (Letter dated Aug. 25, 1874). Cf. below, pp. 357 *et seq.*
  [1] *Modern Painters*, I, Part II, Sec. I, Chap. VII, para. 6 (First Edition).
  [2] *Modern Painters*, I, Part II, Sec. VI, Chap. III, para 24 (First Edition).
  [3] *Modern Painters*, V, Preface, para. 8.

HIS THEORY OF ART

public to expect and the artist to intend, an earnest and elevating *moral* influence in all that they admire and achieve.'[1]

'God gives every man certain gifts which enable him to fulfil some particular function, and I don't think my fondness for hills and streams—being, as it is, so strong in me as to amount to an instinct—was given me merely to be thwarted.'[2]

'God appoints to every one of His creatures a separate mission, and if they discharge it honourably, if they quit themselves like men and faithfully follow that light which is in them, withdrawing from it all cold and quenching influence, there will assuredly come of it such burning as, in its appointed mode and measure, shall shine before men, and be of service constant and holy . . .'[3]

It was because he was confident that his descriptions of phenomena would 'shine before men and be of service constant and holy' that Ruskin delivered himself to the writing of them with such whole-hearted gusto. The writing of *Modern Painters*, *I*, satisfied every need of his nature and his mind. It satisfied his manic confidence, his impulse to preach, and his social conscience; and as he always enjoyed 'making some sort of melodious noise' about his experiences[4] he had that pleasure too. Moreover, as we know, he enjoyed writing about himself—and the real subject of *Modern Painters*, *I*, is 'Ruskin among the Mountains'. It was in this state of mind that he started on *Modern Painters*, *II*.

When he began to make plans for this second volume his avowed purpose was nothing less than to 'communicate . . . the love and knowledge of the universal system of nature'.[5] And looking ahead he decided that when he had done this he would become a White of Selborne and a lay preacher rolled into one.[6]

[1] Letter to the Rev. Osborne Gordon, March 10, 1844. The italics are Ruskin's.
[2] Letter to the Rev. Osborne Gordon, March 10, 1844.
[3] *Modern Painters*, I, Part II, Sec. I, Chap. VII, para. 8.
[4] *Præterita*, I, Chap. VII, para. 139.
[5] Letter to the Rev. Osborne Gordon, March 10, 1844.
[6] Letter to the Rev. Osborne Gordon, March 10, 1844, and MS. of proposed addition to *Præterita*.

Meanwhile the title of his book remained the same. But now to his discomfort he began to learn more about one half of his nominal subject—the paintings by 'The Ancients'. He was invited here and there by literary people and found to his astonishment that their acquaintance with 'every important work of art from Antwerp to Naples' was considerably wider and more familiar than his own. He visited various collections, including those of Samuel Rogers, and of the Duke of Marlborough who at that time still had Raphael's *Ansidei Madonna* at Blenheim.[1] He began to read art history, which he had never done before. He went to Paris; made notes for the first time in the Louvre; and discovered that if generalisations about art were to mean anything he must take account of figure painting as well as of landscape.[2]

In the following year, 1845, when he made his first foreign tour without his parents, he really began to look at the paintings in Italy. He spent a week in Lucca, another in Florence, a fortnight in Pisa, and a month in Venice; he also visited Milan, Bologna, Parma, Padua, Verona, Brescia and other places and looked at pictures and frescoes wherever he went. He was soon overwhelmed with shame at the thought of that 'Antwerp to Naples' in his Preface. Each day brought new cause for humiliation. Giotto, Fra Angelico, Orcagna, Gozzoli, the masters of the frescoes in Florence, the Bellinis, Titian and Tintoretto in Venice, came one after another to beat him to the ground.[3] In the end he decided that he must alter what he had written and insert references to all these Ancient Masters whom he had just discovered.

The revised version of the first volume appeared in 1846. Some of the more flamboyant references to Turner (including the Angel-of-the-Apocalypse image) and many other passages were cut out; several sections were largely rewritten; and a new long passage of some eighty pages—with allusions to the landscape and flora in the works of Fra Angelico, Giotto, Francia,

---

[1] Letter to a College Friend, Oxford, June 17, 1843.
[2] *Præterita*, II, Chap. V, para. 103, and Letter to Liddell, Oct. 12, 1844.
[3] Diaries and Letters to his father, 1845, and *Modern Painters*, II, Epilogue (1883).

Ghirlandajo, Masaccio, Cima, Leonardo, Giorgione, Giovanni and Gentile Bellini, Titian, Tintoretto, Nicholas Poussin and Gainsborough—was put in.[1]

This revision was of no real service to the book. The long passage about the Italian painters did not remove the fundamental absurdity of Ruskin's treatment of 'The True'; it contributed nothing to the book's first purpose—the exaltation of Turner; or to its second purpose which arose in the course of writing—the exaltation of Ruskin among the Mountains, because it was not inserted to contribute to one or the other, but merely to justify the claims in the Preface.

The new passage had on the contrary a weakening effect because it attracted attention from the present to the past. *Modern Painters, I,* in its original form had been a manic but at the same time an inspiring performance. It was a gesture of generous indignation; a call to the world to stop staring at the past and to begin to stare at the present; an ebullient tribute to the originality of a living man whose later work was misunderstood; and as such it revealed an author who had the stuff within him of a good and useful critic, with the courage to attack the worship of the past by artists 'who are glad to obtain credit for generosity and humility by exalting those who are beyond the reach of praise, and thus escape the more painful necessity of doing homage to a living rival'.[2] Condivi, writing a life of Michelangelo in the artist's lifetime, said of his contemporaries that they 'admired antiquity without criticism through a kind of jealousy toward the talents and industry of their own times'.[3] Ruskin setting out to defend Turner against the academic critics said exactly the same thing. He knew that 'he who would maintain the cause of contemporary excellence against that of elder time, must have almost every class of men arrayed

[1] *Modern Painters,* I, Part II, Sec. I, Chap. VII, paras. 6–47 (3rd edition). This occupies eighty-five pages in the Library Edition. Many commentators on Ruskin (Mrs. Meynell for example in her *John Ruskin,* London, Blackwood, 1900) have evidently mistaken this revised edition for the original text.

[2] *Modern Painters,* I, Preface to Second Edition written before Ruskin's work in the Louvre and Italy in 1844 and 1845.

[3] Cf. my *The Meaning of Modern Sculpture,* p. 56.

against him'.[1] But he faced the odium. His first book was inspiring when it appeared, and remains inspiring to-day, because it was written in this spirit. But when he wrote the revision he had ceased to 'follow the light that was in him' and failed to 'withdraw from it all cold and quenching influence'. He had allowed the flame of his enthusiasm for contemporary creativity to be damped down in Italy by his new experience of the past . . .

The inquiry into the True, the Beautiful and the Intellectual begun in *Modern Painters, I*, had been abandoned half-way through the book, as we have just seen. But before Ruskin left hard thinking and began to enjoy himself in descriptive discursions he had arrived at doctrines which can be set down as follows:

Great works of art are aspects of God.[2]

The greatest art is that which conveys . . . by any means whatsoever, the greatest number of the greatest ideas.[3]

The greatest artist is the man who has embodied, in the sum of his works, the greatest number of the greatest ideas.[4]

Great art is a creative not an illusionist imitative activity.[5]

The pleasure resulting from imitation is 'the most contemptible that can be derived from art'.[6]

Modern Painters, II, was written about the same time as the revision of the first volume. It continues the inquiry into the True, the Beautiful and the Intellectual until, as before, Ruskin became tired of hard thinking and began to enjoy himself—this time by describing the pictures which he had just discovered in Italy.

In *Modern Painters, I*, he had demonstrated 'the True' in the strange way just examined, and he had postponed consideration of the Beautiful and the Intellectual. When he took up the

[1] *Modern Painters*, I, Preface to Second Edition, as above.
[2] *Modern Painters*, I, *passim.*
[3] *Modern Painters*, I, Part I, Sec. I, Chap. II, para. 9.
[4] *Ibid.*
[5] *Modern Painters*, I, Part I, Sec. I, Chap. IV.
[6] *Ibid.*, para. 4.

second volume he had therefore to begin with 'the Beautiful'.

We have encountered his attitude to æsthetic pleasure in those undergraduate days when his conscience would not allow him to devote himself to artistic or scientific studies with any peace of mind.[1] In Rome in 1840, when he was twenty-one, he was already convinced that æsthetic pleasure, in itself, is a bad thing, and that it must be subordinated to the admiring-contemplative faculty, called Theoretic by Aristotle.[2] His attitude to the problem, at twenty-seven, was still the same. In *Modern Painters, II*, we read:

'The term "æsthesis" properly signifies mere sensual perception of the outward qualities and necessary effects of bodies . . . the mere animal consciousness of the pleasantness . . . And the general law for all these pleasures is that, when they are sought in the abstract and ardently they are foul things; but when received with thankfulness and with reference to God's glory they become Theoretic.'[3]

To Æsthesis he opposes Theoria, 'concerned with moral perception and appreciation of ideas of beauty'; Theoria which is 'exultant, reverent and grateful' perception; and concerning which the error is 'the considering and calling it Æsthetic, degrading it to a mere operation of sense, or perhaps worse of custom, so that the arts which appeal to it sink into a mere amusement, ministers to morbid sensibilities, ticklers and fanners of the soul's sleep'.[4]

But what *is* this Beauty which is properly apprehended by 'exultant, reverent and grateful' perception? Here is Ruskin's answer:

'By the term Beauty . . . properly are signified two things.

[1] Cf. above, pp. 38, 48 and 49.
[2] Letter to a College Friend, Rome, Dec. 3, 1840.
[3] *Modern Painters*, II, Part. III, Sec. I, Chap. II, paras. 1, 6 and 7.
[4] *Modern Painters*, II, Part III, Sec. I, Chap. I, para. 9. When Ruskin republished this book in 1883 (after it had been out of print for fourteen years), he added a footnote to this passage attacking the Æsthetic Movement: 'It is one of the principal reasons for my reprinting this book, that it contains so early and so decisive warning against the incipient folly, which in recent days has made art at once the corruption and the jest of the vulgar world' (cf. below, p. 254).

First, that external quality of bodies . . . which, whether it occur in a stone, flower, beast, or in man, is absolutely identical, which . . . may be shown to be in some sort typical of the Divine attributes, and which therefore I . . . call Typical Beauty: and secondarily, the appearance of felicitious fulfilment of function in living things, more especially of the joyful and right exertion of perfect life in man; and this kind of beauty I . . . call Vital Beauty.'[1]

Beauty and the manner of its apprehension being thus defined Ruskin asked himself how the artist's superiority or inferiority in its apprehension can be discovered in a particular work of art. And in answering this his mind soared again into manic flight. The degree of Beauty, he decided, could be discovered by comparing the work of art with nature and thereby discovering how much Beauty the artist had apprehended. Was this possible? Certainly—for John Ruskin. Had he not made geological and botanical studies and stared at mountains and sunsets? Had he not recently supplemented these experiences with studies of the human figure? Was he not specially equipped to apprehend and explain 'the universal system of nature' and 'the perfection, desirableness and instructiveness of all features, small and great'?[2] Was he not Divinely appointed for just this work? Had not God just given him a sign by curing him of diptheria?[3] All he had to do was to continue his appointed work and gradually 'examine and illustrate by examples', the mode in which the characteristics of Beauty appear 'in every division of creation, in stones, mountains, waves, clouds, and all organic bodies, beginning with vegetables, and then taking instances in the range of animals, from the mollusc to the man'.[4]

Here he again paused for breath and postponed this detailed examination and illustration for a later volume.[5]

Here we too may pause and inquire in what way his concept

[1] *Modern Painters*, II, Part III, Sec. I, Chap. III, para. 16 (cf. above, p. 189).
[2] Cf. above, p. 204.
[3] *Præterita*, II, Chap. VII, para 147 (cf. below, p. 331).
[4] *Modern Painters*, II, Part III, Sec. I, Chap. XI, para. 1.
[5] *Ibid.*

of 'the Beautiful' in this second volume differs from his concept of 'the True' in the first, and in what way the method now proposed for demonstrating the one differs from the method previously employed in demonstrating the other. If we so pause we find that there is really no essential difference between the two concepts; that the second in fact absorbs the first and gives it another name. Even Bosanquet, a specialist student of Theories of Beauty can discern nothing in the concept of Truth in the first volume which is outside the concept of Beauty in the second.[1] For when Ruskin proposed to demonstrate 'the Beautiful' by a gigantic scheme of empirical descriptions he was really only proposing to continue as descriptions of 'the Beautiful' those descriptions of natural phenomena which he had previously put forward as demonstrations of 'the True'.

At this point we must also ask: Where was the artists' position in this Ruskinian cosmos? The answer is that, in Ruskin's view, it was their function to apprehend and communicate *some* of the Divine characteristics of that Truth-Beauty of which it was his own mission to reveal the universal system and all the details. In Ruskin's view the artists were Ruskinettos. And thus he was led to another doctrine in his theory. Since the artists were engaged to some extent in the same Divinely inspired mission that he was engaged in they must be to some extent the same kind of men. It was clear that 'No supreme power of art can be attained by impious men'.[2]

Then another thought occurred to him. In the demonstration of 'the universal system of nature' by the examination of every division of creation—from the pebble to the mountain,

[1] *A History of Æsthetic*, Bernard Bosanquet (London, George Allen & Unwin), p. 459.
[2] *Modern Painters*, II, Part III, Sec. I, Chap. XV, para. 4. This doctrine was developed and changed as Ruskin's own religious thought developed and changed. In 1858 he decided that a great artist could not be a religious man in the ordinary sense of the word and that the 'monkish' painters were weak artists compared with Titian and Veronese. In 1874 when he was reverting to his earlier attitude he decided that Giotto's religion was an element of strength to him (cf. below, p. 234). The doctrine all the time was fundamentally the idea as put down in my summary of his art theory as a whole (cf. below, pp. 235–239).

the weed to the tree, and the mollusc to the man—which he had undertaken (and postponed), he would doubtless not have time for specific study of every detail. He would have to make assumptions and come to conclusions in some cases without specific study. By what power would he be able to make these assumptions and come to these conclusions?

In the manic confidence of this period the question was answered by his belief in himself as a divinely inspired interpreter of nature. He had no doubt that he would be able to do this because it was to do this that God had specially equipped him with the instinct for looking at sunsets, and for collecting geological fragments and for drawing ivy round a tree. He might possibly 'fall into many small errors' in empirical demonstration, but he would, of course, be 'right in tendency all the while and entirely right in the end'.[1]

From this he was led to grant a similar power to the great artists—the Ruskinettos. In their case he called the power Imagination—the faculty which is 'the highest intellectual power of man',[2] the faculty which knows instinctively the laws of Nature and Truth-Beauty, and sets all other laws or limits 'at utter defiance'.[3]

Here the theoretic section of the second volume ends—with Ruskin's theory of art much what it was at the end of the first volume. In these books, he said later, he 'declares the perfectness and eternal beauty of the work of God: and tests all work of man by concurrence with or subjection to that'.[4] He really believed at the time that he was doing this and could do it. He believed that a great work of art is the conscious revelation of aspects of God and that he, John Ruskin, had been appointed by God to set standards in such revelation and to decide in the case of particular paintings whether the revelation was accurate or not.

For the rest *Modern Painters, II,* expresses a conflict between Ruskin's social conscience and his manic impulse to

---

[1] *Modern Painters*, III, Preface, para. 3.
[2] *Modern Painters*, II, Part III, Sec. II, Chap. III, para. 4.
[3] *Modern Painters*, II, Part III, Sec. II, Chap. II, para. 15.
[4] *Modern Painters*, V, Preface, para. 8.

preach, both driving him to serve the present, and his new-found pleasure in escaping from the present to contemplation of the past.

He satisfied his social conscience and his impulse to preach by inserting some criticisms of pictures by living men in the Royal Institution (followed in the second edition by criticisms of some pictures in the Royal Academy of 1848); by sundry technical instructions to artists—on the proper uses of anatomical knowledge, pure and blended colour, and so forth; and in satisfaction of the same impulses he inserted a protest against railways in the Lake District, and another against 'those accursed sports in which man makes of himself, cat, tiger, serpent, chætodon and alligator in one; and gathers into one continuance of cruelty, for his amusement, all the devices that brutes sparingly and at intervals use against each other for their necessities'.[1]

This done he felt free to leave the present and to wallow in the past. The original purpose of the book—the demonstration of the superiority in landscape painting of the modern painters over 'all the Ancient Masters'—is now forgotten; Turner is only casually mentioned; and records of his own experiences before the phenomenal genius of Tintoretto and the dancing angels in Fra Angelico's pictures, replace the earlier records of his experiences of skies and mountains.[2]

In the first volume he had abandoned his subject half-way through for the new subject, 'Ruskin among the Mountains'. In the second volume he abandoned it half-way through for yet another subject, 'Ruskin and old Italian pictures'. And he was, for the moment, so far a captive of the past that he moans over the perishing and destruction of old buildings and places of historical interest, and gives examples of such perishing and

[1] *Modern Painters*, II, Part III, Sec. II, Chap. III, para. 33, Addenda; and Sec. I, Chap. I, Addenda; Sec. I, Chap. XII, para. 2; Sec. II, Chap. V, paras. 15 and 17. For a later reference to hunting, cf. above, p. 102.

[2] For his reactions to pictures by Tintoretto cf, below, p. 224. The celebrated purple passage about Fra Angelico's angels which ends *Modern Painters*, II, is a dressed-up version of a letter to his father. cf. below, p. 358.

destruction in Beauvais, Rouen, Tours, Geneva, Pisa, Florence Padua, Venice and other places.[1]

After publishing *Modern Painters, II*, he fell into the depressed and unhealthy condition when the evening sky seemed covered with 'swimming strings and eels'.[2] Then he married, and recovered, and wrote *The Seven Lamps of Architecture* and *The Stones of Venice* with his old assurance, tempered by a little caution.[3]

The main theories advanced in these books are well known. Architecture is treated as the moral and psychological expression of the nations and men *who carved and painted* the buildings into Divine significance; and 'the preference accorded finally to one school over another, is founded on a comparison of their influences on the life of the workman.'[4] In *The Seven Lamps of Architecture* we read: ' I believe the right question to ask respecting all ornament, is simply this: "Was it done with enjoyment, was the carver happy while he was about it?"'[5] And writing later of *The Stones of Venice*, Ruskin states that 'it taught the laws of constructive Art, and the dependence of all human work, or edifice, for its beauty, on the happy life of the workman'.[6]

We have here two separate concepts: first the idea of architecture as an art expressive of Divinity through its sculpture and colour and painting, and second the idea of the happiness of the workman being in some essential way concerned in it.

The first concept is explained in the Preface to the Second Edition of *The Seven Lamps of Architecture* and in the *Addenda* to the first two Edinburgh Lectures.[7] To understand its genesis

---

[1] *Modern Painters*, II, Part III, Sec. I, Chap. I, para. 7.
[2] Cf. above, p. 52.
[3] There is an 'Antwerp to Naples' passage in the Preface to *The Seven Lamps of Architecture*, but this time it is qualified: 'I could as fully, *though not with the accuracy and certainty derived from personal observation*, have illustrated the principles . . . from the architecture of Egypt, India or Spain . . .' (Italics mine.)
[4] *Modern Painters*, V, Part IX, Chap. I, para. 7.
[5] *The Seven Lamps of Architecture*, Chap. V, para. 24.
[6] *Fors Clavigera*, Letter 78.
[7] *Lectures on Architecture and Painting* (1854).

we must remember that Ruskin's mind had swung back to belief in himself as a special authority on aspects of God; and that, in his view, architects, in so far as they were properly called artists, were Ruskinettos. But he was not an architect. He had no practical experience of construction. Confronted with a building his admiration was not aroused by the sight of 'good and neat masonry' or the 'perception of proportion in lines, masses and mouldings'. It was aroused by 'reading the sculpture or painting on walls, capitals, friezes, etc.'.[1] He therefore decided that sculpture, painting and mosaic were 'the divine part of the work' which turned the 'dead walls into living ones' and that this part of the work could only be done by 'Deity, that is to say, those who are taught by Deity'.[2] Hence his doctrine:

'A great architect must be a great sculptor or painter'[3]; all high art consists in the carving or painting of natural objects, chiefly figures[4]; sculpture and painting are 'the all in all of the thing to be done'; the only admiration, properly bestowed on architecture, is admiration 'attached *wholly* to the meaning of the sculpture and colour on the building, admiration very regardless of general form and size, but intensely observant of the statuary, floral mouldings, mosaics and other decorations'.[5]

Ruskin denied the artistic character to proportions, relations of lines, masses and so forth in architecture; in his view these factors were within the province of mere building. He took this view because his interest was not aroused by these factors; and his interest was not aroused by these factors firstly because he was not an architect and secondly because he falsely assumed some opposition between geometrical and organic form, not realising that the first may be symbolic of the second.[6]

[1] *The Seven Lamps of Architecture*, Preface to the Second Edition (1849), para. 2.
[2] *Lectures on Architecture and Painting*. Addenda to Lectures I and II, para. 60.
[3] *Ibid.*, para. 61.
[4] *The Seven Lamps of Architecture*, Preface to the Second Edition, para. 7.
[5] *Ibid.*, para. 6. Italics are Ruskin's.
[6] Cf. below, pp. 224, 225, 239 and 240.

He started at the point where his interest began. He stared at the paintings, mosaics and coloured marbles on the walls, and the sculptures on the exterior of buildings. Then, to arrive at their meaning, he worked through them, as it were, to the mind and spirit of the men who made them, and then further back to the mind and spirit of the nation that wanted the workmen to make them in this way, and then still further back to the significance of the whole thing as a revelation or a denial of some aspect of God. And it was, of course, John Ruskin, Deity, 'that is to say taught by Deity', who was charged with the mission to decide what aspects of God were in question and whether the nations and the architect-sculptors had ignored or revealed them.

When we examine the genesis of Ruskin's second concept we find it still more personal. He was led to insist upon the happiness of the workman as a generalisation from, and a rationalisation of, his own conditions at the time when he was writing these architectural books. He wrote *The Seven Lamps of Architecture* in his house in Park Street, Mayfair, and when he wrote *The Stones of Venice* he was leading the pleasant life in a Venetian palace already described.[1] In these conditions he was happy and he was doing good work. When he had been unhappy in Italy, expecting to die of consumption at the age of twenty-one, and again in the year before his marriage, he had not been able to gather himself together for good work. It was therefore clear that no good work could come from a workman who was unhappy. Thus he arrived at the notion that men must be happy if they are to produce good architecture.

This Happiness-of-the-Workman theory had other aspects. It would not have been accurate for Ruskin to say that his own happiness in writing these books was *solely* the result of the agreeable conditions of his life at the time of writing. He was also happy, and he knew himself also happy, because he was enjoying his work, because he believed the work worth doing, and because the habits which the work involved were stimulating, varied and agreeable. And thus he arrived at the notion

[1] Cf. above, pp. 55 and 56.

that if architecture is good in kind then the work which it involves will make the workman happy.

Then we get the result of Ruskin's social conscience, which told him that no work was worth doing which was done for itself alone. Good work in his mind was serviceable work—work that 'would be of service constant and holy'.[1] He was happy at this time because he persuaded himself that—in cultivating his own happiness and contentment by accepting his agreeable life in London and Venice, by making drawings and notes of sculpture and mosaics, by dipping into archives and producing expensive and elegant illustrated volumes—he was really cultivating his power of service. And thus he arrived at a third aspect of the 'Happiness of the Workman' theory—the idea that the happy man is also the serviceable man and that 'the training which makes men happiest in themselves also makes them most serviceable to others'.[2]

These several ideas about the happiness of the workman are fused and confused one with another when they first appear in Ruskin's writings. Thus in *The Seven Lamps of Architecture* we read:

'We are, perhaps, hardly enough in the habit of inquiring, with respect to any particular form of luxury or any customary appliance of life, whether the kind of employment it gives to the operative or the dependant, be as healthy and fitting an employment as we might otherwise provide for him . . . We should endeavour, as far as may be, to make all our needs such as may, in the supply of them, raise, as well as feed the poor. It may be doubted . . . whether the habits of luxury which necessitate a large train of menservants be a wholesome form of expenditure . . .', and whether the jewellers 'whose dexterity' is 'simply burned out in the blaze of the tiara . . .' might not be 'far more healthily and happily sustained by being set to carve stone . . . I believe that most women would, in the end, prefer the pleasure of having built a church, or contributed to the adornment of a cathedral, to the pride of bearing a certain quantity of adamant on their foreheads.'[3]

[1] Cf. above, p. 205.
[2] *The Stones of Venice*, III, Appendix 7.
[3] *The Seven Lamps of Architecture*, Chap. VII, para. 9.

In this passage it is not clear whether the main objective of the meditation recommended is the happiness of the workmen, the abolition of menservants, the building of more churches, or Mrs. Ruskin's ultimate satisfaction at finding it impossible to mend her tiara because the jeweller who made it has become an ecclesiastical stone carver. Moreover, what if some second footman were to say that he was perfectly happy in opening the carriage door, and that the habits of cleanliness imposed upon him and the smart clothes which he was able to wear had given him a degree of self-respect which distinguished him from a gin-drinking labourer in a suit of torn shoddy? Might it not be argued that if the footman spoke thus it is clearly the rich man's duty to engage a few more footmen and make them clean, happy and self-respecting too?

These ideas, tortuously evolved to achieve peace of mind at the moment, were of great importance in Ruskin's subsequent work. They determined the character of his teaching in the 'fifties at the Working Men's College where he proclaimed it his object not to turn carpenters into artists, but to make carpenters happier as carpenters.[1] They influenced all his lectures in the 'fifties.[2] When he worked at Social-Economics between 1855 and 1862, he re-examined them and separated them one from another and made them an inherent feature of his social-economic theory.[3] And he fell back upon them for comfort in the 'seventies when he started *Fors Clavigera* to ease his conscience, and, as he put it, through his own happiness 'rightly help others'.[4]

In *The Stones of Venice* we meet another doctrine which was of great importance in his subsequent work. Ruskin always found it impossible to work in a precise, accurate and patiently constructive way. He consoled himself with the reflection that though he shirked regular precise labour and made mistakes in detail he was 'always entirely right in the end'.[5] Rationalisation

---

[1] Evidence to National Gallery Site Commission (1857), cf. p. 375.
[2] Cf. below, pp. 280–282.
[3] Cf. below, pp. 282–287.
[4] *Fors Clavigera*, Letter 61 (cf. above, p. 108).
[5] Cf. below, p. 230.

of this personal shortcoming now played a part in the formulation of a general law that 'Men are not intended to work with the accuracy of tools, to be precise and perfect in all their actions'[1]; that it is 'ignoble . . . to prefer the perfectness of the lower nature to the imperfection of the higher' seeing that 'in the works of man, those which are more perfect in their kind, are always inferior to those which are, in their nature, liable to more faults and shortcomings'.[2] We get this in a celebrated passage:

'In our dealings with the souls of other men, we are to take care how we check, by severe requirement or narrow caution, efforts which might otherwise lead to a noble issue; and, still more, how we withhold our admiration from great excellencies because they are mingled with rough faults . . . This is what we have to do with our labourers; to look for the *thoughtful* part of them, and get that out of them, whatever we lose for it, whatever faults and errors we are obliged to take with it . . . You must either make a tool of the creature or a man of him. You cannot make both . . . If you will make a man of the working creature you cannot make a tool. Let him but begin to imagine, to think, to try to do anything worth doing; and the engine-turned precision is lost at once.'[3]

This passage comes from the chapter in *The Stones of Venice* called 'The Nature of Gothic' which was reprinted, forty years later, in the 'nineties, by William Morris with a preface of his own. The doctrine became the creed of the Arts and Crafts Movement which has encouraged countless young ladies to assume that the value of a hand-made object is to be found in its imperfection and that the virtue of a hand-drawn straight line resides in its wobbliness. But though Ruskin was responsible for the doctrine, and derived satisfaction from it, he must not be held responsible for its misapplication in this way. In theory he accepted the 'rough faults' of the amateur workman. But in practice he would not tolerate them *in other people*. He drew attention, at all periods, in scores of passages, to the ex-

[1] *The Stones of Venice*, II, Chap. VI, para. 12.
[2] *The Stones of Venice*, II, Chap. VI, para. 11.
[3] *The Stones of Venice*, II, Chap. VI, paras. 11 and 12.

quisite accuracy and precision of fine craftsmanship; and he always set incipient craftsmen to outline leaves and twigs with the greatest accuracy possible, as a training in precision for eye and hand.

This personal inability to work with patient constructive accuracy was thus partly responsible for his view that the workman must be treated as a creative being and must not be degraded to a tool. But other factors, of course, contributed to the evolution of this doctrine which was to stand near the centre of all his subsequent work.

Ruskin recognised from the outset that great art was a creative, not imitative, activity. He assumed that its essence, the creative element, must inevitably be non-existent in the machine-made object. He did not conceive the possibility of a work of art designed, i.e. created, by a man and executed by a machine designed, i.e. created, for the purpose. He looked around him and saw that machine production had already destroyed craftsmanship, and he assumed that, because the manufacturer used machines to execute bad designs, all objects produced by machinery must always inevitably be badly designed.[1]

As he did not recognise the symbolic relation between geometric form and organic form (which I discuss later), but assumed on the contrary an opposition between their characters, he also assumed that the precision of the machine is in itself an evil and thus started the notion that the fallibility of handcraftsmanship is in itself a merit. Later when studying the social structure he saw that, in practice, the production of machine-made objects tends to involve the principle of division of labour whereby each man is continuously employed in monotonous gestures producing some minute part of an object without exercising the creative faculty at all. This confirmed his dislike of machine production. The founders of the Arts and Crafts Movement, followed by their descendants to-day, failed to see that Ruskin's three charges against machine production were different in kind; that though the practice of the

[1] He corrected this error later. 'Your manufactures become base, because no well-educated person sets hand to them,' *Aratra Pentelici*, I, para. 6 (1870).

division of labour destroys the creative instinct—and is therefore a bad practice—it does not follow that a straight line is metaphysically less good than a wobbly line or that the design, i.e. the created element, in a machine-made carpet is of necessity inferior to the design, i.e. the created element, in a carpet made by hand.

The architectural volumes of the eleven-volume work we are considering also contain, as is well known, an historical theory which Ruskin himself summarised as follows:

'The architecture called "Gothic", though in conception perfect, like the theory of a Christian character, never reached an actual perfection, having been retarded and corrupted by various adverse influences; but it reached its highest perfection ... about the close of the thirteenth century, being then indicative of a peculiar energy in the Christian mind of Europe.

'In the course of the fifteenth century ... the Christianity of Europe was undermined; and a Pagan architecture was introduced in imitation of that of the Greeks and Romans.'[1]

'The architecture of the Greeks and Romans themselves was not good, but it was natural and ... good in some respects and for a particular time. But the imitative architecture introduced first in the fifteenth century and practised ever since was neither good nor natural ... All the architects who have built in that style have built what is worthless ... We must give up this style totally ... and build henceforward only in that perfect and Christian style hitherto called Gothic, which is everlastingly the best.'[2]

This historical theory was wildly paradoxical at the time when it was written. But it has been generally assumed to be correct since the time when Ruskin's popularity set in. We find it echoed in Wilde's *De Profundis* and in Clive Bell's *Art*.

[1] Cf. *The Stones of Venice*, III, Chap. II, para. 101. 'This double creed of Christianity confessed and Paganism beloved was worse than Paganism itself.' And for the 'adverse influences' on Gothic, cf. *The Flamboyant Architecture of the Valley of the Somme*, where Ruskin states that the Reformation and the Renaissance were hostile to each other and both hostile to Gothic.

[2] *Explanatory Note* at the end of the *Venetian Index* (a collection of Plates with Notes supplementary to *The Stones of Venice*).

RUSKIN AS ART CRITIC

In so far as it has been contested since the 'seventies it has been
so mainly by derivative architects in the period which has followed the Venetian-Gothic building of the later nineteenth century—by architects that is to say who have not been willing to
build in Venetian-Gothic, but who have been unable to think
of any other way of building except the pseudo-classical style.
As an historical summary Ruskin's theory is as good and as
bad, as false and as true, as complete and incomplete, as any
other. It is one of those convenient historical finality-forms to
which I have drawn attention in *The Meaning of Modern Sculpture*, defensible if it is made to serve the useful purpose of encouraging contemporary creativity, but indefensible and dangerous if it is used to impede that force.[1]

Ruskin was not an historian; and the theory was not the
purpose of the book. In *Modern Painters, II*, he had never
been happy in his capture by the past and he had inserted topical exhortations to ease his conscience, as we have seen. In the
same way he could not be happy in concocting Venetian history
until he had persuaded himself that he was using it for some
present serviceable end. The historical finality-form in *The
Stones of Venice* was put together in order to introduce and
justify a programme of present action. Hence the famous opening sentence; and hence the programme for a Venetian-Gothic
renaissance in architecture.

This programme was, of course, an astonishing blunder.
Ruskin's historical finality-form would have been defensible if
the programme which it was designed to introduce had been a
means of furthering contemporary creativity. But his programme in fact advocated not *creative* but *imitative* architecture;
and he thus recommended the exact error which his historical
finality-form had exposed and condemned in the pseudo-
classical building of Renaissance and post-Renaissance times.

I have called this blunder astonishing because Ruskin nevertheless had a clear idea of the lines on which contemporary creative architecture would most naturally proceed—the lines on
which, in fact, it might have proceeded much earlier but for the
fanatical attention paid to Ruskin's writings in the last quarter

[1] *The Meaning of Modern Sculpture*, pp. 14–16 and 78–80.

of the nineteenth century. We know that he had seen those lines clearly before he started work on *The Stones of Venice;* for in *The Seven Lamps of Architecture* we read:

'There is no law, no principle, based on past practice, which may not be overthrown in a moment, by the arising of a new condition, or the invention of a new material . . . The time is probably near when a new system of architectural laws will be developed, adapted entirely to metallic construction.'[1]

Yet he did not see the significance of the Crystal Palace. He saw that metal and glass were destined to be cardinal materials in architecture, but he blustered against the Crystal Palace, saying feebly, that though buildings, largely of glass, might be Aladdin's palaces, and strike a new note in the annals of human splendour, they could never be admirable because all good colour is colour applied to opaque surfaces, and because 'the delight which we receive from glass painting is one . . . in which we should degrade ourselves by over-indulgence'.[2] When the Crystal Palace was opened at Sydenham in 1854 and the address presented to the Queen claimed that the building represented 'an entirely novel order of architecture', producing its effects by mechanical ingenuity—Ruskin replied with a pamphlet in which he described it as 'a magnified conservatory' and urged not the development of this new creative art and its organisation into dignity and style but—the formation of a Society for the Preservation of Ancient Buildings.[3] This was the more astonishing because Ruskin saw that this desire to develop metal and glass architecture was part of the natural creative energy of the time—comparable with the building of 'a screw frigate or a tubular bridge'.[3] Why did he not realise that new conditions and materials had already come to overthrow the laws and principles of past architectural practice, and that the

[1] *The Seven Lamps of Architecture,* Introductory, para. 2 and Chap. II, para 9.
[2] *The Stones of Venice,* I, Appendix 17.
[3] Twenty-three years later William Morris founded a past-loving Society of this kind.
[3] *The Opening of the Crystal Palace considered in some of its Relations to the Prospects of Art* (1854).

real task of creative contemporary architecture was the formulation of new principles and laws for those materials?[1]

The answer is partly to be found in his inability to conceive proportions, relation of lines, masses and so forth as the essence of architecture. He could not imagine an architecture symbolic of universal form, because he was held back by the presumed opposition between metaphysically evil geometrical form and metaphysically good organic form which was not 'precise and perfect' and which included 'carving or painting of natural objects chiefly figures'.

With his power of grasping first principles he saw at once the lines on which metal and glass architecture would naturally develop; but he spoke contemptuously of 'endless perspective of black skeleton and blinding square'.[2] His mind leapt, that is to say, eighty years ahead to the point where architecture stands to-day. But it did not leap to the point where architecture will stand to-morrow—to buildings growing from the top of shafts and leaving the ground free for vegetation and uncongested transport. He did not see that the concept of a town as a group of steel and glass boxes would have to give way in its turn to the concept of a town as a group of buildings in the form of trees or open umbrellas; or that houses would eventually hang from their roofs and not cumber the earth by standing upon it.[3]

Ruskin's concept of sculpture as the God-taught part of architecture, the only part revealing organic form, the 'all in all of the thing to be done', also played a part in his hostility to the new forms which the new materials would inevitably, as he realised, create. He saw that the steel and glass boxes, the 'endless perspective of black skeleton and blinding square'

---

[1] *Imagination in Architecture (The Two Paths)*, 1857.
[2] *The Two Paths*, IV, 1857.
[3] In such buildings, constructed high in the air round central shafts, the shafts will doubtless contain the lifts and services, and the foundations of the shafts the subterranean garages, storehouses and so forth. It should also be possible to erect shafts containing the central services and attach to and remove houses from them as bird boxes are attached to and removed from trees.

would have no organic need of sculpture, and in his view this meant that such architecture could never be an art.

His personal concept of architecture thus kept him from appreciating contemporary creativity in that art; but it led him to a profound appreciation of one kind of sculpture. He thought of sculpture at this period, and always, as sculpture on buildings. He was never interested in free sculpture in the round. He cared little or nothing for the fragmentary remains of real Greek sculpture in the round or for the so-called Greco-Roman 'copies',[1] or, later, for the concoction called 'Mausolus' in the British Museum.[2] He avoided writing about the sculpture at the Royal Academy and stated his view plainly—'I ought not to speak of Sculpture because I have little pleasure in it when unconnected with architecture; so that I only go into the Sculpture room to look at my friends' works . . .'[3]

Since he thought of sculpture fundamentally as sculpture on buildings he was led to the study of abstraction in art—to the consideration, that is to say, of art as a formative activity by means of which the artist's experience of phenomena is symbolised. And he came to the following conclusions:

'Symbolical expression which appeals altogether to thought, and in nowise trusts to realisation . . . is the *only one allowable in noble art*.'[4]

[1] Cf. above, p. 104.

[2] 'Charles Newton's pride in discovering Mausolus and their engineers' whistling over his Asiatic mummy, have entirely corrupted and thwarted the uses of the British Museum Art Galleries . . . If I showed you a photograph of the head of Mausolus without telling you what it was, I will undertake that you saw with candid eyes in it nothing more than the shaggy poll of a common gladiator' (Letter to the Rev. F. A. Malleson, April 23, 1881. For the British Museum's construction and reconstruction of the *Mausolus* in 1860, cf. my *The Meaning of Modern Sculpture*, p. 77. Ruskin has another tilt at it in *Præterita*, II, Chap. VIII, para. 155.

[3] *Academy Notes*, 1857. He stated this attitude again later: 'Sculpture which is prepared for private persons, to be kept under cover, will of necessity, degenerate into the copyism of past work, or merely sensational and seasonal forms of present life, unless there be a governing school addressing the populace, for their instruction, on the outside of buildings,' *Aratra Pentelici*, IV, para. 132.

[4] *The Stones of Venice*, III, Conclusion para. 19. (Italics Ruskin's.)

'Perfect sculpture must be part of the severest architecture . . .[1] the first office of that sculpture is not to represent the things it imitates but to gather out of them those arrangements of form which shall be pleasing to the eye in their intended places . . .[2]'

'Noble abstraction is taking first the essential elements of the thing to be represented, then the rest in order of importance, and using any expedient to impress what we want upon the mind, without caring about the mere literal accuracy of such expedient . . .[3]'

'The general definition of the true forms of conventional ornament is that they consist in the bestowal of as much beauty on the object as shall be consistent with its Material, its Place, and its Office.'[4]

He arrived at this understanding of the nature of sculpture at the price, as it were, of non-appreciation of contemporary creativity in architecture. And in this non-appreciation there was yet another factor. In spite of himself, and in spite of his resistance, he was recaptured by the past when he was studying the sculpture on buildings in Venice. The Siren city (then much more romantic in appearance than she is to-day after eighty years of 'making up' with restorations) had seduced him and clouded his brain. Just as in 1845 he had forgotten Turner and lost interest in creative contemporary energy in painting when he began to enjoy looking at old Italian pictures, so in 1850 when he began to enjoy looking at old Venetian architecture, he lost interest in the creative aspect of contemporary architecture. And thus instead of urging the creation and development of a new metal and glass architecture analogous to, though different from, the stone and glass architecture of the Gothic cathedrals—he urged the imitation of Venetian Gothic.

I must mention one other point before I leave these architectural volumes. Both *The Seven Lamps of Architecture* and *The Stones of Venice* contain violent attacks on the Roman Catholic

[1] *The Seven Lamps of Architecture*, Chap. IV, para. 34.
[2] *The Seven Lamps of Architecture*, Chap. IV, para. 31.
[3] *The Stones of Venice*, I, Chap. XXI, para. 10.
[4] *The Two Paths*, III, para. 76.

religion and Catholic Emancipation in England. These attacks have no connection with Ruskin's theory of art, and such connection as he managed to provide for them he admitted later to have been arbitrary and historically wrong. The attacks were the relief of his own fear of seduction by Roman Catholic ritual and I discuss them later in relation to the development of his religious ideas at various periods of his life.[1]

While Millais and Ruskin's wife were falling in love with one another at Glenfinlas, Ruskin was writing his *Lectures on Architecture and Painting* which he delivered in Edinburgh at the end of 1853. These lectures—in which he introduced the work of Millais and other Pre-Raphaelites to his audience— were mainly summaries of the theories put forward in the books just considered, and the student may therefore find it convenient to read them as an introduction to the theoretical sections of *The Seven Lamps of Architecture*, and *The Stones of Venice*.

After his wife's desertion in 1854 Ruskin returned, as will be remembered, to Denmark Hill. For the rest of the 'fifties he suffered more and more, as chronicled, from mobility of interest, and inability to work continuously at any one subject. His father continually urged him to continue *Modern Painters;* and to please him he resumed the book about 1855.

He was thus once more faced with the formidable programme which he had postponed half-way through the second volume —the plan to exhibit 'the perfection, desirableness and instructiveness of all features small or great, of external nature'; and the examination and illustration by examples of the mode in which Divine characteristics appear 'in every division of creation, in stones, mountains, waves, clouds, and all organic bodies, beginning with vegetables, and then taking instances in the range of animals, from the mollusc to the man'.[2]

He now began to see that this gigantic scheme of empirical demonstration could never conceivably be carried out; and also to suspect that his personal experience of phenomena could not

[1] Cf. below, pp. 329 *et seq.*
[2] Cf. above, p. 210.

constitute a criterion for assessing the degree of Truth-Beauty in particular pictures or other works of art.

We see his quandary in an essay of this period:

'A great artist represents many and abstruse facts; it is necessary in order to judge of his works, that all those facts should be experimentally (not by hearsay) known to the observer; whose recognition of them constitutes his approving judgement. A young man *cannot* know them. Criticism of art by young men must, therefore, consist either in the more or less apt retailing and application of received opinions, or in a more or less immediate and dexterous use of the knowledge they already possess, so as to be able to assert of given works of art that they are true up to a certain point; the probability being then that they are true farther than the young man sees. The first kind of criticism is, in general, useless, if not harmful; the second is that which the youths will employ who are capable of becoming critics in after years.'[1]

Ruskin knew that he had never indulged in the first kind of criticism. He knew that he had never been guilty of 'retailing and application of received opinions'. But he also knew now that in *Modern Painters*, *I*, and *II*, he had been guilty of making 'a more or less immediate and dexterous use' of his personal experience. He therefore said characteristically that of the two inadequate procedures the second was the one which would be employed by youths capable of becoming critics in after years.

He was, however, committed to his programme of demonstrating the perfectness of phenomena from the stone to the mountain, the weed to the tree, and the mollusc to the man; and as he liked dipping into geology and botany and zoology, and staring at the sky, and as the study of sunsets in High Savoy provided an excuse for escaping from Denmark Hill, he decided to continue the old scheme.[2]

---

[1] *The Arts as a Branch of Education*, 1857.

[2] When he republished *Modern Painters*, II, in 1883, he put the following note to the passage where the programme was set down: 'This was indeed the original plan of the book—formed . . . in 1845. I reflected upon it for fifteen years—and then gave it up. In another fifteen years the scientific world professed itself to have discovered that the mollusc was the Father of the Man; and the comparison of their modes of beauty be-

But now he felt lost in this vast, formless project with its countless facets. He found it difficult to select a subject to begin on and still more difficult to continue with a subject once he had begun. There were always a dozen subjects calling for his attention at the same time; and in his neurotic restlessness he could not resist the temptation to turn continually from one to another.

We have his confession of this written at this moment when the habit began to settle upon him:

'When I say I "have not time" for a thing I don't mean . . . that I have worked since five in the morning and that it is now twelve at night. But I mean that I have worked for four hours and that it is my time for going to see how the grass grows and what the ants are about and that I haven't time for anything but that.'[1]

That was the truth of the matter. Excessive mobility of interest, and inability to concentrate really began at this time, as I have already noted.[2] And in order to rationalise this continual turning from one thing to another, he now chose 'To-day' as his motto—though he might with greater accuracy have chosen 'This Hour' or still more accurately 'This Minute'.[3]

Hence the inconsequent and chaotic form of *Modern Painters, III, IV* and *V*. These books are really collections of essays —extremely readable and interesting—but not arranged in their logical order, or all connected with the main thesis of the work as a whole. Excluding numerous digressions and excursions the books contain the continuation of the passages on Imagination in *Modern Painters, II*[4]; a sketch for a history of

came invidious; nevertheless, it is possible I may have a word or two to say, on the plan of the old book, yet' (*Modern Painters*, II, Part III, Sec. I, Chap. XI, para. 1, 1883 edition).
[1] Letter to Mrs. Acland, July 10, 1855. For a reference to the crowding thoughts in his head, mentioned in the same letter, cf. above, p. 60; cf. also above, pp. 122, 156, 160, 165.
[2] Cf. above, p. 60.
[3] *Præterita*, II, Chap. VIII, para. 160, where he says that he inscribed this motto on his seal between 1855 and 1857—the time which we are now considering.
[4] *Modern Painters*, Vol. III, Part IV, Chaps. I-X; Vol. IV, Part V, Chaps. I-V; and Vol. V, Parts VIII and IX.

man's reactions to natural scenery as deducible from art and literature throughout the ages[1]; the continuation of the descriptions of Ruskin's experience of natural phenomena begun in *Modern Painters, I*, with special reference to mountains, tree forms and foliage, and clouds[2]; and the continuation of the praise of Turner with expositions of the concept of Art as conscious revelation of aspects of God.[3]

This Ruskin prefaced with the apology for his method from which I have already quoted and which I must now set down in full:

'The labour of a critic who sincerely desires to be just, extends into more fields than it is possible for any single hand to furrow straightly. He has to take *some* note of many physical sciences; of optics, geometry, geology, botany and anatomy; he must acquaint himself with the works of all great artists, and with the temper and history of the times in which they lived; he must be a fair metaphysician and a careful observer of the phenomena of natural scenery. It is not possible to extend the range of work thus widely without running the chance of occasionally making mistakes; and if I carefully guarded against that chance, I should be compelled both to shorten my powers of usefulness in many directions . . . and to lose much time over what work I undertook. All that I can secure, therefore, is rightness in main points and main tendencies; for it is perfectly possible to protect oneself against small errors and yet to make great and final error in the sum of work; on the other hand it is equally possible to fall into many small errors and yet be right in tendency all the while and entirely right in the end.'[4]

In the late 'fifties he delivered some lectures and addresses in circumstances which I detail in the Appendix.[5] These parerga fall into two classes: lectures called 'The Political Economy of Art' (afterwards published as *A Joy for Ever*), which really be-

---

[1] Vol. III, Part IV, Chaps. XI–XVIII; and Vol. IV, Part V, Chaps. XIX and XX.
[2] Vol. IV, Part V, Chaps. VI–XVIII; and Vol. V, Parts VI and VII.
[3] Notably Vol. V, Part IX.
[4] *Modern Painters*, III, Preface, para. 3.
[5] Cf. below, pp. 380 *et seq.*

gan his writings on Social and Political Economy and are accordingly discussed in that connection[1]; and miscellaneous lectures afterwards published as *The Two Paths*, which summarise, and in some points develop, the art theory contained in the five volumes of *Modern Painters* and the architectural books.

In 1858—1859 he enjoyed the sensual art of Veronese, and the promenade of pretty women round the bandstand at Turin, and 'Moët's champagne with Monte Viso ice in it'; he walked out of the Waldensian Chapel; and felt a manic desire to tell the world that the Bible was not the Word of God and that all Churches were forms of idolatry; he fell in love with the child Rosie; and he was 'seriously and despairingly thinking of going to Paris or Venice and breaking away from all modern society and opinion, and doing I don't know what'.[2]

This phase in his development extended his theory of art:

'Certainly it seems intended that strong and frank animality, rejecting all tendency to asceticism, monachism, pietism, and so on, should be connected with the strongest intellects. Dante, indeed, is severe, at least, of all nameable great men, he is the severest I know. But Homer, Shakespeare, Tintoret, Veronese, Titian, Michael Angelo, Sir Joshua, Rubens, Velasquez, Correggio, Turner, are all of them boldly Animal. Francia and Angelico, and all the purists, however beautiful, are poor weak creatures in comparison. I don't understand it; one would have thought purity gave strength, but it doesn't. A good, stout, self-commanding, magnificent Animality is the make for poets and artists, it seems to me . . .

'Is this mighty Paul Veronese, in whose soul there is a strength as of the snowy mountains, and within whose brain all the pomp and majesty of humanity floats in a marshalled glory, capacious and serene like clouds at sunset—this man whose finger is as fire, and whose eye is like the morning—is he a servant of the devil; and is the poor little wretch in a tidy black tie, to whom I have been listening this Sunday morning expounding Nothing with a twang—is he a servant of God? It is a great mystery. I begin to suspect we are all wrong to-

[1] Cf. below, pp. 280–286.
[2] Cf. above, pp. 66 and 75, and below, p. 275.

gether—Paul Veronese in letting his power waste into wantonness, and the religious people in mistaking their weakness and dulness for seriousness and piety. It is all very well for people to fast, who can't eat; and to preach, who cannot talk or sing; and to walk barefoot, who cannot ride, and then think themselves good. Let them learn to master the world before they abuse it.'[1]

'A great painter must necessarily be a man of strong and perfect physical constitution. He must be intensely sensitive, active, and vigorous in all powers whatever; gifted especially with a redundant nervous energy, able to sustain his eye and hand in unbroken continuousness of perception and effort . . .

'He is gifted by his exquisite sensibility with continual power of pleasure in eye, ear, and fancy; and his business consists, one half of it, in the pursuit of that pleasure, and the other half in the pursuit of facts, which pursuit is another kind of pleasure, as great, and besides sharp and refreshing when the other is at all deadened by repetition. Farther, it not only is his business to seek this pleasure, but he has no trouble in seeking it, it is everywhere ready to his hand, as ever fruit was in Paradise. Nothing exists in the world about him that is not beautiful in his eyes, in one degree or another; so far as not beautiful it is serviceable to set off beauty; nothing can possibly present itself to him that is not either lovely, or tractable, and shapeable into loveliness; there is no Evil in his eyes;—only Good, and that which displays good. Light is lovely to him; but not a whit more precious than shadow—white is pleasant to him, as it is to you and me; but he differs from you and me in having no less delight in black, when black is where black should be. Graceful and soft forms are indeed a luxury to him; but he would not thank you for them unless you allowed him also rugged ones . . .

'May he not be led, without suffering, but in his own work and his own way to that happy religion . . . in which this world may be enjoyed without forgetting the next? No; by no manner of means—at least of means hitherto brought to bear in this world's history . . . You may have religious shepherds, labourers, farmers, merchants, shopmen, manufacturers—and re-

[1] Notes on the Turin Gallery. Diary, 1858.

ligious painters, so far as they make themselves manufacturers
—so far as they remain painters—no . . . .

'Unless a painter works wholly to please himself, he will
please nobody;—he must not be thinking while he is at work
of any human creature's likings, but his own . . . "I alone here,
on my inch of earth, paint this thing for my own sole joy, and
according to my own sole mind. So I should paint it, if no
other human being existed but myself. Let who will get good
or ill from this—I am not concerned therewith. Thus I must
do it, for thus I see it, and thus I like it, woe be to me if I paint
as other people see or like." This is the first law of the painter's
being; ruthless and selfish—cutting him entirely away from all
love of his fellow-creatures, till the work is done. When done
he may open the door to them, saying calmly, "If you like this
—well, I am glad. If you like it not, away with you, I've nothing for you." No great exertion of benevolence, even in this.
But farther. In order to the pursuit of this beauty rightly, our
great painter must not shrink in a timid way from any form of
vice or ugliness. He must know them to the full, or he cannot
understand the relations of beauty and virtue to them. . . .

'As the great painter is not allowed to be indignant or exclusive, it is not possible for him to nourish his (so-called) spiritual
desires, as it is to an ordinarily virtuous person. Your ordinarily good man absolutely avoids, either for fear of getting
harm, or because he has no pleasure in such places or people,·
all scenes that foster vice, and all companies that delight in it.
He spends his summer evenings on his own quiet lawn, listening to the blackbirds or singing hymns with his children. But
you can't learn to paint of blackbirds, nor by singing hymns.
You must be in the wildness of the midnight masque—in the
mystery of the dark street at dawn—in the crowd when it rages
fiercest against law—in the council chamber when it devises
worst against the people—on the moor with the wanderer, or
the robber—in the boudoir with the delicate recklessness of
female guilt—and all this, without being angry at any of these
things—without ever losing your temper so much as to make
your hand shake, or getting so much of the mist of sorrow in
your eyes, as will at all interfere with your matching of colours;

never even allowing yourself to disapprove of anything that anybody enjoys, so far as not to enter into their enjoyment. Does a man get drunk, you must be ready to pledge him. Is he preparing to cut purses—you must go to Gadshill with him—nothing doubting—nowise thinking yourself bound to play the Justice, yet always cool yourself as you either look on, or take any necessary part in the play . . . Does a man die at your feet—your business is not to help him, but to note the colour of his lips; does a woman embrace her destruction before you, your business is not to save her, but to watch how she bends her arms.'[1]

In the 'seventies, when he himself reverted to something approaching the attitude usually called religious, he decided that Giotto though religious was as powerful an artist as Titian and that 'the Religion in him, instead of weakening, had solemnised and developed every faculty of his heart and hand'.[2] But for sixteen years, from 1858 to 1874, he believed that no great painter could be a religious man—in the ordinary sense of the word religious; and that—though no man could be a great artist who was not metaphysically speaking a good man—the great artist had a form of morality of his own.[3]

[1] The passages are from a Brantwood MS. dating from this period marked by Ruskin 'Part of unpublished old Modern Painters'; the full text is printed in the Library Edition as an Appendix to *Modern Painters*, II, though the editors draw attention to its later date.

[2] *Fors Clavigera*, Letter 76 (cf. below, pp. 352, 355 and 356).

[3] It was this attitude, combined with other factors, which led him to surprise people by defending Swinburne's *Poems and Ballads* against those who called them immoral and who asked him to protest against them in 1866. His replies on that occasion, published as addressed 'to a correspondent', are well known: 'He is infinitely above me in all knowledge and power, and I should no more think of advising or criticising him than of venturing to do it to Turner if he were alive again' (Letter of Sept. 14, 1866); 'Swinburne . . . in power of imagination and understanding simply sweeps me away before him as a torrent does a pebble. I'm righter than he is—so are the lambs and the swallows, but they're not his match' (Letter of Sept. 17, 1866). Ruskin was mentally and physically well at this moment. But three months later he had fallen into one of his bad depressions and we get characteristic transference of his morbid state to the object in comments on W. M. Rossetti's appreciation of Swinburne: 'I . . . entirely concur with you as far as you have carried it.

We have now reached the point where Ruskin's theory of art can be contemplated as a whole, and briefly summarised as follows:

Great art reveals aspects of God.

Great art cannot be produced by the æsthetic faculties isolated. The concept of an Æsthetic Man for purposes of art production and appreciation is an abomination and an absurdity. A great work of art is the product of the whole man. It is only possible when the whole man is, on balance, metaphysically speaking, good—though he need not in the ordinary sense of the words be religious or behave in a respectable way.

The value of a work of art resides in this metaphysical goodness of the artist who is Deity—because taught by Deity.

The great artist is a phenomenon of nature. He is of necessity 'a seeing and feeling creature . . . an instrument of such tenderness and sensitiveness, that no shadow, no hue, no line, no instantaneous and evanescent expression of the visible things around him, nor any of the emotions which they are capable of conveying to the spirit which has been given him' escapes him.[1] He sees life steadily and sees it whole.

But you have left the fearful and melancholy mystery untouched, it seems to me . . . the corruption which is peculiar to the genius of modern days' (Letter to W. M. Rossetti, Dec. 2, 1866). The other factors which contributed to Ruskin's appreciation of Swinburne were his natural enthusiasm for a man who had, as he himself had, the gift of rhythmic and emotive speech in a superlative degree; and the fact that Swinburne who was eighteen years his junior was to an extent his protégé. Ruskin had met him in 1858 when he was in Oxford in connection with the painting of the Oxford Union by Rossetti and his friends (cf. below, p. 380), and again, doubtless frequently, at Rossetti's; Brantwood papers included MS. copies of several of the poems in *Poems and Ballads;* a copy of the *Itylus* is dated 1863; he had received from Swinburne a MS. version, in his own hand, of *Before the Mirror* (verses on a picture by Whistler) in 1865 (cf. above, p. 78). He also owned MS. copies of *Félise* and *Dolores* (Letters to C. A. Howell, Feb. and April 2, 1866). He had already praised Swinburne's *Atalanta* in 1865 and had written in that connection: 'The grandest thing ever yet done by a youth—though he is a Demoniac youth. Whether ever he will be clothed and in his right mind, Heaven only knows. His foam at the mouth is fine, meantime' (Letter to C. E. Norton, Jan. 28, 1866). Swinburne was twenty-nine in 1866. Ruskin was forty-seven.

[1] *The Stones of Venice*, III, Chap. II, para. 10.

The great artist delights in his material and is influenced by it. 'Whatever the material you choose to work with, your art is base if it does not bring out the distinctive qualities of that material.'¹ 'All Art working with given materials must propose to itself the objects which, with those materials, are most perfectly attainable; and becomes illegitimate and debased if it propose to itself any other objects better attainable in other materials.'² 'Not only is it more laborious to carve granite delicately, than a softer rock; but it is physically impossible to bring it into certain refinements of form . . . Hence the sculptor of granite is forced to confine himself to, and to seek for, certain types of form capable of expression in his material; he is naturally driven to make his figures simple in surface . . . and colossal in size . . .'³

The great artist must have the art gift. He must start by mastering brush and chisel that he may evolve a technique for his purpose. The technique or language evolved by a great artist for his purpose is admirable in itself. 'It is well . . . when we have strong moral or poetical feeling manifested in painting, to mark this as the best part of the work; but it is not well to consider, as a thing of small account, the painter's language in which that feeling is conveyed.' The man who cannot manage his brush 'had much better have put his morality into sermons, and his poetry into verse, than into a language of which he was not master . . .'⁴ There can be no great painting except by men

---

¹ *The Two Paths*, V, para. 160.
² *The Stones of Venice*, I, Appendix 12.
³ *Modern Painters*, IV, Part V, Chap. VIII, para. 17. Whistler annotating the report of his libel action quoted the concluding words of this passage among his examples of Ruskin's absurd dicta. The conclusion reads: 'Had granite been white and marble speckled (and why should this not have been, but by the definite Divine appointment for the good of man?) the huge figures of the Egyptian would have been as oppressive to the sight as cliffs of snow, and the Venus dei Medici would have looked like some exquisitely graceful species of frog.' Isolated, this may seem silly enough. But the passage as a whole is simply a statement of that collaboration between sculptor and material which Michelangelo wrote about and which modern sculptors so well understand (cf. my *The Meaning of Modern Sculpture*, pp. 92–104).
⁴ *The Stones of Venice*, I, Appendix 15.

who know—apart from everything else—that 'a painter's business is to paint'. But there is no standard language of art. 'Nothing is a great work of art for the production of which either rules or models can be given.'[1]

Great artists are never concerned with illusionist imitation. Nothing worth revealing can be revealed in this way. 'We can "paint a cat or a fiddle so that they look as if we could take them up"; but we cannot imitate the ocean or the Alps . . . We can imitate fruit, but not a tree; flowers but not a pasture . . . And the pleasure resulting from imitation is the most contemptible that can be derived from art.'[2] 'Great art never deceives.'[3] 'The moment that art has reached a point at which it becomes sensitively and delicately imitative . . . its deceptions, its successes, its subtleties, become interesting to every condition of folly, of frivolity, and of vice . . . the largest bribes of gold as well as of praise are offered to the artist who will betray his art, until at last . . . it sinks into the cabinet ivory and the picture kept under lock and key.'[4]

Great art is a formative, inventive, imaginative activity. It is achieved by the artist's formative power combined with his power of sensitive apprehension of phenomena, and his power of abstraction. 'Form is form, *bona fide* and actual, whether in marble or in flesh—not an imitation or resemblance of form, but real form.'[5] 'To a painter the essential character of anything is the form of it.'[6] 'As soon as a great sculptor begins to shape his work out of the block, we shall see that its lines are nobly arranged and of noble character. We may not have the slightest idea for what the forms are intended . . . their likeness to anything does not affect their nobleness. They are magnificent forms, and that is all we need care to know of them, in

[1] *The Stones of Venice*, II, Chap. VI, para. 28.
[2] *Modern Painters*, I, Part I, Sec. I, Chap. IV, paras. 4 and 5.
[3] *The Seven Lamps of Architecture*, Chap. II, paras. 4 and 14.
[4] *The Study of Architecture*, Address to the Royal Institute of British Architects, 1865.
[5] *Modern Painters*, I, Part I, Sec. I, Chap. IV, para. 3.
[6] *Ethics of the Dust*, X, para. 107 (1865), quoted *Aratra Pentelici*, III, para. 99 (1870).

RUSKIN AS ART CRITIC

order to say whether the workman is a good or bad sculptor.'[1]
Great art must be inventive.[2] Those who have no invention
'are excluded from the first rank of artists'[3] and 'nothing can be
starker nonsense than the idea of practice being needed for invention.'[4]

All great art is in a sense and to a degree conventional, and
involves abstraction. 'The chalk outline of the bough of a tree
on paper is not an imitation; it looks like chalk and paper—not
like wood . . .[5] The arrangement of colours and lines is an art
analogous to the composition of music, and entirely independent of the representation of facts. Good colouring does not
necessarily convey the image of anything but itself. It consists
in certain proportions and arrangements of rays of light, but
not in likenesses to anything. A few touches of certain greys
and purples laid by a master's hand on white paper will be good
colouring; as more touches are added . . . we may find out that
they were intended to represent a dove's neck . . . but the good
colouring does not consist in that imitation but in the abstract
qualities and relation of the grey and purple . . .[6] There is not
any distinction between the artists of the inferior and the
nobler schools more definite than this:—that the first *colour for
the sake of realization* and the second *realize for the sake of
colour* . . .[7] Take any noble musical air, and you find, on examining it, that not one even of the faintest or shortest notes can be
removed without destruction to the whole passage in which it
occurs; and that every note in the passage is twenty times more
beautiful so introduced, than it would have been if played
singly on the instrument. Precisely this degree of arrangement
and relation must exist between every touch and line in a great
picture . . .'[8]

[1] *The Stones of Venice*, II, Chap. VI, para 42.
[2] *Modern Painters*, III, Part IV, Chap. III, para. 21.
[3] *Modern Painters*, III, Part IV, Chap. XVI, para. 26.
[4] Letter to Miss E. F. Strong (Lady Dilke), March 3, 1860.
[5] *Modern Painters*, I, Part I, Sec. I, Chap. IV, para. 3.
[6] *The Stones of Venice*, II, Chap. VI, para. 42.
[7] *The Stones of Venice*, III, Chap. IV, para. 27. The italics are Ruskin's.
[8] *The Two Paths*, I, para. 44.

'. . . Noble abstraction is taking first the essential elements of the thing to be represented, then the rest in order of importance, and using any expedient to impress what we want upon the mind . . .[1] Symbolical expression which . . . appeals altogether to thought and in nowise trusts to realisation . . . is the only one allowable in noble art.'[2]

Abstraction, in the hands of artists who are not metaphysically good, produces geometric art which is dead art. In the hands of a great artist it produces organic art containing 'fullness of life'.[3]

The life which the great artist reveals is organic life, the life which is identical throughout the universe, which is God in natural phenomena and God in animals and men.[4]

The noblest art is the art which reveals most of that Universal Life—and is 'thus capable of arousing the greatest number of the greatest ideas'.[5]

That as I understand it was Ruskin's theory of art. It is overlaid in the eleven volumes with countless discursions and obscured by what Ruskin called later 'the mischief of fine writing', and sometimes by writing which is bad with the badness of writing that does not say what the writer set out to say when he began the sentence or paragraph.[6] It is never stated clearly in its simplicity and the doctrines which comprise it are never related one to another. But it exists nevertheless scattered in the eleven volumes with one or two additions from other writings and the later works. And, as I see things, it is complete except in the following three points.

Ruskin had Baudelaire's concept of the Universal Analogy. The concept in itself was the product of his genius—though his assumption that he could demonstrate that Analogy in the whole system of nature from the weed to the oak tree, and the mollusc to the man—was born of the manic aspect of his illness.

[1] *The Stones of Venice*, I, Chap. XXI, para. 10.
[2] *The Stones of Venice*, III, Chap. IV, para. 19.
[3] *The Seven Lamps of Architecture*, Chap. V, para. 1.
[4] *Modern Painters*, II, Part III, Sec. I, Chap. III, para. 16.
[5] *Modern Painters*, I, Part I, Sec. I, Chap. II, para. 9..
[6] Cf. below, pp. 360 *et seq*.

That concept as I have tried to show in *The Meaning of Modern Sculpture* stands at the centre of the modern artists' creed. But the modern artists do not draw Ruskin's distinction between geometric and organic art. They regard the distinction as a fallacy inherent in the Romantic Movement, which postulated a wild, free, ragged 'nature' with no formality in its structure and opposed in its essential character to unity, harmony, and order. Science has shown more and more the amazing formality of natural form in the weed and the tree, the mollusc and the man; and the modern artists look upon geometric form as symbolic of this formality in organic life.[1]

That is one point where Ruskin's system can be amplified. In approaching the study of architecture he allowed himself to be seduced by his interest in sculpture on buildings which seemed to him metaphysically good because revealing organic form; he never arrived at the concept of architecture as a revealing art because he could not think of geometry—of abstract proportions, relations of lines, recessions, and so forth, as symbolic of organic form and life.

Then, his neglect of sculpture in the round must be remedied. He looked on contemporary sculpture, I fancy, as a species of 'escaped subsidiary', a power formerly evolved for a specific purpose, i.e. to render architecture revealing, but now continuing without relation to that purpose—like a wheel rolling for a time though detached from a car. There is really nothing in his theory which excludes the concept of sculpture in the round as a type of art different from but not less metaphysically good than sculpture on buildings.

Ruskin regarded sculpture on buildings as 'addressing the populace for their instruction'; and sculpture in the round as 'prepared for private persons, to be kept under cover' and so bound to 'degenerate into the copyism of past work, or merely sensational and sensual forms'. This concept of sculpture in the round was parallel to his concept of skilful imitative painting bound to degenerate to the picture 'kept under lock and key'.[1] It assumed the influence of the spectator as a factor determining the character and value of the work. And it was

---

[1] Cf. my *The Meaning of Modern Sculpture*, pp. 155–164.

connected with the third point where his theory needs amplification.

Ruskin did not draw a distinction between Intrinsic Value and Acquired Value in works of art. He saw that the value of the work of art derives from the metaphysical goodness of the artist, and that it cannot be assessed by its effects upon the spectator. But he did not press this to its logical conclusion and say that no one but the artist who revealed it could receive the full revelation of a work of art—though he got near to it at the moment when he said that 'great Art is of no real use to anybody but the next great Artist . . . it is wholly invisible to people in general'.[1] He did not advance from this to the concept of a different kind of value altogether presented to the work after its completion by the good or bad, wise or stupid, gross or sensitive spectator; and so to the contrast between the permanent invariable character of Intrinsic Value and the transitory variable character of Acquired Value.

He was held back here, I fancy, by his manic confidence which induced him to believe that he himself could assess all types of Value in works of art. He was always ready to say that a picture was or was not 'worth' so much money. He said that Whistler's *Nocturne in Black and Gold: The Falling Rocket* was not worth two hundred guineas because it disagreeably affected him. He did not realise that in so doing he was really assessing on the basis of his judgement of Intrinsic Value and thus confusing *Intrinsic Value* and *Exchange Value*. He would have been saved from this confusion if he had distinguished between the Intrinsic Value of a work of art which is unalterable and *not expressible in terms of Exchange Value* (which is what we mean when we say that a great picture is 'priceless') and the Acquired Value of a work of art which is variable and which *determines the Exchange Value* at any given moment in any given place.[2]

These, it seems to me, are the points where Ruskin's Theory of Art needs reinforcement. In the two books where I have

[1] Letter to Mrs. Browning, Nov. 5, 1860 (cf. above, p. 64).
[2] Cf. below, pp. 290, 293, 300 and 301.

attempted to contribute to the study of art—*The Modern Movement in Art* and *The Meaning of Modern Sculpture*—I have tried to complete his system in these particulars. With these additions his system seems to me to provide a basis for that psychological study of the art activity which is now in its infancy and will soon be developed. But that development, of course, will only be achieved by people who see, as Ruskin saw, that the postulate of an Æsthetic Man is as useless for serious study of the art activity as the concept of the Economic Man is useless in Economics.[1]

[1] Cf. below, pp. 290, 291–292, 300–301.

RUSKIN AS ART CRITIC

HIS PRACTICE AS ART CRITIC

With Ruskin's theory of art before us we can now turn to his pronouncements on particular works. But we are still not provided with a means of understanding those pronouncements—firstly because his theory set up an exceedingly high standard which could rarely be applied in particular cases; secondly, because his particular pronouncements have always to be examined in relation to the conditions of his life and the state of his mind at the moment; and thirdly because after the age of forty he cared so little about art, was so incapable that is to say, of reacting to contemporary creativity, that his pronouncements were mainly automatic attempts to capture personal satisfactions or to escape from personal distresses.

Up to the age of forty he was able to react to certain aspects of contemporary creativity. Thereafter he could no longer make that effort, and he only looked at old pictures—and that with an ever-increasing tendency to perseverate in certain grooves. After forty he took no interest at all in contemporary production; and even before that age there were times when he escaped from the hard task of understanding the present to the easy pastime of pretending to understand the past. After forty he became one of the thousands of people who imagine that they can understand the original art created by dead cultures though they cannot understand the original art of the living culture around them. In his early years he knew that no one can understand any aspect of human activity unless he can understand it in men who are alive. He knew this as late as 1856, when he pointed out that Shakespeare had learned to understand the past by reading the hearts and minds of his own day.[1] But when he began to lose the power of understanding contemporary creativity he tried to escape from his own dictum by

[1] *Modern Painters*, III, Part IV, Chap. VII, para. 20.

suggesting that in the nineteenth century it might be necessary for 'great men, having sympathies with earlier ages, to act, in this, differently from their predecessors'.[1] This was the signal that he had ceased to be able to understand or react to original art either of living men or dead men; because he had ceased to look to contemporary creativity for the standards.

In his boyhood he had been taught by Turner to look at mountains and skies. At twenty-three he had discovered the essential character of a great artist and summed it up by describing Turner as 'a great natural force in human frame'.[2] When, at twenty-six, he came upon the work of Tintoretto he saw the same character that he had discovered in Turner. 'None of the changes or phenomena of Nature herself', he wrote, 'appear to me more marvellous than the production of one of his pictures. Tintoret's work is actual creation; it seems one of the Powers of the Divine Spirit granted to a creature.'[3] Turner had given him the key to Tintoretto's pictures.

At thirty-nine, when he suddenly understood Veronese in Turin, it was the same character that he discovered; and if the reader will compare the Angel-of-the-Apocalypse passage about Turner quoted on page 204, with the passage about Veronese quoted on page 231, he will see that Ruskin expressed the same understanding and reactions in the same rhythms and almost the same words, though the second passage was written fifteen years later than the first.

His pronouncements on particular works of art were healthy and, as far as his influence went, useful, up to 1860; but thereafter they were unhealthy and harmful. I have said elsewhere: 'The study of art history is stupid and dangerous pedantry unless it helps us to understand and appreciate the original painting of our own day';[4] and elsewhere again: 'If the critic's studies of the past help his contemporaries to understand and so appreciate the original art of their day he is a good and useful critic; if his studies of the past do not affect the comprehension

---

[1] *Modern Painters*, IV, Part V, Chap. XX, para. 32.
[2] Letter to Susan Beever, undated, 1874.
[3] Letter to his father, March 13, 1852.
[4] *French Painting*, by R. H. Wilenski (Medici, 1931), Preface.

and appreciation of the original art of his day he is a critic of no consequence; if his studies of the past militate against the comprehension and appreciation of the original art of his day he is a bad and harmful critic.'[1] For sixteen years—from 1843 to 1859—Ruskin, led by his understanding of certain aspects of contemporary creativity, was able to understand certain aspects of creativity in the past; and he used that and his other experience of the past as a means of serving the present. Up to 1859 he did not bring back his experiences of the Old Masters in Italy and use them as a rod with which to chastise the creative artists of his own day. In the early days he used his experience of the fifteenth century Italian painters to further the cause of the Pre-Raphaelites. In 1851 he did not say that the essential good of Italian fifteenth-century painting could not be equalled by living artists whether they insolently called themselves Pre-Raphaelites or anything else—as the bad and harmful critics said at the time and as he himself would have said if he had encountered the Pre-Raphaelites for the first time in 1871; he said that these young artists were admirable because they were aiming stubbornly at Pre-Raphaelite honesty and attempting to bring a creative spirit into English art. And in so saying he was doing something healthy and useful.

It is easy nevertheless to exaggerate his services as critic of particular pictures even in the early period when his weight in the main was thrown on the useful side. To begin with, his influence in the 'fifties, as I show in the Appendix, was smaller than is commonly supposed.[2] Nor, as is sometimes suggested, did he present the Pre-Raphaelites with their artistic doctrines; on the contrary, he allowed himself to be diverted by them, for a moment, from his own. He did not 'discover' the Pre-Raphaelites of his own volition. The Brotherhood was formed in 1848. In 1849, at the Royal Academy, Millais exhibited *Lorenzo and Isabella* and Holman Hunt *Rienzi;* and Rossetti exhibited *The Girlhood of the Virgin* in the Hyde Park Gallery. Ruskin did not see any of these pictures because he was abroad

[1] *The Meaning of Modern Sculpture*, p. 19.
[2] Cf. pp. 369 *et seq.*

from April to September in that year. Rossetti's picture was highly praised by the art critic of the *Athenæum*, who described it as 'creditable to any exhibition' and continued: 'Its spiritualised attributes, and the great sensibility with which it is wrought, inspire the expectation that Mr. Rossetti will continue to pursue the lofty career which he has here so successfully begun. The sincerity and earnestness of the picture remind us forcibly of the feeling with which the early Florentine monastic painters wrought.' *The Times* had no notice of the Academy that year. The *Athenæum* gave Hunt and Millais advice and lukewarm praise. In the 1850 Academy Millais had *Jesus in the House of His Parents* (The Carpenter's Shop) and Hunt had *Claudio and Isabella* and *A Converted British Family sheltering a Missionary;* Rossetti's *Ecce Ancilla Domini* was rejected and shown at the Free Exhibition of the National Institute. Ruskin went to the Academy in 1850, but he was not attracted by the Pre-Raphaelite pictures. He confessed later that he did not notice 'The Carpenter's Shop': 'Mr. Dyce, R.A. . . . dragged me, literally, up to the Millais picture . . . which I had passed disdainfully and forced me to look for its merits.'[1] Even then he did nothing about it, though Dickens was thundering against the picture in a celebrated tirade in *Household Words* and other papers were equally hostile. It was not till 1851 that he was induced by Coventry Patmore (who was friendly with Millais) to write his letters to *The Times*, and these letters contained as much criticism and advice as praise.[2]

These letters to *The Times* and the pamphlet called *Pre-Raphaelitism* published the same year refer to the Academy pictures by Millais and Hunt. They do not refer to Rossetti who, as noted, had not exhibited at the Academy; and Ruskin does not seem to have been acquainted with Rossetti's pictures at that time. He does not seem to have interested himself in Rossetti until the Belfast shipper and collector, Francis McCracken, who had been persuaded by Hunt to buy Rossetti's *Ecce Ancilla Domini* in 1853, bought Rossetti's water-colour

[1] Letter to Ernest Chesneau, Dec. 28, 1882.
[2] Letters to *The Times*, May 13 and May 30, 1851.

Dante drawing an Angel in 1854 and sent the drawing to Ruskin for his opinion.[1]

Ruskin as an amateur champion of the Pre-Raphaelites thus began by encouraging Millais and Hunt. In 1851 he was thirty-two, full of confidence, plentifully supplied with money, and enjoying social distractions with his wife in Venice and London. Millais was twenty-two and Hunt was twenty-four. Ruskin looked upon them as beginners, and it was as beginners that he felt justified in praising them. His view then, as always, was that *beginners*, in order to acquire precision of hand and humility of spirit, should 'go to nature, rejecting nothing, selecting nothing and scorning nothing'.[2] Turner and Tintoretto were phenomena of nature who could make cosmic gestures; and he himself was engaged in the exhibition of the whole system of nature from the leaf to the mountain and the mollusc to the man; but the incipient artist, the Ruskinettino, though he might eventually be able to do likewise, must begin very humbly and precisely with the mollusc and the leaf. The pictures by Hunt and Millais in 1851 seemed to him beginners' studies

[1] This seems to have been what happened because, Rossetti wrote to Madox Brown on April 14, 1854: 'McCracken, of course, sent my drawing to Ruskin, who the other day wrote me an incredible letter about it, remaining mine respectfully (!!) and wanting to call. His manner was more agreeable than I had always expected . . . He seems in a mood to make my fortune . . .'

McCracken had been acquainted with Ruskin for about ten years, as we know from a letter from Ruskin to his father in 1845, where he says that he has picked up some bits of black marble thrown away by restorers of the Pisa Baptistery, and is sending them 'home to McCracken' (Letter from Pisa, May 21, 1845). McCracken presumably was his father's shipping agent for his sherry from Spain, and Ruskin knew him in this way and used his organisation for sending cases from Italy.

Ruskin does not seem to have seen Rossetti's *Girlhood of the Virgin* when it was exhibited in 1849, nor his *Ecce Ancilla Domini* either when it was exhibited in 1850, or before McCracken bought it, or indeed till 1878 when he saw it at Dunira in William Graham's collection to which it had presumably passed from McCracken's (cf. *The Three Colours of Pre-Raphaelitism*, paras. 1 and 2). The first mention of Rossetti in Ruskin's published writings seems to be in the Addenda to the 1853 *Lectures on Architecture and Painting* added in April, 1854.

[2] *Modern Painters*, I, Part II, Sec. VI, Chap. III, para. 21.

of this admirable kind. In his letters to *The Times* he praised the artists as beginners who had set about the regeneration of English art in the only right and possible way. Then yielding to his impulse to preach he told the artists the points where they had gone wrong and how to improve their painting on future occasions.[1]

His second letter in *The Times* had been printed with an editorial protest charging him with inconsistency in having praised both Turner, who was commonly regarded as essentially the painter of misty and indistinct effects, and the Pre-Raphaelites whose pictures were considered hard and crude. When he wrote the pamphlet *Pre-Raphaelitism* later in the year he was not really concerned with defending the Pre-Raphaelites but with defending himself against this charge of inconsistency. The pamphlet accordingly points out that in so far as Hunt and Millais are good artists they are good for the same reason that Turner was good, i.e. because they painted the truths around them as they appeared to their minds, not as they had been taught to see them 'except by the God who made both him and them';[2] Ruskin then improves the occasion by examining the relation of the young artists' works to Italian fifteenth-century painting in a useful way; and he hails Hunt and Millais as the founders of a new school of English art:

'The current fallacy . . . is that the Pre-Raphaelites imitate the *errors* of early painters. . . . The Pre-Raphaelite pictures are just as superior to the early Italian in skill of manipulation, power of drawing, and knowledge of effect, as inferior to them in grace of design . . . there is not a shadow of resemblance between the two styles . . . the Pre-Raphaelites imitate no pic-

---

[1] 'No defence can . . . be offered for the choice of features in the left-hand figure of Mr. Millais' *Dove returning to the Ark* . . . Next to this . . . is to be noted the defect in the colouring of the flesh . . . much of this evil may arise from the attempt to obtain too much transparency . . . close study of minor details is unfavourable to flesh painting . . . Mr. Hunt has a slight tendency to exaggerate reflected lights . . . if Mr. Millais has ever been near a piece of good painted glass he ought to have known that its tone is more dusky and sober than that of Mariana's window . . .' Letter to *The Times*, May 30, 1851.

[2] *Pre-Raphaelitism*, para. 54.

tures . . . they paint from nature only . . . but they have opposed themselves . . . to the entire feeling of the Renaissance schools, a feeling compounded of indolence, infidelity, sensuality, and shallow pride. . . . If they adhere to their principles and paint nature as it is around them, with the help of modern science, with the earnestness of the men of the thirteenth and fourteenth centuries, they will . . . found a new and noble school in England. If their sympathies with the early artists lead them into mediævalism or Romanism, they will of course come to nothing.'

Even in this pamphlet it is as one addressing beginners that Ruskin exhorts Hunt and Millais to 'paint nature as it is around them' as a necessary factor in their progress. Had he not felt bound to rebut the charge of inconsistency he would not have been so false to his own concept of great art as to write in a way that might lead people to assume that he ranked them with Turner. To defend himself he accepted for a moment the Pre-Raphaelite doctrines which could not be defended by his own art theory. And he has paid heavily for so doing. Because it has often been assumed that his 'go to nature, rejecting nothing, selecting nothing and scorning nothing' was the sum and substance of his art theory and that he supported the Pre-Raphaelites because they conformed to it. I have not been guiltless myself in thus misrepresenting him in days when my acquaintance with his works was casual. But as anyone can satisfy himself by checking the reference,[1] when Ruskin wrote the celebrated phrase in *Modern Painters, I*, at the age of twenty-three, he was addressing beginners and giving them practical—perhaps good, perhaps bad—advice. He was not there describing the procedures of great artists. Even at that early date he had already written 'The pleasure resulting from imitation is the most contemptible that can be derived from art.'[2]

The next stage was the discovery of Rossetti. Here Ruskin's attitude was quite different. He never looked on Rossetti as a beginner or as a Pre-Raphaelite. He recognised him as a genius —'a great natural force in human frame'; he felt it a privilege to

[1] *Modern Painters*, I, Part II, Sec. VI, Chap. III, para. 21.
[2] *Modern Painters*, I, Part I, Sec. I, Chap. IV, para. 4.

praise and finance him—though as always, with his manic impulse to preach, he spoiled everything by silly pedagogic advice and criticism.[1]

The third stage was *Academy Notes*. In these pamphlets Ruskin drew attention to still obscure artists with Pre-Raphaelite tendencies and upbraided a number of the most popular artists of the day. He picked out and praised *Burd Helen* by W. L. Windus, *The Stone-breaker* by John Brett, and *The Wounded Cavalier* by W. S. Burton at a time when all these artists were unknown and when Burton's picture was hung without title or artist's name because the labels had been lost. He discussed in detail the pictures shown by the Pre-Raphaelite leaders—Hunt's *Scapegoat*, Millais' *Autumn Leaves*, *Sir Isumbras at the Ford*, *The Vale of Rest*, etc., and he had the courage to risk the accusation of indulging in personal malice by describing Millais in 1857 as an artist who was becoming false to his own gifts. In 1855 he described the President of the Academy, Sir Charles Eastlake, as an imitator of the Venetians who had absorbed the errors of his masters but none of their virtues. In 1858 he wrote of Frith's *Derby Day*—(which was protected from an admiring crowd by a brass rail and a policeman)—as 'a kind of cross between John Leech and Wilkie, with a dash of daguerreotype here and there, and some pretty seasoning with Dickens's sentiment'. In the same year, of Abraham Cooper, R.A., then aged seventy-two, he said: 'It is interesting . . . to see that . . . one may write R.A. after one's name, yet not be able to paint a gutter.' Of David Roberts, a personal friend, he wrote in 1855: 'Is it altogether too late to warn him that he is fast becoming nothing more than an Academician?'

When he decided at the end of the 'fifties that English artists were not worth preaching to, he was led mainly by disappointment at his failure to capture Art Dictatorship. But there were also grounds for disappointment with the Pre-Raphaelites. It is undeniable that Millais had degenerated by 1857, as Ruskin indicated in his *Academy Notes* of that year; and it is arguable that Rossetti painted his best pictures and made his loveliest

[1] For Ruskin's personal relations with Rossetti and other artists, cf. below, pp. 264–278.

drawings between 1850 and 1860. When Ruskin wrote in 1860 that Rossetti was doing 'absurd things in the midst of his beautiful ones', and that Pre-Raphaelitism had been side-tracked into 'Mediævalism', as he had predicted it might be, he was not only rationalising a personal disappointment but writing defensible art-criticism as well.[1]

But though in the 'fifties his influence was useful in tendency, his pronouncements on particular pictures even at that time often reveal superficiality of interest and elements which were less in the nature of artistic judgements than attempts to capture psychic satisfactions or reliefs from psychic distresses. Take, for example, his well-known comments, in 1854, on Hunt's *The Awakening Conscience:*

'The poor girl has been sitting singing with her seducer; some chance words of the song, "Oft in the stilly night", have struck upon the numbed places of her heart; she has started up in agony; he, not seeing her face, goes on singing, striking the keys carelessly with his gloved hand.

'I suppose that no one possessing the slightest knowledge of expression could remain untouched by the countenance of the lost girl, rent from its beauty into sudden horror; the lips half open, indistinct in their purple quivering; the teeth set hard; the eyes filled with the fearful light of futurity, and with tears of ancient days. But I can easily understand that to many persons the careful rendering of the inferior details in this picture cannot but be at first offensive, as calling their attention away from the principal subject. It is true that detail of this kind has long been so carelessly rendered, that the perfect finishing of it becomes a matter of curiosity, and therefore an interruption to serious thought. But, without entering into the question of the

[1] The unhealthy Wardour Street 'Mediævalism' in painting which can still be seen in some aspects of popular art-production, began as a political gesture officially encouraged by the Bourbon regime in France in 1816, when it was desired to obliterate the Empire and the Revolution and join up with the old history of France—with Henri IV as a national hero. The first painters who responded to this official demand were some Lyonnais pupils of David; and the gesture was continued by Ingres. This unhealthy movement became entwined with the healthy Romantic Movement (cf. my *French Painting*, pp. 194–195).

general propriety of such treatment, I would only observe that, at least in this instance, it is based on a truer principle of the pathetic than any of the common artistical expedients of the schools. Nothing is more notable than the way in which even the most trivial objects force themselves upon the attention of a mind which has been fevered by violent and distressful excitement. They thrust themselves forward with a ghastly and unendurable distinctness, as if they would compel the sufferer to count, or measure, or learn them by heart. Even to the mere spectator a strange interest exalts the accessories of a scene in which he bears witness to human sorrow. There is not a single object in all that room—common, modern, vulgar (in the vulgar sense, as it may be), but it becomes tragical, if rightly read. That furniture so carefully painted, even to the last vein of the rosewood—is there nothing to be learnt from that terrible lustre of it, from its fatal newness; nothing there that has the old thoughts of home upon it, or that is ever to become a part of home? Those embossed books, vain and useless—they also new—marked with no happy wearing of beloved leaves; the torn and dying bird upon the floor; the gilded tapestry, with the fowls of the air feeding on the ripened corn; the picture above the fire-place, with its single drooping figure—the woman taken in adultery; nay, the very hem of the poor girl's dress, at which the painter has laboured so closely, thread by thread, has story in it, if we think how soon its pure whiteness may be soiled with dust and rain, her outcast feet failing in the street.'[1]

Here we have to some extent concocted interpretations, indulged in to conceal a fundamental boredom with the actual picture—a procedure rather like the interpretations to which Ruskin's boredom with Greek art and his automatic pleasure in the Spanish Chapel impelled him later in *The Queen of the Air* and *Mornings in Florence*.[2] We must also note here the image of the wet eyes and half-open lips—the image that was once Adèle and was soon to be Rosie; and the intrusion of a personal confession—the experience of morbid observation of

[1] This was published as a letter in *The Times*, May 25, 1854.
[2] Cf. above, pp. 89, 90, 193 and below, pp. 260 and 261.

details when the 'mind has been fevered by violent and distressful excitement'—which we also find three years later in a reference to moments when 'under some strong excitement of feeling, all the details—of visible objects presented themselves with a strange insistence and intensity whether you would or no, urging themselves upon the mind, and thrust upon the eyes, with a fascination which you could not refuse',[1]—and which we get yet again in his own accounts of his attacks of madness which I have already quoted.[2] Moreover even at this early stage we already get here an ingenious rationalisation of a personal characteristic. The words 'those embossed books, vain and useless—they also new—marked with no happy wearing of beloved leaves' are a defiant excuse for his own habit of buying mediæval manuscripts and writing upon them in ink and cutting out pages on the plea that books are for use and not for pleasure.[3]

We thus fall into error when we try to assess Ruskin's judgements of particular pictures even at this early period by relating them to his artistic theory—because it may be that there was never a time when he could look at a picture uninfluenced by his personal disquietudes. And, of course, if we assess his pronouncements on particular pictures by relating them to any theory *other* than his own we are simply not attempting to understand them.

When Ruskin was acting as to some extent a useful critic of contemporary art, i.e. from 1843 to 1859, his influence was relatively small. From 1859 to 1869 he wrote practically nothing about art; and he published no pronouncements on contemporary painting—though he alluded to Rossetti and Burne-Jones at the British Institution in June, 1867—in an unpublished lecture really delivered to please and help Burne-Jones.[4] Then for another sixteen years, from 1870 to 1885, when his reputation was daily becoming wider and his influence more

[1] *The Two Paths*, IV, para. 128 (Jan. 23, 1857).
[2] Cf. above, pp. 145 and 188.
[3] Cf. above, pp. 38 and 59.
[4] Printed from Brantwood MSS. in the Library Edition, Vol. XIX. For Ruskin's personal relations with Burne-Jones, cf. below, pp. 264 *et seq.*

powerful, he was an art critic who at his best was of no consequence and who at his worst was exceedingly harmful and bad—though his influence in other fields was altogether healthy.

When he ceased to be able to appreciate contemporary art, he persuaded himself, characteristically, that there was no contemporary art to appeciate. In his Oxford lectures I can recall no useful word reminding the youth of England that the past can only be understood when we have learned to appreciate the present. He praises the works of dead men—Turner, the Greeks, the Florentines, and so forth—but on the rare occasions when he speaks of living artists he speaks only words of derision and contempt, and this contempt and derision extend to members of the public who look at contemporary work at all. With the weight of his notoriety and the respect aroused by the republication of the books containing his art theory behind him, and the halo of an Oxford professorship round his head, he now talks of people who 'waste any quantity of time' in looking at contemporary work—at 'Mrs. A's sketches or Mrs. B's photographs',[1] at *Ramsgate Sands* and *Paddington Station* (Frith),[2] at the absolute rubbish professing to be a 'harmony in pink and white' (Whistler),[3] at Cattermole and Browne's illustrations to Dickens, in which 'every species of distorted folly and vice, the idiot, the blackguard, the coxcomb, the paltry fool, the degraded woman, are pictured for . . . the Cockney reader's itch for loathsomeness'.[4] He lashes out at the Æsthetic Movement—'pigs' flavouring of pigs' wash'— sought now in the model room and formerly in the Parc aux Cerfs;[5] and he tells his audience that contemporary artists are 'struggling to occupy a position of equality in wealth with the noblesse; that they are paid irregular and monstrous prices by an entirely ignorant and selfish public, and compete with each other to supply the worst article they can for the money'.[6]

[1] *Ariadne Florentina*, II, para. 47.
[2] *Ariadne Florentina*, IV, para. 40.
[3] *Val d'Arno*, III, para. 79.
[4] *Ariadne Florentina*, Appendix, para. 234.
[5] *Love's Meinie*, III, para. 130 (cf. above, p. 209).
[6] *Val d'Arno*, III, para. 79. When he resigned his Oxford Professorship after his 1878 madness, he gave as his official reason the fact that the judge-

The sum of Ruskin's services to contemporary creativity in art is thus really much smaller than is frequently supposed; and it is ludicrously small in relation to his opportunities both at home and abroad.

When he was on the Continent year after year, for months at a time, he might have familiarised himself with the creative artistic production of his day in all countries. But he only made one visit to Germany (in 1859, when he toured the galleries of *old* pictures after he had been made to look foolish at the National Gallery Site Commission where he had to admit that he had not seen Raphael's *Sistine Madonna*). He never set foot in Holland or Spain. He never paid any attention to contemporary Italian production; and he never troubled to look at contemporary work in Paris even in the 'forties and 'fifties.

He was in Paris in '35, '44, '48, '49, '52, '58, '63, '68, '69, '70, '72, '74, '76, '80 and '82. On all these occasions he was perfectly free to stay as long as he liked and to see what he liked; also he could always have made as many more visits to Paris as he chose and seen the annual and special exhibitions which were so widely and heatedly discussed. As a rich man, a collector and the author of *Modern Painters* and *The Stones of Venice* the doors of all the studios were open to him. But he

ment in the Whistler trial had nominally gone against him. 'I cannot hold a Chair', he wrote, 'from which I have no power of expressing judgement without being taxed for it by British Law. It is not owing to ill health that I resign, but because the professorship is a farce, if it has no right to condemn as well as praise' (Letters to Liddell, Nov. 28 and undated, 1878). His first act after recovery was a gesture of defiance in the shape of articles to the *Nineteenth Century* on contemporary painting (*The Three Colours of Pre-Raphaelitism*). But the articles were really perseverations in his former interest in Turner and the Pre-Raphaelites with whom he associated Burne-Jones. When he was re-elected (after his two following attacks) in 1883, the Oxford authorities proposed as a gesture of politeness and confidence that he should lecture on 'Recent English Painting', and thus it came that he talked of Rossetti and Holman Hunt, Burne-Jones, Leighton, Alma Tadema, Mrs. Allingham, Kate Greenaway, Francesca Alexander, Leech, Tenniel, Du Maurier, George Robson and Copley Fielding (*The Art of England*, 1883). In the choice of names here factors entered that had nothing to do with art criticism. I have referred to some in connection with Kate Greenaway and Francesca Alexander above (cf. pp. 173 and 174).

neglected these opportunities. He did not go to the *Exposition Universelle* in 1855 when Delacroix had a gallery of his own filled with thirty-five of his most celebrated pictures, and Ingres had another, and Courbet had a pavilion of his own; and there are no references to Ingres, or Delacroix or Courbet in his writings and correspondence.[1] He never mentions the name of Corot whose works were features of the Salons and in dealers' windows from 1850 onwards. He did not visit Manet's one man show at Martinet's in 1863 or the much-talked-of *Salon des Refusés* in that year—though the Salon was due to the personal initiative of the Emperor and Empress whom he so much admired.[2] He did not visit the *Exposition Universelle* of 1866 where Manet had his own pavilion, or any of the notorious Impressionist Exhibitions of '74, '76, '77, '79, '80, '81 and '82. He never mentions the names of Manet, Renoir, or Degas, nor even the names of Pissarro, Monet and Sisley, whose work, as an admirer of the light effects and atmosphere in Turner's later pictures, he might have been expected to appreciate. In 1883, when the Impressionists had already revolutionised modern painting by a system of colouring based on the spectrum, Ruskin talks of 'the darkness and distortion of the vicious French schools of landscape'.[3]

It was, of course, because he never made the effort to understand *contemporary* French painting that he never understood French painting of the past. He could never open the doors to the French old masters because he neglected to secure the necessary keys. 'The French, properly speaking,' he wrote in about 1878, 'have no school except of decorative art . . . and have never produced a single great painter. Watteau their best is still a mere room decorator.'[4] In the 'seventies the good critics began by understanding Renoir who led them to

[1] He refers to the pulling down of the Colonne Vendôme in *Fors Clavigera*, Letter 6. But he does not mention Courbet's name even in this connection.

[2] Cf. below, pp. 308 and 367.

[3] Note (1883) to *Modern Painters*, II, Part III, Sec. I, Chap. XV, para. 6.

[4] Note intended for the *Laws of Fésole*, 1877–1879. There is no other mention of Watteau in his works.

Watteau (and thence to Rubens if they wanted to travel further). Ruskin might have arrived at Watteau through Turner who told their common friend the Rev. W. Kingsley that he had learned more from Watteau than from any other painter. But he missed the key thus offered. In the same way he missed the key offered by Corot to Chardin and by Ingres to Clouet— though as Rossetti had published a poem on Ingres' *Roger and Angelica* it is odd that Ruskin paid no attention to that artist.[1]

For the same reason he was incapable of 'discoveries' among the old masters after about 1860. From that date onwards he looked exclusively at old pictures, but he had no power or desire to enlarge his experience. He went abroad year after year, but he always travelled on the old routes. As he never went to Madrid, he remained ignorant of the Spanish and Italian pictures in the Royal Collection. He included photographs of Titian's *Charles V at Mühlberg* and Velasquez's *Margarita of Austria on Horseback* (both in the Prado) in his 'Standard Series' in Oxford, but he had never seen the originals.[2] He knew nothing of Morales or of El Greco to whom he never refers; and the only reference to Goya is a letter from which we learn that he burned a set of the *Caprichos* in 1872.[3]

He went year after year to Italy and perseverated in old grooves. As he had no key to Piero dei Franceschi, and as none of the figures in his pictures reminded him of Rose, he never 'discovered' him and never refers to him except in one passage in *Fors Clavigera* where he states that his name meant 'Fran-

[1] In the same way it is odd that he paid no attention to Delacroix— because Rossetti, who saw his work in Paris with that of Ingres in 1849, was enthusiastic about Delacroix, much to Hunt's surprise. (Holman Hunt, *Pre-Raphaelitism*, I, p. 130.)

[2] Had he seen the portrait of *Margarita of Austria* he might have realised that only the horse and part of the background are by Velasquez. The picture is No. 1177 in the Prado. Margarita of Austria died in 1611 when Velasquez was twelve. Ruskin, showing this photograph with other examples of portraiture at an Oxford lecture said: 'If you do not like them, I cannot help myself, for I can find nothing better for you' (*Lectures on Art*, VII, para. 181).

[3] Letter to E. S. Ellis, Sept. 19, 1872.

cesca's Peter' because he was chiefly trained by his mother Francesca.[1]

He claimed to have 'discovered' Carpaccio in 1869; but his appreciation of the St. Ursula pictures was not an artistic judgement, but the relief of the Rose obsession as we have seen, and Carpaccio was quite well known and highly esteemed in England before that date, the National Gallery having bought one of his pictures in 1865 for the equivalent of £10,200 in present money.[2]

His first reference to Botticelli, whom he also claimed to have 'discovered', is in an Oxford lecture delivered in the spring of 1871, when he exhibited a copy by himself of some leaves in the background of the *Spring*.[3] But his interest in Botticelli's pictures soon became purely the relief of his obsessions. In 1872 and 1874 he began to see Rose images in his pictures, and then he copied the Zipporah in Rome, and the roses on Flora's dress in Florence as we have also seen.

[1] *Fors Clavigera*, Letter 22 (October, 1872). Vasari, who says that Piero was brought up solely by his mother, is responsible for this legend. Piero's mother's name was not in fact Francesca but Romana; and his own name was Piero dei Franceschi—Francesco being his father's family name. He was not exclusively brought up by his mother, as his father, who was a cloth merchant and calcolatore, was still alive nearly fifty years after his marriage. Piero was also sometimes called Piero Borghese because he was associated with Borgo San Sepolcro, where he was probably born. Ruskin might have been expected to take an interest in Piero because he must have been familiar with his two pictures—*The Baptism* and *The Nativity*, acquired for the National Gallery in 1861 and 1874 respectively, the second for the equivalent of £7,245 (£2,415) paid at Christie's on express instructions from Disraeli, who insisted that the picture should be acquired by the National Gallery (Sir William Fraser, *Disraeli and his Day*). I doubt if he ever saw Piero's works at Borgo San Sepolcro, which he seems never to have visited. He was at Arezzo in 1840 when he would not look at the frescoes in churches (cf. above, p. 197).

[2] The picture is No. 750 in the National Gallery, *The Madonna and Child with SS. John Baptist and Christopher and the Doge Giovanni Mocenigo*. It was bought as by Carpaccio for £3,400 from the Mocenigo family in Venice. It is now catalogued as ' School of Gentile Bellini'. Ruskin had nothing to do with the purchase.

[3] *Lectures on Landscape*, I, paras. 10 and 11. He placed the sketch in the Oxford Drawing School collection.

He arrived at Botticelli in the first place through his appreciation of Burne-Jones' pictures; and it is often assumed that he started the cult of Botticelli which prevailed in the later decades of the nineteenth century as a result of the popularity of Burne-Jones (concurrently with the cult of Velasquez which was a result of the popularity of Whistler). But Ruskin did not launch the Botticelli cult. It was already launched when in 1867 Rossetti had 'picked up' a Botticelli somewhere and hung it in his house. Swinburne's *Notes on Designs of the Old Masters at Florence* were published in the *Fortnightly Review* in 1868. The London National Gallery had bought a work ascribed to Botticelli (*Madonna and Child*, No. 275) in 1855, the *Adoration of the Magi* (No. 592) in 1857, the *Portrait of a Young Man* (No. 626) in 1859, and the *Madonna and Child* (No. 782, now considered a school piece) in 1867; *The Nativity* (No. 1034) bought in 1878 had been lent by Fuller Maitland to the Manchester Art Treasures Exhibition in 1857, where *A Young Man*, lent by Lord Northwick, had also been exhibited. Ruskin had nothing to do with the purchase of any of these pictures. He visited the Manchester Exhibition (though he had not been invited to assist in its organisation), but he did not notice *The Nativity*.[1]

The student must, in fact, discount all Ruskin's pronouncements of the 'seventies and 'eighties on Italian pictures and regard them not as serious contributions to the study of creative art, but as the result of potterings and as the reliefs of obsessions. And though he will find valuable flashes and incidentals in the later lectures and writings about art, he must not attempt to substitute them for Ruskin's main theory as put forward in the eleven volumes between 1843 and 1860.

On the other hand, to the students of the whole man Ruskin, the later lectures and writings about art are intensely significant, because in page after page we meet his secret shames and angers, fears and obsessions, his perseverations, and the curious

[1] Cf. below, p. 381. For his claim to have 'discovered' Botticelli and Carpaccio, cf. *Modern Painters*, II, Epilogue (1883), where he also claims—equally without foundation—that Turner, Tintoretto and Luini were unknown till he discovered them.

cross-flittings of his mind. It is pathetically intriguing to recognise the familiar features as they appear and reappear; to come upon a rant against Rose La Touche's theological pretensions in the Oxford Inaugural Lectures on Art,[1] and to read an attack on Faraday,[2] and references to Ruskin's relàtions with his parents, to Rose's relations with hers, and to Spurgeon's influence on Rose's father—in the Guide Book called *Mornings in Florence*.[3]

This little Guide Book is really a mosaic of autobiographical allusions and rationalisations. Ruskin had discovered the frescoes in the Spanish Chapel of Sta. Maria Novella when he was twenty-six, in 1845; and he had written a long description of the Virtues and Sciences, Prophets and so forth in a letter to his mother at that time.[4] In 1874, when he was fifty-five, he spent five weeks in the Chapel copying bits and pieces.[5] In 1882 he returned once more to the Chapel on the plea that *Mornings in Florence* was in need of revision. But he was not interested in the frescoes on the later visits, and he scarcely noticed anything more than he had noticed thirty years before. He looked at them again and again because he was impelled to repeat the old experiences. His reactions were automatic; and he relieved the tedium by concocting interpretations and falling back on subjects which really did interest him—himself, and Rose, and the 'bestial howling and entirely frantic vomiting of hopelessly damned souls through their still carnal throats', i.e. the Italians talking outside the window of his hotel.[6]

The whole life of *Mornings in Florence* resides in the autobiographical interpolations. In writing this short book over a period of four years and revising it five years later, he was reliving his experiences—he was once more avoiding the tricky step where he had formerly stumbled, and once more lifting the curtain to go behind the marble altar in Sta. Maria Novella,[7]

[1] 1870 (cf. below, p. 349, where the passages are quoted).
[2] *Mornings in Florence*, II, paras. 33 and 34 (cf. above, p. 167).
[3] *Mornings in Florence*, III, paras. 48–50.
[4] Letter to his mother from Florence, June 9, 1845.
[5] Cf. above, pp. 113 and 122.
[6] *Mornings in Florence*, V, para. 102 (cf. above, p. 123).
[7] *Mornings in Florence*, II, para. 17 .

and once more bribing the sacristan to get everything arranged
for him exactly as he wanted it. These things are more real in
the book than the pseudo-expert talk about restorations, and
the fantastic interpretations, because they *meant more to Ruskin*.
The tips to the sacristan were for him a really important matter
because his conscience always plagued him in regard to them.
In *Mornings in Florence* we read:

'Pay your sacristan well and make friends with him: in nine
cases out of ten an Italian is really grateful for the money, and
more than grateful for human courtesy; and will give you some
true zeal and kindly feeling in return for a franc and a pleasant
look. How very horrid of him to be grateful for money, you
think! Well, I can only tell you that I know fifty people who
will write me letters full of tender sentiment for one who will
give me ten pence.'[1]

The transferences here are like the transferences of his
mother's blindness and old age to himself and the theory that
nature had deteriorated because he had lost his delight in
mountains and skies. The tourists are to do as he has always
done, (whether they can afford it he does not consider), and thus
redeem the unfair advantage which he has always purchased
with his wealth. He knew all too well that he had always called
for ladders and scaffolding and paid too much for them, and
kept pictures obscured by them from travelling students (who
perhaps could only afford two days in Florence or Venice once
in a lifetime); that he had always bribed sacristans everywhere
not only to admit him anywhere at any time, but to keep other
people out while he was inside. But if everybody were to do
the same then his fault would be redeemed—'Give anybody
who follows you anything they want', he says elsewhere in the
Guide Book, 'to hold their tongues or go away.' And the transference of the conscientious tourist's objection, 'But isn't it
rather horrid and unfair of me, Mr. Ruskin, to bribe the sacristan to get what I want?' into 'How very horrid of him to be
grateful for money' is also, of course, both characteristic and
significant.[2]

[1] *Mornings in Florence*, Preface.
[2] The passages in *Mornings in Florence* about tips to the sacristans

Reality peers through many passages in the Guide Book that seem merely silly or obscure. For example, addressing young people:

'You may properly speak before you have been taught how to think. For indeed it is only by frank speaking that you *can* learn how to think. And it is no matter how wrong the first thoughts you have may be, provided you express them clearly and are willing to have them put right.'

That is what he wrote. What he meant was, 'I have recently brought out a new edition of *Modern Painters*, *I*, a book in which I prattled a lot of nonsense before I had learned to think, but which was fine frank writing for all that; and I am preparing a new edition of *The Seven Lamps of Architecture* with footnotes apologising for my earlier absurdities which were nevertheless admirable because they were brave and frank.'

It is this autobiographical undercurrent that makes the later writings on art so intensely interesting for the student of Ruskin's mentality. But it also makes them useless for the student of creative art. And it made them definitely harmful to the general public who followed Ruskin's lead in the days of his maximum renown. In the 'seventies and 'eighties Ruskin induced thousands of English and American spinsters and others to turn their backs on the creative art of their own day and spend their holidays in places and in front of pictures where he had found reliefs from his personal obsessions. When de la Sizeranne visited the Spanish Chapel at that time he could see nothing of the fresco of the Sciences because a crowd of English

should be compared with a letter which Ruskin wrote to an artist-assistant who was copying something in Siena on his instructions the year before: 'Do not spare fee to custodes, and put them down separately to me. People talk so absurdly about bribing. An Italian cannot know at first anything about an Englishman but that he is either stingy or generous. The money gift really opens his heart, if he has one. You can do it in that case without money, indeed, eventually, but it is amazing how many people can have good (as well as bad) brought out of them by gifts, and no otherwise' (Letter to an artist, May 20, 1873). At the beginning of the 'eighties when he had his troop of protégés copying bits 'for Sheffield' at the expense of St. George's Guild, 'Fee the sacristan' is a regular refrain in his letter of instruction.

schoolgirls were reading *Mornings in Florence* with their governess before it. But Ruskin meanwhile—though his social conscience drove him to confess in *Fors Clavigera* that his business and everybody else's was with art in England 'now' and not with art 'in Florence then'[1]—was relieving a complex at the expense of Whistler.

[1]*Fors Clavigera*, Letter 37, cf. above, p. 103.

RUSKIN AS ART CRITIC

HIS RELATIONS WITH ARTISTS

Ruskin first met Turner in 1840. He was then twenty-one and Turner was sixty-five. He was introduced by Turner's agent as a young man whose rich father had given him a Turner drawing on his twenty-first birthday; but he failed at the first fence with Turner by assessing degrees of goodness in his pictures. Ruskin spoke reverently of 'a leading drawing of the England series' and was surprised that Turner made no reply, and said nothing to him for the rest of the interview—except 'Good-bye'.[1]

As the Ruskins continued to be eager and regular customers, Turner began to take an interest in them, and he allowed the enthusiastic Ruskin junior who was writing a book called *Turner and the Ancients*[2] to keep in touch with him while he was composing it—as we know from Ruskin's diaries of 1843:

Jan. 27. 'Called on Turner; found him in, and in excellent humour and will come to me on my birthday.'

Feb. 24. 'Called at Turner's . . . insisted on my taking a glass of wine, but I wouldn't; excessively good-natured to-day. Heaven grant that he may not be offended with the work!'

Then *Modern Painters, I*, was published and Ruskin enters:

May 15. 'Called on Turner to-day, who was particularly gracious. I think he must have read my book, and have been pleased with it, by his tone.'

But Turner made no reference to the book for fifteen months as we know from a passage in Ruskin's diary which I have already quoted.[3]

After the publication of *Modern Painters, I*, Ruskin senior

[1] *Præterita*, II, Chap. IV, para. 67.
[2] Cf. above, p. 199.
[3] Cf. above, p. 50.

began to cultivate artists on his son's behalf; he gave dinner parties which Turner himself attended, and sometimes Turner would come and dine with the Ruskins *en famille*.[1]

Ruskin has left us records of Turner's behaviour at Denmark Hill.

'I never saw him at my father's house look for an instant at any of his own drawings: I have watched him sitting at dinner nearly opposite one of his chief pictures [*The Slave Ship*]—his eyes never turned to it. But the want of appreciation, nevertheless, touched him sorely; chiefly the not understanding his meaning . . .'[2]

Turner was dining at the house on the day when his *Snowstorm* had been described in the Press as 'a mass of soapsuds and whitewash':

'After dinner, sitting in his arm-chair by the fire, I heard him muttering low to himself at intervals "Soapsuds and whitewash" again and again and again. At last I went up to him asking why he minded what they said. Then he burst out " 'Soapsuds and whitewash'. What would they have? I wonder what they think the sea's like? I wish they'd been in it." '[3]

'To censure . . . Turner was acutely sensitive, owing to his own natural kindness; he felt it, for himself, or for others, not as criticism, but as cruelty . . . and the attacks made upon him in his later years were to him not merely contemptible in their ignorance, but amazing in their ingratitude. "A man may be weak in his age", he said to me once at the time when he felt he was dying; "but you should not tell him so." '

Ruskin's enthusiasm, on the other hand, gave him 'no ray of pleasure'. He made it clear that he did not think he understood his work:

'He could not make me at that time understand his main meanings . . . He tried hard one day for a quarter of an hour to

---

[1] *Præterita*, II, Chap. IX, para. 172.

[2] *Modern Painters*, V, Part IX, Chap. XI, para. 30, note.

[3] This picture is now in the National Gallery, Millbank, No. 530. Turner had been on the steamboat in the storm depicted and had had himself tied to the mast that he might remain on deck to observe it. (*Notes on the Turner Gallery at Marlborough House*, 1856.)

make me guess what he was doing in the picture of *Napoleon* before it had been exhibited, giving me hint after hint in a rough way; but I could not guess and he would not tell me . . . he loved me but cared nothing for what I said, and was always trying to hinder me from writing because it gave pain to his fellow-artists.'[1]

Turner's love for the Denmark Hill establishment was, doubtless, mainly cupboard love. In his eyes it was obviously the function of prosperous city people to buy his pictures; the Ruskins understood their function—that was good; they also gave one a capital meal with excellent sherry—that was also good—though Ruskin junior was really very comic and tiresome with his flamboyant enthusiasm and his ridiculous habit of setting the merits of one picture against those of another.[2] What did he know about 'modern painters'? no more than he knew about 'all the Ancient Masters'—which was obviously next to nothing.

Ruskin, on his side, looked on Turner as 'a great natural force in human frame'. But he could not leave it at that. He brought himself into the matter—and spoilt everything.

The creative artist regards himself as part of life and his pictures as part of himself and so part of life. Sickert has said this with twentieth-century terseness: 'One's pictures are like one's toe nails—they're one's own and that's all there is to it.' Ruskin knew this, but he could not leave it there—because that left him

[1] *Modern Painters*, V. Part IX, Chap. XII, para. 11, and Part IX, Chap. XI, para. 30, note.

The *Napoleon* is the picture known as *War: the Exile and the Rock Limpet* now in the National Gallery, Millbank, No. 529. Turner exhibited this picture in the Academy with the following lines in the catalogue:

'Ah, thy tent-formed shell is like
A soldier's nightly bivouac, alone
Amidst a sea of blood . . .
. . . But *you* can join your comrades.'

It represents Napoleon on Saint Helena contemplating a limpet. *Punch* caricatured it as 'The Duke of Wellington and the Shrimp', adding the lines:

'And can it be, thou hideous imp,
That life is, ah! how brief, and glory but a shrimp?'

[2] *Modern Painters*, V, Part IX, Chap XI, para. 30, note.

out altogether. He often forgot that as the creative artist sees things there *is* no place for the spectator; that the creative artist regards himself as the only spectator who can possibly tell whether his picture is 'good' or 'bad', because goodness in any of his pictures is the fulfilment of his intention and badness the failure to fulfil it. Ruskin knew that the intrinsic value of a picture derives from the whole-man-artist; but he often failed at the next stage in understanding. He never distinguished between the Intrinsic Value of a Turner water-colour that derived from Turner at the time of creation and the Acquired Value which he, John Ruskin, put upon it when it hung at Denmark Hill.[1]

He rarely understood why the creative artist cares so little about his own work once he has decided—(whether it consists of three lines or of ten square yards of elaborately painted canvas)—that it is 'finished'. Twenty years after Turner's death he wrote to Norton:

'Mr. Kingsley's cousin was in Turner's own gallery with him. They came to the *Crossing the Brook;* a piece of paint out of the sky, as large as a fourpenny piece, was lying on the floor. Kingsley picked it up, and said, "Have you noticed this?" "No," said Turner. "How can you look at the picture and see it so injured?" said Kingsley. "What does it matter?" answered Turner; "the only use of the thing is to recall the impression." Of course it was false, but he was then thinking of himself only, having long given up the thought of being cared for by the public.'[2]

'Of course it was false'. Ruskin had forgotten that to a creative artist it is the painting of the picture and not what happens to it afterwards that matters—though he had realised this in 1858–1859 when he wrote the additional passage for *Modern Painters* quoted above.[3]

Then again he was always puzzled by the way in which the creative artist behaves about money. He knew that creative artists set their work before money. He distinguished between

[1] Cf. above, p. 241.
[2] Letter to C. E. Norton, Aug. 7, 1870.
[3] Cf. above, p. 233.

'Work-First' and 'Fee-and-Fame-First' artists[1]; and he put down the distinction thus also:

'The test is absolute, inevitable—Is your art first with you? Then you are artists; you may be, after you have made your money, misers and usurers; you may be, after you have got your fame, jealous, and proud, and wretched and base; but yet, *as long as you won't spoil your work* you are artists. On the other hand—Is your money first with you, and your fame first with you? Then, you may be very charitable with your money, and very magnificent with your money, and very graceful in the way you wear your reputation, and very courteous to those beneath you, and very acceptable to those above you; but you are *not* artists. You are mechanics and drudges.'[2]

He understood so far. But no further. He left unanswered the question why Turner took such pains to sell his pictures for the highest possible sums, why he became a miser, why he was so eager to amass the money that could not seduce him from his work. He could not answer the question because he did not realise that, though the creative artist does not permit the spectator to criticise his pictures, or expect him to be able to appreciate or understand them, he expects him to *buy* them, saying as Ruskin said of the scholars, 'that is what the spectators are there for.'[3] The creative artist thinks his 'good' pictures above all price because their intrinsic value, as life, cannot be translated into terms of money; he never wants to part with such pictures—though he also never wants to look at them once they are finished. But he needs money; and so he sells his 'good' pictures and hates the world for parsimony however large the sum which he gets for them. On the other hand he always wants to part with his 'bad' pictures as quickly as possible. These he regards as intrinsically valueless and so again not assessable in terms of money. But he needs money—the equivalent of the time he has spent in producing these failures; therefore he sells these also for the highest price he can get for them, and hates the world for its idiocy in paying money

[1] *The Crown of Wild Olive*, I, para. 32.
[2] *The Two Paths*, IV, para. 135. Italics are Ruskin's.
[3] Cf. above, p. 187.

for anything so worthless. All the purchaser sees in the one case and the other is exactly the same thing. The artist seems to be behaving in exactly the same way. But in fact the procedures are quite different. And there is another difference also. If the creative artist does not sell a 'good' picture, he hoards it for ever —though he never looks at it and he does not mind if it crumbles to pieces. But unless he sells a 'bad' picture at once— a few weeks after it is painted—he destroys it, always, inevitably.

Ruskin could never understand why Turner hoarded those thousands of sketches which no one ever saw till the cases were unpacked in the National Gallery. He was still puzzling over this when he wrote in *Mornings in Florence:*

'It is a characteristic—(as far as I know, quite a universal one) —of the greatest masters, that they never expect you to look at them—seem always rather surprised if you want to, and not over pleased. Tell them you are going to hang their picture at the upper end of the table at the next great City dinner, and that Mr. So-and-So will make a speech about it; you produce no impression upon them whatever, or an unfavourable one. The chances are ten to one they send you the most rubbishy thing they can find in their lumber-room. But send for one of them in a hurry, and tell him the rats have gnawed a nasty hole behind the parlour door, and you want it plastered and painted over;—and he does you a masterpiece which the world will peep behind your door to look at for ever. I have no time to tell you why this is so; nor do I know altogether; but so it is.'[1]

It was always the same thing. He always dragged in the spectator. He continually forgot that from the standpoint of the creative artist the spectator is not a man but a purse.

And then, of course, there was his manic impulse to preach. He did not, presumably, tell Turner to his face that he ought to give up wasting his time in sketches—though he wrote it in *Modern Painters, I,* as we have seen.[2] But when he was in contact with Rossetti—though once more he recognised 'a great

[1] *Mornings in Florence,* III, para. 45.
[2] Cf. above, p. 204.

natural force in human frame'—he could not resist the impulse to tell him how and how not to paint his pictures.

He met Rossetti, as noted, in 1854 when he himself was thirty-five and Rossetti was twenty-six. He went frequently to Rossetti's studio; he guaranteed him an annual allowance for some years in exchange for the first refusal of his drawings up to that amount; he commissioned pictures from him; and he financed the publication of his *Early Italian Poets*. 'He attempted', says a recent biographer, 'to buy the soul of Rossetti in order to take possession of it.'[1] This does him an injustice. Ruskin did not attempt to buy Rossetti's soul. He knew he was a genius and he wanted to help him; and in a moment of comprehension he saw that the only way to help a genius is to provide him with money. He himself had more money given him by his father than he knew what to do with, and he passed some of it on to Rossetti. He also passed some on to Elizabeth Siddal to whom he guaranteed the equivalent of £400 a year in present values that she might look after her health, and not worry, and give him in exchange the refusal of any drawings that she might care to produce. He made this arrangement at a time when he did not expect that her health would permit her to make any drawings at all. He gave her the money because he wanted to save Rossetti anxiety, because he believed that Rossetti 'would not have given his soul to her unless she had been both gentle and good', and because she had more the look of a Florentine fifteenth-century lady than anything he had ever seen out of a fresco.[2] He sent her to Nice and Switzerland and defrayed the expenses. As Evelyn Waugh says, 'Whatever pain and difficulty Rossetti did not suffer in his wretched engagement and marriage was saved him by Ruskin's tenderness and generosity.'[1]

[1] David Larg, *John Ruskin* (London, Davies, 1932).
[2] Letter to Dr. Acland, *circa* 1855.
[1] Evelyn Waugh. *Rossetti: His Life and Works* (London, Duckworth, 1928). Another biographer of Rossetti, R. L. Megroz (*Dante Gabriel Rossetti, Painter poet of Heaven in Earth*. London, Faber, 1928), suggests that Ruskin was in love with Elizabeth Siddal. For that I can find no evidence.

The actual sum which he allowed her was £150 a year. I cannot find

Ruskin in the 'fifties was confident in his own 'perfect judgement' of pictures and assumed that Rossetti would welcome his opinions on his work. He plagued Rossetti with pedagogic criticisms:

'Please put a dab of Chinese white into the hole in the cheek and paint it over. People will say that Beatrice has been giving the other bridesmaids a "predestinate scratched face" . . . also, a white-faced bridesmaid in mist behind is very ugly to look at— like a skull or a body in corruption . . . Never put raw green into *light* flesh.'[1]

Rossetti failed to comply with these instructions and Ruskin writes a few days later:

'I was like to tear everything in the room to pieces at your daubing over the head in that picture . . . it is no use to me now till you have painted it again . . . you have deprived me of a great pleasure by your absurdity. I never, so long as I live, will trust you to do anything again, out of my sight.'[2]

'I was put out to-day, as you must have seen, for I can't hide it when I am vexed. I don't at all like my picture now; the alteration of the head from the stoop forward to the throw back makes the whole figure quite stiff and stupid; besides, the off cheek is a quarter of a yard too thin.'[3]

'Please oblige me in two matters or you will make me ill again. Take all the pure green out of the flesh in the *Nativity* . . . and try to get it a little less like worsted-work by Wednesday when I will send for it. I want the Archdeacon of Salop, who is coming for some practical talk over religious art for the multitude, to see it . . . If you would but do the things I *want*, it would be much easier.'[4]

It did not occur to Ruskin that Rossetti might resent these letters and take no interest at all in the Archdeacon of Salop.

Rossetti, of course, did not care whether Ruskin was ill, or

how long it was continued. A year or two has been suggested by Rossetti's biographers.

[1] Letters to Rossetti, 1856 and 1857.
[2] Letters to Rossetti, 1856 and 1857.
[3] Letter to Rossetti, 1856 or 1857.
[4] Letter to Rossetti, October, 1855.

puzzled, or angry as long as he continued to fulfil his function. In his view Ruskin was a person who gave him money, and who received in return not only his failures (to which he was welcome) but also some of his good drawings—which neither he nor anyone else deserved; the fellow was certainly most kind to 'Guggum' (which was perhaps all right and perhaps not) but at bottom he was obviously an idiot or he would not imagine that a dab of Chinese white or a streak of emerald green, placed where *he* wanted it, would make any difference to the real goodness or badness of a picture.

When, as sometimes happened, Rossetti felt moved to give Ruskin pleasure he was equally unable to understand his man. He praised Ruskin's prose style thinking to make him happy, and he really made him miserable, because what Ruskin wanted to hear from him, and never did hear, was: 'You, my dear Ruskin, are a quite infallible critic of the arts.'

Ruskin was still more unsuccessful in the case of Ford Madox Brown with whom he never achieved even the semblance of friendship. Here he fell at the outset because he did not recognise Brown as a creative artist. The first meeting between them took place in Rossetti's studio. It is described by Brown, who was then thirty-four, as follows:

'While I was smoking a pipe in shirt sleeves "enter to us" Ruskin. I smoke; he talks divers nonsense about art hurriedly in shrill flippant tones. I answer him civilly, then resume my coat and prepare to leave. Suddenly upon this he says: "Mr. Brown, will you tell me why you chose such an ugly subject for your last picture?" I, dumbfounded at such a beginning from a stranger, look in his face expectant of some *qualification*, and ask "What picture?" To which he looking defyingly, answers, "Your picture at the British Exhibition. What made you take such a very ugly subject? It was a pity, for there was some nice painting in it." I . . . being satisfied that he intended impertinence, replied contemptuously, "Because it lay out of a back window," and turning on my heel took my hat and wished Gabriel good-bye! Ruskin . . . would not look at me as I left the room.'[1]

[1] Madox Brown's Diary, Dec. 31, 1855.

It is clear from Madox Brown's diaries that he hated Ruskin. He pays a tribute to his 'Homeric' eloquence, but describes him as 'in appearance a cross between a fiend and a tallow chandler' —(which contrasts curiously with Carlyle's description of Ruskin at this period as 'a bottle of beautiful soda water').[1] Brown was present at some Committee meeting at Denmark Hill and the diary reads:

'Ruskin was playful and childish and the tea table overcharged with cakes and sweets as for a juvenile party. Then about an hour later cake and wine was again produced, of which Ruskin again partook largely, reaching out with his thin paw and swiftly absorbing three or four large lumps of cake in succession.'

Ruskin on his side never wrote about Brown's pictures, and not only did not assist him to sell them, but advised people privately not to buy. We know this from a letter to Miss Heaton: 'Do not buy any Madox Brown at present. Do you not see that his name never occurs in my books—do you think that would be so if I *could* praise him seeing that he is an entirely worthy fellow?'[2]

He failed also to win the friendship of G. F. Watts, though by 1848 he had discovered him as 'the only real painter of history or thought we have in England', Watts who was a couple of years his senior being then thirty-one. In 1851 he commissioned him to draw his wife's portrait. He had some contact with him at other periods; and there was respect on both sides; but here again intimacy was killed by Ruskin's preaching: 'From long drawing with chalk point', he wrote to Watts, 'you have got a mottled and broken execution and have no power of properly modulating the brush. Well the way to cure yourself of that is not by trying for Titian or Correggio ... but take a piece of absolute modulation—the head of the kneeling figure in Sir Joshua's *Three Graces* at Kensington for instance, and do it twenty times over and over again, restricting yourself wholly to his number of touches ... Again the chalk drawing has materially damaged your perception of the subtlest qualities of

---

[1] Letter of Carlyle to his brother, Nov. 27, 1855 (cf. above, p. 40).
[2] Letter to Miss Ellen Heaton, March 12, 1862.

local colour . . . you should paint the purest and subtlest coloured objects on a small scale till you can realise them thoroughly. I say on a small scale . . .' etc., etc. I need not continue the letter; Watts, doubtless, did not read as far.[1]

With Burne-Jones the position was quite different. Jones was twenty-three when he met Ruskin who was then thirty-seven; he was wildly enthusiastic about Ruskin's writings, and still at the very beginning of his own career. He knew that he was over-praised by Ruskin and delighted in the over-praise. He was not angry when Ruskin told him exactly what colours he should use—he thanked him for the advice, and sometimes took it. When Jones married, Ruskin told his wife, Georgiana, how to look after her baby; she was not angry—she thanked him for the advice, and went on as before. Ned and Georgiana allowed Ruskin to manage them and looked on his services to them—the trips on the Continent and the public praise of Ned's pictures—as kindnesses. They liked him as a man and he liked them as a pair of amiable friendly children. He thought Ned a good and docile artist and Georgiana a dear. That friendship held. There was a moment about 1871 when Jones showed signs of outgrowing his boots. He had 'arrived', and he began to think himself an important artist. 'Ruskin I see never,' he writes at this moment, ' and when I see him he angers me . . . he quarrels with my pictures and I with his writing, and there is no peace between us—and you know all is up when friends don't admire each other's work.'[2] But Ruskin's personality won in this encounter. Jones was too dependent on other people to be able to stand on his two feet. He fell back to docility and gave evidence for Ruskin against Whistler at the trial.[3]

The manageableness which Ruskin found so agreeable in Ned and Georgiana was a quality that he longed to find and could not find in Rossetti and 'Guggum'. He was fascinated by them but also annoyed and bewildered by them because he could not manage them:

[1] Letter to G. F. Watts, Feb. 5, 1861.
[2] Letters from Burne-Jones to Norton, 1871.
[3] He was really Ruskin's official representative on this occasion; Ruskin was touched by his willingness to play the role; and retained a great affection for him to the end.

'These geniuses are all alike, little and big. I have known five of them—Turner, Watts, Millais, Rossetti and this girl [Elizabeth Siddal]—and I don't know which was, or which is, wrong-headedest. I am with them like the old woman who lived in the shoe, only that I don't want to send them to bed, and can't whip them—or else that is what they all want . . .'[1]

The same applied to Rossetti's friends. Ruskin went to Oxford while the Union fresco-painting was in progress and saw Topsy Morris performing, and met Swinburne, and became more and more bewildered:

'You know the fact is they're all the least bit crazy and it is very difficult to manage them.'[2]

This experience was extremely good for him. By studying Rossetti his outlook on life was broadened. It was this study that helped him to the temporary understanding of the artist's attitude which is seen in the passage written about 1858 as an addition to *Modern Painters* but never added[3]; it was Rossetti who made it possible for him to understand and champion Swinburne's poems[4]; and it was with his arm in the arm of Rossetti, metaphorcially speaking, that he walked out of the Waldensian Chapel, and copied Veronese and tipped the ballerina in Turin.[5]

In the 'fifties he took up some other artists and tried to manage them and make them accept his 'teaching'. One was J. W. Inchbold and another was John Brett. The following letters show his procedures:

'The two little drawings of which you speak in my bedroom are Inchbold's; the cottage, one I chose and made him draw at Lauterbrunnen; the Thun, bought when he couldn't sell anything, to help him a little. I wanted and ordered of him (paying him when he was at Chamouni last year) four more cottages; but he got entirely off the rails at Chamouni, and the cottages are failures. I stayed with him some time, or rather made him

---

[1] Letter to Mrs. Acland, July 10, 1855.
[2] Letter to W. M. Rossetti, Dec. 29, 1857.
[3] Cf. above, pp. 231–234.
[4] Cf. above, pp. 234 and 235.
[5] Cf. above, pp. 65 and 66.

stay with me, at Bellinzona, in order to make him understand where he was wrong . . . It was a delicate and difficult matter to make him gradually find out his own faults (it's no use *telling* a man of them) and took me a fortnight of innuendos. At last I think I succeeded in making him entirely uncomfortable and ashamed of himself . . .'[1]

That 'it's no use *telling* a man of them' was of course the result of his experience with Rossetti. But though the technique of the error is different—the error is just the same.

'I mentioned that Mr. Brett was with me at La Tour . . . I sent for him at Villeneuve, Val d'Aosta, because I . . . thought he wanted some lecturing like Inchbold: besides that, he could give me some useful hints. He is much tougher and stronger than Inchbold, and takes more hammering; but I think he looks more miserable every day, and have good hope of making him completely wretched in a day or two . . .'[2]

Ruskin had commissioned Brett to paint *Val d'Aosta;* and he wrote glowing praise of it in *Academy Notes*, 1859, when the artist had presumably fulfilled his instructions. He had the picture in his collection for many years. When he exhibited it in 1880 he stated in a note 'Mr. Brett visited me at Turin to consult about this picture.' Brett's toughness came out in 1864 when he stood up to Ruskin who replied by calling him a fool and ending the friendship.[3]

Between 1861 and 1864, absorbed in his own depression, and living mostly abroad, Ruskin saw little of Rossetti. He was not in a frame of mind to be shocked by his liaison with Mrs. Schott—he had known of it before and learned to understand in the revealing years of 1858 and 1859. But he could not take Rossetti and Fanny Schott to Winnington—as he took Ned and Georgiana; and I suspect that when he saw Rossetti at this period he did not refer to his visits to the school. And now of course Rossetti, who was making £2,000 a year by his paintings, had no more need of him. Other purses were available. When Ruskin told him that his handling of oil paint was coarse,

[1] Letter to his father from Turin, Aug. 9, 1858.
[2] Letter to his father from Turin, Aug. 26, 1858.
[3] Cf. above, p. 78.

he resented it as before, and now expressed his resentment in plainer terms, and accused him, quite unjustly, of trying to sell or get rid of the drawings bought in the 'fifties. Attempts were made on both sides to avoid a quarrel. But both men were mental invalids; and in 1865 the quarrel came.[1]

After this Ruskin made no more attempts to associate with wrong-headed geniuses. He consoled himself with the young ladies to whom he gave precise instructions in his Drawing School in Oxford, with Kate Greenaway to whom he explained in hundreds of letters exactly how her 'girlies' should be drawn; and all through the 'seventies and 'eighties he gradually surrounded himself with a troop of artist-assistants who did exactly what he told them to do 'for Oxford" and 'for Sheffield'—in exchange for his money and the money of the Guild. There had been a moment when he thought that he could group the creative artists of England in a circle round him hanging on his words and waiting for his instructions. He found that they would not submit to the formation. So he turned his back on them; and, as it was the grouping more than the art that he stood in need of, he achieved the grouping in another way. In the 'fifties he failed to capture Art-Dictatorship of England. In the 'seventies and 'eighties he had all the pleasures of the office within his own four walls. Allen, Rooke, Bunney, Ward, Burgess, Hackstoun, Randal, Newman, Alessandri, and the rest of them—took their places in the formation as neatly and readily as the children had taken theirs in the crystal-game he had worked out for them at Winnington.[2] He was indefatigable in his instructions; and they were obedient and docile in response—all except Ward, whom he had to reprimand sharply more than once:

'My dear Ward—*I* don't want *any* of these leaves painted. You are to work on them for practice, doing one or two over and over again—fifty times, if needful . . .'[3]

But in the end he wore down Ward as he wore down Kate Greenaway (who struggled against leaf-drawing for some

[1] Cf. above, p. 79.
[2] *Ethics of the Dust*, III and IV.
[3] Letter to William Ward, Aug. 9, 1870 (cf. above, p. 88).

years), and when he had worn him down then he smiled and caressed him in a letter that reached him on the morning of Christmas, 1873:

'Dear Ward—I am intensely delighted with your sketches —finished sketches I ought to say . . . they are a complete reward to me for all my patience and work with you, as I hope they will bring reward to you for all your patience and faith in me . . . Attend to your health, be as cheerful as you can, and in the beginning of the year . . . I will set you to correct work . . . In the meantime make pencil outlines of any portion of cloud that stays long enough, especially upper ones of delicate ramification. This is the only work I will prescribe at Christmastime—I wish you all good, with your family, and am, your faithful Master, John Ruskin.'

RUSKIN AS SOCIAL AND POLITICAL ECONOMIST

INTRODUCTORY COMMENTS

Reading the English papers in Venice in 1852 Ruskin decided that everyone in authority in England was so 'ridiculous' that he must set aside some hours for three days in order to cram wisdom into their empty heads.[1] He carried this out in three letters to *The Times* on *Taxation, Election and Education*. The writing of these letters was a hyper-confident gesture, and he began by stating that the principles involved were 'so clear and simple that he who runs may read'. Ruskin wrote without any study of the problems involved, but the proposals which he made nevertheless foreshadow his subsequent attitudes to social and political economy—for they included a graduated income tax, a capital levy, abolition of all import and export duties, universal suffrage with graduated voting power, and State education for all children.[2]

He sent the texts to his father, who refused to send them to *The Times* and wrote back explaining his reason:

'All attacks on your books are only as the waves beating on Eddystone Lighthouse, whereas your politics are Slum Buildings liable to be knocked down, and no man to whom authority is a useful engine should expose himself to frequent defeat by slender forces.'[3]

---

[1] Letter to his father from Venice, March 6, 1862.

[2] The first two papers were not published till the Editors of the Library Edition printed them from MSS. The third was used by Ruskin as Appendix 7 to *The Stones of Venice*, III.

[3] Letter from J. J. Ruskin to Ruskin, March 30, 1852 (cf. above, p. 71).

Ruskin acquiesced in this decision, but it rankled for years, and was a cause contributing to his collapse into depression in 1861–1863.

In the period following the writing of these letters he was occupied with posing to Millais for his portrait, with his wife's desertion, and with his own re-establishment at Denmark Hill. Between 1855 and 1859 he was working intermittently at this, that and the other connected with the miscellaneous essays published as *Modern Painters, III, IV* and *V*. But he never forgot for a moment that his ideas on political economy had been described as 'Slum Buildings'; and he was determined to demonstrate the absurdity of the accusation. By 1855 he had already started to read the text books on political economy, and he was already convinced that the writers were quite ignorant of the science they professed. 'My studies of political economy', he writes to Mrs. Carlyle, 'have induced me to think . . . that nobody knows anything about that, and I am at present engaged in an investigation, on independent principles, of the Natures of Money, Rent, and Taxes, in an abstract form, which sometimes keeps me awake all night.'[1]

The first 'independent principles' that emerged from these studies were rationalisations of the conditions of his own life which he put forward as ideal conditions for the body politic in lectures called *The Political Economy of Art*, delivered in Manchester in 1857.[2]

To understand these lectures—*A Joy for Ever*—we must visualise the Ruskin establishment at Denmark Hill in the middle of the 'fifties. It was a large house with seven acres of gardens, and a troop of servants, each with his or her appointed station and appointed work, and all obedient to the appointed

[1] Letter to Mrs. Carlyle, 1855.
[2] For the circumstances of the delivery of these lectures cf. Appendix p. 381. They were delivered in July and published as *The Political Economy of Art* in the same year at half a crown (seven and sixpence in present values). This book was a failure, the second edition, ten years later, being made up of remainder sheets. It was republished as *A Joy for Ever* in 1880 at eighteen shillings (say fifty shillings); again in 1882 at thirteen shillings and in 1887 at five shillings. By 1893 an edition labelled 13th thousand was brought out.

government of the best and most serviceable people in the house, the people who handed out the money and decided what was to be done with it—Mr. and Mrs. Ruskin and John Ruskin. There was no competition between the Ruskin establishment and those of their neighbours, or between one servant within the establishment and another. Each servant had but to do his or her own work in the rank appointed by Providence and the governing body. In return the governing body looked upon and treated the servants as members of the household to whom they had responsibilities and duties. The Ruskins chose servants from families known to them, they engaged them as children, trained them to efficiency in their several types of work, fed them and gave them money for other necessities, kept them in their service up to middle life, and never dismissed them as superannuated.[1]

The Denmark Hill establishment was not only a well-ordered house and gardens; it was also a temple of Art. There was a nice balance between the functions of Ruskin's father and mother, and those of Ruskin himself who made drawings, and

[1] *Præterita*, I, Chap, IV, para. 80 There were regular dynasties of servants at Denmark Hill. Ruskin describes some in *Præterita* II, Chap. VI, para. 108. The two old servants whom he installed in his teashop in 1874 (cf. above, p. 111) were a parlourmaid who had worked at Denmark Hill for forty-five years and her sister who had worked there for forty. His nurse, Anne, who came as a child, died at Denmark Hill as recorded (cf. above, p. 127); in her later years she was quite useless and took delight in annoying his mother, who was 'very imperative and particular about having her teacup set on one side of her little round table'; Anne would 'observantly and punctiliously put it always on the other', and Mrs. Ruskin said 'every morning after beakfast, gravely, that if ever a woman was possessed by the Devil, Anne was that woman' (*Præterita*, I, Chap. I, para. 31). When Anne died Mrs. Ruskin said, 'She always persecuted *me*. But one must hope there are intermediate kinds of places where people get better ... I ought to have sent her away three months after she came' (Ruskin's Diary, March 31, 1871). She had, however, not dismissed her because the Ruskins made it a point of honour never to dismiss a servant. A visitor to the house once asked what the duties were of one of the aged maidservants and Mrs. Ruskin answered 'she puts out the dessert' (Collingwood's *Life of Ruskin*). Ruskin also kept his own valets for a great many years. He only had three, I think, all his life. We have seen his varied employment of the gardener, Downs.

wrote books, and hung the walls with works of art, and exercised an influence on the production of the artists with whom he came in contact. In the exercise of this influence he had commissioned particular water-colours from Turner,[1] and told Rossetti exactly what he wanted him to do, and made him an allowance while he was doing it[2]; and he was training young artisans at the Working Men's College to draw and look at nature and works of art, and discover the happiness yielded by creative work while remaining content with their appointed position in the world as artisans[3]; and by his expensive books and his relations with rich people he believed that he was encouraging the upper classes to respect art and try to understand it. His interest moreover was not restricted to the works of living men. Some of the works of art that he brought to Denmark Hill were by artists who had lived in the past. Since his wife had deserted him he had spent the money formerly allocated to her ball dresses—(so much admired when she curtseyed to Royalty in London and Venice)—on adding to his collections. He now had nearly a hundred water-colours by Turner as well as a number of drawings by Rossetti and other living artists, a number of mediæval manuscripts, a valuable collection of minerals, one or two Italian pictures, and so forth. Finally, we must remember, he was a traveller; he was not insular; he looked with interest on foreign lands; he sympathised with their distresses and deplored the bad conditions of their monuments. Had he not written *The Stones of Venice* and drawn attention in *Modern Painters*, *II*, to neglected monuments in France?[4]

In *A Joy for Ever* he tells us that precisely the same laws of economy which apply to a house, a farm, or an estate apply to a province, or a country or a continent.[5] The government of a state must be a Paternal Government not a *Laisser Faire* Government. The Paternal Government must tolerate no preten-

[1] Catalogues of the Ruskin collection of drawings by Turner (1878).
[2] Cf. above, pp. 270–272.
[3] Cf. above, pp. 61 and 218 and below, pp. 286–287.
[4] Cf. above, p. 214.
[5] *A Joy for Ever*, I, paras. 9, 10, 12, 17.

sions of Equality; each man must have his allotted task of service. In return the governing body, the best people in the highest places, must 'completely and unstintingly' recognise each soul's claim to 'protection, and education in childhood, help or punishment in middle life, reward or relief, if needed, in old age'. The Paternal Government must aim at securing 'a fair balance between the use and the pleasure of its possessions'. It thus requires artists. It must discover its artists' young, train them in trial schools, and set them to the various forms of art-production which it requires, providing them with good materials, and regulating the rewards of their efforts. The best people, the Pilots of the State, must be allowed the benefits of their labours: 'It would be hard if a man who has passed the greater part of his life at the desk or counter could not at last innocently gratify a caprice.'[1] The State in its concern for the pleasure as well as the usefulness of its possessions must not restrict itself to the discovery, training and employment of living artists. It must also be a collector of works produced in the past: 'There was much complaining last week of the vast sum the nation has given for the best Paul Veronese in Venice—£14,000; I wonder what the nation meanwhile has given for its ball dresses. Suppose we could see the London milliners' bills, simply for unnecessary breadth of slip and flounce, from April to July; I wonder whether £14,000 would cover *them*.'[2] There ought to be 'a great National Society' constituted for purchasing old pictures and presenting them to the various galleries . . . 'You should stand, nationally, at the edge of Dover Cliffs— Shakespeare's—and wave blank cheques in the eyes of the nations on the other side of the sea, freely offered, for such and such canvases of theirs.' Here in England we are making enormous and capricious efforts to produce new art of all kinds,

---

[1] *A Joy for Ever*, II, Addenda.

[2] The Veronese referred to is *The Family of Darius* (National Gallery, No. 294). The exact sum paid was £13,650 (say £40,000 in present values). It was bought from the Count V. Pisani, whose ancestors are shown in the picture. Ruskin had not been consulted in the purchase. In a letter to *The Times* (July 7, 1857) approving it, he said that the picture was worth one third more than the sum paid for it.

knowing and confessing all the time that the greater part of it is bad, 'all the while taking no thought whatever of the best possible pictures, and statues, already in existence, which require nothing but to be taken common care of'. Nations, like neighbours, must live at peace with one another and not quarrel. No State profits from the misery of its neighbour. A wise State is not ignorant and insular and impervious to its neighbours' distresses, or neglectful of its neighbours' monuments. 'The personal efforts of Englishmen to redeem the condition of foreign nations, are among the most direct pieces of duty which our wealth renders incumbent upon us.'

This was where Ruskin stood in political economy in 1857. He had arrived at the idea of a Paternal Government (as opposed to a *Laisser Faire* Government), and at the ideas of State Education (including technical training), and of old-age pensions. The taxation and suffrage schemes of his 1852 letter to *The Times* had dropped out.

It is important to note the advocacy in these lectures of national purchase and preservation of the art of the past. His conscience was uneasy about his own capture by the past and he was attempting rationalisation in this way. Instead of hailing the Crystal Palace as a sign pointing to a new style in architecture he had advocated a Society for preserving old buildings.[1] And now instead of urging a national Society for the purchase of contemporary art he calls for a Society for the purchase of old pictures. When he became unable to understand and react to contemporary creative architecture he became the pioneer of the Society for the Preservation of Ancient Monuments (destined to be founded in 1877); when he began to lose interest in contemporary creative painting he became the pioneer of the National Art-Collections Fund (destined to be founded in 1903).

We now reach 1858 and 1859 when he realised that his bid for Art-Dictatorship had failed; and when he ascribed the fault to the obstinate stupidity of the architects and artists who had not done as he bade them and to the general conditions of life in England which, he decided, made the production and appre-

[1] Cf. above, p. 223.

284

ciation of great art impossible and rendered art criticism useless and ridiculous. At this time, it will be recalled, he decided to talk no more of art and to begin at the other end 'with moral education of the people and physical'.[1] In 1859 he drove to the North through the manufacturing and industrial regions and was shocked at the ugliness which was blackening the country; and his social conscience was set in motion by the gloomy squalor of the workmen's life. In the lectures which he delivered at this period he protested both against the ugliness and against the squalor. He told his audience at Bradford that just as the first question about growing wheat is to discover whether the ground and weather are suitable for wheat, so the first question about growing artists is to see whether the conditions can possibly produce them. No art can be produced by men who see nothing but ugliness. Men must see the fields and the sky and breathe fresh air in clean cities before they can produce art.[2] If the manufacturers want designs they must begin with moral and physical care of the designers. 'Inform their minds, refine their habits, and you form and refine their designs.'[3]

Ruskin's proclamation of his first ideas on social economy in the lectures called *The Political Economy of Art* (1857) and his protest against the ugliness and squalor of industrial England in the lecture just discussed (1859) were addressed to small audiences, and when the texts were published they fell flat.[4] These gestures did not bring him into conflict with the official world or with the public as a whole. For this his father, who still thought his political opinions jerry-built, was grateful. But Ruskin in his defiant mood of 1858–1860 was thirsting for a fight. He was now convinced that he could construct a polygon of social-economic doctrines which, like his polygon of

[1] Cf. above, p. 64.
[2] *The Two Paths*, III, paras. 86–92.
[3] *The Two Paths*, III, para. 92. For the circumstances of the delivery of this lecture, cf. Appendix, p. 382. The other lectures published in *The Two Paths* are part of Ruskin's main theory of art and really constitute an appendix to *Modern Painters* (cf. above, p. 193). *The Two Paths* was published in 1859. It was not reprinted till 1878. Republished in various editions in the 'eighties it reached the fifteenth thousand in 1901.
[4] Cf. above, note p. 280 and Appendix p. 381.

artistic doctrine, would be an 'Eddystone Lighthouse'. Though he denied having studied the text books of the professional economists, he was really well acquainted with their contents.[1] He had at last brought *Modern Painters* to some sort of an end and presented it with expressions of filial piety to his father. And he now resolved to go away to his favourite Chamonix and construct his Eddystone Lighthouse from the notes which he had already made.

But before starting he appeared before a House of Commons Committee on Public Institutions which had invited him, as an instructor at the Working Men's College, to give his views on proposals to open Museums in the evenings for 'healthful recreation and improvement of the people'. Here was a chance for a fight with the higher powers. The Chairman of the Committee was Sir John Trelawny and its members included Sir Robert Peel (son of the statesman who had died in 1850). Ruskin took the chance with gusto and he made the Committee angry. He told them that it was useless to open museums in the evenings while the working hours were so long that they left the workmen exhausted at the end of the day; that the museums could not help designers to work with the taste of foreign designers because the conditions and surroundings in which the designer worked here 'blunted his senses'—apart from the fact that the French naturally had better taste and more invention in design than the English; that the English workman had 'a thirsty desire' to improve himself in every direction; but the idea that knowledge is power, and the hope of rising out of his class, were at the back of this desire; he must be helped to rise in his class and not out of it; all efforts to help him would be vain while he was allowed to be 'entirely crushed in mind and body' by the principle of competition on which English commerce was conducted; 'an acquaintance with what foreign nations have accomplished may be very use-

---

[1] In the Preface to *The Political Economy of Art* (1857) he declared that he had not read any author on political economy except Adam Smith whom he read many years earlier. But he had been reading Mill and the others since 1855 as we know from his letter to Mrs. Carlyle (cf. above p. 280).

ful to our workmen, but a spirit of competition is useful to no one; we ought not to try to grow claret here or to produce silk; we ought to produce coal and iron and the French should give us wine and silk in exchange.'[1]

An incident in the course of this evidence is thus related by Ruskin:

'You would have been amused at seeing some of their faces as I got out, in repeated and clear answers, my hatred of Competition. At last, on my saying finally that all distress mainly came from adopting for a principle the struggle of man with man instead of the help of "man by man", Sir Robert Peel burst out with "most extraordinary sentiments, I must say, Mr. R". "Do you think so, Sir Robert?" (To the reporter) "I hope that comment is down." "It's all right," said the Chairman laughing. What he meant by "all right" I don't know.'[2]

After this he left for Chamonix where he began the essays that we know as *Unto This Last* and *Munera Pulveris.*

[1] The full text of the evidence was published in the Committee's Report, March 27, 1860. It can be found in the Library Edition, Vol. XVI.

[2] Letter to Mrs. John Simon, March 21, 1860. Ruskin had rashly said that the workmen on the Continent were happier than in England, that they were not ashamed to be seen in places where the upper classes forgathered as they were in England, that they were better dressed, and that the upper classes abroad took more interest in the condition of the working classes than the upper classes did in England. Sir Robert Peel, who was decidedly rude to him, said that this was casting a slur on the English upper classes and called upon him to substantiate or withdraw. Ruskin virtually withdrew by describing his comments purely as personal impressions not based on specialised study. Sir Robert Peel's exclamation, 'Most extraordinary sentiments' does not appear to have been recorded in the minutes.

RUSKIN AS SOCIAL AND POLITICAL ECONOMIST

RUSKIN'S THEORY OF ECONOMY

'No measures are practical except those which touch the source of the evil opposed.'

Fors Clavigera, Letter 10.

Ruskin wrote his treatise on Social and Political Economy between the beginning of 1860 and the end of 1862. His theory can be read in or rather extricated from *Unto This Last* and *Munera Pulveris*.

I say 'extricated from' because both books are badly arranged and badly written; and the arguments in both are obscured by digressions and quotations from the Bible. These faults are far more conspicuous in *Munera Pulveris*. When *Unto This Last* was written, Ruskin's mind was still in a mood of defiance and the book though badly constructed is yet relatively clear. But when he wrote *Munera Pulveris*, his mind was already in the unhealthy condition that culminated in 1863.[1] *Munera Pulveris* is the first of his books in which he deliberately indulged himself in flight of ideas, in purely fantastic interpretations, in word-jingling and obscurantism. His mind at the time was not capable of hard thought, or of even the degree of precise expression achieved in the earlier books and *Unto This Last*. And characteristically he rationalised this failing of his powers; at the very moment when he was abandoning hard thought for the fantastic discursions and obscurities of *Munera Pulveris* he wrote to his father:

'The best wisdom of the world has been spoken in strange enigmas—Dante's, Homer's, Hesiod's, Virgil's, Spenser's—

[1] Cf. above, pp. 67–74.

and no one listens, and God appoints all his best creatures to speak in this way: "that hearing they may hear and not understand"; but *why* God will always have it so, and never lets any wise or great man speak plainly—Ezekiel, Daniel, St. John being utter torment to anybody who tries to understand them, and Homer scarcely more intelligible—there's no guessing.'[1]

But within *Unto This Last* and *Munera Pulveris* there is nevertheless a polygon of social and political economic doctrines. That polygon I must now try to summarise and set in relation to the conditions and doctrines prevailing at the time.

We are so familiar with the spectacle of organised labour and high wages on the one hand, combined with enormous national expenditure on social services and unemployment on the other, that we find it hard to visualise the England of 1860, where labour was unorganised and entirely without security, and the State had not yet felt called upon to organise social service on the present socialistic scale. In 1860 there were no minimum wages in industry, no eight-hours day, no early closing, no provision for unemployment or illness, no old-age pensions, no free State elementary and technical education as we understand it, no free libraries. The Trades Union Act dates from 1871, the Public Health Act and the Artisans Dwellings Act from 1875, the educational system from the 'seventies, and the unemployment and pensions services, as everyone knows, are relatively recent. Ruskin was familiar with the dismal conditions in which labour in 1860 worked and lived; he had seen them with his own eyes in the manufacturing districts. He was also familiar with the views of business men, because he came from the business world and knew his father's business acquaintances. He analysed the situation and decided that it was simply the exploitation of the hunger, laziness and sensuality of labour by the stupidity, greed, dishonesty and insensibility of the employers; and that the official political and social economists had evolved a creed which was nothing but a series of excuses for that exploitation.

[1] Letter to his father, October, 23, 1862.

The creed evolved by the economists of that time can be summarised as follows:

I. The Postulate of the Economic Man

For economic problems man must be postulated as an Economic Man, a machine capable of so much labour costing a fluctuating price. The social affections and moral ingredients in man, inconstant and variable factors, must be left on one side in the consideration of economic questions. They may be considered separately by people whose concern they are—women, parsons, and so forth. But they must not be allowed to confuse the issue in the Science of Economics which is exclusively concerned with constant factors, and is in fact the Science of Making as Much Money as possible out of the Products of Labour, with the aid of Capital and of Business Enterprise.

II. The Law of Wages

The right price to pay for labour is the lowest price rendered possible by the Law of Supply and Demand. When labour is abundant, wages are therefore lower than when labour is scarce.

III. The Science of Catallactics

The value of a commodity is its Exchange Value in goods or money. Its value is what you can get for it. The character of the commodity does not affect this Law. It is the same for a cannon ball or a pudding, a silk flounce or a woollen petticoat. The Science of Catallactics, or Exchange Value, must control all economic operations between man and man, firm and firm, and country and country.

IV. Money and Wealth

Money and Wealth are interchangeable terms—because Wealth can be turned into money and money into Wealth. If individuals or firms accumulate money, especially money from other countries, the wealth of the country is *ipso facto* increased.

V. Unfetterd Competition

Competition is the most productive of all incentives. There must be no restrictions upon it.

VI. The Doctrine of Laisser Faire

The industry and trade of the country are the affair of the people engaged in industry and trade. They are not the business of the State or the Government. The economic problems involved are too difficult and technical for a Government to understand. The industry and trade of the country can only prosper when Supply and Demand, Competition, and Catallactics are allowed to operate without Government interference.

Ruskin's reply can be summarised as follows:

RUSKIN'S REPLY[1]

I. The Postulate of the Economic Man

This postulate is an absurdity and falsifies every calculation to which it is applied. It is an absurdity because man is not purely an economic man, and cannot act as such. The social and moral factors cannot be extracted from him and handed to the care of women and parsons. They remain inevitably with him in economic activity. If you have four healthy men, working with a will and an interest in their work, and four underfed men working without interest and loathing their work, and you calculate that you have added the second four men to the first four and thus have eight Economic Men, your calculation is false because the qualitative difference affects the quantitative calculation. If you have a business employing a thousand underfed casual underpaid hands, taking no interest in the business, and with no respect or affection for their employer, and another business employing a thousand well-fed men, with security of pay and tenure, taking an interest in the business, and with respect and affection for their employer (an organisation with *esprit de corps* like that of a well-run household or a regiment in a well-ordered army)—you are entirely wrong if you calculate that the business value of the first thousand men

---

[1] In the summary which follows I have taken the substance of Ruskin's answers, using sometimes Ruskin's examples and sometimes my own, and sometimes Ruskin's actual words and sometimes my own. But there is no idea in the summary that is not contained in the books themselves, as I understand them.

is equal to the business value of the second or, if (assuming that you own both businesses) you make any plans on the basis of two thousand Economic Men. Inclusion of the social affections and moral factors in economic calculations is not sentimental and does not confuse the issue; it is simply common sense and scientific procedure.

II. The Law of Wages

The application of the law of Supply and Demand to wages is the exploitation of hunger. The system is unjust because a bricklayer has the same right to be sure of fair pay for his labour, irrespective of the amount of labour available, as a Bishop, a soldier, a doctor or a lawyer. The system is also bad business because the qualitative factor, in such circumstances, must inevitably operate against the employer who will always suffer loss from disaffection and hostility and in extreme cases from sabotage.

In place of this system it is imperative to devise a system whereby the workman can count on a fixed rate of pay irrespective of the demand for labour and the amount of labour available; and on security of tenure if he works well.

The devising of such a system is not a matter of difficulty. It can be easily achieved by co-operative organisation of labour. The honesty of the employers is however an essential condition. The only difficulty is how to meet the 'sudden and extensive inequalities of demand which necessarily arise in mercantile operations'.

What is required is a system whereby labour agrees to a reasonably low scale of wages in return for permanency and security in employment, and the employers refrain from speculation and rapacity in fat times and accumulate reserves for lean ones.

It may seem unjust that the bad workman should receive the same wages as the good workman, but in practice the system would really mean that the good workman would be engaged and employed and the bad workman not engaged and unemployed. Bad workmen, like idlers and rogues, are largely manufactured by bad conditions. Education could ensure a minimum of such production. At its worst the system of paying a bad workman the same as the good workman is better than the system when the bad workman 'is allowed to offer his work at half-price, and either takes the place of the good, or forces him by his competition to work for an inadequate sum'.

III. The Science of Catallactics

This so-called science is based on the assumption that Exchange Value and Real Intrinsic Value are identical. This is quite false. Real Intrinsic Value is capacity for service. The Real, Intrinsic Value of a piece of silk flounce of which the Exchange Value is a guinea, is not the same as the Real, Intrinsic Value of a woollen petticoat of which the Exchange Value is also a guinea—because the one commodity is useless and the other is useful.

The Real Intrinsic Value of any form of labour or any commodity is the extent to which 'it avails towards life'.

Exchange Value is merely the price which its possessor will take for it.

'You may grow for your neighbour, at your liking, grapes or grape-shot; he will also catallactically grow grapes or grape-shot for you, and you will each reap what you have sown.' The Exchange Value of a cannon ball and a pudding may be the same, but the Real Intrinsic Value is different because the second contributes to life and the first distributes death.

To exclude Intrinsic Value from economic calculations is unscientific.

To confuse it with Exchange Value, which is merely the market price at the moment, is absurd.

IV. Money and Wealth

Money and Wealth are not interchangeable terms.

Money is a documentary promise ratified and guaranteed by the nation to give or find a variable claim to unspecified labour and commodities on demand.

The use as money of substances with worth of their own, such as gold, is a relic of barbarism.

Money will always be a variable claim, will be liable that is to say to fluctuations in worth, but might be much steadier if based on something other than gold—for example food, if a standard in food could be fixed.[1]

Wealth is the possession of useful articles which we are able to use. It is the possession of Intrinsically Valuable things by people able and willing to put them to serviceable purpose.

A horse is not wealth unless it is attached to a man who can bridle and ride or drive it, and that to some serviceable end.

The Wealth of a nation includes its stores of serviceable men and serviceable commodities.

All countries possess Wealth in some quantity. They also all possess Illth in some quantity.[2]

Their stores of Illth consist in unserviceable men and unnecessary, useless, and harmful commodities. Stores of Illth cause all kinds of devastation and trouble and act as impediments to the production, accumulation, and distribution of Wealth.

If all the money in the world, notes and gold, were destroyed in an instant, the Wealth of the world would remain the same.

As Money is a claim to unspecified types of labour and com-

---

[1] 'I have long been considering how to fix a standard for bread and fuel ... I should only be laughed at for proposing a currency founded on the ultimate standard of a ship's biscuit' (Letter to his father, Sept. 27, 1863). Ruskin foresaw our present troubles and proposed solutions on the lines of those now being put forward by the American economists as 'Technocracy' and by English economists like F. W. Pethick-Lawrence who has recently advocated a Multiple-commodity standard (*The Money Muddle*, London, Allen & Unwin, 1933). In *Munera Pulveris*, III, he wrote: 'The right of debt ought not to rest on a basis of imagination; nor should the frame of a national currency vibrate with every miser's panic, and every merchant's imprudence. There are two methods of avoiding this insecurity, which would have been fallen upon long ago, if, instead of calculating the conditions of the supply of gold, men had only considered how the world might live and manage its affairs without gold at all ... One is, to base the currency on substances of truer intrinsic value; the other, to base it on several substances instead of one ... ultimately the steadiness of currency depends upon the breadth of its base; but, the difficulty of organisation increasing with this breadth, the discovery of the condition at once safest and most convenient can only be by long analysis ...'

[2] 'Illth' was a word coined by Ruskin. He used it rarely. His ecomonic writings would have been much clearer if he had used it more often. He arrived at it by seeking an antithesis to Weal-th.

modities, it represents a power to affect both Wealth or Illth. An accumulated store of such claim in the hands of an individual or a firm may become *in the use* an increase of the country's Wealth; or it may become *in the use* an increase in the country's Illth; till *it is used* it is neither one nor the other, but remains merely a store of money, i.e. of variable claim on unspecified types of labour and commodities.

The accumulation of large sums of money in the hands of individuals is thus not in itself a good thing or a bad thing. It merely establishes an inequality in such variable claim. Such inequality is useful and desirable if the people with the maximum store of claim are also the people with the maximum ability, the maximum honesty, and the maximum sense of social duty.

Exactly the same thing applies to States. Inequalities of accumulation of money between States are inevitable. Whether the inequality is useful or harmful depends on the degree of ability, honesty, and sense of duty to other States exhibited by the State with the maximum store of claim.

The fundamental thing is to avoid the confusions between Wealth and money—and money and gold.

The market value of 'a pound' depends less on the supply of gold than on the extravagance or economy of the persons holding documentary currency, i.e. claim to goods.

War and Waste cause the worth of money to fall.

When Wealth increases, but not money, the worth of the money increases. When money increases, but not Wealth, the worth of the money diminishes.

'Lowered worth of money is often indicated not so much by a rise in the price of goods, as by a fall in that of labour. The household lives as comfortably as it did on a hundred a year, but the master has to work half as hard again to get it. Distress and crime spread in silent channels. But the old lady of Threadneedle Street does not so much as ask for "My fan, Peter".'[1]

[1] Ruskin's main examination of the relation of supplies of gold to money are contained in a letter to his father, Sept. 27, 1863, a letter published in *The Times*, Oct. 8, 1863, and a paper called *Gold. A Dialogue*, intended for *The Times* but suppressed by his father, 1863 (cf. above, p. 71).

V. Unfettered Competition

Competition in all forms is childish and abominable, and should be everywhere restrained. There is only One Economy for the world and for all units within the world. Separate and separatist economic systems within the main unit are offences against it. The existence of Custom Houses at frontiers shows that mankind economically is still in its childhood.[1] World Political Economy consists in the recognition of the fact that men acquire wealth by helping one another, and not by preying upon one another. Free Trade is right because it puts an end to destructive trade competition between nations. All countries should specialise in their national products and exchange them for national products of their neighbours. They should not compete and unfairly undersell one another.

'*Government and Co-operation are the Laws of Life. Anarchy and Competition are the Laws of Death.*'

VI. The Doctrine of Laisser Faire

This doctrine is the rationalisation of Anarchy, and so against the interests of any and every country.

The doctrine required to replace it is a doctrine which will uphold Paternal Government against Anarchy and define the duties of such Government.

A Paternal Government is a government in which the best and most serviceable people all work together to produce' accumulate, distribute and consume Wealth; and to prevent the production, accumulation, and distribution and consumption of Illth. It is a government organised in hierarchies, each level executing its appointed duties. The nominal form of the government does not matter, because, in the event, the working of the hierarchy depends on the whole nation. Such a government will leave serviceable private enterprise alone, but will 'sharply interfere' with any private enterprise that is against the public good.

The functions of such a Paternal Government are:

(*a*) To define what is and is not to be *done* in order that Wealth may be produced, accumulated, distributed and consumed.

[1] Cf. *The Stones of Venice*, III, Chap. IV, para. 3.

People who could work and don't, should be made to work.

(b) To define what may and may not be *possessed* by individuals; to regulate and control the use of possessions; and prevent useless accumulations and waste.

Nothing foments revolution more than useless and harmful extravagance by the rich. It is as essential that the rich should not be allowed to steal from the poor by extravagance, dishonesty and vice, as that the poor should not be allowed to steal from the rich by sloth, dishonesty and sensuality.

(c) To define what is and is not to be *suffered* by individuals for the public good.

A Paternal Government of this kind must register its people and know all about them; it must educate them and look after them; encourage good ethics and refinement of sensibility; look after the housing and the health of the people; regulate the relations between employees and employed, and the hours and conditions of labour. It must reduce foul and mechanical employment to a minimum—(such work as far as possible being relegated to criminals); it must provide national work for the unemployed; it must pay pensions to the old and destitute, just as it pays pensions to its own servants; and it must encourage the rank and file, as well as the captains, not only to do serviceable work, but also to employ their leisure in serviceable and not trivial ways.

It must do all this and thus make the people 'soldiers of the ploughshare as well as soldiers of the sword'. And it must see to it that the masters in agriculture, industry and commerce behave like real captains in a well-organised army.

As immediate measures the Government must institute:

(1) Free State-controlled national schools for the young; and regulations for the health of the young.

(2) Compulsory subsequent training in some trade or calling, for which purpose Government workshops must be established where a high standard of workmanship and a high quality of material used must prevail.

(3) Employment of the unemployed, male and female, in these Government workshops.

(4) Fixed minimum rates of pay in all employments.

(5) Old-age pensions.

To the expenses of such Social Services, State enterprise must contribute. No demonstrably profitable public enterprises should be left in the hands of private companies who tax the nation as a whole to pay dividends to the shareholders. The Railways for example should immediately be taken over by the State, the holders receiving the amount which they paid for their holdings.[1]

We have no right to complain that our governments are expensive as long as we allow individuals and private companies to run all the profitable public enterprises, and sacrifice our wealth to governments for unproductive purposes such as the payment of interest on war debts and the preparation for further wars.

The largest interests of money and the occupations of it which are most profitable to the lender by no means necessarily involve productive industry in the borrower.

Public wealth should be invested in a true Paternal Government engaged in productive enterprises that avail towards life and not in enterprises that make for death.

Such a government is never expensive; but governments engaged on enterprises that make for death are always ruinously expensive everywhere.

Such was the general theory which Ruskin put together between 1860 and 1862 and wrote in *Unto This Last* and *Munera*

---

[1] The clearest statement of this is a little later; it will be found in a letter to the *Daily Telegraph*, May 8 and 10, 1868. There he said: 'Competition will make two railways (sinking twice the capital really required); then, if the two companies combine they can oppress the public as effectively as one could; if they do not, they will keep the said public in dirty carriages and in danger of its life, by lowering the working expenses to a minimum in their antagonism . . . Neither the roads nor the railroads of any nation should belong to any private persons. Neither road, nor railroad, nor canal, should ever pay dividends to anybody . . . All dividends are simply a tax on the traveller and the goods levied by the person to whom the road or canal belongs, for the right of passing over his property. And this right should at once be purchased by the nation, and the original cost of the roadway—be it of gravel, iron or adamant—at once defrayed by the nation . . . If railway property is a good and wise investment of capital, the public need not shrink from taking the whole off their hands.'

Pulveris. To this theory he added little in after life. In the lectures and writings of the 'sixties, notably in *Sesame and Lilies* and *Time and Tide*, we get the addition of some constructive details and numerous fantastic touches. And in the lectures and writings of the 'seventies and 'eighties we get the stressing of the doctrine that there can be no one-sided profit in true exchange, and also—especially in periods of mental excitement near his illnesses—the stressing of a doctrine that *all* interest on money is usury and that all lending of money is unproductive —a rationalisation, of course, of his own position at the end of the 'seventies when as he had spent, given away, lost and frittered away his fortune, he no longer had dividends but a large income instead from his produce, i.e. his books.

After 1861 he worked mainly at one aspect of Economics— the problem of War. I discuss the development of his ideas on that subject in the next section. Here I need only mention that, whereas in *Munera Pulveris* he suggests ironically that the State should leave the unprofitable business of War to private enterprise, in his later writings he appears as a bitter opponent of the private manufacture of arms.[1]

---

[1] In relation to Ruskin's doctrine of the unproductive nature of the interest on War Debt (cf. *Munera Pulveris*, Preface and paras. 127–129), it is perhaps worth noting that the same point is made by G. D. H. Cole in *The Intelligent Man's Guide through World Chaos* (1932) where we read that the debt service in Great Britain at present absorbs considerably more than the total amount paid in Income Tax and not much less than the product of Income Tax and Surtax; that by far the greater part of direct taxation is thus promptly redistributed to holders of the debt at home and abroad; that the people who get the tax back again in the form of interest on War Debt are in the main rich people and rich corporations, while the poorer Income-Tax payers in the main do not get it back in this way; that the payment of the interest of War Debt thus results in 'a redistribution of income through taxation which instead of equalising incomes, tends to make them more unequal', and that a very small proportion of the War Debt interest paid to individuals and corporate bodies, is spent on charitable, educational or other social service.

It is also perhaps relevant to recall that 70 per cent of the total Revenue of both France and England is now spent on War Debt and preparations for War. In Great Britain the expenditure from the Budget on Social Services is now 6 per cent. In other European countries it is less (League of Nations World Economic Survey, 1931–1932). For the rest, readers

In regard to his main economic thesis it will be observed that his refusal to begin the study of economics by postulating an Economic Man is equivalent to his former refusal to begin the study of art by postulating an Æsthetic Man. His concept of work was creative work; and he postulated at the outset in both cases that creative work is inevitably the product of the whole man. For the rest his reply to the postulate of the Economic Man is, of course, a development of the Happiness-of-the-Workman theories put forward in the architectural books of his art theory.

Then again his concept of an Intrinsic Value in commodities is related to his concept of an Intrinsic Value in works of art. But in the case of the work of art the Intrinsic Value, in his theory, is the result of the Intrinsic Value of the Artist *qua* Man, who is Deity because taught by Deity. The value, that is to say, is the value of the source, an aspect of *origin*. But in the field of economics the Intrinsic Value of activities and commodities, in his theory, resides in the extent to which the activity or commodity '*avails towards life*'. It is thus an aspect of *result*. He held that the good picture has Intrinsic Value because it is the production of a good man. But he did not say that the good pudding has Intrinsic Value because it is the production of a good man. The Intrinsic Value in the first place is established in the process of production by the fact of the value of the maker; and that Intrinsic Value cannot be afterwards completed or destroyed. In the second case the Intrinsic Value does not arise in the course of production but only begins when some useful purpose is fulfilled by the product. The exact equivalent would have been a concept of Economic Intrinsic Value residing in the *Cost* of the commodity, i.e. the amount of Intrinsic Value in terms of human goodness and skill and labour that went to the making of it. But though this idea was in Ruskin's head he did not get much further with it than his early confused statements about the happiness of the workman, and the dictum that nothing is 'cheap'

of Wells' *The Work, Wealth and Happiness of Mankind* will realise that his concept of White War as a real form of war was anticipated and sketched in its main lines by Ruskin.

which is produced by misery, degradation and hunger.

In his theory of art, as noted, he did not point out the distinction between the fixed Intrinsic Value (deriving from the value of the artist) and the variable Acquired Value determining the Exchange Value of works of art. He was able to merge the second value with the first, and say vaguely that the one *should* be the equivalent of the other, and claim that he, John Ruskin, had the power to determine both in every particular case. But he could not do this in the wider field of general Economics, because even in his most hyper-confident moods he could not claim the power to determine the variable Acquired, i.e. Exchange Value, at any given moment, of every conceivable commodity.

We must also observe that when he worked out his theory of Art in the 'forties and early 'fifties he claimed the power to assess the degree in which every artist was in fact valuable as Deity taught by Deity; and he made this claim because he regarded himself as an appointed authority on Aspects of God. When he worked out his Economic Theory in 1860 he also claimed the power to make assessments of Intrinsic Value, to determine what activities and commodities were Wealth and what Illth; to determine, that is, what avails towards life and what does not. But in 1860 he was less confident in his power to obtain contact with Deity; and in Economics he claimed the power to assess Intrinsic Value not on the ground of his equipment as an authority on Aspects of God, but on the ground of his equipment as a just, wise and honest man.[1]

His Social Theory, with its insistence on the increase of Government powers and responsibilities, and on the necessity of social services, was wildly paradoxical in 1860 when nineteenth-century Individualism was the prevailing attitude. But as the century drew towards its end, more and more people began to realise the hardships and chaos created by the Individualist system, and Ruskin's ideas were then found to correspond to the social conscience of the time. While this was going on he was secluded at Brantwood and becoming daily

[1] Cf. below, pp. 341, 345, 352 and 356.

more and more imaged as the white-bearded Prophet. His books of all periods were then republished, and his writings on economics began to find numerous readers. But as *Unto This Last* and *Munera Pulveris* are badly arranged and written, and as to understand his system it is necessary to read a number of his other writings as well, and to read them all in the right order—few people at the time of his great popularity rightly understood what he was driving at in this particular field. Casual readers were content to react to the emotive language and derive a vague thrill from contact with the passion of the Prophet of Brantwood.

But to-day we either do not read his Economic writings or read them in order to discover his Economic Theory as a whole. And if we read with patience and construct the polygon of which he scattered the component parts we find, I submit, something of substance and of service for problems not only of his own time, but also—and perhaps still more—for problems that confront the world to-day.

RUSKIN ON WAR

On February 16, 1866, Ruskin lectured on War to the Cadets at Woolwich. He probably owed the invitation to his friendship with Colonel Edwardes who had been created K.C.B. in 1859 on his return from India, and had finally retired in England shortly before the lecture was delivered.[1]

Ruskin wrote the lecture at a moment when his mind was particularly well balanced, and when he had just completed *Ethics of the Dust* and the later essays in *The Cestus of Aglaia*. It is one of his most interesting productions. But to understand it we must first look at the development of his ideas on war.

When he was born, Napoleon was on St. Helena. When he died, the Boer War was in progress. He thus lived through all the wars of the nineteenth century and witnessed the growth of modern methods in their conduct and finance. Alfred Krupp (1822–1877) and Sir William Armstrong (1810–1900) were his exact contemporaries; and the business interests which we associate with the names of Sir Basil Zaharoff (who was born in 1850) and the firm of Vickers, came into existence in his time.

As a result of his travels and his friendships he had some personal knowledge of the places and people concerned in several of the nineteenth-century wars and conflicts; and he took an

---

[1] Cf. above, p. 152. Sir Herbert Edwardes appears to have done very fine administrative work in India and to have been a man of high ideals. He read Wordsworth's *The Happy Warrior* to Ruskin as the type of what a soldier's life and every man's life should be (Letter from Ruskin to Joseph Toynbee, Feb. 8, 1866, and Appendix to *The Crown of Wild Olive*). He wrote *A Year on the Punjab Frontier*, 1848–1849, and this book was made the subject of a lecture which Ruskin delivered in Coniston in 1883 (*A Knight's Faith*).

interest in and made pronouncements upon all of them—except the Boer War which he was too ill to follow. The progress of his thought in this field was slow. He was held up by his education, as we in all countries have been held up by ours, and as our sons in all countries are now being held up by theirs. His thought, moreover, was side-tracked, as happens to all of us, by respect for professional soldiers of marked gentleness and high character among his personal acquaintance. But his progress in this field, though slow, was real and continuous; and it continued to develop right up to the 'seventies—though, as we have seen, his thought in the field of social economics developed little after the age of forty-three, and in the field of art scarcely at all after the age of forty.

When he went to Oxford as a gentleman commoner, the Cult of Napoleon was already launched. Wells has discussed the later consequences of that Cult; he has told us that it is partly responsible for the office-boy-to-millionaire ideal that is now so widespread in Europe and America; that the thought of Napoleon's unscrupulous directness still reassures 'the business man hesitating over a more than shady transaction . . . the clerk fingering a carelessly written cheque . . . the trustee in want of ready money . . . the manufacturer meditating the pros and cons of an adulteration'; he has reminded us that the ex-Emperor of Germany was 'Napoleonic', that we live in a world where would-be Napoleons of finance, the Press, and so on still abound; and that 'half the cells in our jails and many in our mad-houses are St. Helenas'.[1] But the consequences of that Cult were not foreseen in Oxford in 1838 when the dons chose 'The Exile of St. Helena' as the subject for the Newdigate Prize Poem of the year.

Ruskin competed unsuccessfully for this prize. In his poem we read:

> 'Strengthen thy shackles, Grave! They'll quake to keep,
> Thy captive's breast from heaving in its sleep.'

Further we read:

> 'Still to thy lot the hearts of thousands cleave
> Fierce to avenge, or eager to retrieve;

[1] H. G. Wells, *Outline of History*, p. 500.

RUSKIN ON WAR

Still at thy name the warrior fires arise
Glow in the heart and lighten in the eyes;
From quiet swords their rusty scabbards fall,
And blunt spears tinkle on the idle wall.
Oh! if the hope of France's wounded heart
Clings to thee, crushed and fall'n as now thou art
How had she rallied, in thy dangerous hour
To save thine honour, or to prop thy power!
Had the stern will of thine ambition spared
Her life, to love thee, or her strength to guard,
Had the high soul, which all the earth subdued
Learned but to rule its own inquietude—
The cries of men, and all the noise of war
Had shrunk in whispers from thy throne afar . . .'[1]

The poem concluded with the image of:

'. . . England pointing to her chiefest pride
Her guard in battle and in peace her guide—'

i.e. the Duke of Wellington in his double role of Victor at Waterloo and Leader of the Tories.

After this Ruskin swung to the romantic attitude in *The Battle of Montenotte* written a little later:

'Though narrower yet their guarding grows
And hot the heaps of carnage close,
In death's faint shade and fiery shock
They stand, one ridge of living rock,
Which steel may rend, and wave may wear,
And bolt may crush and blast and tear,
    But none can strike from its abiding.
The flood, the flash, the steel may bear
Perchance destruction—*not* despair
And death—but not dividing.'

Then Napoleon himself is introduced:

[1] That there might be no mistake about it he added as a footnote: 'For the opinions expressed in this passage I hope no lengthened apology will be thought necessary. Surely, could his ambition have been restrained, the government of Napoleon was peculiarly adapted to the genius of the French nation. His power was sufficient to check their restlessness, because it was based on their vanity, and his powerful intellect, wherever it turned (and it turned everywhere) called into action innumerable energies which had before been wasted in frivolity and indolence.'

'But still, along the cumbered heath
A vision strange and fair
Did fill the eyes that failed in death
And darkened in despair;
Where blazed the battle wild and hot,
A youth, deep-eyed and pale,
Did move amidst the storm of shot,
As the fire of God through hail.
He moved, serene as spirits are,
And dying eyes might see
Above his head a crimson star
Burning continually.'

This did not last. Ruskin discovered that Napoleon had destroyed innumerable marbles and bronzes and a hundred and sixty churches in Venice,[1] and he began to look closely at the legend of his greatness. Ten years later he writes of him as a brigand who changed 'loyalty into licence, protection into plunder, truth into treachery, chivalry into selfishness . . .' and so forth.[2]

Meanwhile there was bloodshed among people and in places that he knew. He travelled all over Italy on the tours of 1840–1841 and 1845. In 1840, though he was in a depressed condition, he had nevertheless used his eyes, and he had been anything but the conventional English tourist who 'if he can gather a black bunch of grapes with his own fingers and have his bottle of Falernian brought him by a girl with black eyes, asks no more of this world, nor the next; and declares Naples a Paradise'.[3] He had observed, not only that the volcanic landscape was a morbid phenomenon and that the blue sea broke on black sand, but also that the Neapolitans were dejected and oppressed.[4] In Florence he had noted that the people had been crushed to 'vegetables'.[5] But these observations seem only to have increased his Toryism in those days. The sufferings of the Italians under the various tyrannies set up by Napoleon's victors were caused in his view by neglect and lack of firmness

[1] *Modern Painters*, Vol. I, Part II, Sec. I, Chap. VII, para. 30, 1843.
[2] Edinburgh, *Lectures on Architecture and Painting*, II, para. 32, 1853.
[3] *Præterita*, II, Chap. III, para. 51.
[4] *Præterita*, II, Chap. III, para. 50 (first and second drafts).
[5] Letter to his father, Aug. 24, 1845.

in the governing powers. In his old age, when he wrote *Præ-terita*, he claimed that he and Byron had alone seen that this mis-government had made 'all the modern life of Italy one captivity of shame and crime, alike against the honour of her ancestors, and the kindness of her God'.[1] But the realisation at the time did not move him to sympathy with the early gestures of the Risorgimento. He regarded the Italian efforts of 1848 in the same way that he regarded the French efforts of the same year —namely, as shoddy outbreaks of deplorable discontent and disorder. He was in Paris in the autumn of 1848 after the flight of Louis Philippe, the proclamation of the Second Republic, and the Battle of the Barricades; he described what he saw there as 'the unhappy traces of a slaughterous and dishonourable contest'.[2] He viewed the Italian attempt to dislodge the Aus-trians from Venice from the same standpoint at the time. There was no romance, he complained, in the Battle of Custozza (1848), it was not a fine affair like Agincourt or Bannockburn, it was 'mere feebleness and distrust on the one side and mere physical force on the other'.[3] And what were the results of that contest? A hole in every palace on the Grand Canal and three through Tintoretto's paintings on the ceiling of the Scuola di San Rocco.[4] It will be recalled that in his married life he spent many agreeable months in Venice under Austrian rule. He found the Austrians excellent administrators, the very officers who had made holes in the palaces most charming fel-lows, and their commander, Marshal Radetsky, a model of old-world courtesy who introduced Mrs. Ruskin to the Archduke Charles Ferdinand, and was uncommonly civil to her on several occasions.[5] This confirmed his coldness to the Risor-gimento; he denounced the complaints of the Italian Liberal Party as 'groundless and ridiculous'; and he was sure that if measures taken by the Austrians to repress sedition had in-

[1] *Præterita*, II, Chap. III, para. 51. (An automatic echo from Macau-lay's *Lays of Ancient Rome*.)
[2] Letter to W. H. Harrison, Oct. 24, 1848.
[3] Edinburgh, *Lectures on Architecture and Painting*, II, para. 31, 1853, and *The Stones of Venice*, III, Appendix 3, 1851–1853.
[4] *The Stones of Venice*, III, Appendix 3, 1851–1853.
[5] Cf. above, pp. 55 and 56.

flicted hardships, the blame lay 'with those whose occupation is the excitement of sedition'.[1]

In this frame of mind he made a hero of Napoleon III. His Austrian friends warned him of his error. The Emperor's crown, they said, could only be retained by wars. But Ruskin would not listen.[2] He thought that everything the Emperor did was right; he cites the negotiations which led to the Crimean War as proof of his honesty, strength, and prudence[3]; and when the Crimean butchery was at its height he calls him 'a great Emperor', in a Jingo parson's harangue in *Modern Painters, III*.[4]

The insensibility into which, at the end of the 'fifties, he rationalised his disappointment and failure to capture Art-Dictatorship, comes out in a reference to the Indian Mutiny in 1858. Addressing a South Kensington audience he contrasted the noble Highlander of Scotland, who had no art, with the 'bestial, degraded' Indian, whose art 'enriches alike, with one profusion of enchanted iridescence, the dome of the pagoda, the fringe of the girdle and the edge of the sword'. Out of the peat cottage, he said, 'come faith, courage, self-sacrifice, purity and piety and whatever else is fruitful in the work of Heaven. Out of the ivory palace' come 'corruption festered to its loathsomest in the midst of the witnessing presence of a disciplined civilisation' and 'treachery, cruelty, cowardice, idolatry, bestiality—whatever else is fruitful in the work of Hell'.[5]

---

[1] *The Stones of Venice*, III, Appendix 3 (1851–1853). Letter to *Scotsman*, June, 1859, and letters to his father, Jan. and Feb., 1852.

[2] Letter to his father, Dec. 23, 1851.

[3] Edinburgh, *Lectures on Architecture and Painting*, II, para. 32, 1853, and pamphlet on *The Opening of the Crystal Palace*, para. 7, 1854.

[4] *Modern Painters*, III, Part IV, Chap. XVIII, para. 37 (cf. above, p. 41, and below, pp. 367–368). He apologised for this in 1873 when he called the Crimean War a 'prolonged piece of temporary meddling'. (*Love's Meinie*, III, the Dabchicks, para. 133; cf. below, p. 323.)

[5] *The Two Paths*, I, paras. 1–4, Jan. 13, 1858. He apologised for this the next year as we shall see (cf. below, p. 314), and he apologised again, perhaps too handsomely, in 1884 when he said that the British rule in India had mainly resulted in the introduction of Paisley instead of Cashmere shawls and that 'every mutiny, every danger, every terror, and every crime occurring under or paralysing our Indian Legislation, arises

The fact was that at the age of thirty-nine in 1858, Ruskin had not yet begun to study the problem of war. He still looked on the Crimean War as the execution by the Czar of his 'appointment' to attack 'for confirmation of all our greatness, trial of our strength, purging and punishment of our futilities'[1]; and he still visualised other conflicts as impertinent and seditious revolutions, or as intriguing games of chess.

He still thought of war fundamentally as a form of play-like art. 'It is not . . . easy', he had written, 'to distinguish the respect paid to the Power from that rendered to the Art of the soldier; the honour of victory being more dependent, in the vulgar mind, on its results, than its difficulties. I believe, however, that taking into consideration . . . the subtleties both of apprehension and stratagem constantly demanded by it . . . it must indeed rank as far the first of the arts of the second order . . .'[2]

He had acquired this concept (which is that of people who stick flags into maps when wars are being fought) from reading military history and from playing chess—two pastimes in which he took pleasure at all periods of his life. He was intrigued and amused by the play-like art or art-like play which military historians call strategy and tactics; like a child playing with tin soldiers he was always fond of inventing and reconstructing battles 'geometrically'.[3] We meet traces of this amusement at all periods of his writings—at thirty he describes an architectural feature in the Broletto of Como as 'cut across in several places like General Zach's column at Marengo'.[4] and at

directly out of our national desire to live on the loot of India, and the notion always entertained by English young gentlemen and ladies of good position, falling in love with each other without immediate prospect of establishment in Belgrave Square, that they can find in India, instantly on landing, a bungalow ready furnished with the loveliest fans, china and shawls—ices and sherbet at command—four-and-twenty slaves succeeding each other hourly to swing the punkah, and a regiment with a beautiful band to "keep order" outside, all round the house' (*The Pleasures of England*, III, para. 81).

[1] *Modern Painters*, III, Part IV, Chap. XVIII, paras. 33–37.
[2] *The Stones of Venice*, I, Appendix 14 (1848–1851).
[3] *A Knight's Faith*, Part III, Chap. VII, 1885.
[4] *The Stones of Venice*, I, Chap. XXVIII, para. 13 (1849–1851).

sixty-six he discourses of Napoleon's misuse of cavalry and Lord Raglan's fluke at the Battle of Alma.[1] Up to 1858 he generally thought of war as a game of chess, and of armies as rows of pieces properly disposed in their first formation on the board.

It is important to get quite clear about this concept which stayed with Ruskin to the age of forty, in order that we may follow the way in which he adapted and changed it as the years went on. What we have then up to 1858 is this:

The image of peace-time armies as the four rows of pieces in their first formation on the chess board;

The image of war as a game of chess in progress.

The first of these images must be further defined. Ruskin believed that in the processes of being carved, as it were, to the required shapes and arranged in the required peace-time positions on the board, the human pieces were perfected in their bodies and their mind.[2] He thought of peace-time armies as rows of pawns with fine bodies and fine hearts ready to obey the commands of similar Court pieces; and he believed that all their fineness was the result of army discipline. He never suspected the opposite view which has thus been expressed by Wells:

'This drilling of millions of young men . . . mentally as well as physically to kill . . . is not a good thing . . . There is a real breaking down of initiative in the well-trained common soldier . . . army discipline exaggerates mental suggestibility until it may even induce that type of hysteria which is accompanied by partial paralysis and kindred crippling functional disorders . . .'[3]

Ruskin did not think of this; it did not occur to him that the sergeant-major's power might not make for 'truth, gentleness, and simplicity'[4] in the sergeant-major's mind and heart. He believed, as we have seen, in co-operative discipline between graded ranks,

[1] *A Knight's Faith, loc. cit.*
[2] *Modern Painters*, Vol. III, Part IV, Chap. XVI, para. 16, 1855–1856, and *The Two Paths*, V, para. 194, 1857–1858.
[3] *The Work, Wealth and Happiness of Mankind*, p. 609.
[4] *Præterita*, II, Chap. VIII, 151.

and he assumed—having no experience of an army either in peace or war—that army discipline was a fulfilment of this ideal. Also, like most people who have no experience of army training and like all non-combatants in wars, he persuaded himself that army training aims at teaching men how to be killed with fortitude. He could not face the idea, set down by Wells, that men are not sent into battle to get killed but to kill, and that soldiers are not sent up in aeroplanes that they may come down in flames but that they may drop bombs and cause flames to arise elsewhere. And it was of course his respect for the gentleness and kind-heartedness among the professional soldiers whom he had met—respect shared by Wells and stressed by him in another passage in the same book—which helped him to rationalise the unpleasant idea in this very usual way.

We must also look more closely at Ruskin's second image— war as a game of chess.

Military historians always write as though a war were a game of chess played *by the pieces themselves*—a game in which the pawns, on each side, representing the rank and file, are moved about by the Court pieces who move of their own volition. They concentrate, that is to say, on the movements of armies and leave out the war.

Ruskin to the age of forty accepted this concept. He did not reflect on what made the armies move. Or—to put it differently—he imaged a war as a game of chess at Denmark Hill, and he omitted the figures of himself and his opponent from the image. As long as this image dominated Ruskin's attitude, he thought of war as a game that cost no wealth and made no money; and he felt no need to inquire who paid the bill and who pocketed the money—because in the game thus envisaged there was no bill to pay.

But when, from 1859–1862, he studied the social structure for *Unto This Last* and *Munera Pulveris* he decided that the knights and castles in war move no more of their own volition than do the pawns. And he came gradually to the conclusion that the players who moved them all were greedy, cheating, panic-stricken, competing tradesmen; selfish and unimaginative women; and 'capitalists' who subscribe money to governments for expenditure on armaments. Behind the neat rows of pieces, he now saw competitive piles of bombs; and he reflected with horror that every bomb, in its nature, must sooner or later blow somebody's head off.[1]

This new attitude found early expression in a famous passage in *Unto This Last:* 'You may grow for your neighbour . . . grapes or grape-shot; he will also, catallactically, grow grapes or grape-shot for you, and you will each reap what you have sown . . .'[2]

He now reflected also that bombs and grape-shot cost a lot of money and that soldiers must be paid and fed. He asked himself where the money came from. And, in attempting to answer it, he arrived at a very singular position.

His economic studies had led him to the conclusion that modern wars are financed in the following way: first the people are taxed to prepare armaments, and 'capitalists' lend further money to governments for expenditure in the same field; then the money is spent in this way; and then the people's taxes are increased to pay the interest to the 'capitalists'.

Every war thus financed he thought of as an 'unjust' war.

But he was still far from believing that all modern wars were unjust wars. On the contrary he still believed that there was always justice on one side or the other.

As a result he was forced to the conclusion that there were two types of wars:

(1) Unjust wars, supported firstly by the greed of a nation willing to be taxed for armaments in the hope of gain in war, and secondly by loans from 'capitalists'—wars which were paid for afterwards by further taxation for the benefit of the 'capitalists' alone;

(2) Just wars—to which these conditions did not apply.

We get the statement of this curious confusion in *Unto This Last:*

'It is entirely capitalists' cash which supports unjust wars. Just wars do not need so much money to support them; for most of the men who wage such, wage them gratis; but for an

[1] *Unto This Last,* IV, para. 76.
[2] *Unto This Last,* IV, *loc. cit.* (cf. above, p. 293).

unjust war men's bodies and souls have both to be bought, and
the best tools of war for them besides . . . not to speak of the
cost of base fear and angry suspicion . . . All unjust war being
supportable, if not by pillage of the enemy, only by loans from
capitalists, these loans are repaid by subsequent taxation of the
people, who appear to have no will in the matter, the capitalists'
will being the primary root of the war; but its real root is the
covetousness of the whole nation . . .'[1]

Meanwhile wars and armed conflicts were taking place each
year. There was the Franco-Sardinian war against Austria
(1859), the Franco-British expeditions in China and Japan
(1860–1863), the Polish-Russian conflict (1863), the Circassian
trouble (1864), the Prussian-Danish conflict (1864) and the
American North and South War (1861–1865). Ruskin decided
for himself where justice lay in all these conflicts and proclaimed
his decisions to the world.

He was in Germany at the time of the Franco-Sardinian war
against Austria. Public feeling in England was then being
worked up to hysterical fear of the French; Portsmouth and
Plymouth Hoe were being fortified; and volunteers were marching up and down the country chanting the emotive doggerel
called *Riflemen Form*, which Tennyson wrote for the occasion
in *The Times:*

> There is a sound of thunder afar,
> Storm in the South that darkens the day!
> Storm of battle and thunder of war!
> Well if it do not roll our way.
> Storm, storm, Riflemen form!
> Ready, be ready against the storm!
> Riflemen, Riflemen, Riflemen form!
>
> Be not deaf to the sound that warns,
> Be not gull'd by a despot's plea!
> Are figs of Thistles? or grapes of Thorns?
> How can a despot feel with the Free?
> Form, Form, Riflemen form!
> Ready, be ready to meet the storm!
> Riflemen, Riflemen, Riflemen form!

[1] *Unto This Last*, IV, para. 76. Ruskin wrote 'Capitalists' wealth', but
he said later that of course he meant 'cash', as he distinguished wealth
from money.

Let your reforms for a moment go!
Look to your butts and take good aims!
Better a rotten borough or so
Than a rotten keel and a city in flames!
Storm, Storm, Riflemen form!
Ready, be ready against the storm!
Riflemen, Riflemen, Riflemen form!

Form, be ready to do or die!
Form in Freedom's name and the Queen's!
True we have got—*such* a faithful ally
That only the Devil can tell what he means.
Form, Form, Riflemen form!
Ready, be ready to meet the storm!
Riflemen, Riflemen, Riflemen form!

Ruskin took an independent view. He saw no justice in the
Austrian cause; and he published his decision in a letter written
from Berlin between the battles of Magenta and Solferino:

'For a long time I regarded the Austrians . . . as the only
protection of Italy from utter dissolution . . . and I should have
looked upon them as such still, if the Sardinian Government
had not shown itself fit to take their place. And the moment
that any Italian Government was able to take their place, the
Austrians necessarily became an obstacle to Italian progress,
for all their virtues are incomprehensible to the Italians and
useless to them. Unselfish individually [the Austrians in Italy]
. . . would have given, any of them, life and fortune unhesitat-
ingly at their Emperor's bidding, but their magnanimity was
precisely that of the Highlander or the Indian, incognisant of
any principle of action but of devotion to his chief or nation.'[1]

Ruskin was thus for immediate intervention on the side of
Italy and France. But there is no talk now of Napoleon III as
'a great Emperor'.[2] There is no complaint now that the battles
of the Italian Risorgimento lack romance.[3] There is no antithesis now between Highlanders as servants of Heaven and
Indians as servants of Hell.[4] What we have now is the very

[1] Letter in the *Scotsman*, July 20, 1859.
[2] Cf. above, p. 308.
[3] Cf. above, p. 307.
[4] Cf. above, p. 308.

different suggestion that 'patriotism is not enough' and that service loyalties may be misapplied.

In the same way he called for intervention on behalf of the Poles who were being murdered with Russian arms paid for by British loans to the Russian Government[1]; on behalf of the Circassians[2]; and of the Danes.[3] He winked at the exploits of the *Alabama* because he had decided that the war was waged by North America for dominion and money and not for liberty[4]; and he protested against the British selling opium 'at the cannon's mouth' in China.[5]

In these pronouncements there is no suggestion that the side to which Ruskin ascribed justice *required less money* than the other side. He had found his theory of the just war as, ipso facto, a cheap war, an embarrassment—and he had dropped it.

In place of this theory he was now reasoning as follows:

In the modern world there are just wars and unjust wars. Both are prepared for, waged, and paid for in the same way. Both involve the same misuse and waste of labour and life;

There is no difficulty about deciding what war is just and what unjust. It is merely a matter of being just oneself. He himself was 'nearly as just as it is possible for a man to be in this world'.[6] If everyone were just every nation would always see where justice lay in every conflict.

It is only the influence of unjust people that continues to make war a necessity.

We get this in *Munera Pulveris:*

'Precisely according to the number of just men in a nation is their power of avoiding either intestine or foreign war. All disputes may be peaceably settled, if a sufficient number of persons have been trained to submit to the principles of justice, while the necessity for war is in direct ratio to the number of

[1] Letter published in *Liverpool Albion*, Nov. 2, 1863, and *Sesame and Lilies*, I, paras. 29 and 30, 1864, and *The Crown of Wild Olive*, I, para. 35, 1865.

[2] *Sesame and Lilies*, II, para. 72, 1864.

[3] Letter published in *Morning Post*, July 7, 1864.

[4] Letter to C. E. Norton, Feb. 10, 1863.

[5] *Sesame and Lilies*, I, para. 30, 1864.

[6] Letter to D. G. Rossetti, 1855.

315

unjust persons who are incapable of determining a quarrel but by violence. Whether the injustice take the form of the desire of dominion, or of refusal to submit to it, or of lust of territory, or lust of money, or of mere irregular passion and wanton will, the result is economically the same;—loss of the quantity of power and life consumed in repressing the injustice added to the material and moral destruction caused by the fact of war . . .' and 'the mere dread of distrust resulting from the want of the inner virtues of Faith and Charity prove often no less costly than war itself.'[1]

This was where he stood when the invitation came to him to address the Cadets of the Royal Military Academy at Woolwich. It was unfortunate for the Woolwich authorities that they had delayed the invitation till Ruskin was forty-six. Had they invited him ten years earlier they would have got a sentimental jingo harangue like the passage on the Crimean War in *Modern Painters, III*, or the speech on the Indian Mutiny at South Kensington. Had they approached him twenty years earlier he might have read them *The Battle of Montenotte*—which perhaps they would have liked still better. But educational authorities tend to proceed with caution and to arrive too late. This, as we have seen, was again the case in 1869 when the Oxford authorities made Ruskin a Professor of Fine Art; had they offered him the post in 1849 they would have got what they wanted—a professor whose chief interest was art.

Ruskin's brief at Woolwich was 'to strengthen the young soldiers' trust in the virtue of their profession'[2]—and it was obvious that he would have to be careful what he said; that he would have to hold himself in check and not cry to them 'Look on the map of Europe and count the bloodstains on it between Arcola and Waterloo'[3]; or read them the passage from *Munera Pulveris* which I have just quoted, or tell them that the army is composed of some 'fiery and headstrong youths' who offer themselves for service, and of others 'weak and unserviceable in the civil capacity' who are 'tempted or trapped into it'.[4] He

[1] *Munera Pulveris*, Appendix I.
[2] *The Crown of Wild Olive*, Appendix, para. 161 (1873).
[3] *Modern Painters*, Vol. V, Part IX, Chap. IX (1860).
[4] *The Two Paths*, V, para. 194.

tried hard to stick to his brief and avoid indiscretions. But he hardly succeeded, as we shall see, and the Woolwich authorities filed no account of his lecture in their records, hoping, no doubt, that the young gentlemen would soon forget it.

A LECTURE TO CADETS

The lecture, afterwards published in *The Crown of Wild Olive*, was called 'War'—though its contents would be more accurately entitled 'The Soldier's Part in Peace and War'.

After a polite introductory bow in which, as the distinguished art critic, and the guest of a military institution, he built up a fantastic theory that war is the foundation of the arts and 'of all the high virtues and faculties of men'—the lecture proper began as follows:

There are three forms of war. War for exercise or play; war for dominion; war for defence.

War for exercise or play:

War is not a game to the conscript. But 'to the governor who determines that war shall be and to the youths who voluntarily adopt it as their profession, manly war has always been a grand pastime; and chiefly pursued because they had nothing else to do . . . No youth who was earnestly busy with any peaceful subject of study, or set on any serviceable course of action, ever voluntarily became a soldier. Occupy him, early and wisely, in agriculture or business, in science or in literature, and he will never think of war otherwise than as a calamity. But leave him idle, and the more brave and active and capable he is by nature the more he will . . . find, in the passion and peril of battle, the only satisfying fulfilment of his unoccupied being.' Thus there are and always have been two types of men—the workers who provide for the necessities of life and the players who are 'proudly idle, and continually therefore needing recreation in which they use the productive and laborious orders partly as their cattle and partly as their puppets or pieces in the game of death'.

Grant that wars at present are inevitable, and that there may be virtue and goodliness in the right playing of this game, there is nevertheless no excuse for playing it 'with a multitude of human pawns'. Gentlemen should be ashamed to 'set up these unhappy peasant-pieces upon the chequer of forest and field'. Ladies should blush to chatter wittily among themselves while, as Carlyle says in *Sartor Resartus*, a group of peasants are shipped away to kill and be killed by another group with whom they have no quarrel. This war-game must be played by gentlemen against other gentlemen in personal combat to prove who has the finer frame, the stronger arm and the steadier heart and, who is consequently the better man. 'You must not make of it a question which of the combatants has the longest gun, or which has got behind the biggest tree or which has the wind in his face, or which has gunpowder made by the best chemists, or iron smelted with the best coal, or the angriest mob at his back.' There is no measure of your guilt if you wage war in this way, 'if you have to take away masses of men from all industrial employment—to feed them with the labour of others—to provide them with destructive machines varied daily in national rivalship of inventive cost, if you have to ravage the country which you attack—to destroy for a score of years its roads, its woods, its cities, and its harbours, and if finally . . . you tear masses to pieces with jagged shot.'

If the game of war is again to be rightly played you must play it as the Spartans played it at Corinth when they won a decisive battle with the loss of eight men, not as the Americans played it in 1863 when 30,000 men were killed in an indecisive fight at Gettysburg . . .

We can hear the nervous coughs of the Woolwich authorities, and see the crossing and uncrossing of their legs, as they listened to this account of the game of war. The authorities were doubtless grateful for the tactful use of 'governor' instead of 'King'; but all this was certainly not what was expected from the author of that 'right-minded' sermon on the Crimean War. They doubtless took comfort in the thought that the idea of single combat was so silly that the Cadets might be trusted to take the measure of the rest.

Yet, considering his real views on war at the time, Ruskin was speaking with deliberate restraint. He was trying to get back to his old concept of the chess board on which the Court pieces with loyal hearts moved about the loyal pawns geometrically in play-like art; and to keep on one side his new concept of tradesmen, women, and 'capitalists' as the real movers of all the pieces in the game. He was almost succeeding—but not quite; and in the failure he was throwing all the guilt of the tradesmen, women, and 'capitalists' on the unfortunate Court pieces.

Moreover he was restraining his ironical wit. He was not addressing the young men at Woolwich in the same terms that he had used at the Working Men's Institute at Camberwell a month or so before, when he spoke of 'the play of plays, the great gentlemen's game, which ladies like them best to play at—the game of War'—the game for which they 'dress . . . in scarlet and gold and all manner of fine colours . . . all paid for by hard labourers' work . . . in the furrow and furnace'.[1]

The lecture continued as follows:

War for dominion:

Human nature is naturally noble; the strength of a country does not depend on its size or population but on the number of its noble men. A King who is noble will realise that his real power is power to help, and he will be fully occupied in increasing the happiness of his subjects and improving their land; but a King who is false to his natural nobility will imagine that his power is power to meddle and destroy. The noble King will not want to extend his territory by war for dominion; the ignoble King will always be seeking larger fields in which to meddle and destroy. No nation is strengthened by seizing dominion over races whom it cannot benefit . . . Whether England is to be weakened or strengthened by the possession of India will depend on the degree in which her influence on the native race proves 'benevolent and exalting'.

'But as it is at their own peril that any race extends their dominion in mere desire of power, so it is at their own still greater peril that they refuse to undertake aggressive war, according to their force, whenever they are assured that their authority would be helpful and protective. To a nation whose

---

[1] *The Crown of Wild Olive*, I, para. 28.

conscience is clear these situations will always be obvious.'[1]

War for defence:

You young gentlemen have become defenders of England in sentimental 'peacocky' enthusiasm for the idea that it is nobler to die for her in a red coat than to live for her in a black one. But 'if you cared to do your duty to your country in a prosaic and unsentimental way . . . there is now truer duty to be done in raising harvests than in burning them; more in building houses than in shelling them—more in winning money by your own work, wherewith to help men, than in other people's work, taxing for money, wherewith to slay men.'

By your soldier's vow you have made yourselves slaves 'driven to your work without thought at another's bidding'. But who are your masters? You were too proud to become shop-keepers; are you content to become the servants of shop-keepers, and 'stand at the shop door to protect shop-boys cheating inside'?

You must not submit to be a mercenary army because that would be fatal to England. A state which uses a mercenary army, a state in which the brave go out to fight and the cowards stay at home to think—is doomed. Remember that you are a part of England, not her tool. It may well be that you are the noblest part. See to it that you become the wisest. 'You must think and feel for England, as well as fight for her'—and if necessary you must rule her . . .

The peroration was as follows:

If it is not yet possible to beat swords into ploughshares it is the fault of the mothers and wives and maidens of England, because no war could continue without their approval. If the usual course of war instead of unroofing peasants' houses and ravaging peasants' fields merely broke the china on the women's drawing-room tables no war in civilised countries would last a week . . .

---

[1] I have extracted the argument here from a mass of emotive verbiage in the actual text. Ruskin, I fancy, was not anxious to be too clear. He had lived, we must remember, a good deal abroad, and he may have met people who suggested that the English were in a delicate position in discussing the ethics of War for Dominion.

It will be observed that two cats—the covetous cheating shop-keepers and the selfish unimaginative women—at last hopped out of Ruskin's bag. But he managed to keep the 'capitalist' subscribers to loans for armaments inside.

The distinction drawn in this lecture between voluntary and conscript service and the insistence on the wholesale destructiveness of modern guns marks the directions in which Ruskin's attitude to the war problem was about to develop. In concentrating on these aspects he was in line with the conscience of the time. Since his youth the Cult of Napoleon had been steadily growing and those who viewed it with alarm were pointing out that the Napoleonic omelette was made with conscript eggs. Sadowa, won instantaneously by Prussians with the new breech-loading guns, came six months after Ruskin's address to the Cadets. Thereafter all thinking men realised that when victory could only be won by advancing against these weapons, the eggs in future wars would always have to be not only conscripts but also very numerous indeed.[1]

In Ruskin's view the new weapons made the modern conduct of war an abomination. In 1868 he writes:

'If war is to be waged by money and machinery, the nation which is the largest and most covetous multitude will win. You may be as scientific as you choose; the mob that can pay more for sulphuric acid and gunpowder will at last poison its bullets, throw acid in your faces, and make an end of you—of itself also in good time, but of you first. And to the English people the choice of its fate is very near now. It may spasmodically defend its property with iron walls a fathom thick, a few years longer—a very few . . . against the multitude that is breeding and spreading, faster than the clouds, over the habitable earth. We shall be allowed to live by small pedlar's business and ironmongery—since we have chosen those for our line of life—as long as we are found useful black servants to the Americans; and are content to dig coals and sit in the cinders;

[1] Ruskin referred to Sadow (Königgratz) and its 'sudden and appalling demonstration of the power of a new weapon' a few years later in his letter on *Modern Warfare* in *Fraser's Magazine*, 1876 (cf. below, p. 326).

and have still coals to dig—they once exhausted or got cheaper elsewhere, we shall be abolished.'[1]

He had not however lost his respect for what Wells calls the *persona* of the soldier, and he still clung to the image of the disciplined army as a type of Government and Co-operation— as distinguished from all types of Anarchy and Competition.[2] The crime of war, as he now saw it, resided in the relation between the combatants—voluntary and conscript—and the non-combatants. He decided that all war is abominable unless the whole manhood of the nation, led by their King, is fighting in the field; and he tried to demonstrate that the wars of the past were noble because they had been conducted in that way:

'All great nations first manifest themselves as a pure and beautiful animal race, with intense energy and imagination. They live lives of hardship by choice and by grand instinct of manly discipline; they become fierce and irresistible soldiers; the nation is always its own army and their King or chief head of government is always their first soldier—Pharaoh, or David, or Leonidas, or Valerius, or Barbarossa, or Cœur de Lion, or St. Louis or Dandolo or Frederick the Great.'[3]

This nonsense was written in one of the periods when he allowed himself to be captured by the past. It was written at the time when he was angling for an appointment at one of the Universities, and fiddling with Greek coins in the British Museum, and inventing fantastic interpretations of Greek myths. By indulging in this silly and dangerous notion of past wars *nobly conducted*, contrasted with *ignobly conducted* wars of the present, he was, of course, still evading the central theoretical question of the whole problem, 'What is a just and what an unjust war?' And he was still answering it as heretofore by 'A war which I, Ruskin—or failing me other just men —decide to be just or unjust in relation to the circumstances.' It was in this position that he was caught by the Franco-Prussian War in 1870.

[1] *The Queen of the Air*, III, paras. 114 and 116. (1869).
[2] Cf. above, p. 296.
[3] *The Queen of the Air*, III, para. 105, 1869.

When the war broke out he was in the Alps, with Mrs. Hilliard, and Connie and Joan, a maid, a valet and the gardener Downs, and he hurried back as already chronicled.[1] On the way he took the ladies to the *Comédie Française* where the *Marseillaise* was sung and he found 'the cry of the audience '*à genoux*' most touching'.[2] For the rest he still believed in Napoleon III, and finding the question of where justice lay in the conflict extremely difficult, he flew, for the moment, to the usual refuge of the addle-pated, and said vaguely that the war was 'all men's fault' as much as the Emperor's.[3]

But Ruskin was not the man to take cover in this way for long. After Sedan he regarded Napoleon III as 'a shadow of a King',[4]—'a feeble Pan's pipe or Charon's boatswain's whistle, instead of a true King',[5]—a fool whose Crimean War had been nothing but 'a prolonged piece of temporary meddling'[6]; the creature had not only surrendered at the head of his army, but he had abandoned his country to the Republicans. Ruskin still thought he knew all about French Republicans. Had he not seen them in 1848 in Paris 'roaming about the streets at night, spitting about them by day, throwing stones at statues and windows, and confiscating any property that could be got hold of'.[7] There could be no longer doubt where justice lay, now that the war had become a contest between Republicans and Monarchists.

We get this in letters to the *Daily Telegraph:*
'The war on the French side is now being conducted by a government which for the time renders all political treaty with it practically impossible' . . . The world is confronted with 'a simple and testing struggle between pure Republicanism on the one side, expressed in the most exquisite, finished, and exemplary anarchy yet achieved—under earth—and one of the

---

[1] Cf. above, p. 106.
[2] Letter to C. E. Norton, July 29, 1870.
[3] *Ibid.*
[4] *Fors Clavigera*, Letter 10, Oct., 1871.
[5] *Fors Clavigera*, Letter 31, July, 1873.
[6] *Love's Meinie*, III, para. 133, 1873.
[7] *Fors Clavigera*, Letter I (first draft), Jan., 1871.

truest Monarchies and schools of honour and obedience yet
organised under heaven.' The Prussians can be trusted to spare
what they can and ought . . .

But before the ink was dry the news came that the Prussians
were marching on Paris. And Ruskin concluded his letters by
declaring that the Prussians were pressing their victory too far,
that their demand for Alsace and Lorraine as 'guarantees' was
ridiculous since their annexation would 'guarantee' nothing,
and that England must intervene at once to insist that Prussia
should offer an immediate armistice and acceptable terms of
peace.[1]

In the months that followed he became yet more indignant
at the Prussian conduct. This 'true Monarchy's' ideas of what
it ought to spare were extremely curious. The Prussians had
not spared the Library at Strasbourg; and now they were bom-
barding Paris and threatening the Sainte-Chapelle and Notre
Dame. He wrote again to the *Daily Telegraph*, and he joined
the Mansion House Committee for Relief Work in Paris.[2]

Looking back on the Franco-Prussian War, Ruskin concentrated on three ideas.

The first was the idea that in spite of the wholesale destruction made inevitable by modern weapons, there is less deliberate
'frightfulness' in modern war than was the case in the wars of
the past. 'Of wilful destruction', he wrote, 'I most thankfully
acknowledge the cessation in Christian warfare.' Frankly
abandoning the silly noble-wars-of-the-past theory he now
contrasts the Prussian entry into Paris in 1871, when no damage was done and no lives taken, with the capture of Magdeburg in the Thirty Years War in 1631 when the conquerors
burned practically the whole town and executed 30,000 out of
the 36,000 inhabitants without regard to age or sex.[3]

Here events have shown that his vision for once failed him.
He did not foresee the German conduct in Belgium in 1914.

[1] Letters to the *Daily Telegraph*, Oct. 6 and 7, 1870.
[2] Letters in *Daily Telegraph*, Jan. 12 and 19, 1871, and *Fors
Clavigera*, Vol. I, Letter 1, Jan., 1871.
[3] Letter on *Modern Warfare* in *Fraser's Magazine*, July, 1876.

The second idea that was pressed upon him by the Franco-Prussian War came from the spectacle of Englishmen willing to sell arms both to France and Prussia. As he now saw it, since one side or the other, or both sides, in a war must be perpetrating crime, these Englishmen were patently willing to aid and abet the crime if only thereby they could make some money. In the 'seventies, his attacks on the armament dealers abound. In *Fors Clavigera* he writes:

'There is no physical crime to-day, so far beyond pardon—so without parallel in its untempted guilt, as the making of war-machinery, and invention of mischievous substance. Two nations may go mad, and fight like harlots—God have mercy on them; you, who hand them carving knives off the table, for leave to pick up a dropped sixpence, what mercy is there for *you?*'[1]

'*You must simply rather die than make any destroying mechanism or compound.*'[2]

He reminded his readers that Armstrong guns, sold to all and sundry, were in fact being sold to people who might fire them down English throats.[3] To his audience in Oxford he said:

'The misuse we have made of our discoveries will be remembered against us in eternal history . . . The practical fact which will remain for the contemplation of the future is that we have invented gun-cotton and nitro-glycerine . . . We shall be remembered as the most cruel and . . . the most unwise generation that ever troubled the earth:—the most cruel in proportion to our sensibility and the most unwise in proportion to our science.'[4]

He then examined the post-war finance and brought the 'capitalists' into relation with the gunmakers:

'Capitalists when they do not know what to do with their money persuade the peasants in various countries that the said peasants want guns to shoot each other with. The peasants

[1] *Fors Clavigera*, Letter 7.
[2] *Fors Clavigera*, Letter 7. Italics are Ruskin's.
[3] *Fors Clavigera*, Letter 29.
[4] *The Eagles' Nest*, II, paras. 34–35.

accordingly borrow guns, out of the manufacture of which the capitalists get a percentage and men of science much amusement and credit. Then the peasants shoot a certain number of each other, until they get tired; and burn each other's homes down in various places. Then they put the guns back into towers, arsenals, etc., in ornamental patterns (and the victorious party put also some ragged flags in churches). And then the capitalists tax both, annually, ever afterwards, to pay interest on the loan of the guns and gunpowder.'[1]

The third idea impressed upon him by the Franco-Prussian War was the power of propaganda:

'We improve contention of arms with contention of tongues and are able to multiply the rancour of cowardice and mischief of lying in universal and permanent print.'[2]

His position by 1876 was thus largely summed up in the following passage:

'Nowadays persons who quarrel fight at a distance with mechanical apparatus for the manufacture of which they have taxed the public and which will kill anybody who happens to be in the way; gathering at the same time, to put into the way of them, as large a quantity of senseless and innocent mob as can be beguiled or compelled to the slaughter . . . the persons in arms led out for mutual destruction are by no means the whole nation on either side, but only the individuals of it who are able-bodied, honest and brave, selected to be shot from among its invalids, rogues and cowards . . . The nations minded thus to try their quarrel should at least raise the stakes for their match before they make the ring, instead of drawing bills for them upon futurity.'[3]

And he added the warning:

'That the money-lenders whose pockets are filled while everybody else's are emptied by recent military finance, should occultly exercise irresistible influence not only on the development of our armaments but also on the deliberation of Cabinets and the passions of the populace is inevitable under present cir-

---

[1] *Munera Pulveris*, 1871, Preface (cf. also *Fors Clavigera*, Letter 8).
[2] *Fors Clavigera*, Letter 4.
[3] Letter on *Modern Warfare* to *Fraser's Magazine*, July, 1876.

cumstances; and the exercise of such influence, however advantageous to contractors and projectors, can scarcely be held consistent either with the honour of a Senate or the safety of a State.'[1]

In the final construction of his polygon of doctrine about war, Ruskin linked up the experience of the Franco-Prussian war with his general social-economic theory in *Unto This Last* and *Munera Pulveris*.

He linked it in the first place with his old enemy—Competition:

'The first reason for all wars, and for the necessity of national defences, is that the majority of persons, high and low, in all European nations, are Thieves, and, in their hearts, greedy of their neighbours' goods, land, and fame. But besides being Thieves, they are also fools, and have never yet been able to understand ... that the prosperity of their neighbours is, in the end, their own also; and the poverty of their neighbours, by the communism of God, becomes also in the end their own.'[2]

And he looked forward to a future when all the energies now devoted to war will be diverted to peaceful production of Wealth instead of Illth; when there will be 'Soldiers of the Ploughshare as well as Soldiers of the Sword'; and when the virtues of loyalty and obedience that now appear in armies and in the *persona* of the soldier, will be employed in policing the world and repressing knaves.

He had put forward this solution in *Unto This Last* and *Munera Pulveris*.[3] It lay, of course, behind the Hincksey digging in Oxford, and he had stated it specifically in *Time and Tide:*

'To punish knaves and make idle persons work ... that is indeed the ultimate and perennial soldier-ship; that is the essential warrior's office to the end of time ... The soldier's office at present is indeed supposed to be the defence of his country

---

[1] Letter on *Modern Warfare* in *Fraser's Magazine*, July, 1876.
[2] *Fors Clavigera*, Letter 7.
[3] For example, in *Munera Pulveris*, VI, para. 149.

against other countries; but that is an office which—Utopian as you may think the saying—will soon now be extinct.'[1]

But now he was less optimistic:

'How long is it before these virtues of loyalty and obedience shall be conceived as capable of development, no less in employments which have some useful end and fruitful power than in those which are simply the moral organisation of massacre and the mechanical reduplication of ruin?'[2]

It was this solution that lay behind his lecture on Sir Herbert Edwardes' *A Knight's Faith*[3] which he delivered in 1883. And he thus arrived, in the end, at the precise position where Wells now stands in *The Work, Wealth and Happiness of Mankind.*[4]

And then we get this epilogue:

'The time is certainly drawing near for the workmen, who are conscious of their own power and probity, to draw together into action. They ought first in all Christian countries to abolish, not yet *War*—which must yet be made sometimes in just causes,—but the Armaments for it, of which the real root cause is simply the gain of manufacturers of instruments of death.'[5]

Ruskin died in 1900. After the 1914–1918 war the conscience of the world framed the Covenant of the League of Nations. There we read:

'The Members of the League agree that the manufacture by private enterprise of munitions and implements of war is open to grave objections . . .'

[1] *Time and Tide*, XXIV, para. 160.
[2] *Fors Clavigera*, Letter 79.
[3] Cf. above, p. 303.
[4] Cf. below, p. 368.
[5] Letter for publication to Thomas Barclay, 1887.

RUSKIN'S RELIGION

'The claim ... of the Personal relation of God to man, as the source of all human, as distinguished from brutal, virtue and art ... must be carefully and clearly distinguished by every reader who wishes to understand either *Modern Painters* or any of my more cautiously written subsequent books, from the statement of any Christian doctrine as commonly accepted ... Man's use and purpose ... is to be the witness of the glory of God, and to advance that glory by his reasonable obedience and resultant happiness. Nothing is here said of any tradition of Fall, or of any scheme of Redemption; nothing of Eternal Punishment, nothing of Immortal Life. It is assumed only that man can love and obey a living Spirit; and can be happy in the presence and guidance of a Personal Deity, otherwise than a mollusc, a beetle, or a baboon.'

Epilogue to *Modern Painters*, Sunday, September 16, 1888.

This passage, one of the last that Ruskin wrote, accurately describes his religion, which was always really personal, and which never fundamentally varied all his life.

It is usually suggested that he was a bigoted Evangelical Protestant till he was thirty-nine in 1858, that he then became a sceptic, and that after 1874 when he was fifty-five, he developed into a broadminded Protestant. There is considerable evidence which, if superficially read, supports this suggestion; and it is what Ruskin himself at certain moments believed to have happened. But if we examine the evidence in relation to the circumstances of his life and the workings of his mind at the different periods, we find that his own final statement is undoubtedly the truth.

In childhood and adolescence his head was crammed with the text of the Bible. He continued to read the Bible all his life, and his familiarity with its text was always exceptional. All his religion was really based on that Bible reading. There is no evidence that he was ever a sectarian bigot like his mother. In

329

his childhood the Pope and Romanism had been held up to him as Evil and Corrupting Forces that must be shunned like the Devil. In adolescence he continued to look upon the Pope and Roman Catholicism in this way. This was a complication in his early passion for Adèle, who was a Roman Catholic; and in 1840 it made him presume the malaria in the Campagna a consequence of Papal wickedness, and to suppose that no Roman Catholic religious painting was worth looking at.[1] But there is no evidence that once he reached the age of conscious religious thought he ever looked on his mother's sect as the appointed medium between himself and God. And, as noted, he could not bring himself to take Holy Orders and accept the Church as his master.[2]

Sectarian bias is not a feature of *Modern Painters, I*. When he wrote that book in a mood of manic confidence he believed that, because he had an exceptional acquaintance with the text of the Bible and a bubbling enthusiasm for phenomena, he had an exceptional knowledge of God, and had been appointed to explain God's Word and Works. There is no evidence that the special claims of any section of the Church came into the picture. Believing himself half-way between earth and heaven he went much further in personal religion than the orthodox Evangelical belief in the divine inspiration, authority, and sufficiency of the Holy Scriptures, and the right and duty of private judgement in the interpretation of them. He visualised himself and God and Turner on the one hand, and the Pope and Roman Catholicism and Claude on the other. That, clearly, is what his religion amounted to in *Modern Painters, I*.

On the tour alone with his guide and valet, which preceded *Modern Painters, II*, he spent six months in Italian churches, looked for the first time at Roman Catholic religious painting, and fell in love with the dancing angels in the pictures by Fra Angelico, who was not only a Roman Catholic but a Dominican. And panic came upon him lest he should be seduced to Romanism by the emotive appeal of Roman Catholic painting, architecture, and ritual.

[1] *Præterita*, II, Chap. II, para. 31.
[2] Cf. above, pp. 47 and 48.

The first result of this panic was renewed zeal in reading the Bible and in professed sectarianism before his valet:

'The steadily read chapters—morning and evening, with the continual comparison between the Protestant and Papal Services every Sunday abroad, made me feel that all dogmatic teaching was a matter of chance and habit; and that the life of religion depended on the force of faith, not the terms of it ... A little more force was also put on Bible study at this time because I held myself responsible for George's tenets as well as my own, and wished to set him a discreet example ... So I read my chapter with him morning and evening; and if there were no English church on Sundays, the Morning Service, Litany and all, very reverently ...'[1]

The second result of the fear of seduction by Rome was a direct appeal to God. When he was ill with diptheria he prayed that he might be cured as a sign—and he believed that this direct appeal was directly answered.[2] This happened on his way back to England. But he tells us he had scarcely reached home before he had 'sunk back into the faintness and darkness of the Under-World'.[3]

Confidence and, with it, faith in his knowledge of God, returned during the writing of *Modern Painters, II*, where he expounded God's intentions in manic passages of 'pious insolence',[4] and indulged in one or two tilts at 'the languid sympathies of the untaught flocks' of 'vulgar Romanism'.

We get the same characters in *The Seven Lamps of Architecture*:

'In the pressing or recommending of any act or manner of acting we have choice of two separate lines of argument: one based on representation of the expediency or inherent value of the work, which is often small and always disputable; the other

---

[1] *Præterita*, II, Chap. VI, paras. 110 and 111. For George, his valet, cf. above, pp. 51 and 55.
[2] *Præterita*, II, Chap. VII, para. 147.
[3] *Ibid.*, para. 148.
[4] *Modern Painters*, II, Part III, Sec. I, Chap. VI, para. 15. Note added, 1883. (For examples of this 'pious insolence' cf. para. 16 and another 1883 note, also Chap. XI of the same section.)

based on proofs of its relations to the higher orders of human virtue, and of its acceptableness, so far as it goes, to Him who is the origin of virtue. The former is commonly the more persuasive method, the latter assuredly the more conclusive; only it is liable to give offence, as if there were irreverence in adducing considerations so weighty in treating subjects of small temporal importance. I believe, however, that there is no error more thoughtless than this. We treat God with irreverence by banishing Him from our thoughts, not by referring to His will on slight occasions. His is not the finite authority or intelligence which cannot be troubled with small things. There is nothing so small but that we may honour God by asking His guidance of it or insult Him by taking it into our own hands; and what is true of the Deity is equally true of his Revelation. We use it most reverently when most habitually; our insolence is in ever acting without reference to it, our true honouring of it is in its universal application.'[1]

Here in his 'pious insolence' he is really saying 'Every problem can be solved by reference to the Bible—the Word of God. I, John Ruskin, know the Bible by heart. Every problem can be solved by asking me for the appropriate quotation.'

With this, at this time, we get fear of Romanism expressed in abuse of Romanist ritual and of Catholic Emancipation:

'We must always fearfully and widely shun the thought that the magnificence of the temple can materially add to the efficiency of the worship or the power of the ministry . . . That is the abuse and fallacy of Romanism by which the true spirit of Christian offering is directly contradicted . . . The danger and evil of their church decoration, altogether, lie . . . in its tinsel and glitter, in the gildings of the shrine and painting of the image, in embroidery of dingy robes, and crowding of imitated gems . . .'[2]

'In expressing my belief of the close connection of the distress and burden which the mass of the people at present sustain,

[1] *The Seven Lamps of Architecture*, Introductory, para. 5 (1848).
[2] *The Seven Lamps of Architecture*, Chap. I, para. 8. Ruskin deleted this and the following quotation from the 1880 edition as 'pieces of rabid and utterly false Protestantism' (1880 Preface).

with the encouragement which, in various directions, has been given to the Papist [Catholic Emancipation (1829) and Maynooth grant (1845)], do not let me be called superstitious or irrational. No man was ever more inclined than I, both by natural disposition and by many ties of early association, to a sympathy with the principles and forms of the Romanist Church ... But in confessing this strength of affectionate prejudice surely I vindicate more respect for my firmly expressed belief, that . . . its lying and idolatrous Power is the darkest plague that ever held commission to hurt the Earth . . . that we never can have the remotest fellowship with the utterers of that fearful falsehood and live . . . England will never be prosperous again . . . the honour of her arms will be tarnished, and her commerce blighted, and her national character degraded, until the Romanist is expelled from the place which has impiously been conceded to him among her legislators . . . England has already made one step full of danger . . . Her foot already hangs over the edge of the precipice. It must be retracted, or the Empire is but a name.'[1]

The fear is still present in *The Stones of Venice*. There he again attacks Catholic Emancipation in England, quoting a newspaper article by his father[2]; and after the well-known description of the emotive glories of the interior of St. Mark's, and of the 'passionate kiss and clasp of the arms given to the feet of the crucifix' by the worshippers, he writes:

'But we must not hastily conclude from this that the nobler characters of the building have at present any influence in fostering a devotional spirit . . . This effect is altogether to be ascribed to its richer assemblage of those sources of influence which address themselves to the commonest instincts of the human mind, and which, in all ages and countries, have been more or less employed in the support of superstition. Darkness and mystery; confused recesses of building; artificial light employed in small quantity, but maintained with a constancy which seems to give it a kind of sacredness; preciousness of

[1] *The Seven Lamps of Architecture*, note 1. The last three sentences are a quotation from *Historical Essays*, by the Rev. Dr. Croly, 1842.
[2] *The Stones of Venice*, I, Appendix 5.

material easily comprehended by the vulgar eye; close air loaded with a sweet and peculiar odour associated only with religious services; solemn music; and tangible idols or images having popular legends attached to them.—These, the stage properties of superstition . . . have been from the beginning of the world, and must be to the end of it, employed by all nations . . . to produce a false awe in minds incapable of apprehending the true nature of the Deity . . . It must . . . therefore be altogether without reference to its present usefulness, that we pursue our inquiry into the merits and meaning of the architecture of this marvellous building.'[1]

In *The Stones of Venice* we also read:

'Of all . . . fatuities, the basest is the being lured into the Romanist Church by the glitter of it, like larks into a trap by broken glass; to be blown into a change of religion by the whine of an organ-pipe; stitched into a new creed by gold threads or priests' petticoats; jangled into a change of conscience by the chimes of a belfry. I know nothing in the shape of error so dark as this, no imbecility so absolute, no treachery so contemptible.'[2]

To understand all this we must read Ruskin's letters and diaries at the time. For then it becomes clear that he himself was really fascinated by the characters which he abused. He had prefaced the writing of *The Seven Lamps of Architecture* by several months' study in the French cathedrals where he attended services, and was obviously moved and attracted by the ritual and processions, the 'saintly and sublime' music and the large and attentive congregations. After a service in Rouen Cathedral he wrote in his diary:

'I felt convinced that, freed from abuses, this *mode* of service was the right one . . . that all these proud pillars and painted casements, all these burning lamps and smoking censers, all these united voices and solemn organ peals had their right and holy use in this their service, and that all these white-robed priests and young troops of novice and chorister could be, and

[1] *The Stones of Venice*, II, Chap. IV, paras. 19 and 20 and 22.
[2] *The Stones of Venice*, I, Appendix 12.

ought to be, devoted to their lofty duties and separated from the common world without offence—yes and with high honour before God . . . I never felt more strongly the non-importance of all these things as subjects of dispute or of law. In some respects they are little other than matters of taste in religion . . .'[1]

After another service in the same cathedral he wrote to his father:

'Vespers in the cathedral . . . are very nearly our English evening service magnificently chanted . . . all the priests, novices, etc., coming down from the altar, and the Archbishop from his throne, to sit before the pulpit—his crozier and the crucifix held before him by two priests in white stoles and the little choristers, Paul Veronese-like, with their crimson caps, grouped round him; all of which gives me intense pleasure . . . We receive his blessing with the rest of the congregation—*I* at least very thankfully—and then after some more lovely passages of chanting, we come out into the grey cathedral porch—I trust none the worse for an hour so spent, whatever the portion of the congregation may be who leave that porch for the planked passages of the theatre door.'[2]

The fear of seduction by these characters remained with him in Venice. It lay behind his pamphlet calling on all Protestant sects to unite against the insidious foe (*Notes on the Construction of Sheepfolds*, 1851), behind the querulous 'By our system of education we have made half the youth of our upper classes Roman Catholics'—in his letters intended for *The Times* (1852), and behind his statement in the same letters that four of his fellow-students of Divinity in Oxford had since become 'zealous Romanists'. And it was finally confessed thirty years later when he said that 'the depreciation of ecclesiastical influence, and the strong insistence on the national styles of civil building', which were among 'the chief faults' of his architectural books, were primarily due to his 'dread of ritualist devotion'.[1]

[1] Diary, Oct. 15, 1848.
[2] Letter to his father from Rouen, Oct. 9, 1848.
[1] *Valle Crucis*, II, *Mending the Sieve* (lecture on Cistercian Architecture, Dec. 4, 1882). I think it possible that his Firefly obsession may

Once more he sought refuge in the text of the Bible. But now he feels in its 'poetry' a disturbing obscurantism, a 'Delphic-oracle tone . . . savouring of tripods and hot air below', and adds:

'While I am ready to receive any amount of mystery in *What* is revealed I don't at all like mystery in the *manner* of revealing it. The *doctrine* is God's affair. But the revelation is mine, and it seems to me that from a God of Light and Truth, His creatures have a right to expect plain and clear revelation touching all that concerns their immortal interests. And this is the great question with me—whether indeed the Revelation *be* clear, and Men are blind, according to that "He hath blinded their eyes and hardened their hearts" or whether there be not also some strange darkness in the manner of Revelation itself.'[1]

The day after writing this he went off with his wife to Verona for the aged Marshal Radetsky's ball where Effie 'was allowed by everyone to be the *reine du bal*'[2]; and then he enjoyed the Venetian Carnival and other social distractions. By the end of February he is solving a minor problem of a mundane kind:

'I find that in reality the Marshal was much pleased at our twice coming to Verona merely to go to his ball, and that, while we esteemed it a favour to be asked, he did not less think it polite in us to come.'[3]

On Good Friday the problem of the Bible reappears in his letters to his father. By this time he had conceived the thought that the Bible might not really be the Word of God—and, so, that in quoting it he, John Ruskin, might not really be 'Deity, i.e. taught by Deity'.[4] To recapture his faith in himself he now tried to repeat the experience of the cure from diptheria. But there is no longer the same simplicity of conviction in the result:

have been connected with his early fascinated horror of the points of candlelight in Roman Catholic cathedrals.

[1] Letter to his father from Venice, Jan. 24, 1852.
[2] Cf. above, p. 56.
[3] Letter to his father from Venice, Feb. 28, 1852.
[4] Cf. above, pp. 215 and 216.

'One day last week . . . I began thinking over my past life and . . . I saw that I had always been working . . . either for myself, in doing things I enjoyed, i.e. climbing mountains, looking at pictures, etc.; or for my own aggrandisement and satisfaction of ambition, or else to gratify my mother, but that I had never really done anything for God's service. Then I thought of my investigations of the Bible and found no comfort in that either, for there seemed to me nothing but darkness and doubt in it; and as I was thinking of these things my chest got sore and I began coughing . . . and I thought I was going to have another violent attack . . . So . . . I resolved that at any rate I would act as if the Bible *were* true . . . that to disbelieve the Bible was quite as difficult as to believe it . . . And when I had done this I fell asleep directly. When I rose in the morning the cold and cough were gone; . . . and everything has seemed to go right with me ever since.'[1]

On Easter Day he continues:

'By saying I had come to the place where the "two ways met" I did not mean the division between religion and no religion: but between Christianity and philosophy . . . The higher class of thinkers . . . for the most part have given up the peculiarly Christian doctrines, and indeed nearly all thought of a future life . . . They set themselves actively to improve this world and do as much good in it as they can. This is the kind of person that I must have become, if God had not appointed me to take the *other* turning . . .'[2]

In the Good Friday letter of 1852, it will be observed, he laments that he has so far done nothing for God's service. By November 16 of 1853 he was lamenting that he had so far not 'visited the poor nor fed them'.[3] And then on November 18 he made a desperate attempt in his Edinburgh lecture to recapture the old manic confidence of *The Seven Lamps of Architecture:*

'What is the custom of your British Parliament in these days? You know that nothing would excite greater manifestations of

[1] Letter to his father from Venice, Good Friday, April 9, 1852.
[2] Letter to his father, Easter Day, April 11, 1852.
[3] Cf. above, p. 58.

contempt and disgust than the slightest attempt to introduce the authority of Scripture in a political consultation . . . God will put up with many things in the human heart, but there is one thing He will *not* put up with in it—a second place. He who offers God a second place, offers Him no place . . . He who makes religion his first object, makes it his whole object; he has no other work . . . in the world than God's work.'[1]

But there is evidently the same difference in degree of conviction between this and the earlier statement, as between the degrees of conviction in the case of the second direct answer to prayer and the first. And it is from about this period that his faith in the Bible as the Word of God really begins to disappear.

In the later years of the 'fifties he was rationalising his failure to capture Art-Dictatorship by the assumption that art and art criticism were absurdities if not crimes in prevailing conditions. This with other factors, as we have seen, led to a mood of defiance expressed in various ways. In 1858 this mood of defiance caused the episode of the Waldensian Chapel in Turin.

He has left us four accounts of this episode. The first is a diary entry of the time; the second is in a letter to his father written at the time; the third is in *Fors Clavigera* written in 1877; and the fourth is in *Præterita* written in 1888. Here they are in chronological order:

'Is this mighty Paul Veronese . . . a servant of the devil? and is the poor little wretch in a tidy black tie, to whom I have been listening this Sunday morning expounding Nothing with a Twang—is he a servant of God?'[2]

'I went to the Protestant church last Sunday . . . and very sorry I was that I did go. Protestantism persecuted or pastoral in a plain room, or a hill chapel whitewashed inside and ivied outside, is all very well: but Protestantism clumsily triumphant, allowed all its own way in a capital like this, and building itself vulgar churches with nobody to put into them, is a very disagreeable form of piety. Execrable sermon—cold singing, a

[1] *Lectures on Architecture and Painting*, IV, paras. 119 and 120. Delivered Nov. 18, 1853.
[2] Notes on the Turin Gallery, Diary, 1858 (cf. above, p. 231).

nice-looking old woman or two . . . three or four decent French families; a dirty Turinois here and there, spitting over large fields of empty pew; and three or four soldiers, who came in to see what was going on, and went out again, very wisely, after listening for ten minutes, made up the congregation.'[1]

'In 1858 it was, with me, Protestantism or nothing: the crisis of the whole turn of my thoughts being one Sunday morning, at Turin, when, from before Paul Veronese's Queen of Sheba, and under quite overwhelmed sense of his God-given power, I went away to a Waldensian chapel, where a little squeaking idiot was preaching to an audience of seventeen old women and three louts, that they were the only children of God in Turin; and that all the people in Turin outside the chapel, and all the people in the world out of sight of Monte Viso, would be damned. I came out of the chapel, in sum of twenty years of thought, a conclusively *un*-converted man—converted by this little Piedmontese gentleman, so powerful in his organ-grinding, inside-out, as it were. "Here is an end to my 'Mother-Law' of Protestantism anyhow!—and now—what is there left?" You will find what was left, as, in much darkness and sorrow of heart I gathered it, variously taught in my books, written between 1858 and 1874.'[2]

'One Sunday morning I made my way to a little chapel which by a dusty roadside gathered to its unobserved door the few sheep of the old Waldensian faith who had wandered . . . into the worldly capital of Piedmont. The assembled congregation numbered in all some three or four-and-twenty . . . Their solitary and clerkless preacher . . . put his utmost zeal into a consolatory discourse of the wickedness of the wide world, more especially of the plain of Piedmont and city of Turin, and on the exclusive favour with God, enjoyed by the between nineteen and twenty-four elect members of his congregation . . . Myself neither cheered nor greatly alarmed by this doctrine, I walked back into the condemned city, and up into the gallery where Paul Veronese's Solomon and the Queen of Sheba glowed in full afternoon light. The gallery windows being

[1] Letter to his father from Turin, Aug. 4, 1858.
[2] *Fors Clavigera*, Letter 76 (April, 1877).

open, there came in with the warm air, floating swells and falls of military music, from the courtyard before the palace, which seemed to me more devotional, in their perfect art, tune, and discipline, than anything I remembered of evangelical hymns. And as the perfect colour and sound gradually asserted their power on me, they seemed finally to fasten me in the old article of Jewish faith, that things done delightfully and rightly were always done by the help and in the Spirit of God.

'Of course that hour's meditation in the gallery of Turin only concluded the courses of thought which had been leading me to such end through many years. There was no sudden conversion possible to me, either by preacher, picture, or dulcimer. But, that day, my evangelical beliefs were put away, to be debated of no more.'[1]

It is clear that what really happened to Ruskin in the chapel was not a sudden revolt against Protestantism, but a manic desire to *proclaim* his loss of faith in the Bible as the Word of God, and to charge *all* Churches with idolatry.[2] This was the gesture that he desired to make in 1858; and it was from this gesture that he was dissuaded by Mrs. La Touche.[3]

When he recovered from the excitement of this defiance his earlier personal religion became a simple belief in God and in a Religion of Humanity— a religion in which man serves his Creator by doing kindness and justice on earth. He adopted, that is to say, the religion of the philosophers referred to in his letter to his father on Easter Day, 1852[4]—the religion from which the concepts of the Bible as the Word of God, of the Fall, of Redemption, of Eternal Punishment and Immortal Life are all eliminated. In this religious temper he decided in 1858 that 'to be a first-rate painter—you *mustn't* be pious, but rather a little wicked and entirely a man of the world',[5] and wrote the chapter intended as an addition to *Modern Painters* in which he insisted that the great artist must be broadminded

---

[1] *Præterita*, III, Chap. I, para. 23 (1888).
[2] Letter to Mr. and Mrs. Browning, March 29, 1858 (cf. above, p. 66).
[3] Cf. above, p. 66.
[4] Cf. above, pp. 329 and 337.
[5] Cf. above, p. 65.

and cannot be a religious man.[1] It was in this temper also that he worked at social-economics for *Unto This Last* and *Munera Pulveris*. His religion at that moment is best summarised as follows:

'Human work must be done honourably and thoroughly, because we are now Men;—whether we ever expect to be angels or ever were slugs, being practically no matter. In resolving to do our work well, is the only sound foundation of any religion whatsoever. We *are* now Human creatures, and must, at our peril, do Human—that is to say affectionate, honest and earnest work.'[2]

And to this we must add:

'All true nobleness and worthiness only comes out when people cease to think of another world.'[3]

Depression came upon him during the writing of *Munera Pulveris*. From 1862–1864 he used his new religious attitude as a rod with which to chastise his parents, and moaned about his lack of faith in orthodox doctrines, just as he moaned about his incompetence, his frustrations, his languor and his indigest-tion.[4] In these years of depression he fancied himself martyred for his independent religious thought and ranked himself with Bishop Colenso, Wilson and Williams.[5]

When his morale recovered after his father's death in 1864 he paraded his personal Religion of Humanity with defiance. He told Spurgeon not to preach about the next world but this one,[6] and he poured ridicule on Keble who defended the concept of Hell as a necessary way of frightening people into piety.[7]

---

[1] Cf. above, pp. 231–234.

[2] *Fors Clavigera*, Letter 76 (passage written in 1877 referring to his attitude between 1858 and 1874).

[3] Letter to his father, Nov. 9, 1862.

[4] Cf. above, pp. 66 *et seq.*

[5] Colenso's *Commentary on the Epistle to the Romans* appeared in 1861. The publication of his *Critical Examination of the Pentateuch* began in 1862. He was deposed and excommunicated in 1863. Wilson and Williams were both prosecuted in 1862 for denying the doctrine of eternal punishment (cf. above, pp. 68 and 71).

[6] Cf. above, pp. 81 and 82.

[7] At the Church Congress in Bristol, 1864. Ruskin refers to this

In 1864 he told a Manchester audience that 'the Word of God, by which the heavens were of old, and by which they are now kept in store, cannot be made a present of to anybody in morocco binding'.[1] In 1866 he tilts at average thinking about a future life:

'If you address any average modern English company as believing in an Eternal life; and then endeavour to draw any conclusions from this assumed belief, as to their present business, they will forthwith tell you that "what you say is very beautiful, but it is not practical". If, on the contrary, you frankly address them as *un*believers in Eternal life, and try to draw any consequences from that unbelief, they immediately hold you for an accursed person, and shake off the dust from their feet at you.'[2]

At the beginning of the 'sixties he decided to use no more Biblical quotations in his writings:

'There is ... little use and much harm in quoting Bible now; it puts religious people in a rage to have anything they don't like hammered into them with a text, and the active men of the world merely think you a hypocrite or a fool.'[3]

But he could not abandon the habit. In the 'sixties he continued to quote from the Bible as frequently and indeed more frequently than before.[4]

His own explanation of this is provided by two passages—one in a private letter and the other in *Time and Tide*. Here is the first:

'I notice in one of your late letters some notion that I am coming to think the Bible the "Word of God" because I use it ... for daily teaching. But I never was farther from thinking and never can be nearer to thinking, anything of the sort. Nothing could ever persuade me that God writes vulgar Greek. If an angel all over peacocks' feathers were to appear in the bit

speech more than once (cf. *Ethics of the Dust*, VII, para. 80 (1865), and *Time and Tide*, Letter X (1867).

[1] *Sesame and Lilies*, I, para. 17.
[2] *The Crown of Wild Olive*, Introduction.
[3] Letter to his father, Nov. 15, 1861.
[4] Cf. below, pp. 363–365.

of blue sky now over Castle Crag and to write on it in star letters "God writes vulgar Greek," I should say "*You* are the Devil, peacocks' feathers and all."

'If there is any divine truth at all in the mixed collection of books which we call the Bible, that truth is, that the Word of God comes *directly* to different people in different ways; and may to you or me to-day, and has nothing whatever to do with printed books, and that, on the contrary, people may read the same collection of printed books all day long all their lives, and never, through all their lives, hear or receive one syllable of "God's Word".'[1]

Here we observe first a frank confession that he is using the Bible without believing it to be the Word of God and secondly the persistence of his fundamental belief in the possibility of direct contact between himself and God. In *Time and Tide* at the same period he explains his continued use of the Bible in his books and lectures in a more elaborate passage which can be summarised as follows:

There are only four possible theories respecting the Bible.

The first, held only by the uneducated, regards 'The Bible' as dictated by God and in every syllable 'His Word'.

The second, held by most good and upright clergymen and the better class of the professedly religious laity, admits verbal error, but regards the substance of the whole collection of books called the Bible as absolutely true and furnished to man by Divine inspiration of the speakers and writers of it, and believes that such truth as is necessary for man's salvation can be found in the Bible by those who honestly and prayerfully seek it there.

The third, held by 'many active leaders of modern thought', believes that the books were neither written nor collected under any Divine guidance, securing them from substantial error; that they contain like other human writings false statements mixed with true; but that they nevertheless relate the dealings of the one God with the first races of man, and His dealings

[1] Letter to Joan Agnew, August 18, 1867. The words omitted between 'because I use it' and 'for daily teaching' are regrettably omitted in the Library Edition (cf. above, p. 170).

343

with them in after time through Christ; and that they record true miracles and bear true witness to the resurrection of the dead, and the life of the world to come.

The fourth, held 'for the last half-century by the soundest scholars and thinkers', regards the mass of religious Scripture as merely the best efforts made by men towards the discovery of some relations with the spiritual world; and holds them only trustworthy as expressions of the enthusiastic visions or beliefs of earnest men, and only worthy of study, with other religious speculations, as containing a portion, divinely appointed, of the best wisdom which human intellect, earnestly seeking for help from God, has hitherto been able to gather between birth and death.

To this he adds a fifth view, which indicates 'a natural incapacity for receiving certain emotions' and is held nevertheless by many honest and good, though 'mechanical or animal' men —the view that no belief can be put in inspiration in any sense, or in help given by any Divine power to the thoughts of men.[1]

Having set down what he held to be the four attitudes to the Bible which he regards as worthy of consideration, he states that in using quotations from the Bible in his work he imagines himself addressing people with the fourth attitude: 'If I can persuade or influence them I am logically sure of the others' because 'whatever power a passage . . . may have over the mind of a person holding the fourth theory, it will have a proportionately greater over that of persons holding the third or the second'. He quotes the Bible, he says, because it 'has been the accepted guide of the moral intelligence of Europe for some fifteen hundred years', because it forbids pride, lasciviousness, and covetousness and enjoins truth, temperance, charity and equity. Finally he says:

'Let it not offend you if, deducing principles of action first from the laws and facts of nature, I nevertheless fortify them also by appliance of the precepts . . . of this Book, of which the authority is over many around you, more distinctly than over you, and which, confessing to be divine, *they* at least can only disobey at their mortal peril.'

[1] *Time and Tide*, VIII, March 7, 1867 (cf. above, p. 190).

RUSKIN'S RELIGION

Thus Ruskin who had said in *The Seven Lamps of Architecture* that all questions of expediency were most conclusively solved by reference to God's Revelation, and told his Edinburgh audience in 1853 that 'he who offers God a second place, offers Him no place'—had reached a point in 1867 where he admits that he deduces the principles of action first from the laws and facts of nature—i.e. on the basis of his personal experience and ethics—and then reinforces his precepts by quoting from the Bible which some of his audience think the Word of God.

I shall refer to the technical aspect of Ruskin's use of quotations from the Bible and the extent to which it was partly habit, and partly exhibitionism, and partly showmanship, when I discuss his methods as a writer.[1] Here we are concerned with its relation to his religious attitude and there is no need, on that point, to add anything to his own words that I have quoted.

But at this point we must distinguish between his use of Biblical quotations, to reinforce his ethical precepts, and the numerous rants against pietistic religion which occur at this time. In the letter to Joan Agnew, quoted on page 342, he also says this:

'One must above all things be cautious of allowing one's vanity to meddle in the matter—or of expecting a perpetual Divine help and interference. Most people's religion is so inwoven with their vanity that it, their religion, becomes the worst thing about them.'

Here he was thinking of Rose La Touche, and we misunderstand many passages of his lectures and writings between 1864 and 1873 unless we realise that all the attacks on self-righteous piety that occur in them were really directed against this girl.

In the early days of his acquaintance with the child Rosie he had written her letters full of his personal 'Religion of Humanity'; and during the depression that followed he had wallowed in her childish prattle about God and her efforts to rescue him from 'Bye-Path Meadow'.[2] But when the child Rosie became

[1] Cf. below, pp. 363–365.
[2] 'Little Rosie is terribly frightened about me, and writes letters to get me to come out of Bye-Path Meadow—but I won't.' Letter to C. E. Norton, June 2, 1861.

the girl Rose and the pietistic Rose who expounded theology to him in her letters and sent him her own selection of texts from the Bible,[1] he became extremely angry and doubtless wrote her that 'most people's religion is so inwoven with their vanity that it, their religion, becomes the worst thing about them'.

Ruskin said that *Sesame and Lilies* had been written 'to please one girl'.[2] But he really wrote the lectures to scold her. They were delivered in December, 1864, when she was nearly seventeen and working up to the frame of mind when she was making people at parties all kneel down and pray.[3] In *Sesame and Lilies* we read accordingly as follows:

'There *is* one dangerous science for women—one which they must indeed beware how they profanely touch—that of theology. Strange, and miserably strange, that while they are modest enough to doubt their powers, and pause at the threshold of sciences where every step is demonstrable and sure, they will plunge headlong and without one thought of incompetency into that science in which the greatest men have trembled, and the wisest erred. Strange, that they will complacently and pridefully bind up whatever vice or folly there is in them, whatever arrogance, petulance, or blind incomprehensiveness, into one bitter bundle of consecrated myrrh. Strange, in creatures born to be Love visible, that where they can know least, they will condemn first, and think to recommend themselves to their Master, by crawling up the steps of His judgement-throne to divide it with Him. Strangest of all that they should think they were led by the Spirit of the Comforter into habits of mind which have become in them the unmixed elements of home discomfort.'[4]

Matthew Arnold said that *Sesame and Lilies* was 'not to be borne'; and a recent biographer of Ruskin—Mrs. Amabel Williams Ellis—finds the lectures 'unreadable in their entirety'

---

[1] Quotation from a letter from Rose to Ruskin published by Cook from an intended Addendum to *Præterita* (cf. above, p. 83).
[2] *Sesame and Lilies*, 1871, Preface.
[3] Cf. above, p. 81.
[4] *Sesame and Lilies*, II, para. 73.

because in them 'we are being "spoken to" in the most odious sense of that idiom'.[1] But it is not Mrs. Williams Ellis who is really being 'spoken to', nor was it the audience at Manchester —it was and it is—Rose.[2]

So again in *The Ethics of the Dust* it is not the children at Winnington, nor the reader of the book, but Rose, whom he is addressing when he says:

'There's one point of possible good in the conventual system, which is always attractive to young girls; and the idea is a very dangerous one;—the notion of a merit, or exalting virtue, consisting in a habit of meditation on the "things above", or things of the next world. Now it is quite true, that a person of beautiful mind, dwelling on whatever appears to them most desirable and lovely in a possible future, will not only pass their time pleasantly, but will even acquire, at last, a vague and wildly gentle charm of manner and feature, which will give them an air of peculiar sanctity in the eyes of others. Whatever real or apparent good there may be in this result, I want you to observe, children, that we have no real authority for the reveries to which it is owing ... I do not deny, though I cannot affirm, the spiritual advantages resulting, in certain cases, from enthusiastic religious reverie, and from the other practices of saints and anchorites. The evidence respecting them has never yet been honestly collected, much less dispassionately examined: but assuredly, there is in that direction a probability, and more than a probability, of dangerous error, while there is none whatever in the practice of an active, cheerful, and benevolent life.'[3]

The Winnington children felt doubtless crushed, but not very guilty, when he said: 'Here is Violet thinking she ought to

[1] Mrs. Williams Ellis, *The Tragedy of John Ruskin* (London: Cape, 1928).

[2] In *Sesame and Lilies* we also read: 'Among all the principal figures in Shakespeare's plays, there is only one weak woman—Ophelia; and it is because she fails Hamlet at the critical moment, and is not, and cannot in her nature be, a guide to him when he needs her most, that all the bitter catastrophe follows' (II, para. 58).

[3] *The Ethics of the Dust*, VII. *Home Virtues*, paras. 83 and 87. (December, 1865).

leave *her* tasks to help God in His—unless she takes Lily's more modest view, and thinks only that He ought to learn something from her'; and when he said 'there is no way in which His name is more guiltily taken in vain than by calling the abandonment of our own work, the performance of His,' and 'there's always a considerable quantity of pride, to begin with, in what is called "giving one's self" to God.'[1] But Rose, when she read the passages, though guilty, was not crushed. For when Ruskin proposed marriage to her a few weeks after this book had appeared she told him that in the light of her theology his religion was not Christianity but scepticism.[2]

Then came Ruskin's lecture in Dublin, where he scolded two thousand people in words written when he hoped that Rose herself would be seated before him:

'I will not speak of the crimes which in past times have been committed in the name of Christ, nor of the follies which are at this hour held to be consistent with obedience to Him; but I *will* speak of the morbid corruption and waste of vital power in religious sentiment, by which the pure strength of that which should be the guiding soul of every nation, the splendour of its youthful manhood, and spotless light of its maidenhood, is averted or cast away. You may see continually girls who have never been taught to do a single useful thing thoroughly; who cannot sew, who cannot cook, who cannot cast an account, nor prepare a medicine, whose whole life has been passed either in play or in pride; you will find girls like these, when they are earnest-hearted, cast all their innate passion of religious spirit, which was meant by God to support them through the irksomeness of daily toil, into grievous and vain meditation over the meaning of the great Book, of which no syllable was ever yet to be understood but through a deed; all the instinctive wisdom and mercy of their womanhood made vain, and the glory of their pure consciences warped into fruitless agony concerning questions which the laws of common serviceable life would have either solved for them in an instant, or kept out of their way. Give such a girl any true work that will make her

---

[1] *The Ethics of the Dust*, VI, para. 72, and VII, para. 81.
[2] Cf. above, pp. 80 *et seq.*

active in the dawn, and weary at night, with the consciousness that her fellow-creatures have indeed been the better for her day, and the powerless sorrow of her enthusiasm will transform itself into a majesty of radiant and beneficent peace.'[1]

At the beginning of 1870 Rose asserted her piety and her horror of scepticism and again postponed the answer to his proposal.[2] When this happened Ruskin was writing his In-augural Lectures for Oxford and, as already noted, he was much agitated, more surely in anger than in sorrow, and inserted passages at the last minute.[3] Thus it came that the new Slade Professor, who was expected to talk about the glories of Greek art, astonished the company with a rant against Pride of Faith, and another against women who brood on the sufferings of Christ instead of alleviating the sufferings of men. The under-graduates, like the Winnington children, did not, doubtless, feel particularly guilty—being then, as now, not habitually occupied for the most part in undue theological concentration; and, as they could not know that he was really scolding a young woman in Ireland, they must have been astonished and be-wildered when they heard his passionate delivery of these words:

'The Pride of Faith . . . invests every evil passion of our nature with the aspect of an angel of light, and enables the self-love, which might otherwise have been put to wholesome shame, and the cruel carelessness of the ruin of our fellow-men, which might otherwise have been warmed into human love, or at least checked by human intelligence, to congeal themselves into the mortal intellectual disease of imagining that myriads of the inhabitants of the world for four thousand years have been left to wander and perish, many of them everlastingly, in order that, in fulness of time, divine truth might be preached suffici-ently to ourselves: with this farther ineffable mischief for direct result, that multitudes of kindly disposed, gentle, and sub-missive persons, who might else by their true patience have

---

[1] *Sesame and Lilies*, III. The Mystery of Life and its Arts (1868); cf. above, pp. 90 and 91, 260 and below, p. 365.
[2] Cf. above, p. 127.
[3] Cf. above, p. 128.

alloyed the hardness of the common crowd, and by their activity for good balanced its misdoing, are withdrawn from all such true services of man, that they may pass the best part of their lives in what they are told is the service of God; namely, desiring what they cannot obtain, lamenting what they cannot avoid, and reflecting what they cannot understand.'[1]

But Rose knew what he meant; and she echoed the last words in a letter to the George MacDonalds which I have quoted earlier.[2]

In the same way Rose knew what was meant, though the undergraduates did not feel particularly guilty, when he said in an Oxford Lecture:

'No feathered idol of Polynesia was ever a sign of more shameful idolatry than the modern notion in the minds of certainly the majority of English religious persons, that the Word of God ... may be carried about in a young lady's pocket, with tasselled ribands to mark the passages she most approves of.'[3]

And this:

'Try to conceive the quantity of time, and of excited and thrilling emotion, which have been wasted by the tender and delicate women of Christendom during these last six hundred years, in . . . picturing to themselves; the bodily pain, long since passed, of One Person:—which, so far as they indeed conceived it to be sustained by a Divine Nature, could not for that reason have been less endurable than the agonies of any simple human death by torture.'[4]

After this came the mysterious accusation against him which Mrs. La Touche repeated to Rose, whereby she was induced to refuse to meet him or correspond with him.[5] Ruskin replied in

[1] *Lectures on Art*, II, para. 39.
[2] Cf. above, p. 130. In revising these lectures in 1887, Ruskin, remembering the real meaning of this passage, and realising that it must seem odd to the reader, tried to mend matters by adding as a note: 'This concentrated definition of monastic life is of course to be understood only of its more enthusiastic forms.' He added a similar note referring to the passages I have quoted to *Ethics of the Dust* in the Preface of 1877.
[3] *Aratra Pentelici*, II, para. 64, 1870.
[4] *Lectures on Art*, II, para. 57.
[5] Cf. above, p. 128.

the 1871 Preface to *Sesame and Lilies*. 'Let her read that,' he said in a letter to the MacDonalds. I have already quoted the passage from that singular document where he defends his character and claims the right to dogmatise on ethical subjects.[1] Here I must quote one more passage scolding Rose:

'This . . . . is what I would say to any girl who had confidence enough in me to believe what I told her, or to do what I asked her. First, be quite sure of one thing, that, however much you may know, and whatever advantages you may possess, and however good you may be, you have not been singled out, by the God who made you, from all the other girls in the world, to be especially informed respecting His own nature and character. You have not been born in a luminous point upon the surface of the globe, where a perfect theology might be expounded to you from your youth up, and where everything you were taught would be true, and everything that was enforced upon you, right. Of all the insolent, all the foolish persuasions that by any chance could enter and hold your empty little heart, this is the proudest and foolishest—that you have been so much the darling of the Heavens, and favourite of the Fates, as to be born in the very nick of time, and in the punctual place, when and where pure Divine truth had been sifted from the errors of the Nations; and that your papa had been providentially disposed to buy a house in the convenient neighbourhood of the steeple under which that Immaculate and final verity would be beautifully proclaimed. Do not think it, child; it is not so. . . . You, with all your pretty dresses, and dainty looks, and kindly thoughts, and saintly aspirations, are not one whit more thought of or loved by the great Maker and Master than any poor little red, black, or blue savage, running wild in the pestilent woods, or naked on the hot sands of the earth; . . . of the two, you probably know less about God than she does; the only difference being that she thinks little of Him that is right, and you much that is wrong.'[2]

All through the 'seventies, as we have seen, Ruskin's mind became rapidly more disordered. While his mobility of interest

[1] Cf. above, p. 128.
[2] *Sesame and Lilies*, Preface to 1871 edition, paras. 5 and 6.

and manic tendencies were being satisfied by the planning of the St. George's Guild and a library of publications for a chain of St. George's Schools and a series of collections of representative Examples for Oxford, and so forth, and while he found rest and relief from obsessions by automatic perseverations and the finding of Rose images in Italy—his depressive tendencies were causing more and more a lack of confidence in his right to expound ethical principles and confirm them by Biblical quotations. The doubt really began in 1871 at the very moment that he was embarking on St. George's Guild and the other schemes. It began in the 1871 Preface to *Sesame and Lilies* with: 'Being now fifty-one years old and little likely to change my mind hereafter on any important subject of thought (unless through weakness of age) . . .' and with: 'What I am, since I take on me the function of a teacher, it is well that the reader should know. . . . Not an unjust person; not an unkind one; not a false one; a lover of order, labour, and peace. That it seems to me, is enough to give me right to say all I care to say on ethical subjects.'[1] The doubt began, that is to say, by defiance of itself. And then it grew and grew until in the end he found peace by abandoning the personal religion of the middle period and returning to the personal religion of the 'forties and 'fifties.

The symptoms of this return were characteristic. He began secretly to identify himself with St. Francis. During his delirious illness at Matlock in 1871 he dreamed that he was 'a brother of St. Francis'.[2] This dream was recalled in Rome in 1874 when a Capuchin to whom he had given alms presented him with a relic—a fragment of St. Francis' cloak.[3] From Rome he went to Assisi, where he remained for months spending long hours chatting with the Franciscan friars in the Sacristan's cell, copying bits of Franciscan frescoes and so forth.[4] From this time onwards he referred to himself as 'a brother of the Third Order of St. Francis',[5] and insisted upon the presence of the

---

[1] Cf. above, pp. 128 and 129.
[2] *Ariadne Florentina*, VI, para. 214 (cf. above, pp. 115 and 157).
[3] *Fors Clavigera*, Letter 76.
[4] *Fors Clavigera*, Letter 46 (cf. above, p. 122).
[5] *Deucalion*, I, Chap. X, para. 9.

domestic animals when he conducted family prayers at Brant-wood.

The trend of his thoughts was construed by the Franciscans as a desire to be received into the Church of Rome; one friar prayed daily for this occurrence: 'C'è una piccola cosa', he said, 'ma credo che San Francesco lo farà.'[1] Nor was the friar's optimism quite unfounded. For Ruskin had written from Rome a few weeks earlier: 'I quite begin to understand the power of this place over the most noble class of English religious mind. . . . No matter what takes place *now* around them, the intense reality of the Past becomes to them an irresistible claim on their submission and affection. . . . I verily believe that were I a Christian at all, Rome would make a Romanist of me in a fort-night.'[2] With inverted perseveration of his early diatribes against Romanism he now began to insist on the services which the old faith had rendered the world in the middle ages, and to contrast this with the shortcomings of Protestantism. This came to a climax in the notorious Oxford lecture where he exhibited Carpaccio's St. Ursula as 'a type of Catholic Witness' and pictures of an 'alert little pig' and 'Mr. Stiggins with his concertina' as types of the Protestant spirit.[3] In England in the 'seventies and 'eighties the trend of his thoughts was also mistaken for an inclination to be received by Rome. He denied the inclination in *Fors Clavigera* (Letter 76) in 1877:

'Don't be afraid that I am going to become a Roman Catho-lic, or that I am one, in disguise. I can no more become a *Roman*-Catholic, than again an Evangelical-Protestant. I am a Catholic . . . of the Catholics; holding for sure God's order to his scattered Israel,—"He hath shown thee, oh man what is good; and what doth the Lord thy God require of thee but to do justice, and to love mercy, and to walk humbly with thy God?"'

But the Roman Catholic party in England did not give up

[1] Cook quoting Oscar Browning, who visited Assisi in 1874 shortly after Ruskin had left.
[2] Letter to Joan Severn from Rome, May 5, 1874.
[3] *The Pleasures of England*, Lecture V, Protestantism, November, 1884.

hope. Cardinal Manning, who had been friendly with him for many years, had long been pointing out how close their attitudes were: 'With a theist', he wrote, 'I have sympathy, with an atheist or an agnostic I can find no human hand or heart to lay hold of. What room for the καλόν or "pulchrum" physical, moral, spiritual, ideal in men who feel they may be the Sons of an ape? Your *Fors* is a vigorous and human protest against this degradation of man and of Society; which next after the Church is God's greatest work.'[1] And he reinforced this flattery by attacks on a weak spot as we know from Ruskin himself:

'I lunched with Cardinal Manning, and he gave me *such* a plum pie. I never tasted a Protestant pie to touch it. . . . He gave me lovely soup, roast beef, hare and currant jelly, puff pastry like Papal pretensions—you had but to breathe on it and it was nowhere—raisons and almonds, and those lovely preserved cherries like kisses kept in amber.'[2]

Still the Cardinal did not give up hope. When Francesca Alexander's *The Story of Ida* with Ruskin's introduction was published he renewed the attack: 'It is simply beautiful, like the *Fioretti di San Francesco*. Such flowers can grow in one soil alone. They can be found only in the Garden of Faith, over which the world of light hangs visibly. . . .'[3] Finally, when Ruskin had given a stained-glass window to a Romanist church near Coniston, the rumour of his conversion was widely spread. But Romanist hopes were once more disappointed when he sent this letter to the Press:

'I shall be entirely grateful to you if you will take the trouble to contradict any news gossip of this kind which may be disturbing the minds of any of my Scottish friends. I was, am, and can be, only a Christian Catholic in the wide and eternal sense. I have been that these five-and-twenty years at least. Heaven keep me from being less as I grow older! but I am no more likely to become a Roman Catholic than a Quaker, Evangelical, or Turk.'[4]

[1] Letter to Ruskin, Oct. 21, 1873.
[2] Letters to Susan Beever, Aug. 21 and Sept., 1880.
[3] Letter to Ruskin, May or June, 1883.
[4] Letter published in the *Morning Post* and other papers, April 7, 1887.

We must observe the differences between Ruskin's religious attitude in his middle and last periods. Between 1858 and the beginning of the 'seventies he proclaims his personal Religion of Humanity, uses Biblical quotations to reinforce his ethical precepts, and attacks the pietistic theology of Rose. In the last period, 1871–1889, he professes Christianity in his published writings and draws attention to their increasing 'Christian tone'[1]—while still protesting in his private correspondence that he is not a Christian, as we have just seen; he attacks Atheism— with which he associates Science[2]; he attacks the clergy as men 'preaching a false gospel for hire';[3] and he tends more and more to expound the meaning of the Bible.[4]

The final phase really indicates, as I have said, a return to the attitude before 1858. The doubt of his right to make ethical judgements and reinforce them by the Scriptures, which appeared at the beginning of the 'seventies, gave place to a return of manic confidence in himself as an appointed interpreter of the text of the Bible. Even in the middle period he had never ceased to read the Bible daily, and in his depressed moments he had often consulted *Sortes Biblicae*. In the last period his religious attitude was an automatic return to the confidence of *The Seven Lamps of Architecture*, when he said that all questions of expediency could be solved by reference to the Bible and was convinced that he himself could always find the appropriate quotation.[5] In *Fors Clavigera* after 1874 he expounds text after text, and he assumes in *Mornings in Florence* that he can tell which of the old artists had arrived at the 'innermost

[1] *Fors Clavigera*, Letter 76.
[2] *Ibid.* (cf. above, p. 167).
[3] *Fors Clavigera*, Letters 49, 51, 54, 55. In the last, written just after Rose's death, he writes of the clergyman's profession 'with its pride, privilege, and more or less *roseate* repose of domestic felicity, extremely beautiful and enviable in country parishes' (italics mine). In letter 57 two months later he quotes in full a newspaper account of a clergyman's wedding describing the bride's dress of 'superb white satin', the 100 lb. wedding cake and the display above the communion table of the text 'Jesus was called to the marriage.'
[4] *Fors Clavigera*, Letters 37–96.
[5] Cf. above, p. 332.

meaning' of the Gospels and which had failed to discover it.[1]

The final position summed up in the passage quoted at the head of these notes was really the first position. In the beginning he sought God in the Bible and on the tops of mountains in High Savoy; he believed himself an appointed interpreter of Deity because he knew the Bible by heart and could write rhythmic prose about sunsets and clouds; and he abused Romanism because he was afraid of seduction by its ritual. In the middle period he preached ethical goodness, and he looked to the Bible to help him in his preachings. In his last period, when he decided that Giotto's religion had not weakened him but 'developed every faculty of his heart and hand',[2] he again sought God in the Bible and believed himself an appointed expounder because he knew the text by heart and because he secretly identified himself with St. Francis. He was never really a sectarian in religion; and if being a Christian means acceptance of the Church or any part of it as an intermediary between man and God—he was never a Christian.

Had he lived in days when the Church could burn heretics—his life might have ended at the stake.[3]

[1] *Mornings in Florence*, V, para. 112.
[2] Cf. above, pp. 211 and 234.
[3] Cf. above, p. 40.

RUSKIN AS A WRITER

After the age of forty Ruskin detested his reputation as a fine writer. He said so again and again. He permitted the publication of Harrison's *Selections* in 1861 because his early books had cost his father much money, and brought his publisher next to nothing, and he did not feel justified in withholding his consent to a book from which his publisher expected to make a profit. But he refused to have anything to do with it, and secretly hoped that few people would read it:

'Don't send the book of extracts to *any*body that you can help. Above all—don't send it *here*. It is a form of mince-pie which I have no fancy for.'[1]

In the same way he permitted the publication of Susan Beever's *Frondes Agrestes* in 1875, persuading himself doubtless that any money he might get from it would be spent on work 'for Oxford' or 'for St. George'. But he urged the compiler to go for content and not for the 'fine writing':

'It is the chief provocation of my life to be called a "word painter" instead of a thinker. I hope you haven't filled your book with descriptions. I thought it was the thoughts you were looking for.'[2]

Ruskin knew that his writing attracted attention *towards itself* and *away from* the thought which it was fashioned to communicate, and he always looked on this as a defect and not a merit:

'I have had what, in many respects, I boldly call the misfortune, to set my words sometimes prettily together; and not

---

[1] Letter to his father from Lucerne, Nov. 9, 1861.

In justice to Ruskin's father I must add that he too disliked Harrison's *Selections* when he saw it. 'The sweets are brought together in cloying abundance,' he said, and he called it 'rather a vulgar shop affair, with a too handsome, very questionable likeness' to the works from which it was extracted (Letter from J. J. Ruskin to John Simon, Nov. 11, 1861).

[2] Letter to Susan Beever, Aug. 24, 1874 (cf. above, p. 204).

without a foolish vanity in the poor knack that I had of doing
so: until I was heavily punished for this pride, by finding that
many people thought of the words only, and cared nothing for
their meaning.'[1]

'My vanity is never more wounded than in being called a
fine writer—meaning—that nobody need mind what I say.
. . . My vanity is set on having it *known* of me that I am a good
master, not in having it *said* of me that I am a smooth author.'[2]

He had, of course, the gift of writing musical language.
From childhood he 'had pleasure in making some sort of melodious noise about it'; there is pulse and rhythm in everything
he wrote; and in his early years he took pains to develop this
gift and exploit it in flamboyant elegancies of style. Here is a
letter to his father describing a picture:

'I spent an hour and a half before a Fra Angelico and hadn't
had enough of it either. . . . I saw angels dancing . . . and
so I know how they do it. I wish you could see one of Angelico's, either dancing or singing. One that I saw to-day had
just taken the trumpet from his lips and—with his hand lifted
—listens to the blast of it passing away into heaven. And then
to see another bending down to clash the cymbals, and yet
looking up at the same instant all full of love. And their wings
are of ruby colour and pure gold, and covered with stars, and
each has a tongue of fire on his forehead, waving as he moves.'[3]

This appears in a famous passage in *Modern Painters*, *II*
as follows:

'With what comparison shall we compare . . . the angel
choirs of Angelico with the flames on their white foreheads
waving brighter as they move, and the sparkles streaming from
their purple wings like the glitter of many suns upon a sounding sea, listening in the pauses of alternate song, for the pro-
longing of the trumpet blast, and the answering of psaltery
and cymbal, throughout the endless deep, and from all the
star shores of heaven?'[4]

[1] *Sesame and Lilies*, III, para. 97 (1868).
[2] *Ariadne Florentina* I, para. 2, (1872). For his jealousy of Faraday's
reputation as a master of his own subject, cf. above, p. 167.
[3] Letter to his father from Florence, June 5, 1845.
[4] *Modern Painters*, II, last paragraph.

In writing *The Stones of Venice* he carefully and deliberately
ornamented the plain statements:

'I must manage to put a little more verbiage into the pages
enclosed [*Stones*, II] or they will hardly go down.'[1]

'I am getting rather jealous of the time spent in turning sentences musically.'[2]

'The chapter on the Ducal Palace . . . is still devoid of all
adornment. The whole book . . . is a good deal like a house
just built. I must let it dry before I paint or paper it.'[3]

When at a later period, he revised and annotated his early
books all this seemed to him mere 'literary coxcombry'.[4]

'I find . . . my earlier books disfigured by affected language,
partly through the desire to be thought a fine writer, and
partly, as in the second volume of *Modern Painters*, in the
notion of returning as far as I could to what I thought the
better style of old English literature.'[5]

The Seven Lamps of Architecture then seemed to him a
'wretched rant of book';[6] and in the notes which he added in
1883 to *Modern Painters, II*, he grumbles at 'the mischief of
fine writing'. In the Epilogue (1881) to *The Stones of Venice*
he says:

'Everybody praised their "style" partly because they saw it
was stippled and laboured, and partly because for that stippling
and labouring I had my reward, and got the sentences often
into pleasantly sounding tune. But nobody praised the substance, which indeed they never took the trouble to get at; but
occasionally tasting . . . spat it out, and said "What a pity it
had got in." '[7]

It is thus clear that after the age of forty Ruskin did not
wish to be looked on as a literary artist. And of course with
his social conscience and his manic impulse to preach within

[1] Letter to his father from Venice, April 4, 1852.
[2] Letter to his father from Venice, Jan. 31, 1852.
[3] Letter to his father from Venice, Feb. 25, 1852.
[4] Note (1881) to *The Stones of Venice*, Vol. III, Part IV, Chap. II,
para. 98.
[5] *Sesame and Lilies*, Preface, 1871.
[6] Note (1880) to *The Seven Lamps of Architecture*, Chap. V, para. 3.
[7] Epilogue, para. 2.

him he had never been primarily a literary artist. He had put 'fine writing' into his early books to satisfy his exhibitionism and to obtain the pleasure of making 'some sort of melodious noise about it'.

After forty his desire to communicate his thoughts over-powered the factors that made the earlier 'fine writing'. There-after he is only a 'fine writer' incidentally, by accident, or by habit; and he largely failed in his life's endeavour because he became less and less able to say at the end of a page what he had intended to say when he began at the top.

After forty he could strike out arresting sentences, charm, interest, excite and stimulate the reader. He could use language as a drug to excite emotions. He could communicate his pas-sion. He could make his writing fiery, flowery, witty or ur-bane. But as I understand prose writing he was not a good prose writer—he was unable, that is to say, to use words and sentences as the precise communication of ordered thought.

The reader who has followed me to this point will know the reasons for this failure. The manner of his writing, like the content, was always affected by his circumstances, the condition of his mind at the moment, and the triumph of the fine or the feeble aspects of his character at the moment. To understand it we have to apply the same analysis to the manner of any given page as to matter.

The mobility of interest and the inability to concentrate which increase so continually from 1855 onwards are reflected in his ways of writing.[1] I have already drawn attention to the word-jingling and associative-idea-writing and the obscurity in parts of *Munera Pulveris* (1863), and to the letters which he wrote to his father attempting to rationalise these character-istics.[2] We get the same thing in articles written for the *Art Journal* in the Spring of 1865. In an opening passage in the first of these articles he thus announces their purpose and scope:

'We desire to find by what rule some Art is called good and other Art bad . . . to find the conditions of character in the artist which are essentially connected with the goodness of his

[1] Cf. above, p. 229.
[2] Cf. above, pp. 288 and 289.

work . . . to find what are the methods of practice which form this character or corrupt it; and finally, how the formation or corruption of this character is connected with the general prosperity of nations. And all this we want to learn practically: not for mere pleasant speculation on things that have been; but for instant direction of those that are yet to be. My first object is to get at some fixed principles for the teaching of Art to our youth; and I am about to ask . . . how well, or how imperfectly, our youth of the higher classes should be disciplined in the practice of music and painting—how far, among the lower classes, exercise in certain mechanical arts might become a part of their school life—how far in the adult life of this nation, the Fine Arts may advisably supersede and regulate the mechanical Arts?'[1]

We have here a series of questions to which in 1865 he was well qualified to supply interesting answers. But he begins by raising another question: 'What is the real dignity of mechanical Art?' and then he plunges into a long—and most entertaining—description of a locomotive in a railway station, 'infinitely complex anatomy of active steel, compared with which the skeleton of a living creature would seem, to a careless observer, clumsy and vile—a mere morbid secretion and phosphatous prop of flesh', and into speculations on the relation of the pneuma-steam-spirit which produces the steam-whistle to 'that more ancient spiritus, or warm breath, which people used to think they might be "born of."' He then ends the paragraph as follows:

'After all, this shrieking thing . . . can but pull, or push, and do oxen's work in an impetuous manner. That proud King of Assyria, who lost his reason and ate oxen's food, would he have much more cause for pride if he had been allowed to spend his reason in doing oxen's work?'[2]

Thereafter the articles become discourses on *Modesty, Patience*, and *Haste*; and in the discourse on Patience we read:

'The fire which Patience carries in her hand is that truly stolen from Heaven, in the *pith* of the rod—fire of the slow

[1] *The Cestus of Aglaia*, Chap. I, paras. 7 and 8.
[2] *The Cestus of Aglaia*, I, paras. 7-10.

match; persistent Fire like it also in her own body—fire in the marrow; unquenchable incense of life: though it may seem to the bystanders that there is no breath in her, and she holds herself like a statue, as Hermione "the statue lady" or Griselda "the Stone lady"; unless indeed one looks close for the glance *forward*, in the eyes, which distinguishes such pillars from the pillars, not of flesh, but of salt, whose eyes are set backwards. I cannot get to my work in this paper somehow; the web of these old enigmas entangles me again and again. That rough syllable which begins the name of Griselda, "Gries", the stone; the roar of the long fall of the Toccia seems to mix with the sound of it, bringing thoughts of the great Alpine patience; mute snow wreathed by grey rock, till avalanche time comes— patience of mute tormented races till the time of the Grey league came; at last impatient. (Not that, hitherto, it has hewn its way to much: the Rhine-foam of the Via Mala seeming to have done its work better). But it is a noble colour that Grison Grey— dawn colour—graceful for a faded silk to ride in, and wonderful, in paper, for getting a glow upon, if you begin wisely, as you may some day perhaps see by those Turner sketches at Kensington, if ever anybody can see them.'[1]

We cannot assess this as we assess a page by James Joyce or Gertrude Stein; because it is something quite different. The passage is not the work of a writer exploring the possibilities of a literary form; it is the work of a man who has set out to state 'some fixed principles for the teaching of Art to our youth', and to state them practically 'for instant direction'. It is not the work of a writer who wants to be regarded as a literary artist, but of a writer who wants to be thought of as 'a man who knows his science and his business'[2]; and who yet owing to self-indulgence and mental illness has gone about it in this way.

And indeed in regard to this aspect of his writing we have his own confession: 'I say all that comes into my head for my own pleasure, in the first words that come, retouching them afterwards into (approximate) grammar.'[3]

[1] *The Cestus of Aglaia*, III, paras. 34 and 35.
[2] Cf. above, pp. 118, 162 and 167.
[3] *The Queen of the Air*, III, para. 134.

RUSKIN AS A WRITER

In the 'seventies he learned how to exploit his inability to concentrate, and, advancing on the line of least resistance, he developed a discursive manner of writing which enabled him to fashion *Fors Clavigera* and *Mornings in Florence* as the curious mosaics which seem mere journalism to the casual reader but provide for the student tragically comic discoveries of the kind to which I have drawn attention. We get a good example of this procedure in the lecture on Serpents (*A Caution to Snakes*) delivered in 1880 from which I have already made quotations.[1] Here, beginning with serpents that are 'living waves' he wanders off to the Cockney's dropped H's, the results of Church of England education, the talents of the actress Mrs. Kendal, and the adulteration of beer in a public-house near Oxford; and throws in images of Sir Gorgius Midas scolding his footman and the Scots Greys at Balaclava.[2] As a platform performance the lecture was doubtless entertaining. But what would Ruskin have said had a member of the audience congratulated him with a hearty: 'The most amusing lecture, Professor, that I have heard for years?' We know what his answer would have been because on another occasion when an admirer said to him: 'I must tell you, Professor, how much I have admired your books,' he answered, 'I don't care whether you have enjoyed them or not. Have they done you any good?'[3]

His exceptional familiarity with the text of the Bible and his habit of quoting from it also contributed to his failure to control his writing in the days when he had most to say.

I do not know exactly how many quotations from the Bible can be found in his writings. I once counted up to four thousand eight hundred—and then gave in, with a considerable area not yet explored. But, as everyone knows, such quotations occur not only in early books like *Modern Painters, II*, and *The Seven Lamps of Architecture*, but also in the middle and later period. In the 'sixties he was convinced, as noted, that there was 'little use and much harm' in making such quotations;

[1] Cf. above, pp. 160, 188 and 189.
[2] *Deucalion*, II, *Living Waves* (cf. above, p. 160).
[3] Collingwood, *Life and Work of Ruskin*.

but they are frequent nevertheless in all his writings of the 'sixties, no less than forty-nine appearing in the Dublin lecture of 1868;[1] they run through *Fors Clavigera* in the 'seventies; and they abound in the lecture on snakes in 1880.[2]

With Ruskin the use of these quotations was a form of self-indulgence which soon ceased to bear relation to his religious thought. He had had the text forced into his brain in childhood. He knew the Apocalypse by heart before he was twelve,[3] and he read the Bible continuously all his life both in periods when he looked upon it as the Word of God and in periods when he regarded it in other ways. He was always obsessed with the emotive rhythm, the sonority, the obscurity, the archaism, and awful associations of this living text within his brain; and the remembered language continually intervened between the thought and its expression, and often side-tracked the actual thought itself. There were times when he struggled to use language as a means of precise communication. He tried a half-dozen different 'styles' at different periods. He fussed about derivations in an effort to persuade himself that he was learning to use words with scientific care. But he continually failed to achieve sustained control of his vocabulary. Again and again he began by making sentences in which the words exactly represent the thought; and then some emotive words and phrases from the Bible would rise to his mind's surface, and then, abandoning the hard task of precise exteriorisation of his idea, he would yield to the pleasure of making 'some sort of melodious noise about it' in emotive echoes of the Bible. Again and again the words on the first few pages have no power themselves, but submissively obey the thought; then gradually the words themselves become more Biblical, and so emotive, till, in the end, the thought is dancing to their tune.[4]

[1] *Sesame and Lilies*, III.
[2] Cf. above, p. 363.
[3] *The Stones of Venice*, Epilogue, para. 4.
[4] All readers of his works know his habit of working up to a Biblical quotation as the climax of a paragraph. As I have pointed out in discussing his religious attitudes, this procedure in the middle period was a form of reinforcement of his ethical judgements by scriptural quotation. Here we

RUSKIN AS A WRITER

I have already given his own explanations of his continued use of Biblical quotations after 1860.[1] Here we must realise that from an early period this was largely automatic—a form of perseveration. But his use of these quotations in the 'sixties was also due to other factors. His work at that time was mainly lecturing and he was always a showman when he lectured. In ordinary social life he did not make himself conspicuous— except by his blue ties—and he was unaffected in conversation because he was always unconsciously attempting to appear normal and to conceal his mental ills. But on the lecture platform he was a performer; and the performance had usually started at home at a point when he was half-way through the writing of the text. The parade of his Biblical erudition satisfied his exhibitionism, and at the same time it rendered the performance itself emotive and made the audience feel that though they had not followed the arguments they were probably good ones because the speaker had been able to quote the Bible to support them. Furthermore in the case of the lectures designed as reproofs to Rose for her theological pretensions—the Dublin lecture of 1868 for example—the quotations served a special purpose by demonstrating that though Rose might claim to know more than he knew of God's intentions, he knew more passages than she did of the Book which she venerated as God's Word, and not only knew more passages, but knew much better how to apply them.

There was showmanship also in the force and drive of *Fors Clavigera* in the 'seventies when Ruskin wrote as a propagandist concerned to excite in his readers the passions that he desired to play with and to release within them the inhibitions which it was his purpose to set free. The reader who has followed me thus far will find the ninety-six numbers of *Fors Clavigera* the same intriguing and distressing mosaic that I do. But he will be no more able to read them in cold blood than I am, or than Carlyle was when he wrote of them as 'lightning bolts' and of

are concerned with the procedure as part of his technique as a prose writer.
[1] Cf. above, pp. 342–345.

RUSKIN AS A WRITER

the 'divine rage against iniquity, falsity, and baseness that Ruskin has and that every man ought to have'[1]; because *Fors Clavigera* is not argument but propaganda—and propaganda of the most powerful and effective kind.

The manic quality in *Fors Clavigera* gives a special sting to the irony and a peculiar drive to the invective. Ruskin himself was conscious of this; for when he resumed the magazine in 1880, after his madness in 1878, he said that 'the mental ignition or irritation' all through the 'seventies was 'a great additional force' enabling him 'to discern more clearly and say more vividly' what for long years it had been in his heart to say.[2]

There are people who recoil from the manic quality in Ruskin's propaganda and it may be that this quality is a factor in the neglect of *Fors Clavigera* by the generation to which I belong. But I believe that my generation leave it on one side not as manic propaganda, but simply as propaganda; because they are suspicious of propaganda as such and very passionately resent it. They do not read Ruskin's emotive rhetoric, because with the experience of the 1914–1918 war behind them they know what emotive rhetoric can do.

Ruskin's propaganda is terribly potent. He brought to it all his resources—his gift for sonorous writing, his power to put down an exciting half-truth in an arresting phrase, his generous indignation, his bitter wit. He brought to it all his manic over-stressing and all the devices of the experienced showman to procure his effects. He wrote this for example:

'Though England is deafened with spinning wheels, her people have not clothes—though she is black with digging of fuel, they die of cold—and though she has sold her soul for gain, they die of hunger. Stay in that triumph if you choose[3] . . .'
And this:
'The fishmongers who destroy their fish by cartloads that

[1] Letter to Emerson, April 2, 1872.
[2] *Fors Clavigera*, Letter 88. Ruskin looked on this manic excitement as 'healthy' and curative because it released his inhibitions in this way; and he distinguished it from 'the morbid inflammation of brain which gave rise to false visions'. Here, if my interpretation of his illness is correct, he was wrong (cf. above, p. 146).
[3] *Lectures on Art*, IV.

366

they may make the poor pay dear for what is left, ought to be
flogged round Billingsgate, and out of it. It is not *I* who say
that. Every man's heart on sea and shore says that—if he isn't
at heart a rascal.'[1]

And this:

' "But what are we to do against powder and petroleum
then?" What men may do; not what poisonous beasts may.
If a wretch spit in your face, will you answer by spitting in his?
—if he throw vitriol at you, will you go to the apothecary for
a bigger bottle?'[2]

My generation do not read this kind of writing because they
dare not read it; and they dare not read it because they know
that the man who wrote the last quotation also wrote as follows
when the Crimean War was in progress:

'The cause of this quarrel is no dim, half-avoidable involution of mean interests and errors, as some would have us believe. There never was a great war caused by these things.
There never can be . . . France and England . . . are each of
them beginning to examine . . . the dangerous question respecting the rights of governed and the responsibilities of governing
bodies . . . with the help of a good Queen and a great Emperor;
. . . and to force gradually the discussion of similar questions
into their places of silence. To force it—for true liberty, like
true religion, is always aggressive or persecuted; but the attack
is generally made upon it by the nation which is to be crushed
. . . as now by Russia upon us and our allies, her attack appointed . . . for conformation of all our greatness, trial of our
strength, purging and punishment of our futilities and establishment for ever, in our hands, of the leadership in the political
progress of the world . . . The war is at present productive of
more good than evil. I will not argue this hardly and coldly, as
I might . . . I appeal at once to the testimony of those whom the
war has cost the dearest . . . From prudent economists and careless pleasure-seekers, the cry for peace will rise alike vocifer-
ously . . . But I ask *their* witness, to whom the war has changed
the aspect of the earth, and imagery of heaven, whose hopes it

[1] *Fors Clavigera*, Letter 88.
[2] *Fors Clavigera*, Letter 7.

has cut off like a spider's web, whose treasure it has placed, in a moment, under the seals of clay; those who can never more see sunrise, nor watch the climbing light gild the Eastern clouds, without thinking what graves it has gilded, first, far down behind the dark earthline—who never more shall see the crocus bloom in spring, without thinking what dust it is that feeds the wild flowers of Balaclava; ask their witness, and see if they will not reply that it is well with them and with theirs . . . ask them: and though they should answer only with a sob, listen if it does not gather upon their lips into the sound of the old Seyton war-cry—"Set on." [1]

My generation shun Ruskin's emotive rhetoric, because they know from experience that emotive rhetoric is a drug which can make most men and women everywhere believe anything.

In the last quarter of the nineteenth century thousands of men and women drank Ruskin's rhetoric and having drunk called eagerly for more. My generation who will not drink rhetoric demand a calm parade of arguments and statistical facts; and so they read not Ruskin's *Fors Clavigera*, but Wells' *Outline of History*, and *The Work, Wealth and Happiness of Mankind*.

Wells, as propagandist, is the present-day equivalent of Ruskin, as propagandist. He voices the secret fears and discontents of the men in the street and speaks words that they want passionately to hear. If we make allowance for the happenings in the interval there is astonishingly little in the main thesis of *The Work, Wealth, and Happiness of Mankind* which cannot be found somewhere in the corpus of Ruskin's writings. The difference is in the presentation; and that arises because the men in the street to-day want Wells' presentation and not Ruskin's.

Ruskin voiced not only his own secret fears and disquietudes, but also the secret disquietudes, fears and discontents of his age. As conditions have not improved but grown more menacing since he laid down his pen in 1889, the fears and discontents of our age are still those of the nineteenth century. That is why Ruskin's work belongs to the living present and is not yet part of the dead past.

[1] *Modern Painters*, III, Part IV, Chap. XVIII, 'Of the teachers of Turner', paras. 33–37.

APPENDIX

RUSKIN'S POSITION IN THE 'FIFTIES

Ruskin's biographers generally suggest that he was a kind of Art-Dictator of England in the eighteen-fifties. From the time of Collingwood, who wrote *The Life and Work of Ruskin* in 1892, we have been led to believe that Ruskin in the 'fifties had created the Gothic revival in English architecture, and was widely esteemed as an authority on the old masters and contemporary painting; that the pictures which he praised were sold while those which he condemned or ignored were unsaleable; that he discovered and 'made' the Pre-Raphaelites; and that the official art world and the public were at his feet.[1]

But his real position, as I read the evidence, was different.

He was thirty-one in 1850 and had then published the first two volumes of *Modern Painters*, and *The Seven Lamps of Architecture*. During the 'fifties he published *The Stones of Venice*, the remaining volumes of *Modern Painters*, *Giotto and his works in Padua* (notes on the Arundel Society's reproductions), the pamphlet called *Pre-Raphaelitism*, and the texts of miscellaneous lectures and addresses—*Lectures on Architecture and Painting*, *A Joy for Ever*, and *The Two Paths*. His books at this time were little read; *Modern Painters* and the elaborately illustrated architectural volumes were very expensive; their author's name was not known to the general public; and the number of people interested in their nominal subjects was not greater but smaller than it is to-day.

[1] Even Evelyn Waugh in his careful book, *Rossetti: his Life and Works* (London: Duckworth, 1928), writes of Ruskin in 1851 as 'a very important person indeed in the art world not only with the general cultured public but . . . with buyers'.

The first volume of *Modern Painters* was a success, but mainly among literary people who were intrigued with its combination of juvenile gusto and elaborate writing and who recognised the book as a gesture of value designed to vindicate a living artist against unjust abuse; it was not a success among artists, who, as Ruskin himself says in *Præterita*, were the last to care for it because some were jealous of the praise of Turner and others were scandalised at the contemptuous references to Dutch Art.[1] The second volume of *Modern Painters* was less read than the first; and the sales of the architectural books were also slow. Here are some details in this connection:

The first volume of *Modern Painters* was published in an edition of five hundred copies; only a hundred and fifty were sold in the first nine months.[2] There were intervals of two, three, five, and thirteen years between the various editions of *Modern Painters, II,* and it was then out of print for fourteen years. There was an interval of six years between the first and second editions of *The Seven Lamps of Architecture* which was then out of print for twenty years. There was an interval of eleven years between the first and second editions of the third volume of *Modern Painters,* an interval of twelve years between the first and second editions of the fourth volume, and no second edition of the fifth was called for. It took seven years to use up the first edition of the first volume of *The Stones of Venice* and fourteen years to use up the first edition of the second and third volumes. I have not been able to discover the number of copies in the editions of these books but, as in the case of the first volume of *Modern Painters, I,* it was probably not more than five hundred. Neither *Modern Painters* nor *The Stones of Venice* was reprinted as a complete work till the 'seventies, when, as I have already explained, the demand for Ruskin's books (which grew all through the 'eighties and 'nineties) really began. In the 'fifties these early books were on the drawing-room tables of rich and 'artistic' ladies, in some libraries of men and women of letters, and in some Undergraduates' rooms in Oxford; but they had not penetrated to the

[1] *Præterita*, II, Chap. IX, paras. 169–171.
[2] It had however gone into several editions by 1860.

bourgeois public; and in the studios of artists and architects, where Ruskin most wanted them to be, they were hardly to be found.

There is no evidence that Ruskin had an important influence on English architecture in the 'fifties. He was not a professional architect, he had had no architectural training, and he had never attempted to design a building. By architects he was regarded as a pretentious amateur. He said 'no person who is not a great sculptor or painter can be an architect. If he is not a sculptor or painter he can only be a builder . . . We have no architects.'[1] The architects said 'the entire body cannot but regard him as a common enemy and a malevolent of the worst description . . . obnoxious to the members of the architectural profession one and all.'[2] The architects moreover were scandalised at his praise of St. Mark's, Venice, which was then considered 'a grotesque pile',[3] and 'a barbaric monstrosity'[4] with an exterior 'of extreme ugliness'.[5]

The Gothic revival in English architecture had begun, of course, some thirty years before Ruskin was born. Beckford's opening fête in the jerry-built Gothic Abbey of Fonthill had taken place in 1800. Ruskin was partly responsible for the ultimate triumph of neo-Venetian-Gothic. But the neo-Venetian Gothic villas and the buildings which in 1872, he called 'accursed Frankenstein monsters of indirectly my own making'[6] were not put up in the 'fifties. It was also not till 1874 that Ruskin wrote the celebrated passage where he complained that he had come upon 'a piece of Italian Gothic' and found that 'its total motive was the provocation of thirst and the encouragement of idleness'—the building being a public-house.[7] In the

[1] Edinburgh, *Lectures on Architecture and Painting*, Addenda, para. 61.
[2] Pamphlet, *Something on Ruskinism*, by An Architect, 1851.
[3] *The Builder*, articles entitled 'Ruskin and his Reviewers', May 10 and 24, 1851.
[4] See *The Stones of Venice*, I, Chap. IV, para. 49.
[5] See *The Seven Lamps of Architecture*, Chap. V, para. 14.
[6] Letter in the *Pall Mall Gazette*, March 16, 1872.
[7] Preface to the Third Edition (1874) of *The Stones of Venice* where he also says: 'I would rather . . . for my own part, that no architects had ever condescended to adopt one of the views suggested in this book, than that

'fifties Ruskin was powerless to impose his own architectural taste. He protested in 1854 against the classical design for the Leeds Town Hall,[1] but the design was nevertheless accepted and the building was triumphantly opened by the Queen in 1858. As late as 1859 Lord Palmerston, though he knew Ruskin personally, refused Gilbert Scott's Gothic design for the India Office, saying 'It was all very well for our ancestors to build in that way because they knew no better, but why should we?' The London Law Courts did not rise till 1874.

The only building of consequence, put up in the 'fifties, with which Ruskin was connected, was the Oxford Museum; and his connection with that was due to the accident that the foundation of the Museum was the work of his friend Acland who moved heaven and earth to secure a Venetian-Gothic design especially to please him.[2]

Nor was his taste in the matter of the old masters more influential at this time. After 1870 his writings and lectures about his favourite Italian painters possibly influenced the choice of purchases by the National Gallery. But in the 'fifties the National Gallery set no value on his opinions. He held no official post in those days and the Trustees looked upon him as a tiresome outsider who had made ridiculous attacks on the seventeenth-century artists in the first volume of *Modern Painters*, and who had written to *The Times* to describe Guido Reni's *Susannah and the Elders* (which they had bought for the equivalent of £3,780) as a work with 'no single virtue, no colour, no drawing, no character, no history, no thought . . . and devoid alike of art and decency'.[3] When he was in Venice

any should have made the partial use of it which has mottled our manufacturing chimneys with black and red brick, dignified our banks and draper's shops with Venetian tracery and pinched our parish churches into dark and slippery arrangements for the advertisement of cheap coloured glass and pantiles.' This I submit was the moment when the builders had really begun to be influenced by Ruskin.

[1] Preface to Edinburgh lectures.

[2] When after a long struggle a Venetian-Gothic design was accepted Ruskin, delighted, subscribed £300 for the carving of the windows, and persuaded his father also to contribute.

[3] Letter to *The Times*, Jan. 7, 1847, and *Modern Painters*, II, Part III, Sec. I, Chap. XIV, para. 24. The price actually paid was £1,260.

in 1852 he learned that two pictures by Tintoretto were in the market, and he wrote to the Trustees suggesting that he should buy them on behalf of the National Gallery for the price asked —the equivalent of some £36,000.[1] The Trustees thanked him for having brought the matter to their notice, and Ruskin wrote off to his father: 'I am glad to find that I have *some* power even with such immoveable people as the Trustees for the National Gallery.'[2] But the Trustees never really contemplated the purchase of the pictures on his recommendation. They referred the question to Edward Cheney whom they knew as a reputable antiquarian and collector who had lived for years in Venice and done scholarly work in the archives. Cheney said that he did not concur with Ruskin's valuation of the pictures; and the Trustees thereupon 'communicated to Mr. Ruskin their unwillingness that he should trouble to take further steps'.[3]

His next contact with official art circles was occasioned by the Turner Bequest. The first volume of *Modern Painters*, and the purchases of Turner's works by Ruskin and his father, had brought Turner, in his old age, frequently to Denmark Hill; and when Turner died in 1851 it was found that he had named Ruskin as one of his executors. Ruskin in manic enthusiasm at once conceived a grandiose plan for a 'Ruskin Wing' for the National Gallery, designed by himself, and paid for by his father; of this wing he himself would be Director, and as such he would arrange, frame, and catalogue all Turner's works.[4] But, as the Trustees of the National Gallery saw it, Ruskin under Turner's will had become a representative of the testator but he had no *locus standi* at the reception end of the bequest. When, in 1856, after five years' dispute about the will, the Trustees found themselves faced with the reception of two hundred oil paintings and nineteen thousand water-colours and drawings, they still felt no impulse to call Ruskin to their aid. Sir Charles Eastlake, who at that time held the offices of President of the Royal Academy and Director of the National Gal-

[1] £12,000.
[2] Letter to his father, May 16, 1852.
[3] National Gallery Return, 1847–1852.
[4] Letter to his father, Jan. 1, 1852.

lery, had formerly, as Keeper, been in part responsible for the purchase of the picture by Guido Reni which Ruskin had abused in *The Times*. For this reason and for others, which I note below, he was personally hostile to Ruskin, and he took the line that his own staff was quite competent to deal with the packing-cases of Turner's works;—it was true that the present Keeper, Mr. Thomas Uwins, R.A., had been so much criticised that his health was about to compel his resignation, but there was an excellent successor already ear-marked—Mr. Ralph Wornum, an admirable artist and art-scholar who had travelled abroad as much as young Mr. Ruskin had, and studied in Munich, Dresden, Paris and Rome; and Mr. Wornum would certainly be able to sort the contents of the cases.

Faced with this situation Ruskin set about forcing his way in. He had no doubt that he was the right and only man to deal with, at any rate, the nineteen thousand water-colours and drawings; he knew more about Turner's water-colours than anyone alive; and as the owner of a large number he had made experiments in the best ways of framing and preserving them. So he sat down and wrote to *The Times*:

'I think it . . . my duty to state that I believe none would treat these drawings with more scrupulous care or arrange them with greater patience than I should myself; that I am ready to undertake the task and enter upon it instantly; that I will furnish, in order to prove the working of the system proposed, 100 frames with their cases at my own cost; and that within six weeks of the day on which I am permitted to begin work (illness or accident not interfering) I will have the 100 drawings arranged, framed, accompanied by a printed catalogue and ready for public inspection . . . I will only undertake this task on condition of the entire management of the drawings, in every particular, being entrusted to me . . .'[1]

The authorities of the National Gallery took, of course, no notice of this letter. Even if they had not been actively hostile they would not have contemplated an offer made in such a way. Ruskin therefore had to try again. He knew the Prime Minister, Lord Palmerston, having been introduced to him by Cowper-

[1] Letter to *The Times*, Oct. 28, 1856.

Temple in 1854.[1] He was now told that his letter to *The Times* was irregular and persuaded to write to Lord Palmerston and apologise for the letter and renew his offer in correct form. This he did; the Prime Minister thought he might be useful and said so to the Trustees; and thus, in the end, he was allowed as a favour to spend some months arranging and cataloguing the nineteen thousand water-colours and drawings, with his own assistants, and to provide a hundred mahogany cases at his own expense.

Ruskin worked hard at this task and the nation owes him gratitude—though there is a tradition (for which I can find no authority) that he destroyed a number of genre sketches of low life which he considered improper or obscene. He collaborated loyally with the officials, was careful not to claim credit for parts of the work which he had not done,[2] and as a result he was invited to give evidence before the Commission appointed in 1857 'to determine the site of the New National Gallery and to report on the desirableness of combining with it the Fine Art and Archæological Collections of the British Museum'.

As a witness before this Commission, he was handicapped by his lack of official status. He was treated as an amateur and his comments were clearly regarded as unjustifiably pretentious. He expressed his views on the proper construction of picture galleries, and the proper display of pictures, and was then made to look foolish by having to confess that he was not acquainted with the German museums which were arranged on the latest systems, and that he had never seen Raphael's *Sistine Madonna* or Holbein's *Madonna with the family of Jacob Meyer* in Dresden.[3] And when the Chairman (Lord Broughton) said, 'Will you state precisely what position you hold?' he could only reply, 'I am master of the Elementary and Landscape School of Drawing at the Working Men's Institute.'[4]

[1] *Præterita*, III, Chap. II, para. 29.
[2] Letter to *The Times*, July 9, 1857.
[3] Considered the original up to 1867. Wornum was the first to believe it a copy of the Darmstadt version.
[4] Report of the National Gallery Site Commission, 1857. As a result of this experience Ruskin visited Berlin, Dresden, Munich and other German cities in 1859. Faraday was a member of this Commission (cf. p. 167.)

I have already made some comments about the false assumption that Ruskin 'discovered' and 'made' the Pre-Raphaelites.[1] 'He picked up the timid Pre-Raphaelite Brethren', writes a recent biographer, 'and thrust them blushing and bowing and pocketing handfuls of unexpected money before the public.'[2] I doubt if Hunt, Rossetti and Millais were ever timid. But even if they were the image is misleading. Ruskin, as I have noted, made his first gesture on behalf of Millais and Hunt in 1851; and he began to interest himself in Rossetti in 1854. The Brotherhood was formed in 1848. The first Pre-Raphaelite pictures exhibited in 1849 and 1850 had all been sold before Ruskin appeared upon the scene. Hunt had sold *Rienzi* to a collector named Gibbons for £100, and *A Converted British Family sheltering a Missionary* (which went as the beginning of his Pre-Raphaelite collection to Combe) for £160. Rossetti had sold his *Girlhood of the Virgin* for £84 to the Marchioness of Bath, and Millais had sold his *Lorenzo and Isabella* to a dealer for £150 and his *Jesus in the House of his Parents* (The Carpenter's Shop) to another dealer for just under £300.[3] The artists, that is to say, had not only attracted attention at once, but had sold their pictures for high sums, which must be trebled before we get near the equivalents in present money. When Ruskin, influenced by Dyce and Patmore, decided to make a gesture in favour of Hunt and Millais in 1851, he was not a recognised and influential critic of contemporary art. He had written relatively little about it. He was not in the position of, say, the art critic of *The Times* whose judgements on contemporary exhibitions were read every day by thousands of people. He had not yet started *Academy Notes* and he had no platform on which to make topical judgements. All he could do was to write to *The Times*. That he did, as we have seen, in two letters describing these young artists as promising beginners; and the second letter appeared with an editorial rejoinder, in which he was accused of inconsistency in praising the Pre-Raphaelites after his praise of Turner, and the Pre-Raphaelites were told that if they hoped

---

[1] Cf. above, pp. 245–251, 270 and 271.
[2] *Ruskin*, by David Larg (London: Davies, 1932).
[3] Figures given by Holman Hunt in *Pre-Raphaelitism*.

to 'stand forth as the founders of the illustrious school which our correspondent announces' they must 'throw off the monkish disguise' in which they had been 'fooling'. In the pamphlet *Pre-Raphaelitism*, which was his next gesture, he was concerned with defending himself against this editorial charge, and he was thus carried further in praise of Millais and Hunt.[1] The pamphlet was badly reviewed and did not sell; it was not reprinted in the 'fifties.

Ruskin did nothing for the Pre-Raphaelites in 1852. In 1853 while Millais and Mrs. Ruskin were falling in love he was writing his Edinburgh Lectures, where he called Turner 'the first and greatest of the Pre-Raphaelites'. Meanwhile the Academy had made Millais an Associate and launched him on a separate career away from the Brotherhood which had already disintegrated. In 1854 Ruskin wrote letters to *The Times* on Hunt's *The Light of the World* (May 5) and *The Awakening Conscience*.[2] In that year he began to finance Rossetti, taking his work in exchange, and he continued to help Rossetti for the rest of the 'fifties—his most important contribution to contemporary creativity.[3] In the second half of the 'fifties he interjected references to the Pre-Raphaelites in *Modern Painters, III*, and *IV*, and praised pictures with Pre-Raphaelite tendencies in *Academy Notes*. That is the full extent of his services to Hunt, Millais and Rossetti. Except for the service to Rossetti (which he was able to render because he had an allowance equivalent to £4,500 from his father and no expenses) he really did extremely little for the Pre-Raphaelites—partly because, as I have explained, he always looked on Hunt and Millais as beginners, and partly because his influence was so small that he could not do much.

The pamphlets called *Academy Notes* (1855–1859) are often referred to as evidence of his position as Art-Dictator at this time. But, in fact, they only made him enemies and had little effect on public appreciation of the pictures discussed in them. The Academicians were hostile towards him and in the journals

[1] Cf. above, p. 249.
[2] Cf. above, p. 251.
[3] Cf. above, p. 270.

where they had influence he was always attacked. The *Art Journal*, for example, reviewing his pamphlet *Pre-Raphaelitism*, had been ruthless both in regard to the matter and the manner of his writing, and had concluded by reminding him that 'charitable construction of motive and courteous language are essential to the character of a gentleman'.[1] The Academicians regarded his publication of *Academy Notes* as an impertinence, and they never permitted the sale of them within the Academy. They took the view that he was not a professional critic who had been invited by a Press card to express his views, but an amateur rich enough to pay for the pleasure of seeing himself in print—an amateur moreover who had made unsolicited attacks on Academy hanging and Academy portraiture and on the great Maclise and other contemporary artists in his books.[2]

Academy Notes were full of pedagogic criticism. When Ruskin praised there was invariably a 'but'. He would tell an artist

[1] *Art Journal*, Nov., 1851.
[2] He had attacked the Academy's habit of hanging portraits by its members on the line and placing delicately painted pictures 'above rows of eye-glasses and waistcoats', in *Modern Painters*, I, Part II, Sec. I, Chap. VII, para. 22 (1846 edition). In his Edinburgh lectures in 1853 he attacked 'the base system of Academy teaching . . . which destroys the greater number of its pupils altogether and hinders and paralyses the greatest' and declared that the beginning and the end of Academy portraiture was adulation (Lecture IV, para. 130). His attacks on Maclise were in the first edition of *Modern Painters*, I, (Part I, Sec. I, Chap. I, para. 2, and Conclusion), where he describes his Hamlet as an 'Irish ruffian' and his Ophelia as a person with a 'maudlin expression' which might have 'been properly explained by an empty gin-bottle on her lap'; he followed this by writing of the 'savage recklessness' in his imagination (Preface to Second Edition, 1844); he continued the attacks in *Academy Notes*, 1855, where he described his *As You Like It* as 'energetically and actively bad' with 'every fault usually attributed to the Pre-Raphaelites without one of their excellencies', and in *Academy Notes*, 1857, where he wrote of French-polished brown wood hair in his picture. In the 'forties and 'fifties and 'sixties, Maclise was considered in Academic circles a consummate master. Frith tells us in his *Autobiography* that enthusiasts spoke of him as 'out and away the greatest artist that ever lived'. Ruskin's attacks upon him in *Modern Painters* infuriated the Academicians and their supporters in the Press, who described them as 'scurrilities such as have not disgraced the columns of any newspaper' (*The Art Union Monthly Journal*, June, 1843).

what he was to do and if, next year, the artist had not done it, he did not conceal his amazement and indignation. The artists whom he praised resented the 'buts', those whom he attacked were furious, and those who were not mentioned were the most offended of all. He even lost personal artist friends through the pamphlets because he thought it his duty to point out what he called 'the errors' in their pictures as in others; and when he found that they looked on this, not as justice, but as treachery, he was astonished.[1]

At the end of the 'fifties he thus had numerous and powerful enemies among the artists. After the criticism in *Academy Notes* of Sir Charles Eastlake's pictures, referred to above,[2] the *Quarterly Review* published an anonymous article on Ruskin's writings, which described him as an incompetent critic, and a hard-hearted, bitter, uncharitable and malicious man. The author of the article was found to be Lady Eastlake, the President's wife. Millais had now become an enemy. 'Ruskin will be disgusted,' he wrote in 1859, 'for all the rubbish he has been praising before being sent into the Royal Academy has now bad places . . . He does not understand my work, which is now too broad for him to appreciate, and I think his eye is only fit to judge the portraits of insects.' Frith and, of course, Maclise were other enemies. Frith has revealed in his Autobiography how much he detested Ruskin's activities. And where the President, Frith, Maclise, and Millais led, there was no lack of small fry to follow.

[1] In 1875 Ruskin published an isolated number of *Academy Notes* and wrote as follows of his reasons for abandoning the series in 1859: 'Among various minor, but collectively sufficient, reasons for the cessation of these *Notes*, one of the chief was the exclamation of a young artist, moving in good society—authentically, I doubt not, reported to me, "D—— the fellow, why doesn't he back his friends?" The general want in the English mind of any abstract conception of justice, and the substitution for it of the idea of fidelity to a party, as the first virtue of public action, had never shocked me so vividly before; and thenceforward it seemed to me useless, so far as artists were concerned, to continue criticism which they would esteem dishonourable unless it was false' (Preface to *Academy Notes*, 1875).
[2] Cf. above, p. 250.

Academy Notes had little or no effect on public taste. The pamphlets were of necessity written, printed and published *after* the exhibition had opened, so that the public had the Private View and the Academicians' advice and the professional art critics' Press notices to help them pick 'the pictures of the year' before Ruskin views appeared. And even then the pamphlets were not to be obtained in the Academy itself. They did not prevent the inevitable popular success of the pictures painted to please the popular taste. There were the same crowds year after year before the pictures by Frith and Maclise, and the painters received enormous fees from publishers for the engraving copyrights. Ruskin in the 'fifties had no power to persuade the general public not to like these pictures or to buy the Pre-Raphaelite pictures which he praised. All he could do, and did, was to buy some Pre-Raphaelite pictures and drawings himself and to persuade one or two of his personal friends, notably a Miss Heaton, to buy some of Rossetti's drawings.[1]

It is sometimes supposed that he was responsible for the painting of the Oxford Union Library by Rossetti and his friends in 1857–1858. But this was not so. The initiative came from Rossetti. Ruskin gave the enterprise his blessing and benevolent encouragement when it had been started, and he went from time to time to Oxford to see how the work was progressing.[2]

In the 'fifties he delivered a certain number of lectures in different places. But we must not assume from this that all England was then calling upon him to lecture. If we look into the matter we find that he owed the invitation, in every case, to some special circumstance or to a proposal made by some personal friend.

His first lectures were delivered to the Philosophical In-

---

[1] In 1851 he offered to buy Millais' *The Return of the Dove*, but it had already been sold to Combe. He commissioned *Val d'Aosta* from Brett and had the first refusal of all Rossetti's drawings for some years as already noted.

[2] He was not consulted about the procedure. This was a pity—as he knew something about the technique of fresco painting. Had he been consulted the pictures might not have faded so fast or so completely.

stitution in Edinburgh in 1853.[1] They were the result of a proposal made by the painter, J. F. Lewis, whose works were bought by Ruskin senior in the old days when Turner used to come to dinner and 'there was "frolic wine" in the flask at every right hand such as that never Prince Hal nor Jack Falstaff tasted cup of brighter or mightier'.[2]

In 1857 he lectured in Manchester. On May 5 of that year Prince Albert had opened the Manchester Art Treasures Exhibition to which the most eminent collectors had lent pictures. The opening was a brilliant pageant to which all the notabilities in the art world—all the people whose names are now forgotten—were invited. Ruskin, who was not on the Committee and had not been consulted about the choice of pictures or the arrangement of the exhibition, received no invitation to the opening. But a month later, someone, I have not been able to discover who, suggested that he might be invited to lecture at the Manchester Athenæum on the pictures in the exhibition. Ruskin accepted and read them two lectures called *The Political Economy of Art*—the first sketch for his system of Social and Political Economy—which he had by him; and he made no reference to the pictures in the exhibition. He then published the lectures, which were badly reviewed, did not sell, and were not reprinted till 1880 when they appeared as *A Joy for Ever*.[3]

In January, 1858, he lectured on *The Deteriorative Power of Conventional Art over Nations* at the opening of the Architectural Museum at South Kensington. The Architectural Museum had been founded in 1851 and one of its aims was to train workmen in the crafts. Ruskin had done voluntary work there of the same kind that he did at the Working Men's College in Red Lion Square; and he had given the Museum a number of architectural casts from Rouen and Amiens. As a result he had

[1] *Lectures on Architecture and Painting.*
[2] *Præterita*, II, Chap. IX, para. 172;
[3] He visited the Exhibition on this Manchester visit, but he seems only to have looked at the Reynolds gallery (*Modern Painters*, V, Preface). Botticelli's *Nativity*, lent by Fuller Maitland did not catch his eye (cf. above, pp. 259, 280 and 285).

obtained a footing with the authorities of the Department of Science and Art (then established at Marlborough House) which he regarded as an achievement as we read in a letter: 'The Marlborough House people are fraternising with me.'[1] On the installation of the Museum at South Kensington he offered some prizes for sculptured compositions. There was thus a special reason for inviting him to deliver an address on this occasion; and at the end of the lecture his prizes were distributed.[2]

In February, 1858, he spoke on *The Work of Iron in Nature, Art and Policy*, at the Sussex Hotel in Tunbridge Wells. His cousin, W. S. Richardson, was a well-known doctor at Tunbridge Wells, and had arranged the lecture as an evening's entertainment for his patients and friends.[3]

In October, 1858, he gave an Inaugural Address at the opening of the Cambridge School of Art. This was probably arranged by the Rev. W. Kingsley, with whom he stayed at Sidney Sussex College, or by other Cambridge friends,[4] or it may have been the result of his connection with the Department of Science and Art at South Kensington; or it may have been arranged in the same way as the lectures of the following year.[5]

In 1859 he went on a lecturing tour arranged by the art dealer Ernest Gambart, who ran the French Gallery in London. He travelled by road, in his own carriage, and proceeded north at a leisurely pace. On February 22 he lectured on *The Unity of Art* at the Manchester Art School to which he gave a watercolour drawing of a snail by William Hunt, one of ten drawings which he had commissioned the artist to make for presentation by him to schools of art. From Manchester he drove to various places in Yorkshire, and on March 1 he lectured on *Modern Manufacture and Design* in the Mechanics' Institute in

[1] Letter to C. E. Norton, May, 1857.
[2] The lecture was printed in *The Two Paths* in 1859 and not reprinted till 1878.
[3] This entertaining lecture was printed in *The Two Paths*, 1859, and not reprinted till 1878.
[4] Cf. above, p. 90.
[5] This Inaugural Address was published as a pamphlet. It was not included in a volume till 1885 when it appeared in *On the Old Road*.

RUSKIN'S POSITION IN THE 'FIFTIES

Bradford at the opening of the newly formed School of Design.[1]

These lectures, thus arranged, were delivered to two or three hundred people or less; and when the texts were published they fell flat. It was not till the middle of the 'sixties that he scored his first success as a lecturer with the Manchester addresses that became a 'best seller' as *Sesame and Lilies*.[2]

[1] These lectures were printed in *The Two Paths*, 1859, and not reprinted till 1878 (cf. above, p. 285).

[2] We must assume, I think, the world having been then doubtless much what it is to-day, that in the 'fifties Ruskin was looked upon by many people as a dealer in disguise. There must have been those who spoke insidiously of his association with the dealer Gambart and who pointed out that he appended notices of pictures in Gambart's French Gallery to *Academy Notes*. The same people doubtless pointed out that he was making 'corners' in the works of the artists whom he praised, that he had bought the first refusal of Rossetti's drawings for some years, and that between the publication of the first volume of *Modern Painters* and the last which repeated the eulogies of the first, he had acquired a collection of nearly a hundred works by Turner.

A desire to rebut this line of attack by his enemies was probably one of his motives in giving the collections of Turner water-colours to Oxford and Cambridge in 1861—though there were doubtless other motives also as I have suggested above (cf. pp. 88 and 89).

Ruskin did not of course buy works by Turner or Rossetti with a view to selling them at a profit—though in 1872 he sold Turner's *Slave Ship* (which his father had given him to celebrate the publication of *Modern Painters*, I) for £2,042 to America, saying 'it is right that it should be in America' (Letter to C. E. Norton, Jan. 28, 1872), and he bought, about 1870, a picture by Meissonier for £1,000 which he sold in 1882 for £6,195. His view, repeatedly expressed, of the relation of his praise of Turner to his collection of works by Turner was that by publicly praising Turner he sent up the price against himself. But he came from the business world; his Turners were at first given him by his father; and when he began to buy more for himself it was with money given him by his father; it is clear from the correspondence between them in the 'fifties that Ruskin senior looked upon this expenditure as a form of investment and that Ruskin himself looked upon it partly in the same way and partly as the justifiable satisfaction of a fine passion.

If his enemies hinted or said openly that he was a dealer in disguise they were wrong. But as everyone who knew him knew that he had this collection of Turners, which he was fond of inviting people to see, his enemies must have appeared to be stating facts; and this doubtless was another factor operating against his influence in official circles at that time.

INDEX

Abbeville, 34, 39, 93, 94, 109 n., 148, 152, 195
Abbeydale, 119
Abingdon, 114
Abstract of the Objects & Constitution (of St. George's Guild), (1877), 147
AcademyNotes (1855-1859), 60, 250, 376–8, 380, 383 n.; (1855), 378; (1857), 63 n., 225 n., 250, 378 n.; (1859), 276; (1875), 379 n.
Acland, Sir Henry, 37, 45, 59, 68 n., 87 n., 89, 90, 95 n., 100, 103, 114, 119, 120, 153, 372
Acland, Mrs. (Letters to), 60 n., 229 n., 275 n.
Acquired value (variable character of), 241, 267, 301
Adèle, 45–6, 72–3, 142, 181, 196, 252, 330
Adelphi (Society of Arts), 93
Æsthesis (and Theoria), 209
Æsthetic Man, 235, 242, 300
Æsthetic Movement, the (Ruskin attacks), 209 n., 254
Agnew, Joan (Mrs. Severn), 77, 86 n., 98 n., 106, 114 n., 115, 343 n., 345
Airolo, 141 n.
Aix-la-Chapelle, 195 and n.
'Alabama', the, 315
Albert, Prince, 55, 381
Alessandri, Angelo, 148, 277
Alexander, Francesca (*Roadside Songs of Tuscany*), 148, 173–4, 174 n., 255 n.
'Ali Baba and the Forty Thieves' (pantomime), 83

Allen, George, 37, 67 n., 177, 277
Allen & Unwin, 54 n., 211 n.
Allingham, W. (Carlyle's letters to), 110 n.
Allingham, Mrs., 255 n.
Alpes, Voyage dans les (de Saussure), (1779–96), 43
Alpine Club, the, 99 and n.
Alpine project (water-power), 98, 102, 106
Ambleside, 52
America, Americans, 95, 315, 321
American (Brantwood) edition (22 vols.:1891–93), 177 n.
Amiens, 148, 152, 162
Anarchy, 296, 322, 323
Anderson, J. R. (Letter to), 112 n.
'Angel of the Apocalypse' (i.e. Turner), 206, 244
Annunciation, The (Tintoretto), 95
Ansidei Madonna (Raphael), 206
'Antwerp to Naples', 206, 214 n.
Ape-faced children, 95–6, 123, 174
Apelles, 104
Apollo Belvedere, 104 n.
Apollo Sauroctonos, 104 n.
Aquinas, St. Thomas, 122
Ara Cœli, 153 n.
Aratra Pentelici, 102 n., 104 n., 112 n., 133 n., 220 n., 225 n., 237 n., 350 n.
Architect, An (*Something on Ruskinism*), 371 n.
Architects (and Ruskin), 62, 371
Architectural Association, 63 n.
Architectural Magazine, 47
Architectural Museum (South Kensington), 381

Architecture, 214, 222, 224–5, 371
Arezzo, 258 n.
Ariadne Florentina, 118 n., 157 n.,
254 n., 352 n., 358 n.
Aristotle (Theoretic), 209
Armament makers, 40–1, 325, 328
Armstrong, Lily, 85 n.
Armstrong, Sir William, 303
Arnold, Matthew, 34 and n., 90, 346
Arrows of the Chase (1880), 177 n.
Art dictatorship, 61, 63, 66, 250,
277, 284, 308, 338, 369, 377
Art Journal, 80, 360, 378 and n.
Art of England, The, 153, 173 n.,
255 n.
Art Theory (Ruskin's), 192–242,
300–1
Art Union Monthly Journal, The,
378 n.
Art Work, 156 n.
Arts and Crafts Movement, 219,220
Arts as a Branch of Education, The,
228 n.
Artisans' Dwellings Act (1875),289
Artist (Ruskin as), 34, 39, 48, 96,
122, 186
Arundel Society, 122, 369
Arve, 98
Ashburton, Lady, 60
Aspects of God (great art reveals),
208, 212, 215, 216, 230, 235, 301
Assisi, 116, 122, 123 n., 157 n., 352
Assistants (Ruskin's), 34, 67, 116,
156, 277
Atheism, 155, 354, 355
Athenæum, The, 246
Austria and Austrians, 55, 307, 314
Autobiographical undercurrent (in
Ruskin's books), 10, 190, 262
Automatic use of words (Ruskin's),
85 and n., 86 n., 168, 364
Autumn Leaves (Millais), 250
Auxerre, 148
Avallon, 148
Awakening Conscience, The (Hol-
man Hunt) 145 n., 188, 251, 377

Bacon, 47
Ballerina (in Turin), 65, 84, 275
Bancroft, Squire, 39 and n.
Baptism, The (Piero dei Frances-
chi) 258 n.
Barclay, Thomas (open letter to)
328 n.
Barmouth, 119
Barnum, 165, 166 n.
Barrett, Wilson, 39, 40 n.
Barry, 93, 104 n.
Battle of Montenotte, The, 305, 316
Baudelaire (Universal Analogy),
189, 239
'Beautiful and True, the' (Ruskin's
conception of), 210–11
Beauty, 209
Beauvais, 162, 214
Beever, Susan (*Frondes Agrestes*),
146 n., 151 n., 177, 203 n., 357
Before the Mirror (Swinburne), 78
Bell, Clive (*Art*), 221
Bell, Miss (Winnington), 72, 74–5
Bellini, Gentile, 206–7, 258 n.
Bellini, Giovanni, 206–7
Bellinzona, 276
Bellosguardo, 122
Bennett, Dr. W. C., 112 n.
Benson, A. C. (*Ruskin, A Study in
Personality*), 198 and n.
Berghem, 201
Berlin, 375 n.
Bewdley, 119
Bible, the, 42, 57, 83 n., 91, 101, 110,
329, 336, 343 (four theories on)
Bible of Amiens, The, (1880) 153
Biblical quotation (Ruskin), 332,
342, 345, 363, 364 n.
Bibliotheca Pastorum, 121, 153
Binyon, L. (on Ruskin), 188
Bishop (Ruskin as a), 48
Blackwood's Magazine, 44 n.
Blake, William, 163 and n., 187
Blenheim (*Ansidei Madonna* at),
206
Blumenthal, Carlo (of Venice), 99

Bodley's Librarian (Rev. H. O. Coxe), 100
Boer War, 303–4
Bologna, 206
Bolton Abbey (Turner), 114
Bombay, 44 n.
Bonneville, 169
Booth, General William, 110 and n.
Borghese, Piero *see* Piero dei Franceschi
Borgo San Sepolcro, 258 n.
Bosanquet, Bernard (*A History of Æsthetic*), 211
Both, 201
Botticelli, 39, 121, 135, 198, 258–9 and n., 359, 381 n.
Bourbon regime, the (in France), 251 n.
Bourges, 148
Bowerswell (Perth), 53 n.
Boy Scouts (cf. Companions of St. George), 109
Brabazon (amateur artist), 162
Brackenbury, Captain, 78 n.
Bradford (lecture at), 285, 382–3
Brannackstown (Kildare), 91 n.
Brantwood, 27, 29, 84, 114–16, 121, 125 n., 127, 146–151 and 151 n., 156, 172, 175–6, 179, 301, 353
Brantwood Edition (American), 177 n.
Brescia, 206
Brett, John (*The Stonebreaker*), 78, 250, 275–6, 380 n.
British Institution, 253
British Medical Journal, 145
British Museum, 89, 103, 106, 225 and n., 322
Broadlands (Romsey), 114, 115 n., 131, 134 and n., 141
'Broken Pieces of Sir Philip Sidney's Psalter', 121, 152
Broken Reeds (*Time and Tide*), 132 n.
Broughton, Lord, 375

Brown, Ford Madox, 60, 247 n., 272 and n.
Brown, Dr. John, 65 n., 80 n., 98 n.
Brown, Rawdon (Letter to), 67 n.
Brown, Rev. W. L. (Letter to), 52 n.
Browne, (Dickens illustrator), 254
Browning, Mr. and Mrs., 60; (Letters to), 64–6 nn., 68 n., 241 n., 340 n.
Browning, Oscar (*quoted*), 353
Brunswick Square, 42
Brussels, 195
Builder, The, 371 n.
Bunney, J. W., 96, 148, 277
Burd Helen (W. L. Windus), 250
Burgess, Arthur, 86 n., 94 n., 96, 100 n., 136 and n., 148, 277
Burne-Jones, 60, 67, 76 and n., 78–9, 134 and n., 151, 171, 253 and n., 255 n., 259, 274
Burne-Jones, Lady, 71 n, 74
Burton, W. S. (*The Wounded Cavalier*), 250
Byron, 42, 160

Camberwell (Working Men's Institute), 77
Cambridge, 86 and n., 88, 90, 150
Cambridge School of Art (Inaugural address), 382
Canaletto, 201
Candlelight (Firefly obsession), 335 n.
Canning, Lady, 60
Capitalists, 312–3, 325–6
Caprichos (Goya), 257
Carlyle, Thomas, 28, 37, 40 and n., 68, 71, 90 n., 107, 110 n., 163, 186 and n., 273 and n., 318, 365
Carlyle, Mrs., 280 and n., 286 n.
Carlyle, Dr. John, 40 n., 110 n.
Carpaccio, 34, 105, 134, 152, 172, 258 and n., 259 n.
Carpenter's Shop, The (Millais), 246

Carte blanche (for purchases), 163 n.
Casanova, The Memoirs of (Ruskin reading), 136
Cat (obsession), 146
Catallactics, science of (i.e. exchange value), 290, 293, 312
Catholic Emancipation, 227, 332–5
Cattermole (Dickens illustrator), 254
Caution to Snakes, A (see Living Waves), 160, 188, 189 n.
Cent Ballades (de Queux de Saint-Hilaire), 101
Century Guild Hobby Horse, The, 86 n.
Cestus of Aglaia, 63 n., 73 n., 80 n., 89 n., 139 n., 164 n., 193, 303, 361 n., 362 n.
Cézanne, 35
Chambers' Encyclopædia (article for), 175
Chamouni (Chamonix), 34, 67, 75, 168, 195, 198–9, 275
Champagnole, 28–9, 169
Chardin, 257
Charles V at Mühlberg (Titian),257
Chartres, 162
'Chaucer's Dream', 101
Chelsea (Whitelands), 149, 171
Cheney, Edward, 373
Chesneau, Ernest, 88 n., 246 n.
Chess, 116, 175, 309–10, 318
Christ Church (Oxford), 44, 74
Chubb's lock (and 'Key of Destiny '), 69
Church, the (as 'intermediary'), 47–8, 356
Churches, all ('forms of idolatry'), 66, 81 n., 231
Cima, 207
Cistercian Architecture (Mending the Sieve), 153, 335 n.
City (concept of a modern), 224 and n.
Claude, 62, 201–3

Claudian (Wilson Barrett in), 39
Clayton, Rev. P. B., 110
Clement, Pope (and his mitre), 122
Climacteric (Ruskin's), 65, 71, 181
Clouds and Light (devotional poems by Rose La Touche), 127
Clouet, 257
Cole, G. D. H. (The Intelligent Man's Guide, etc.), 299 n.
Colenso, Bishop, 68, 71, 151 n., 341
Colenso Diamond, the, 151 and n.
Collecting (Ruskin's passion for), 33, 114, 151, 175
Collingwood, W. G. (Life and Work of Ruskin), 37, 61, 118 and n., 121, 151 n., 153, 154 n., 166, 168, 187 n., 281 n., 363 n., 369
Cologne, 195
Colonne Vendôme, 256 n.
College Friend (letters to a), 48 n., 49 n.
Combe (buys Millais' Return of the Dove), 380 n.
Committees (Ruskin and), 94, 273, 286
Como, 195, 309
'Companions of St. George', 109
Competition, 287, 290, 296, 322, 327
Concentrate (Ruskin's inability to), 229, 360
Conclusions (Ruskin's, as to Art), 225–6, 231, 235–9
Coniston, 37, 114–15, 158
Constance, 195
Contemporary Review, 160 n.
Contemporary work (neglected by Ruskin), 34, 243, 250, 254–6
Continuous work (impossible to Ruskin), 127, 227
Cook, E. T. (Life of Ruskin), 37, 40 n., 83 n., 118 n., 175 n.
Cooper, Abraham, R. A. (Ruskin on), 250
Co-operation 296, 322

Copying (Ruskin and Carpaccio's *St. Ursula*), 134, 136, 152, 172–3

Coral mouths (Winnington), 73

Cork High School for Girls, 171

Cornhill Magazine, 65, 69

Corot (neglected by Ruskin), 256–7

Corpus Christi College (Oxford), 114, 127, 150

Correggio, 231, 273

Courbet, 256 and n.

Covent Garden Theatre, 83

Cowper-Temple, the Rt. Hon. W., 37, 100 n., 102, 114, 119–20, 131, 133, 374–5

Cowper-Temple, Mrs. (a spiritualist), 133, 141

Coxcomb (pay 200 guineas, etc.), 143, 198 n., 241

Coxe, H. O., Rev. (Bodley's Librarian), 100

Craftsmanship (happiness necessary), 61, 214, 216–7, 233, 300

Creed (of the economists), 290–1

Crime de Silvestre Bonnard, Le (Anatole France), 187 n.

Crimean War, 41, 308 and n., 309, 318, 323, 367

Critical acumen (selfish cultivation of), 64

Croly, Rev. Dr. (*quoted*), 333

Crowding thoughts (in Ruskin's head), 60, 229 n., 360

'Crown and Thistle, The', (Abingdon) 114

Crown of Wild Olive, The, 41 n., 77, 112 n., 268 n., 303 n., 315 n., 316 n., 317, 319 n., 342 n.

Croydon (Ruskin's maternal grandmother from), 42

Cruelty (*see under* Foxhunting), 213

Crystal Palace, 223, 284

Crystal Palace, Opening of the, etc., 223 n., 308 n.

Cumberland, 86

Curator of University Galleries (Acland's proposal), 90

Custozza, Battle of, 307

Cuttle-fish (and incredulity), 189–90

Cuyp, 201

Czar, the, 41

Daily Express, 91 n.

Daily Telegraph (letters to, etc.), 80 n., 93–4, 102 and n., 107, 298 n., 323–4 and n.

Dale, Rev. Thomas, 47 n., 48 n., 196 n.

Dancing angels (Fra Angelico), 213 and n., 330, 358

Dante, 91, 133, 187, 231, 288

Dante drawing an Angel (Rossetti), 247

Darmstadt (Holbein), 375 n.

David (Lyonnais pupils of), 251 n.

Dawkins, W. Boyd, 104 n.

Deal, 60

Dean and Chapter (Westminster Abbey burial offered), 27

Death (of Ruskin), 27, 179

Degas, 256

Deity ('taught by'), 215–16, 235, 300–1, 336

Delacroix, 256, 257 n.

Della Robbia (*Madonna and Child*), 151

Delusions (Ruskin's), 33, 156, 175

Denmark, The Position of (Letter to *Morning Post*), 80 n.

Denmark Hill, 47, 50–2 n., 56, 59, 65–6, 71, 75 and n., 76–8, 87, 90, 93–4, 97, 100–1, 105–7, 111 and n., 199, 227–8, 265–6, 280

Department of Science and Art, 382

Depression (Ruskin's), 30–1, 34–5, 52, 57, 66, 75, 79, 95, 121, 126, 166, 280, 341

De Profundis (Wilde), 221

Derby Day (Frith), 250

Deterioration of nature (Ruskin's complaint of), 97, 125, 261

INDEX

Deteriorative Power of Conventional Art over Nations, The, 381
Deucalion, 30 n., 113, 121, 123 n., 160, 187–9 nn., 352, 363 n.
Diamond (purchase of the *Colenso Diamond*), 151 and n.
Dickens, Charles, 246, 250, 254
Dijon, 99 n., 195
Dilecta (see *Præterita*), 175
Dilke, Lady (Miss E. F. Strong), 238 n.
Di Ma, 122
Diphtheria (and the 'sign from God'), 210, 331, 336
Disappointments (Ruskin's), 63, 66, 69, 118–20
Disraeli and his Day (Fraser), 258 n.
'Divinely inspired' mission (Ruskin's), 210–12
Dixon, Thomas (letters to: published in *Scotsman*), 88
Domenichino ('abominable') 198
Domestic Servants (letter to *Daily Telegraph*), 80 n.
Don Quixote of Denmark Hill, 176 and n.
Dove returning to the Ark (Millais), 248 n., 380 n.
Downs (gardener), 87, 93, 106, 111–12, 119–20, 135, 281 n., 323
Drawing (Ruskin's 'favourite play'), 34
Drawing School (Oxford), 105, 118 and n., 121, 149, 155, 178, 258 n., 277
Dreams (at Matlock), 157 and n.
Dresden (Holbein), 375 n.
Dress (Ruskin 'a dandy'), 27, 34, and n., 44, 72
Dublin, 90, 92, 95 n., 348
Dulwich Gallery, 199 and n., 200–1
Du Maurier, 255 n.
Dunira (W. Graham's collection at), 247 n.

Dunkeld, 52 n.
Dyce (R.A.), 246, 376

Eagles' Nest, The, 325 n.
Early Italian Poets (Rossetti), 270
Eastlake, Sir Charles (P.R.A.), 250, 373, 379
Eastlake, Lady, 379
Ecce Ancilla Domini (Rossetti), 246, 247 n.
Economic Man (postulate 'useless'), 189, 242, 290–1, 300
Economist (Xenophon), 121, 152
Edinburgh (*Lectures on Architecture and Painting*), 214, 227, 306–7 nn., 345, 371–2 nn., 377, 380–1
Education (letter on, *see under* Taxation), 57
Educational Series, Notes on the, 105 n.
Edwardes, Sir Herbert, 151 n., 303 and n.
Edwardes Ruby, the, 151 n.
Eels ('swimming strings and eels'), 52, 214
Elation (Ruskin's moods of), 31, 35, 156, 162, 166, 175 and n.
Elcho, Lord, 68
Election (letter on, *see under* Taxation), 57
Elements of English Prosody, The, 160
Elgin Marbles, the, 104 n.
El Greco, 257
Ellis, F. S., 104 n., 163 n., 257 n.
Ellis, Mrs. Amabel Williams (*The Tragedy of John Ruskin*), 76, 346–7
Employment of the Destitute and Criminal Classes, Notes for the, 109 n.
English cathedrals, 54
Equality ('no patience with the idea'), 58, 109
Ervine, St. John, 110 n.

INDEX

Esdras II (Ruskin reading Chapter xiv), 122
Ethical judgements (reinforced from Bible, 342–5, 364 n.
Ethical subjects (Ruskin's 'right' to dogmatise on), 128–9, 351
Ethics of the Dust, The, 75, 80, 85 n., 101 n., 177, 185, 237 n., 277 n., 303, 342 n., 347 and n., 348 n., 350 n.
Euphoria, *see* Elation
Exchange value (works of art), 150 n.; and *see also* Catallactics
Exhibitionism (Ruskin's), 34, 70 n., 360
'Exile of St. Helena, The' (subject for Newdigate, 1838), 304
Exposition Universelle (1855 and 1866), 256
Eyesight (Ruskin's always good), 31, 52, 97

Failures (Ruskin's), 63, 66, 118
Family of Darius, The (Veronese), 283 n.
Faraday, 167 n., 260, 358 n.
Father (Ruskin's: J. J. Ruskin), 42–3, 45, 51–2, 55–6 nn., 57–8 nn., 65–6 nn., 67–8 nn., 70–1 and n., 72–7 nn., 80 n., 279, 357 n.
Faunthorpe, Rev. J. P., 28 n.,156 n.
Felstead House, 149
Ferdinand, Archduke Charles, 56
Fiction, Fair and Foul (Scott, Byron, Wordsworth), 160
Fielding, Copley, 255 n.
'Fifties (Ruskin's influence in the, smaller than supposed, 61, 245, 255, 369
Finality-form (Ruskin's), 222
Fine Arts, Museum of (Boston, U.S.A.), 50 n.
Fine writing ('mischief of'), 239, 359
Firefly obsession 32, 86, 138, 141 n., 157 n., 168, 335 n.

Fireworks obsession, 32, 138, 157
Fireworks (Whistler), 32, *see under* Nocturne
First principles (Ruskin's power of grasping), 28, 33, 191, 224
First-rate painter ('mustn't be pious'), 65, 211 n., 234, 340
Flamboyant Architecture of the Valley of the Somme, 94, 221 n.
'Flirtations' (Ruskin's), 165
Florence, 106, 113, 122–3 and n., 135 and n., 196–7, 206, 214
Folkestone 52 n., 53 n., 175
Fonthill, Abbey of ('jerry-built Gothic'), 371
'For Oxford . . . for Sheffield', 39, 116, 119, 277, 357
Fors Clavigera, 27, 30, 38 and n., 41 n., 43 n., 76 n., 90 n., 95 n., 103, 105 n., 107–111 n., 113, 115 n.–117 n., 125 and n., 131–137, 144, 146, 151, 159 n., 178, 218, 234 n., 256 n., 257, 263 n., 323 n., 325–328 n., 339 n., 341 n., 352–3, 355 and n., 366–7 and nn.
Fortnightly Review (Swinburne), 259
Foxhunting, 102, 105, 111, 213 n.
Fra Angelico, 198, 206, 213 and n., 231, 330, 358
France, 32, 34, 41, 46, 51, 60, 93, 98, 123
France, Anatole, 187
Francia, 206, 231
Franco-Prussian War, 106, 322–7
Fraser, Sir William (*Disraeli*), 258 n.
Fraser's Magazine, 65, 69, 321 n., 324 n., 326 n., 327 n.
Freeman, E. A., 104 n.
Free Trade (Ruskin on), 296
French Gothic (Ruskin studies), 54
French painter ('no single great'), 256
French Painting (Wilenski), 244 and n., 251 n.

Frith,W.P. (R.A.), 10, 379; (*Derby Day*), 250; (*Ramsgate Sands and Paddington Station*), 254; (*Autobiography quoted*), 378 n., 379

Frondes Agrestes (Beever), 177, 203 n., 357

Froude, J. A., 28 n., 40 n., 69 n., 71

Furnivall, Dr. F. J., 68 n.

Gainsborough, 151, 198, 199 n., 207

Galileo, 47

Gambart, Ernest, 382, 383

General Principles of Employment for the Destitute and Criminal Classes, The (cf. *Queen of the Air*), 94

Geneva, 169, 195, 214

Genius (Ruskin a), 10, 28, 190

Genoa, 197

Gentleman Commoner (Ruskin at Oxford), 44

Geological Magazine, 101 n.

Geometric and organic form (symbolic relation between), 220, 239, 240

George (Ruskin's valet), 51, 55, 331

Germany (Ruskin visits, 1859),255, 375 n.

German Galleries (Ruskin ignorant of), 167 n., 375

Ghirlandajo, 207

Giorgione, 207

Giotto, 39, 122, 206, 211 n., 234

Girl Guides (cf.'Companions of St. George'), 109

Girlhood of the Virgin, The (Rossetti), 245, 247 n., 376

'Girlies' (Kate Greenaway's), 85 n., 172–4

Girls (Ruskin and), 73, 171

Girton (gifts to), 172

Gladstone, 144

Glenfinlas, 59, 63, 227

God (great art an 'aspect of', *q.v.*), 208

Gogh, Vincent Van, 35

Gold (Ruskin on), 71, 294, 295 n.

Good men (and art: 'monkish' painters comparatively weak artists), 211 n., *and see under* Firstrate

Goodwin, Albert, 116

Gordon, Rev. Osborne, 199 n., 201 n., 205 n.

Gothic architecture, 221 and n.

Gothic revival (in English architecture, 61, 371

Goya, 257

Gozzoli, 197, 206

'Graduate of Oxford, A', (*Modern Painters*), 132 n., 199

Græco-Roman sculpture (in British Museum), 89

Graham, William (collection), 247 n.

Grand Canal (Venice), 55–6

Grant, Sir Francis, 100

Grape-shot ('grapes or'), 312

Gray, Euphemia (Mrs. John Ruskin), 53, 180

Great art (only useful to 'next great artist'), 64, 241

Great man (Ruskin a), 10, 28, 36

Great Victorians, The, 110 n.

Greek art, coins, mythology, sculpture, vases, etc., 89, 102–4, 106, 121, 252 (Ruskin's boredom with)

Green, J. R., 104 n.

Greenaway, Kate, 81 n., 85 n., 167 and n., 171–4, 255 n., 277

Grey, Lady Jane, 131

Griffith (dealer), 45, 50

Grote, 100

'Guggum', 272, 274

Guild of St. George (*see under* St. George)

Guilt (Ruskin's sense of), 156

Hackstoun, W., 148, 277
Hades ('the broad way to'), 96
'Half-open gapes', 73, 252
Hammersmith, 131, 137
Handel, 47
Happiness of the workman (Ruskin's theory), 61, 214, 216–7, 233, 300
Hare-lip, 36
Harker, Mrs. Allen ('Happy Memories' and 'John Ruskin in the 'Eighties'), 155 n., 175 n.
Harrison, Frederic, 93 n.
Harrison, W. H., (*Selections*) 92, 106 n., 111 n., 141 n., 199 n., 307 n., 357 and n.
Harristown, 72, 80 n., 81 n., 91 n.
Harrow School (minerals given to), 150
Hawarden, 144, 157
Haydon (his insanity), 164 n.
Health (Ruskin's good), 31, 46
Heaton, Miss Ellen, 74 n., 273 and n., 380
Hedhead, Robert, 175
Heidelberg, 195
Henri IV, 251 n.
Herkomer, 158 n., 193 n.
Hermes (excavated 1877), 104 n.
Herne Hill, 42, 44, 115–16, 127, 147, 156, 165, 172
Hesiod, 288
Hincksey (road-making), 111–12, 144, 327
High Savoy, 148, 153, 175, 228, 356
Hill, Miss Octavia, 120
Hilliard, Lawrence (secretary), 37, 130, 153, 165
Hilliard, Miss Constance, 95 n., 106, 116
Hilliard, Mrs., 105–6, 116, 134
Historian (Ruskin as), 221–2
Hobbema, 201
Holbein (*Madonna with the family of Jacob Meyer*), 375

Holy Orders (Ruskin considers, but rejects), 47–9, 330
Home, Daniel Douglas (medium), 133
Homer, 231, 288–9
Homes (Ruskin's), 114, 127
Honeymoon (Ruskin's), 54, 130 n.
Hostility (to friends), 165, 175
Hostility (to world at large), 31, 69, 96, 156
House of Commons Committee (on Public Institutions), 286
Household Words (Dickens and Pre-Raphaelites), 246
Howell, C. A. (secretary), 57 n., 77 n.
Hunt, Holman, 95; (*The Awakening Conscience*), 145 n., 188, 251, 377; (lecture on), 153, and *see* 255 n.; (*Rienzi*), 245, 376; (*Scapegoat*), 250; (*Pre-Raphaelitism*), 257 n., 376 n.; (*Light of the World*), 377
Hunter Street (Ruskin's birthplace), 42
Hyde Park (pebble from), 141 n., 151 n.
Hyde Park Gallery, 245

Idolatry (of all churches), 66, 81, 231
Illness (Ruskin's account of his), 86, 145 n., 366 n.
'Illth', 294 and n., 296, 327
Imagination ('highest intellectual power of man'), 212, 229
Imagination in Architecture (Architectural Association), 63, 224 n.
Imitation (Ruskin on), 208, 249
Impious men ('no supreme power of art'), 211; *see also under* First-rate
Impotent (Ruskin?), 54, 130
Impressionist Exhibitions (the seven 'notorious'), 256
Inchbold, J. W., 275–6

393

Income from books (Ruskin's), 178
India (British rule in), 308 n.
India Office (design for), 372
Indian Mutiny, 308, 314, 316
Influence (Ruskin's, exaggerated by biographers), 61
Ingelow, Jean, 95 n.
Ingres, 251 n., 257
Innsbruck, 195
Insanity (Ruskin on), 86, 133
Insensibility (Ruskin's, to other people), 31, 70, 94, 96
Intelligent Man's Guide, etc., *The*, (Cole), 299 n.
Interest and Usury (Controversy with Bishop of Manchester), 160
Interlaken, 90 n.
Intrinsic value (permanent, invariable), 241, 267, 293, 300
Ireland, 72, 92
Iris of the Earth, The, 30 n.
Irritability (Ruskin's 'hostile'), 51, 94, 96, 165
Isabel ('Mousie'), 75
Italian painting (Ruskin's study of) 51, 257 *et seq.*
Italian Question, The (Scotsman), 140 n.
Italian War, the (1859), 65
Italy, 32, 34, 46, 67, 85, 94, 105, 113, 116, 123, 196
Italy (Rogers), 43
Ivy (round tree), 200, 212

Jamaican Insurrection (Daily Telegraph), 80 n.
Jesus in the House of His Parents (Millais), 246, 376
Jingling (with words), 85, 158, 193 n., 360
Jowett (his translation of Plato's *Laws* 'a disgrace'), 159
Joy for Ever, A, 65 n., 230, 280 and n., 282 n., 283 n., 381
Joyce, James, 362

Judgement (Ruskin's claim to 'perfect'), 57, 60, 63, 93
Juliet and her Nurse (Turner), 44 n.
Jumbo (the elephant), 165 and n.

Keble (Ruskin ridicules), 341
Keswick, 87 n.
Kildare, 91 n.
Kingsley, Rev. William, 90, 257, 382
Kitchin, Dean, 44 n.
Knight's Faith, A (Edwardes), 303 n., 309 n., 310 n., 328
Korah ('representative of millions'), 123
Königgratz (Sadowa), 321 n.
Krupp, Alfred, 303

Laisser faire, 282, 291, 296
Larg, David (*John Ruskin*), 49 n., 180 n., 270 n., 376 n.
La Touche, Mrs., 66 n., 75, 81–2 and n., 128, 340, 350
La Touche, Rose, *see* Rose
La Tour, 276
Lauterbrunnen, 275
Law Courts (London), 372
Laws of Fésole, 256 n.
League of Nations, 299 n., 328
Lecturer (Ruskin as), 34, 77, 154–5
Lectures on Architecture and Painting, 193, 215 n., 227, 247 n., 306 n., 307 n., 308 n., 338 n., 371 n., 381 n.
Lectures on Art, 101 n., 110 n., 128, 192, 257 n., 350 n., 366 n.
Lectures on Landscape, 258 n.
Leech, John, 250, 255 n.
Leeds Mercury, 88
Leeds Town Hall, 372
Leighton, Sir Frederick, 255 n.
Leonardo, 207
Leopold, Prince (Duke of Albany), 144, 147
Leslie, C. R. (*Autobiographical Recollections*), 138 n.

Letter to Young Girls, 177
Letters and diaries (Ruskin's), 10, 34, 83 n., 180, 343 n.
Letters to the Clergy, etc., 160 and n.
Lewis, J. F., 381
Library of General Knowledge (projected), 121, 152, 352
Library Edition (Ruskin's works), 9, 11, 91, 120, 145 n., 155 n., 161 n., 185, 207 n., 234 n., 253 n., 279 n., 287 n., 343 n.
Liddell, Dean Henry, 37, 44 n., 45, 89, 100, 201 n.
Light (Ruskin and 'spots of light'), 138; *and see* Fireflies, Fireworks
Light of the World, The (Hunt), 377
'Lily' (i.e. Lily Armstrong, in *Ethics of the Dust*), 85 n.
Lindsay, Lord (*History of Christian Art*), 140 n.
Literary Gazette, The (1842), 198 n.
Liverpool Albion, 315 n.
Living Waves, 160, 363 n.
'Lock and key' (pictures kept under), 240
Lockhart, Miss, 52
Logic, 122
London Institution, 30, 160, 169, 172
Longfellow (Ruskin meets), 95
Lorenzo and Isabella (Millais), 245, 376
Loudon, J. C., 47 n.
Louvre, the, 195, 196, 206
Love's Meinie, 254 n., 308 n., 323 n.
Lowell, J. R., 73 and n.
Lucca, 152 n., 168, 206
Lucian, 104 n.
Lugano, 99
Luini (Ruskin 'discovers'), 259 n.
Lysippus, 104

McCracken, Francis, 246, 247 n.
MacDonald, George, 37, 54 n., 81 n., 129 and n., 350

MacDonald, Dr. Greville (*Reminiscences of a Specialist*), 11, 37 and n., 54 n., 81 n., 128 n., 129 n.
Macdonald, William Macdonald, 53 n.
Machinery (destroys craftsmanship), 220
Maclise (Ruskin's attack on), 378 n., 379
Madness (Ruskin's six attacks of), 27, 34–5, 75, 112, 145, 153, 156, 163, 165–6, 175, 253
Madonna ('with black hair in ringlets'), 64
Madonna with the family of Jacob Meyer (Holbein), 375
Magdeburg, capture of, 324
Maggiore, 195
Magi ('Soldan's discomfited'), 122
Maidstone, 58
Maitland, Fuller, 259, 381 n.
Malaria (and papal wickedness), 197, 330
Malleson, Rev. F. A., 161, 225 n.
Mammon, Victor (and Victor Emmanuel), 85
Manchester Art Treasures Exhibition (1857), 259, 381 and n.
Manchester, Bishop of (Ruskin's controversy with), 160
Manchester Daily Examiner and Times (*Time and Tide*), 88
Manchester lectures (*Political Economy of Art*), 280, 381
Manet, 256
Manic self-confidence (Ruskin's), 35, 52, 68, 98, 191, 199, 205, 212, 241, 330, 337, 355
Manic depression, 10
Manning, Cardinal, 94, 354
Mantegna, 114
Manuscripts (Ruskin and mediæval), 57, 59, 151
Marbles (at Lucca, Ruskin choosing), 152, 168

Margarita of Austria on Horseback (Velasquez), 257 and n.

Marks, H. Stacy (R.A.), 163 n.

Marmontel (*Memoirs*), 101

Marriage (Ruskin's), 53–4, 57, 59, 180, 214

Martinet's (Manet at), 256

Marylebone (teashop in), 111

Masaccio, 207

Master, The (of St. George's Guild), 109, 119, 124, 144, 147, 153

Master's Reports (*ib.*), 110 n., 119 n., 120, 147, 149

Master of Trinity, the (Whewell), 90

Matlock (Ruskin's illness at), 115, 157 and n., 352

'Mausolus' (British Museum), 225

May Queen Festival (Whitelands), 171

Mayfair, 55, 58, 216

Maynooth (grant), 333

Meaning of Modern Sculpture, The (Wilenski), 89 n., 104 n., 207 n., 222, 225 n., 236 n., 240 and n., 242, 245 n.

Mediaevalism, 64, 249, 251

Meersbrook Park (Sheffield), 109 n.

Megroz, R. L. (*Dante Gabriel Rossetti*), 270 n.

Meissonier, 151, 383 n.

Melodious noise, 49, 205, 358

Memoirs (Marmontel), 101

Mending the Sieve (Cistercian architecture), 153, 335 n.

Mercury and Argus (Turner), 44 n.

Merioneth (St. George's Guild property in), 119

Metaphysical Society (paper to, 25th April, 1871), 138 n., 189

Metropolitan Tabernacle Pulpit, 82 n.

Meynell, Mrs. (*John Ruskin*), 207

Michelangelo, 47, 195, 198, 207, 231

Mickley, 119

Milan, 70 n., 195, 206

Mill, John Stuart, 90, 286 n.

Millais, 36, 59, 60, 62, 227; (*Lorenzo and Isabella*), 245; (*Jesus in the House*), etc., 246; (*Dove returning to the Ark*), 248 n., 380 n.; (*Autumn Leaves*), 250; 275, 280, 376, 379, 380 n.

Milton, 91

Minerals (Ruskin's interest in), 33, 45, 57, 148, 151

Mitford, Miss Mary, 52 n.

'Mobility of interest' (Ruskin's), 32, 60, 94, 120, 156, 181, 227, 229, 351, 360

Mocenigo family, the (*The Madonna*, etc.), 258 n.

Modern Movement in Art, The (Wilenski), 242

Modern Painters, 27, 29, 32, 34, 37, 41 n., 49, 50, 51, 60, 62–4, 68, 73, 88, 91–2, 96, 102, 104, 134, 185, 193–4, 198–209, 212–14, 227, 229–30, 234, 236–9, 243–4, 247, 249, 256, 259, 264–7, 280, 285–6, 306, 308–10, 316, 330–1, 340, 358, 368–370, 372, 378, 381

Modern Warfare (*Fraser's Magazine*), 321 n., 324 n., 326 n., 327 n.

'Mollusc to man', 212, 227, 228 n., 239–40, 247

Monastic life, the (Ruskin on), 350 and n.

Monet, 256

Money, (Ruskin's), 28, 45, 54, 57, 67, 76, 115, 178; (creative artists and), 267; (and wealth), 290–3

Money Muddle, The (Pethick-Lawrence), 294 n.

Mont Blanc, 169

Montanvert, 73

Monte Rosa, Society of, 136 and n.

Morales, 257

Mornex, 37, 67, 75, 79

'Morning, Noon and Evening Advertiser', etc., (*Fors Clavigera*), 108

Morning Post, 80 n., 165 and n., 315 n., 354 n.

Mornings in Florence, 113 n., 123 n., 132 n., 139 n., 190, 193, 252, 260, 261, 263, 269, 356 n.

Morris, William, 60, 161, 219, 223 n.

Morte d'Arthur (Pre-Raphaelites and the), 64

Mother (Ruskin's), 36, 38, 42, 44, 48, 51, 53–5, 76–7, 86–7, 90–7, 103, 106, 126, 196

'Mousie', 'Mouse-pet', 75 n., 82–4, 173

Munera Pulveris, 65, 69 n., 109 n., 113, 185, 193 n., 287–8, 298–9, 302, 311, 315–16, 326–7, 341

Munich, 195, 375 n.

Munro of Novar, 151

Murray, C. Fairfax, 148

Murray, Miss, 175

Museums (evening opening of), 286

Music (Ruskin and), 161 n.

'Musical box' (a lively), 118, 162

My First Editor, 50 n.

Myers, Frederic, 170–1

Myron, 104 and n.

Mystery of Life and its Arts, The (Dublin lecture), 90

Naesmyth, Sir John Murray, 73 n., 74 n.

Naples, 116, 196

Napoleon I, 266 and n., 303–6, 310

Napoleon III, 308, 314, 323

National Art Collections Fund (Ruskin a pioneer of the), 284

National Association for the Promotion of Social Science, 93

National Gallery, 172, 199–201, 258–9, 269, 283 n., 372–4

National Gallery Sites Commission, 62 n., 218 n., 255, 375 n.

National Institute (Free Exhibition), 246

Nativity (Botticelli), 259, 381 n.

Nativity, The (Piero dei Franceschi), 258 n.

Newbridge, 91 and n.

Newdigate prize, 44, 304

Newman, Henry R., 148, 150 n., 277

Newton, Charles, 225 n.

Newton, Sir Isaac, 47

'Next great artist' (art useful only to), 64, 241

Nice, 196

Nineteenth century, the ('chiefly memorable', etc.), 28

Nineteenth Century, 160

Norton, Charles Eliot (Ruskin's 'American friend'), 69 and *passim*

Nocturne in Black and Gold (Whistler), 32, 143, 198, 241

Nollekens, 89 n., 104 n.

Normandy, 54

Northwick, Lord, 259

Notes on Designs of the Old Masters at Florence (Swinburne), 259

Notes on his own Drawings (1878), 117 n.

Notes on the Construction of Sheepfolds, 57, 335

Notes on the Educational Series (1872), 139 n.

Nurse (Anne), 127, 145, 187 n., 281 n.

Oberland, the Swiss, 195

Obsessions and delusions, 31–2, 72, 95, 114, 121, 135, 138, 145, 156, 168, 262, 352 (*see also*: fireflies, fireworks, orphan, peacock, Rose, Storm Cloud, St. Ursula, (Plague Wind)

INDEX

Old-age pensions, 284, 289, 298
Old Masters, 43, 172, 194–7, 256–7, 369, 372
Omissions (from letters and from Library Edition, by executors), 343 n.; *see also* p. 83 n.
On the Old Road, 50 n., 160 n., 382 n.
Open Letter to Count Zorzi (1877), 144 n.
Ophelia (Ruskin on), 347 n.
Opium in China (Ruskin's protest), 315
Orcagna, 197, 206
Original artists (Ruskin's relations with), 36, 264–77
Orphan obsession, 126–7, 145
Ottobeuren (monastery), 148
Our Fathers have told us, etc. (History of Christendom), 153, 162
Our Railway System (*Daily Telegraph*), 80 n.
Outline of History (Wells), 304 n.
Outlook, 175 n.
Overwork ('all nonsense'), 31, 112–13, 117, 157, 164
Ownership and Management of Railways (*Daily Telegraph*), 93
Oxford, Bishop of ('rudeness of'), 68
Oxford and Cambridge boat-race, 83
Oxford (Christ Church), 44, 47
Oxford Drawing School (*see* Drawing School)
Oxford Lectures, 106–8, 128, 130 n., 133, 193, 260, 349
Oxford Museum (the building), 372
Oxford professorship (Ruskin's), 90, 100–3, 113, 121–2, 147, 153, 155, 254 and n.
Oxford rooms (Ruskin's), 114
Oxford (Turner drawings to), 88, 150

Oxford University Herald, 118 n., 161, 162 n.
Oxford (Ruskin undergraduate), 44
Oxford Union (frescoes in library), 235 n., 275, 380 and n.

Paddington Station (Frith), 254
Padua, 206, 214
Pagan architecture, 221 and n.
Paint-box (valet holding), 162
Painting ('of our own day'), 244
Pall Mall Gazette, 28 n., 80 n., 371 n.
Palmerstone, Lord, 372, 374–5
Pantomimes, 83 165, 171
Papacy ('and malaria'), 197, 330
Paradise Lost, 85
Paradiso, 133
Parents (Ruskin's relations with), 43–4, 53, 70–1, 76, 93, 94, 96–7, 105–6, 114–15, 126–8
Park Street, Mayfair, 55 and n., 216
Paris, 45, 66, 75, 195
Parma, 206
Parthenon, the, 104 n.
Paternal government, 282, 296
Patmore, Coventry, 62 n., 160–1 n., 246, 376
Patmos (St. John in), 122
Pawns (human, in war), 41, 309–10, 318
Peacock obsession, 145 n.
Pebbles, 33, and *see also* 141 n., 151 n.
Peel, Sir Robert (Junr.), 286–7
Pensions, Old-age, 298
Persecution delusions, 68, 156, 167
Perth, 53 n.
Perugino, 198
Pethick-Lawrence, F. W. (*The Money Muddle*), 294 n.
Phidias, 104 n.
'Phosphor light', 46 n., 139, 141
Piero dei Franceschi, 257
Pietistic religion (Ruskin rails against), 131, 345–50

INDEX

Pisa, 106, 148, 197, 206, 214, 247 n.
Pisani, Count V., 283 n.
Pissarro, 256
Pistoja, 140 n.
Plague-Wind obsession, 32, 124, 168–9 and n.
Plato, 159, 187
'Platted Thorns' (*Fors*), 131
Pleasure (artist and his work), 61, 214, 216–7, 233, 300
Pleasures (Ruskin's), 38–40
Pleasures of England, The, 155, 173 n., 353 n.
Poems and Ballads (Swinburne), 234 n.
Poisonous beasts (fight 'as men, not as'), 41, 367
Poles (Ruskin on the), 315
Political Economy of Art, The, 65, 280 and n., 285–6 n., 381
Polyclitus, 104 and n.
Polygons, 185, 192–3, 285, 289, 302, 327
Portrait (of Ruskin, by Millais), 59, 280
Postillions, 43, 116, 194
Potter, P., 201
Poussin, Gaspard, 201–3
Poussin, Nicholas, 207
Prayer for sick girl, 171, 346
Praxiteles, 104 and n.
Preach (Ruskin's 'manic impulse to'), 29, 54, 57, 92, 212–13, 250, 269, 340, 359
Pre-Raphaelites, 59, 60, 62–4, 138, 227, 245, 248–51, 255 n., 369, 377
Pre-Raphaelitism (Holman Hunt), 257 n., 376 n.
Pre-Raphaelitism (Ruskin's pamphlet), 59, 246, 248 and n.
Præterita, 29, 42–9, 51–2, 65–6, 80, 83, 85, 104, 135, 140, 175, 180, 185, 192, 194–200, 202, 205–6, 229, 264–5, 281, 306–7, 310, 330–1, 340, 346, 370, 375, 377, 381; (above reff. chiefly in nn.)

'Professor, The', 100, 102–3
Propaganda (Ruskin's), 366
Proserpina, 30 n., 113, 121, 133 n., 160, 164
Protestantism ('rabid and false') 332 n., 338–40, 353
Prout, 151, 200
Psalter and Hours of Isabelle of France, The, 59 n.
'Psalter, of St. Louis', 59, 151
Psychasthenia (Rose), 131
Public Health Act (1875), 289
Pullen, F. W., 159 n.
Punch, 266 n.
Punctuation (confused), 132
Purchases (of minerals, shells, etc.), 148–52
Puritan, The, 155

Quarterly Review, 140 n., 379
Queen of Scots Missal, 148
Queen of the Air, The, 89, 90, 94 n., 97 n., 133 n., 193 and n., 252, 322 n.

Radetsky, Marshal, 56, 307, 336
Railways, Ownership and Management of (*Daily Telegraph*), 93; see also 145 n., 213, 298 n.
Ramsgate Sands (Frith), 254
Randal, Frank, 148, 277
Range of Intellectual Conception, etc., The (Metaphysical Society), 138 n., 190 n.
Raphael, 85 n., 174, 206, 375
Rationalisations (Ruskin's), 33, 35–6, 38, 41, 88, 96, 99, 100, 126–7, 152, 168 and n., 174, 191, 218–19, 229, 251, 253, 260, 299, 308, 338, 360
Rawlinson, Rev. G., 100
Reader, The (on glaciers), 29 n.
Readings in Modern Painters, 112 n.
'Recent English Painting' (proposed lecture at Oxford), 255 n.

399

Rede Lecture (Cambridge, 1867), 90
Reference Collection (Sheffield), 109, 148
Reference Series of Examples (Oxford), 105–6, 155
Relation of National Ethics to National Art, The, 90 n.
Relatives (Ruskin 'fond of them'), 77
Religion (Ruskin's personal), 48, 66, 211 n., 227, 329–56
'Religion of Humanity', 66, 80–1, 340–1, 345
Rembrandt, 32, 139, 141; (*Supper at Emmaus*), 195
Reminiscences of a Specialist (MacDonald), 11, 37 n., 54 n., 81, 128 n.
Reni, Guido (*Susannah and the Elders*), 372, 374
Renoir, 256
Resignation (Oxford, reasons for), 158, 254 n.
Return of the Dove, The (Millais), 248 n., 380 n.
Revelation, Book of the, 38 n.
Reynolds, Sir Joshua, 151, 198, 231; (*Three Graces*), 273
Rhine, the, 106
Rhone, the, 98, 102
Rich (Ruskin), 28, 76, 115, 178
Richardson, W. S., 382
Richmond, George (R.A.), 167 n.
Richmond, Miss Julia, 73 n.
Richmond, W. B., 153, 158 n.
Riding (forbidden to Ruskin), 36, 166
Rienzi (Holman Hunt), 245, 376
Riflemen Form (Tennyson), 313
'Right in the end' (Ruskin always), 212, 218
Risorgimento (Ruskin and the), 307, 314
Roadside Songs of Tuscany (Alexander), 148, 174 n., 187 n.

Roberts, David, 200, 250
Roberts, Miss, 101
Robertson, T. W., 39
Robson, George, 255 n.
Rock Honeycomb, 121, 152
Roger and Angelica (Ingres), 257
Rogers, Samuel (*Italy*), 43, 206
Roman Catholicism (Ruskin and), 32, 45, 143, 197, 226, 330, 353–4
Roman de la Rose, Le, 121
Romantic Movement, the, ('fallacy of'), 240; (in France), 251 n.
Rome, 116, 122, 148, 196
Rome from Mount Adventure (Turner), 44 n.
Rooke, T. M., 148, 277
Rosa, Salvator, 201
Rose (La Touche), 72, 74–6 n., 80–6, 91, 95 n., 114, 116 n., 124, 127, 129–31, 133–4, 180, 257, 260, 345–9, 365
Rose and Rosie, 82–3, 131, 171, 181, 187, 345–6
Rose Gardens (and *Broken Reeds*), 132 n.
Rose obsession, 75, 86 n., 128, 132, 156–7, 168, 170, 258
Rose Queen Festival (Cork High School), 171
Roseate, 355 n.
Roses, 127, 135
Rosie, 72, 74, 82–3, 85, 171 n., 231, 252, 345 and n.
Rosina, 85
Rosy, 132, 168
Rossetti, Dante Gabriel, 27, 38, 55, 60, 62–3, 78–9, 151, 153; (*Girlhood of the Virgin*), 245, *see also* 247 n.; (*Ecce Ancilla Domini*), 246, 249, 250, 255 n., 269, 270, 275–6, 282, 315 n., 376–7, 380
Rossetti: His Life and Works (Waugh), 270 n., 369 n.
Rossetti, William Michael, 76, 275 n.
Rouen, 195, 214

Royal Academy, 44, 60, 213, 225, 245–6, 378 and n.; see also 100
Royal Academy Commission, 68 n.
Royal Institution, 94, 101 n., 134 n., 213
Rubens, 195, 198, 231
Ruby (Ruskin's purchase of the Edwardes), 151
Ruskin, A Study in Personality (Benson), 198 and n.
Ruskin Drawing School (see Drawing School), 156 n.
Ruskin, J. J., (Ruskin's father); see Father
Ruskin legend, the, 154, 177
Ruskin Societies (from 1879 onwards), 154
Ruskin, The Prophet (ed. Whitehouse), 11, 185 n.
Ruskinettos ('the great artists'), 211–12, 215
Ruskinettino ('an incipient artist'), 247
Rutherston, Mr. Albert, 156 n.
Ruysdael, 201

Sacristans (Ruskin and), 96, 261
Sadowa (Königgratz), 321 n.
St. Anne (Florence), 122
St. Bernard, the Great, 195
St. Catherine of Siena, 133
St. Cecilia (Raphael), 85 n., 174
St. Cergues, 169
St. Francis of Assisi (Ruskin and), 10, 122, 352, 356
St. George's Fund, 108, 119
St. George's Guild, 30, 88, 109 and n., 110 n., 111, 113, 120, 121, 136 n., 144, 147, 148, 178, 352
St. George's Guild, General Statement of, 109 n.
St. George's Museum, see Sheffield
Saint-Hilaire, de Queux de, 101
St. John (Florence), 122
St. Louis' Psalter, 59, 151
St. Mark's (Venice), 144

St. Paul's, 79
St. Thomas Aquinas, 122
St. Ursula (obsession), 136, 157
St. Ursula's Dream (Carpaccio), 34, 105, 134, 172, 258
Salève, 39, 67
Sallenches, 169 and n.
Salon, the (Paris), 256
Salon des Refusés (1863), 256
Salsette and Elephanta (Ruskin's Newdigate prize), 44 and n.
Salzburg, 195
San Rocco, Scuola di (Tintoretto), 307
Sanger's Amphitheatre, 172
Santa Croce, 122
Saussure, H. B. de (Voyage dans les Alpes), 43
Savoy (annexation, 1860), 98; and see High Savoy
Scapegoat, The (Holman Hunt), 250
Schaffhausen, 195
Schott, Mrs. (Fanny), 276
Schoolgirls (Ruskin and), 43, 73, 171
Scholar (Ruskin 'never a'), 187; and see also 36–8, 48
Scientists (obsession), 156, 167
Scopas, 104
Scotsman, the, 65, 88, 140 n., 308 n., 314 n.
Scott, Gilbert (India Office), 372
Scott MSS., 151, 163
Scott, Walter, 160
Sculpture, 215; (Greek), 225; (on buildings), 225–6, 240
Seascale (Cumberland), 176
Sebastopol, 117
Secretaries (Ruskin's help from), 114, 156; see Assistants
Sedan, 323
Selections, 83, 91, 177, 190, 203 n., 357 and n.
Self-confidence (Ruskin's); see under Manic self-confidence

Self-indulgence (Ruskin's 'one fault'), 36–7, 41
Senlis, 148
Servants (at Denmark Hill), 111 n., 280, 281 n.
Sesame and Lilies, 63 n., 77, 86 n., 91–2, 99, 101–2; ('singular preface' quoted), 128, 177–8, 299, 315 n., 342, 346–7, 349, 351, 358–9, 364, 383
Seven Dials, 111
Seven Lamps of Architecture, The, 32, 54, 57–8, 61, 73, 102, 110, 178, 185, 193, 214–17, 223, 226–7, 237, 239, 332–4, 337; (the 'manic self-confidence of'), 355, 359, 371
Severns, the (*see also* Joan Agnew), 77, 85, 114–16, 122, 130; (in Italy), 170, 179; (at Brantwood), 353
Sexual obsessions (Ruskin's), 32, 65
Shakespeare, 91, 231, 243, 347
Sheffield (Museum), 39, 109, 113, 116, 119, 148–50, 152, 168
Shells (Ruskin and), 149, 151
Sicily, 116
Sickert (*quoted*), 266
Siddal, Elizabeth, 270, 275
Sidney, Sir Philip, 121
Siena, 106, 140–1
'Sign from God' (Ruskin's diphtheria cured), 210, 331, 336
Simon, John, 107 n., 357 n.
Simon, Mrs. John, 98 n., 287 n.
Sir Isumbras at the Ford (Millais), 250
Sirens, the (Art, Science, Scholarship), 48–9
Sisley, 256
Sistine Chapel, the (Botticelli), 135
Sistine Madonna (Raphael), 375
Sizeranne, de la (at the Spanish Chapel), 262
Slade, Felix, 100

Slade Professorship, the, 45, 74, 99, 105, 153
Slave Ship, The (Turner), 50, 138, 265, 383 n.
Smetham, 71
Smith, Adam, 286 n.
Smith, Elder & Co., 178
Snakes, lecture on (Biblical quotations in), 160, 364
Snow Storm, The (Turner), 138
Social conscience (Ruskin's: 'the finest thing about him'), 28–9, 36–7, 40–1, 57, 64, 89, 92, 96, 191, 212, 217, 263, 359
Social economics (Ruskin's 'valuable contributions to'), 41, 61, 69, 89, 90; (*Queen of the Air*), 341
Social services (Ruskin on), 298
Social theory (Ruskin's), 301
Society for Preservation of Ancient Monuments, 223, 284
Society of Arts (*Trade Unions and Strikes*), 93
Society of Mont Rose, 109
Soldan, the, 122
Somerville College, 149, 172
Something on Ruskinism (An Architect), 371 n.
Sortes Biblicæ, 355
Spanish Chapel, the (Sta Maria Novella), 122, 252, 260, 262
Spectators ('what they are for'), 268
Speed (Ruskin's fear of), 32, 145
Spenser, 288
Spielmann, M. H., 40 n., 151 n.
Spiritualism (Ruskin and), 31, 133, 141, 171
Splügen, the, 195
Spring (Botticelli), 258
Spurgeon, 72, 81–2, 260, 341
Sta Maria Novella (*see* Spanish Chapel)
Standard, Multiple-commodity, 294 n.
State education, 284, 289
Statue ('little white'), 81, 142

INDEX

Stein, Gertrude, 362
Stelvio, the, 195
'Stick' ('letting what would'), 143, 198
Stigmata, 133
'Stitch here and patch there' (Ruskin's account of his working methods, 156; see under Mobility of interest
Stonebreaker, The (Brett), 250
Stones of Venice, The, 27, 32, 57–8, 61, 68, 73, 134, 178, 185, 193, 214, 217, 219, 223, 225–7, 235–9, 279, 296, 507–10, 333–4, 359, 364, 371
Storm Cloud (obsession), 32–3, 124, 144, 156, 169, 171
Storm Cloud of the Nineteenth Century, The (lecture), 125 n., 169, 172
Story of Ida, The (Alexander), 174, 354
Strasbourg, 133, 195
Strikes, 93
Strong, Miss E. F. (Lady Dilke), 238
Studies in Ruskin (Cook), 118 n.
Study of Architecture, The, 78, 112 n., 257 n.
Stulz (dresses Ruskin), 27
Supper at Emmaus (Rembrandt), 195
Supply and Demand, The Law of (Daily Telegraph), 80 n.
Susannah and the Elders (Guido Reni), 372
Swinburne, 79 n., 234; (Poems and Ballads), 259; (Notes on Designs, etc.), 275
Switzerland, 51, 53, 60, 85
Symbolical expression, 225; see also Geometric and organic form

Tadema, Alma, 255 n.
Talker (Ruskin a fluent), 34
Tariffs, 296

Taxation, Election and Education (three letters), 57, 279
Tea shop, the, 111, 157 n., 281 n.
Teaching (Ruskin on his own), 29
Teniers, 201
Tenniel, 255 n.
Tennyson, 60, 160, 313
Three Colours of Pre-Raphaelitism, The, 247 n., 255 n.
Three Graces (Reynolds), 273
Time and Tide, 78, 84, 88, 110, 132, 190, 299, 328, 342, 344
Times, The, 44; (obituary notice), 47, 57–8, 63, 71, 246, 248, 252, 279, 283, 295, 313, 372, 374–6
Tintoretto, 95, 97, 138, 151, 206–7, 213, 231, 244, 247, 259, 307, 373
Tips (Ruskin on: see under Sacristans)
Titian, 151; (Ruskin's pictures), 198, 206–7, 211, 231, 234, 257; (Charles V at Mühlberg), 273
'To-day' (motto on Ruskin's seal), 229 n.
Toft, 131
Totley, 119
Tour on the Continent, A, 195 and n.
Tour Through France, A (poem), 195–7 n.
Tours, 214
Townley Venus (the so-called), 89 n., 104 n.
Toynbee, Joseph, 80 n.
Trades Union Act (1871), 289
Trade Unions and Strikes (speech), 93
'Transferences', 31, 32, 97, 261
Travelling, 28, 43, 106, 194
Trelawny, Sir John, 286
Trevelyan, Lady, 60
Trossachs, the, 59
Tubalcain, 122
Tunbridge Wells, 60, 382
Turin, 65–6, 71, 195, 231; (Ruskin and Veronese), 244

Turin Gallery (Ruskin's notes on the), 232 n., 338 n.
Turner, 43–5, 49–51, 57, 62–3, 68, 88, 97, 114, 138 (*Slave Ship* and *Snow Storm*), 187, 196, 198 ('ranked with the great'), 231, 244 ('Angel of the Apocalypse'), 247 ('phenomenon of nature'), 255 n., 259 n., 264, 266 ('great natural force'), 267–9, 275
Turner and the Ancients (first title of *Modern Painters*), 199, 264
Turner Bequest, (Ruskin and the), 373
Turner drawings (Ruskin and), 88, 150–1, 383 n.
Twang ('expounding Nothing with a'), 231, 338
Two Paths, The, 63, 193, 224, 226, 231, 236, 238, 253, 268, 285, 308, 310, 316, 382–3
Two thousand people (Ruskin addresses), 91
Tyrwhitt, Rev. St. John, 90

Uffizi Gallery, the (Florence), 197
Umbrellas ('armed with'), 41
Unemployment (Ruskin on), 289, 292, 297
Unity of Art, The (Manchester Art School), 382
Universal Analogy (Baudelaire), 189, 239
University College, 90
Unjust person (Ruskin 'not an'), 128, 352
Unpopular (Ruskin will 'ruin a man if he takes interest in him'), 62, 374, 377–9
Unsympathetic (Ruskin: *see under* Hostility)
Unto This Last, 27, 41, 65–6, 69, 73, 102, 113, 177, 185, 287–8, 298, 302; ('badly arranged and written'), 311–13, 327, 341

Usury (*Contemporary Review*), 160 n.
Utopian (Ruskin), 30, 105, 108
Uwins, Thomas (R.A.), 374

Val d'Aosta (Brett), 276, 380 n.
Val d'Arno, 254 n.
Val di Serchio, 169
Vale of Rest, The (Millais), 250
Valets (Ruskin's), 51, 162, 281 n.
Valle Crucis (Cistercian architecture), 153, 335 n.
Value (Ruskin's manic confidence in his ability to assess), 241, 301
Van Dyck, 197–8
Vasari, 103–4, 258 n.
Velasquez, 198, 231; (*Margarita of Austria*), 257; (and Whistler), 259
Venetian-Gothic renaissance (in architecture), 222
Venetian Index (to *Stones of Venice*), 134
Venice, 39, 55–8, 66, 75, 85, 94, 97–9, 105–6, 113, 148, 195–6, 198, 206, 214, 216
Venice (poem), 195
Venus (Ruskin 'nicely got up as'), 73
Venus dei Medici, 104 n., 236 n.
Verona, 34, 39, 56, 94–6, 100, 106, 148, 152, 195, 206
Verona and its Rivers (lecture), 101 n., 134 n.
Veronese, Paul, 211, 231–2, 244, 283 n.; (*The Family of Darius*), 283
Vevay (*Queen of the Air*), 97 n.
Vickers, 303
Victoria, Queen, 85
Villeneuve, 276
Virgil, 288
Vivisection (University vote on, and Ruskin's resignation), 155
Voyage dans les Alpes (de Saussure), (1779–96), 43

Wages, law of, 290, 292
Waldensian chapel, 66, 81–2, 231, 275, 338–40
Walkley (Sheffield St. George's Museum), 109, 148, 152
War (1914–18), 40–1; (Ruskin on), 191, 295, 299; (and chess), 310; (three forms of), 317; see also Crimean, Franco-Prussian, Alabama
War debts (Ruskin on), 298, 299 n.
War ('White'), 296, 300 n.
War (Woolwich lecture), 303, 317
War: the Exile and the Rock Limpet (Turner), 266 n.
War loan, 41, 298, 299 n.
Ward, William, 88 n., 277 and n.
Wardour Street 'mediævalism', 251 n.
Waste (Ruskin on), 295
Waterford, Lady, 60
Watteau, 256–7
Watts, G. F., 273, 274 n., 275
Waugh, Evelyn (*Rossetti: His Life and Works*), 270 and n., 369 n.
Wealth (distinguished from money and 'Illth' by Ruskin), 293–5, 298, 313 n.
Weather ('deteriorated'), 97, 126, 169 n.
Webling, Miss Peggy (*A Sketch of John Ruskin*), 147 n., 172 n., 176 n.
Webling, Rosalind and Peggy, 172
Wedderburn, 37, 121
Wells, H. G. (*The Work, Wealth*, etc.), 300 n.; (Napoleonic cult), 304; (*Outline of History*), *ib.* n.; (*quoted*), 310–1; (*persona* of soldier), 322; (Ruskin compared to), 328; (*Outline of History* and *The Work, Wealth*, etc.), 368
Westminster Abbey (burial in, offered for Ruskin), 27
Whewell, Dr., 90

Whistler, J. M., 32, 98, 138; (*Nocturne*), 143; (libel case), 144 n.; (trial), 158; (*Nocturne*), 198; (Ruskin's 'absurd didacticism'), 236 n.; (*Nocturne in Black and Gold*), 241; (Ruskin's Oxford resignation), 254 and n.; (and Velasquez), 259; (Burne-Jones at trial), 263, 274
White of Selborne, 47, 205
Whitehouse, J. H. (ed.: *Ruskin the Prophet*), 11, 185
Whitelands (Chelsea), 149, 163, 171
Wife (Ruskin's behaviour 'perfect' after her desertion), 36; (not mentioned in *Præterita*), 180, 227
Wilde, Oscar (*De Profundis*), 221
Wilenski, R. H. (*French Painting; The Modern Movement in Art; The Meaning of Modern Sculpture*), 89 n., 222, 242, 245
Wilkie, 250
Will (Ruskin's), 179
Willis, Robert 90
Will-o'-the-wisps (girls), 73
Windsor Castle (Ruskin at), 144
Windus, W. L. (*Burd Helen*), 50, 250
Winnington, 46, 67, 70–3, 74–5, 85, 92–3, 101, 140, 150, 161 n., 171, 174, 276–7, 347
Wise ('in his generation': Ruskin), 158
Woolwich, 112, 303; (lecture on *War*), 316 (*ib.*)
'Woolwich infant, the', 108 and n.
Worcestershire (Guild property in), 119
Word painter (Ruskin), 92, 203 and n., 357
Wordsworth, 47, 160, 202, 303 n.
Work (consecutive, impossible for Ruskin), 31–2, 102, 112–7
Work and Wages (Pall Mall Gazette), 80 n.

Work of Iron in Nature, The, 382
Work, Wealth and Happiness of Mankind, The (Wells), 300 n., 310 n., 328
Workmen and Labourers of Great Britain, Letters to the, 107
Working Men's College, 37, 61–2, 218, 282, 286, 381
Working Men's Institute (Camberwell), 77, 319
World Political Economy (Ruskin's theory of), 296
Wornum, Ralph, 374, 375 n.
'Worm and no man', 68
Worry (not the cause of Ruskin's illness), 157
Wounded Cavalier, The (Burton), 250

Writer (Ruskin as a, methods, etc.), 49, 187–8, 203 and n., 345, 357–68

Xenophon (*Economist*), 121, 152, see also 187

Yates Thompson Collection, 59
Year on the Punjab Frontier, A (Edwardes), 303 m.

Zaharoff, Sir Basil, 303
Zipporah (Botticelli), 135, 258
Zoroaster, 122
Zorzi, Open letter to Count (1877), 144 n.